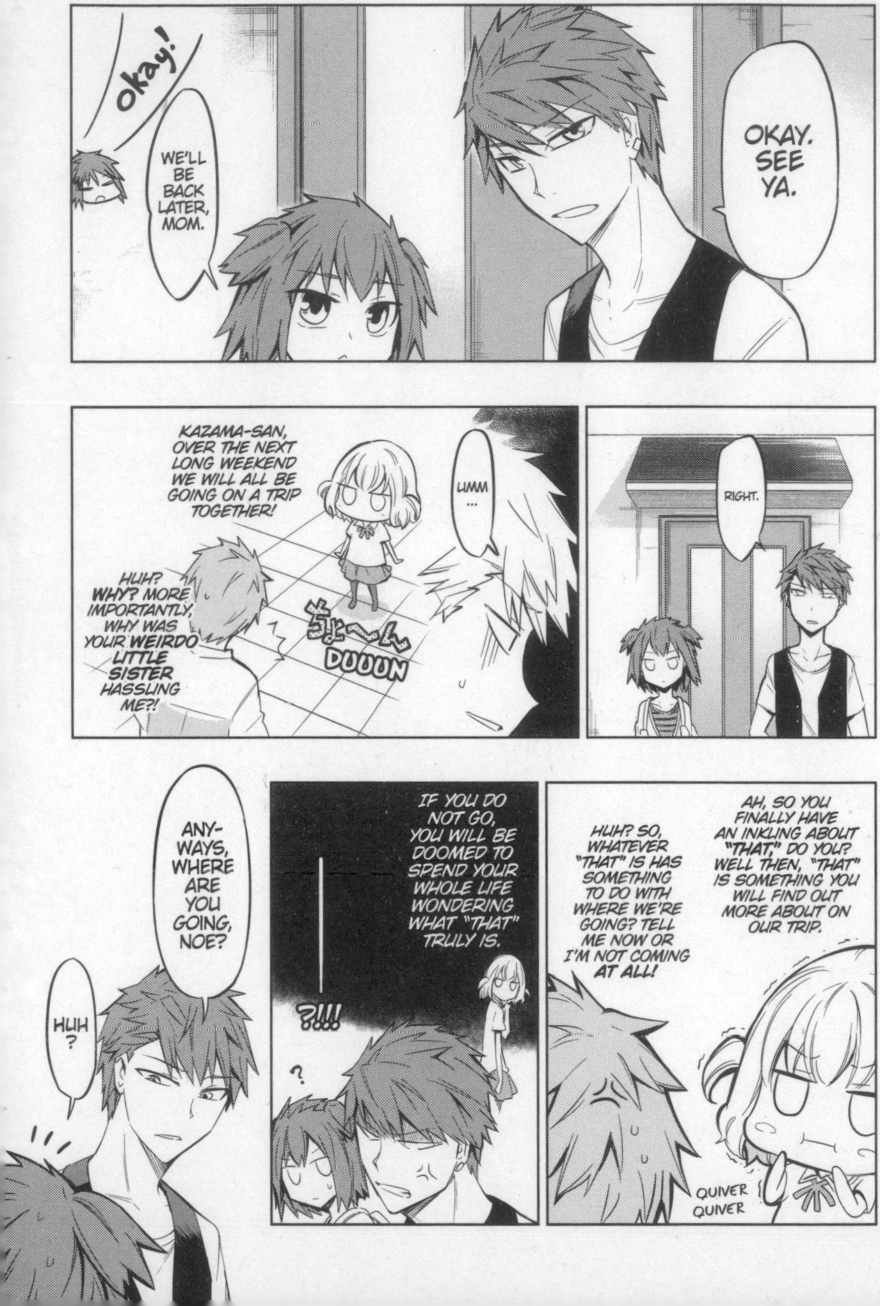
OKAY. SEE YA.
WE'LL BE BACK LATER, MOM.
okay!
RIGHT.
UMM ...
KAZAMA-SAN, OVER THE NEXT LONG WEEKEND WE WILL ALL BE GOING ON A TRIP TOGETHER!
ちょ〜ん
DUUUN
HUH? **WHY?** MORE IMPORTANTLY, WHY WAS YOUR **WEIRDO LITTLE SISTER** HASSLING ME?!
AH, SO YOU FINALLY HAVE AN INKLING ABOUT **"THAT,"** DO YOU? WELL THEN, "THAT" IS SOMETHING YOU WILL FIND OUT MORE ABOUT ON OUR TRIP.
HUH? SO, WHATEVER "THAT" IS HAS SOMETHING TO DO WITH WHERE WE'RE GOING? TELL ME NOW OR I'M NOT COMING **AT ALL!**
QUIVER QUIVER
IF YOU DO NOT GO, YOU WILL BE DOOMED TO SPEND YOUR WHOLE LIFE WONDERING WHAT "THAT" TRULY IS.
?!!!
ANY-WAYS, WHERE ARE YOU GOING, NOE?
HUH?

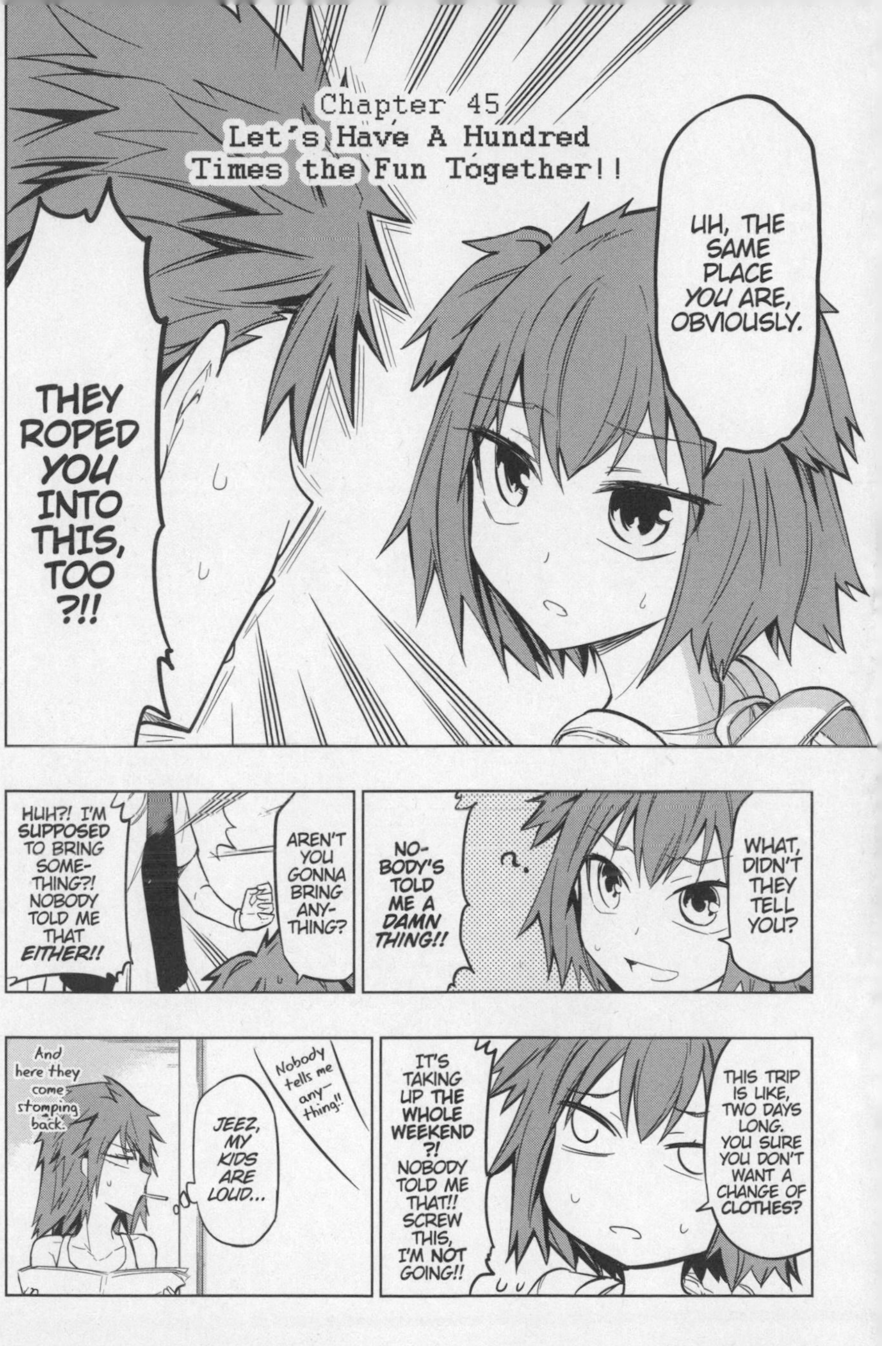
Chapter 45
Let's Have A Hundred Times the Fun Together!!
UH, THE SAME PLACE YOU ARE, OBVIOUSLY.
THEY ROPED YOU INTO THIS, TOO?!!
WHAT, DIDN'T THEY TELL YOU?
NOBODY'S TOLD ME A DAMN THING!!
AREN'T YOU GONNA BRING ANYTHING?
HUH?! I'M SUPPOSED TO BRING SOMETHING?! NOBODY TOLD ME THAT EITHER!!
THIS TRIP IS LIKE, TWO DAYS LONG. YOU SURE YOU DON'T WANT A CHANGE OF CLOTHES?
IT'S TAKING UP THE WHOLE WEEKEND?! NOBODY TOLD ME THAT!! SCREW THIS, I'M NOT GOING!!
Nobody tells me anything!!
JEEZ, MY KIDS ARE LOUD...
And here they come stomping back.

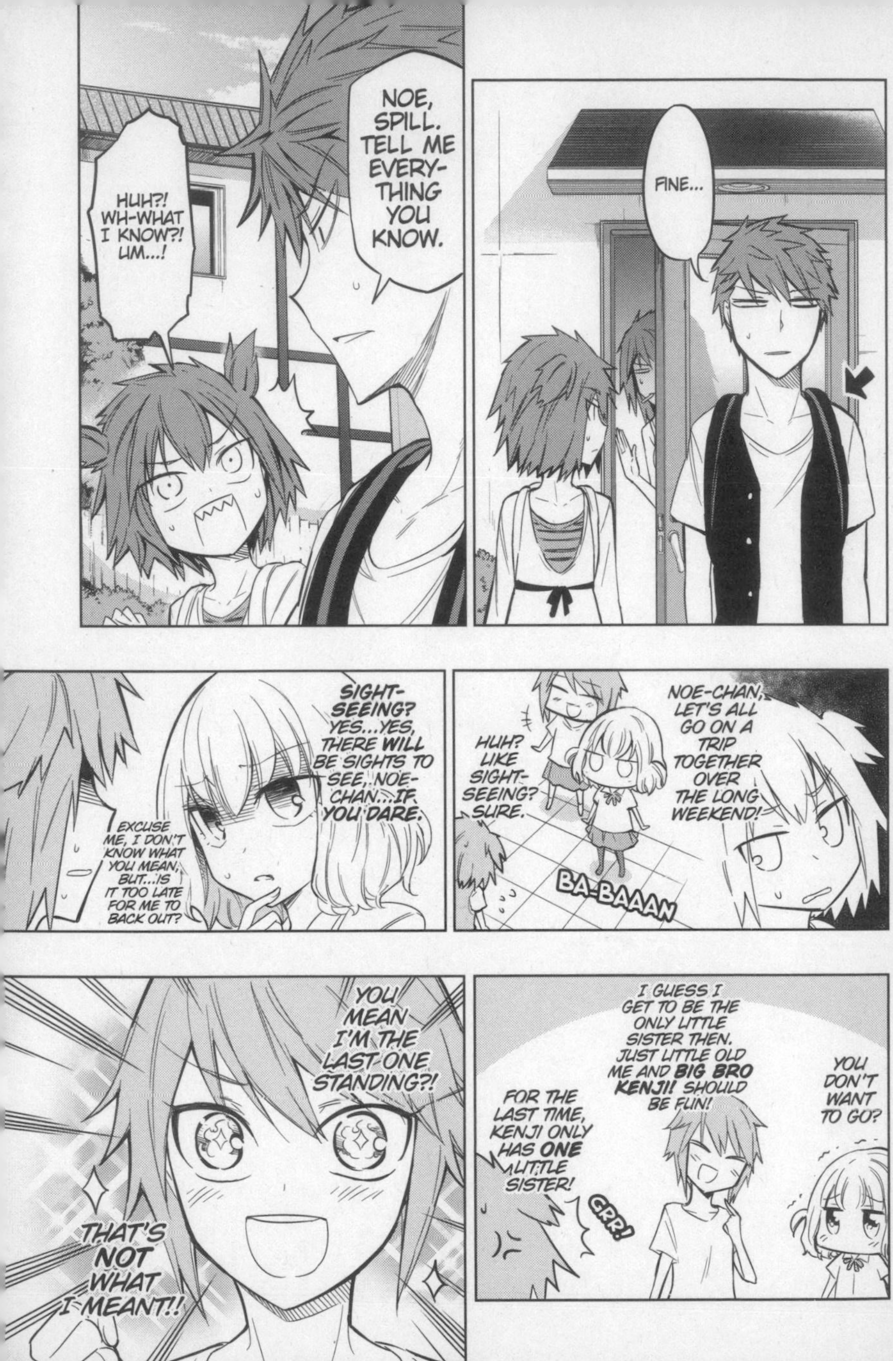
FINE...
NOE, SPILL. TELL ME EVERYTHING YOU KNOW.
HUH?! WH-WHAT I KNOW?! UM...!
NOE-CHAN, LET'S ALL GO ON A TRIP TOGETHER OVER THE LONG WEEKEND!
HUH? LIKE SIGHT-SEEING? SURE.
BA-BAAAN
SIGHT-SEEING? YES...YES, THERE WILL BE SIGHTS TO SEE, NOE-CHAN...IF YOU DARE.
EXCUSE ME, I DON'T KNOW WHAT YOU MEAN, BUT...IS IT TOO LATE FOR ME TO BACK OUT?
YOU DON'T WANT TO GO?
I GUESS I GET TO BE THE ONLY LITTLE SISTER THEN. JUST LITTLE OLD ME AND BIG BRO KENJI! SHOULD BE FUN!
FOR THE LAST TIME, KENJI ONLY HAS ONE LITTLE SISTER!
GRR!
YOU MEAN I'M THE LAST ONE STANDING?!
THAT'S NOT WHAT I MEANT!!

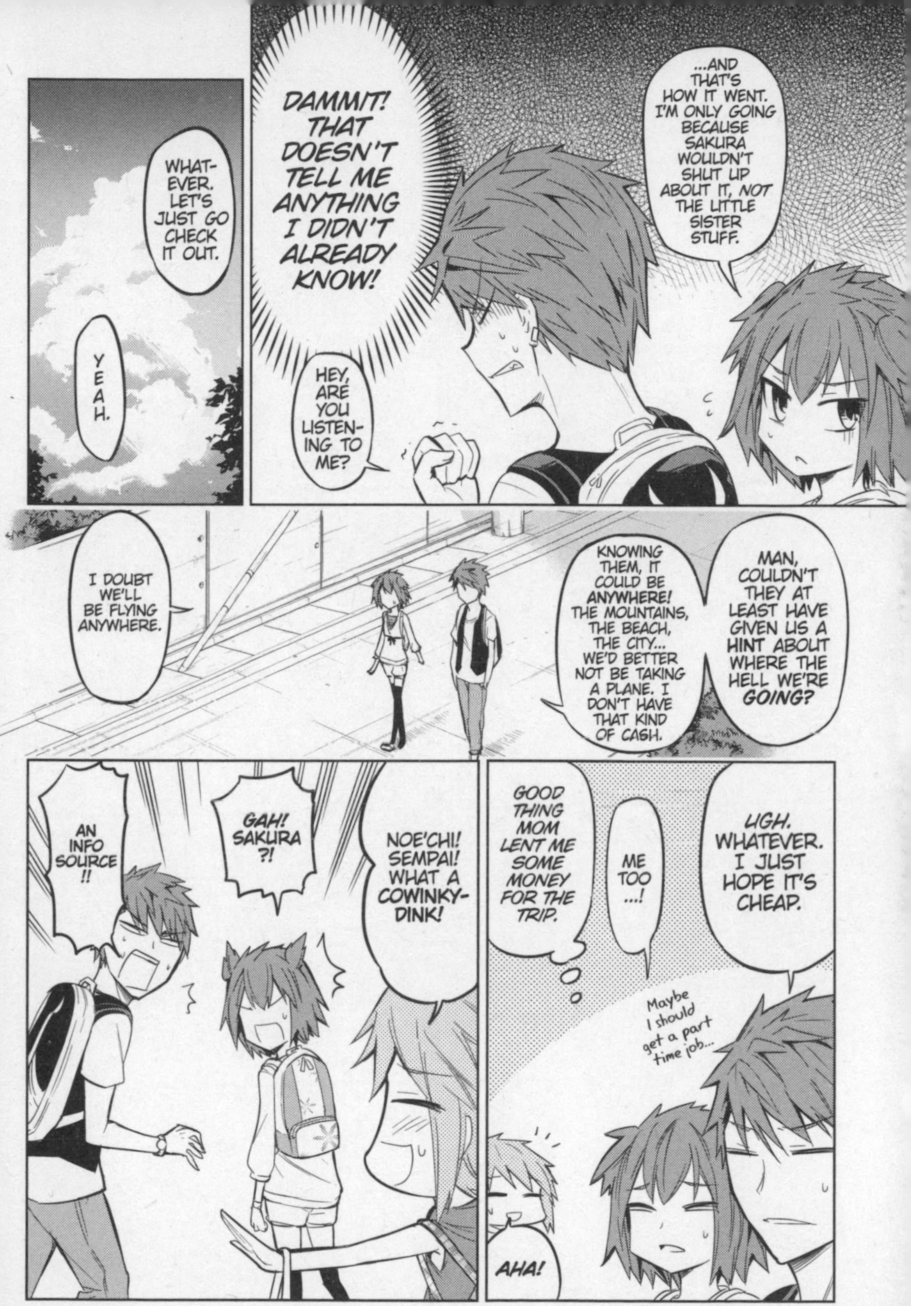
...AND THAT'S HOW IT WENT. I'M ONLY GOING BECAUSE SAKURA WOULDN'T SHUT UP ABOUT IT, NOT THE LITTLE SISTER STUFF.
DAMMIT! THAT DOESN'T TELL ME ANYTHING I DIDN'T ALREADY KNOW!
HEY, ARE YOU LISTENING TO ME?
WHAT-EVER. LET'S JUST GO CHECK IT OUT.
YEAH.
MAN, COULDN'T THEY AT LEAST HAVE GIVEN US A HINT ABOUT WHERE THE HELL WE'RE GOING?
KNOWING THEM, IT COULD BE ANYWHERE! THE MOUNTAINS, THE BEACH, THE CITY... WE'D BETTER NOT BE TAKING A PLANE. I DON'T HAVE THAT KIND OF CASH.
I DOUBT WE'LL BE FLYING ANYWHERE.
UGH. WHATEVER. I JUST HOPE IT'S CHEAP.
ME TOO ...!
GOOD THING MOM LENT ME SOME MONEY FOR THE TRIP.
Maybe I should get a part time job...
AHA!
NOE'CHI! SEMPAI! WHAT A COWINKY-DINK!
GAH! SAKURA ?!
AN INFO SOURCE !!

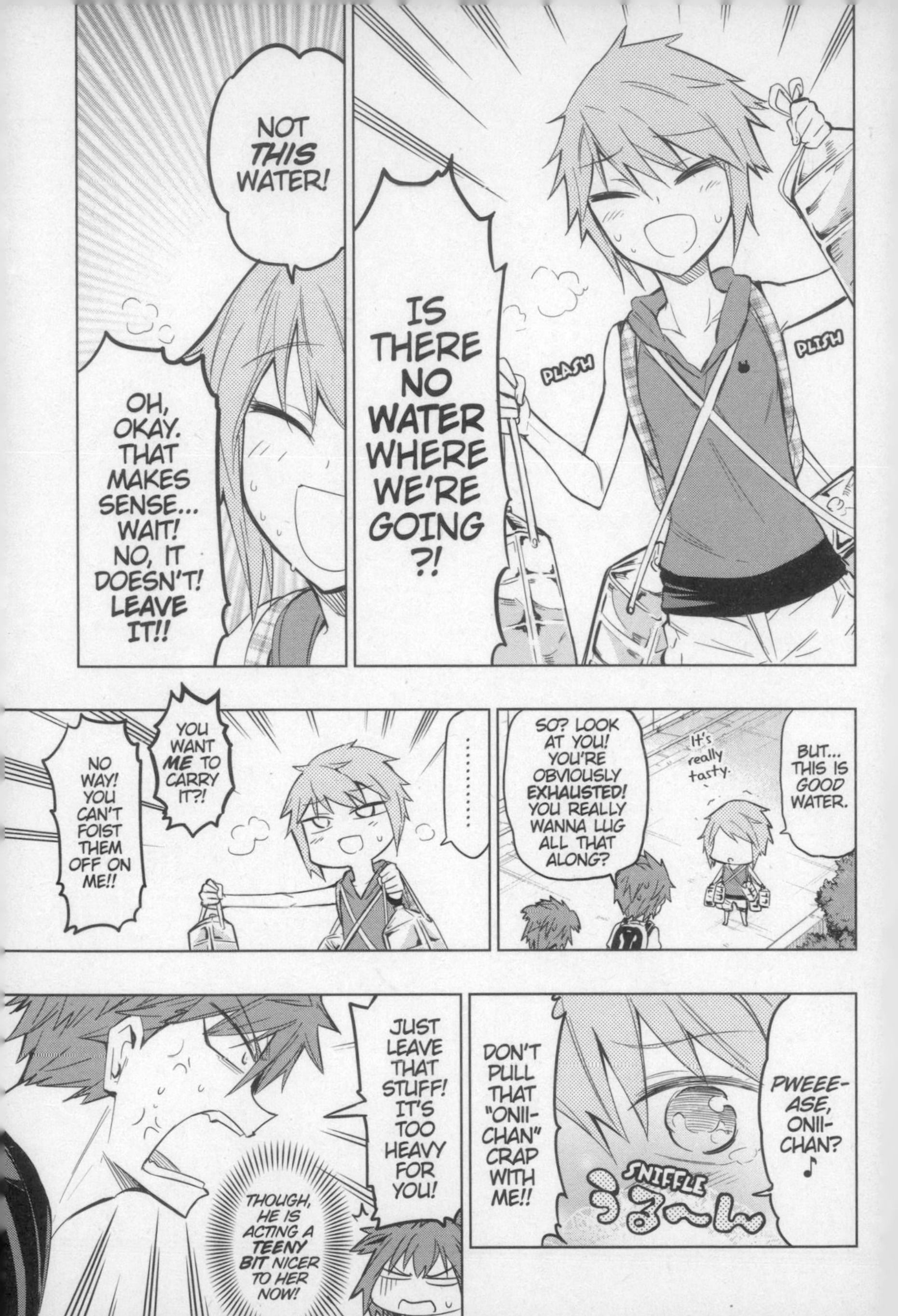
PLISH
PLASH
IS THERE NO WATER WHERE WE'RE GOING?!
NOT THIS WATER!
OH, OKAY. THAT MAKES SENSE... WAIT! NO, IT DOESN'T! LEAVE IT!!
BUT... THIS IS GOOD WATER.
It's really tasty.
SO? LOOK AT YOU! YOU'RE OBVIOUSLY EXHAUSTED! YOU REALLY WANNA LUG ALL THAT ALONG?
......
YOU WANT ME TO CARRY IT?!
NO WAY! YOU CAN'T FOIST THEM OFF ON ME!!
PWEEE-ASE, ONII-CHAN? ♪
SNIFFLE
うる〜ん
DON'T PULL THAT "ONII-CHAN" CRAP WITH ME!!
JUST LEAVE THAT STUFF! IT'S TOO HEAVY FOR YOU!
THOUGH, HE IS ACTING A TEENY BIT NICER TO HER NOW!

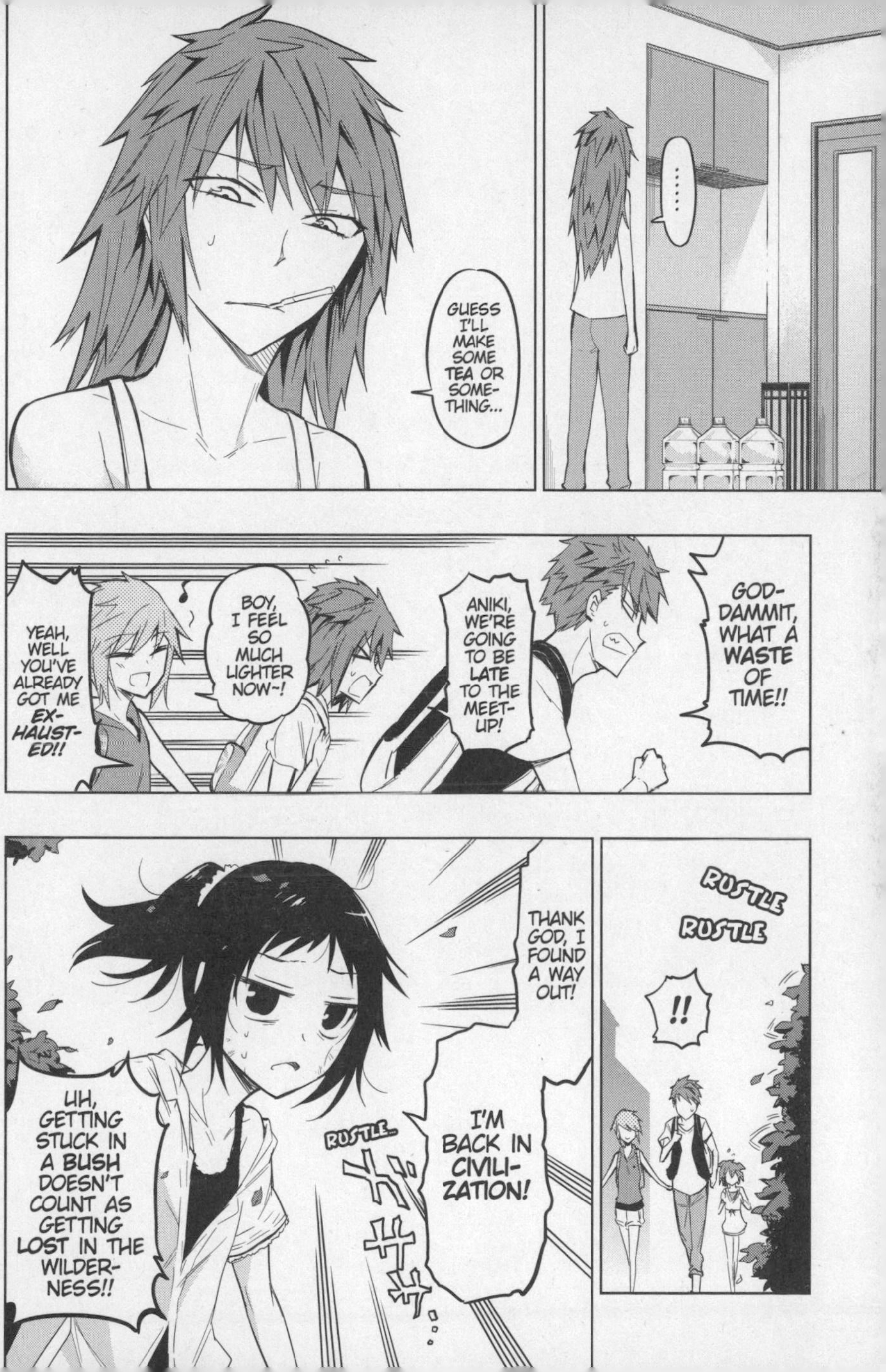
......
GUESS I'LL MAKE SOME TEA OR SOMETHING...
GOD-DAMMIT, WHAT A WASTE OF TIME!!
ANIKI, WE'RE GOING TO BE LATE TO THE MEET-UP!
BOY, I FEEL SO MUCH LIGHTER NOW~!
YEAH, WELL YOU'VE ALREADY GOT ME EX-HAUSTED!!
RUSTLE
RUSTLE
!!
THANK GOD, I FOUND A WAY OUT!
I'M BACK IN CIVILI-ZATION!
RUSTLE...
UH, GETTING STUCK IN A BUSH DOESN'T COUNT AS GETTING LOST IN THE WILDER-NESS!!

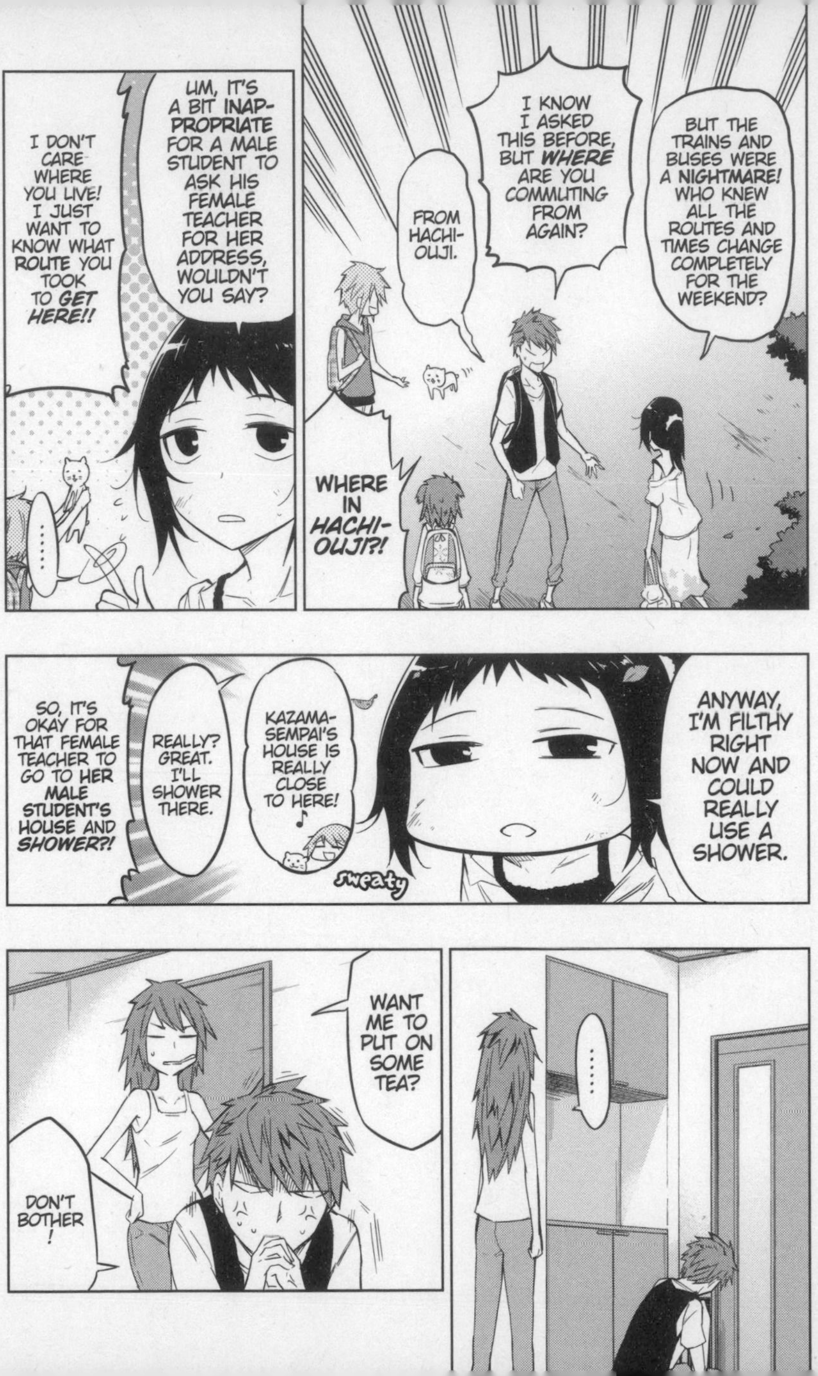
BUT THE TRAINS AND BUSES WERE A NIGHTMARE! WHO KNEW ALL THE ROUTES AND TIMES CHANGE COMPLETELY FOR THE WEEKEND?
I KNOW I ASKED THIS BEFORE, BUT WHERE ARE YOU COMMUTING FROM AGAIN?
FROM HACHI-OUJI.
WHERE IN HACHI-OUJI?!
UM, IT'S A BIT INAPPROPRIATE FOR A MALE STUDENT TO ASK HIS FEMALE TEACHER FOR HER ADDRESS, WOULDN'T YOU SAY?
I DON'T CARE WHERE YOU LIVE! I JUST WANT TO KNOW WHAT ROUTE YOU TOOK TO GET HERE!!
......
ANYWAY, I'M FILTHY RIGHT NOW AND COULD REALLY USE A SHOWER.
KAZAMA-SEMPAI'S HOUSE IS REALLY CLOSE TO HERE! ♪
REALLY? GREAT. I'LL SHOWER THERE.
SO, IT'S OKAY FOR THAT FEMALE TEACHER TO GO TO HER MALE STUDENT'S HOUSE AND SHOWER?!
sweaty
......
WANT ME TO PUT ON SOME TEA?
DON'T BOTHER!

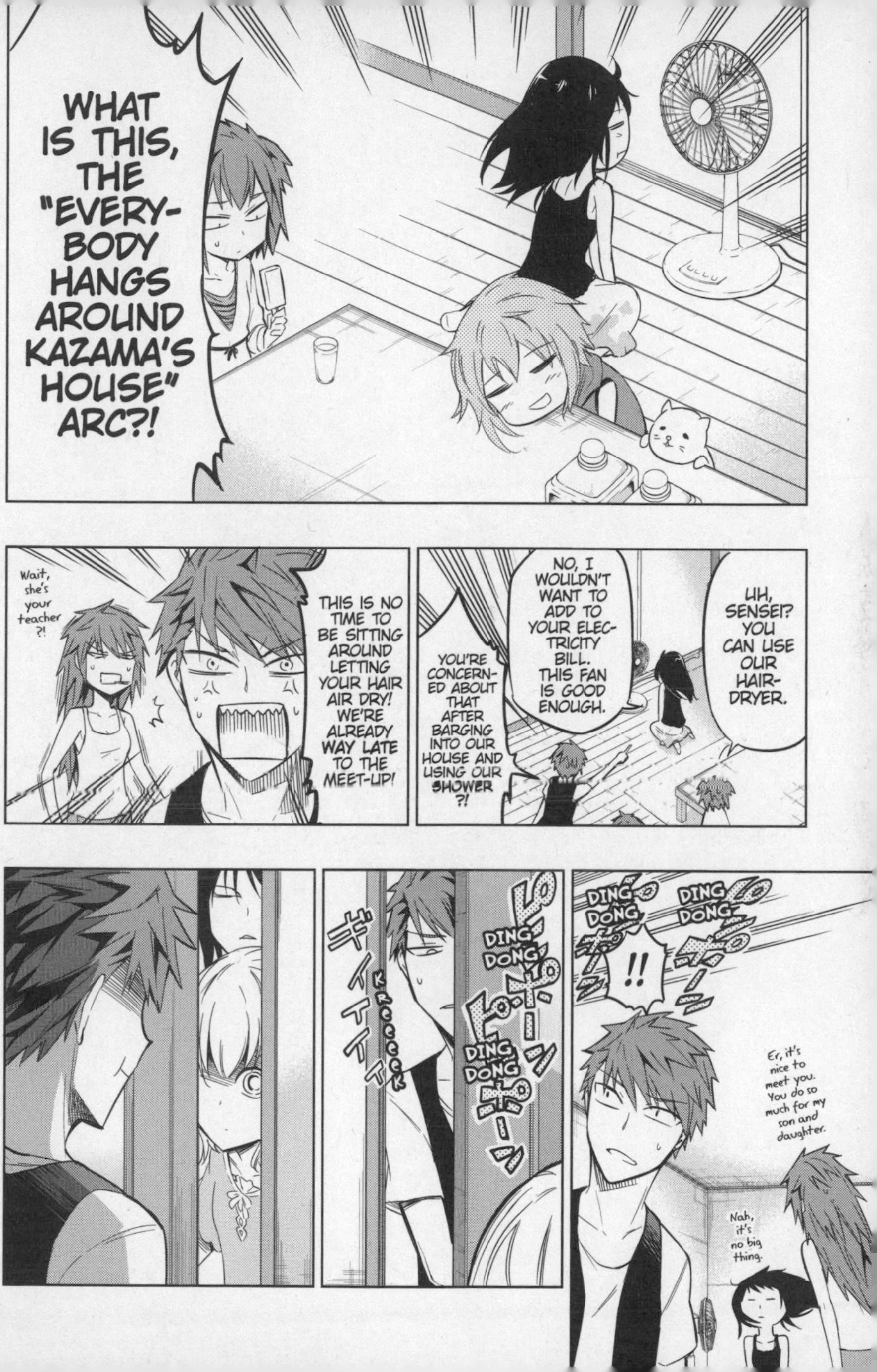
WHAT IS THIS, THE "EVERY-BODY HANGS AROUND KAZAMA'S HOUSE" ARC?!
UH, SENSEI? YOU CAN USE OUR HAIR-DRYER.
NO, I WOULDN'T WANT TO ADD TO YOUR ELEC-TRICITY BILL. THIS FAN IS GOOD ENOUGH.
YOU'RE CONCERN-ED ABOUT THAT AFTER BARGING INTO OUR HOUSE AND USING OUR SHOWER?!
THIS IS NO TIME TO BE SITTING AROUND LETTING YOUR HAIR AIR DRY! WE'RE ALREADY WAY LATE TO THE MEET-UP!
Wait, she's your teacher?!
DING DONG
DING DONG
!!
Er, it's nice to meet you. You do so much for my son and daughter.
Nah, it's no big thing.
DING DONG
DING DONG
KREEEEK

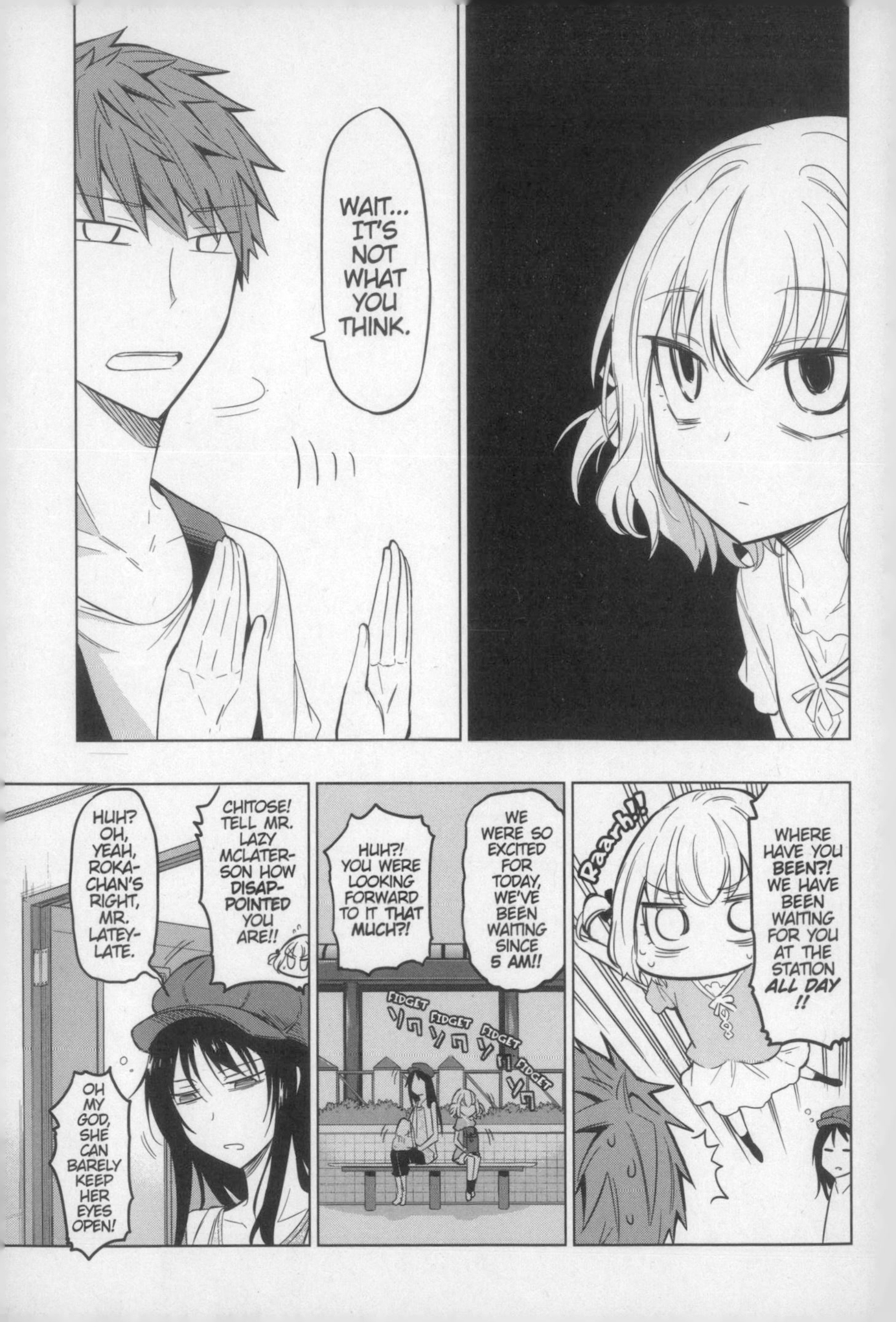
WAIT... IT'S NOT WHAT YOU THINK.
Raarh!!
WHERE HAVE YOU BEEN?! WE HAVE BEEN WAITING FOR YOU AT THE STATION ALL DAY !!
WE WERE SO EXCITED FOR TODAY, WE'VE BEEN WAITING SINCE 5 AM!!
HUH?! YOU WERE LOOKING FORWARD TO IT THAT MUCH?!
FIDGET FIDGET FIDGET FIDGET
CHITOSE! TELL MR. LAZY MCLATERSON HOW DISAPPOINTED YOU ARE!!
HUH? OH, YEAH, ROKA-CHAN'S RIGHT, MR. LATEY-LATE.
OH MY GOD, SHE CAN BARELY KEEP HER EYES OPEN!

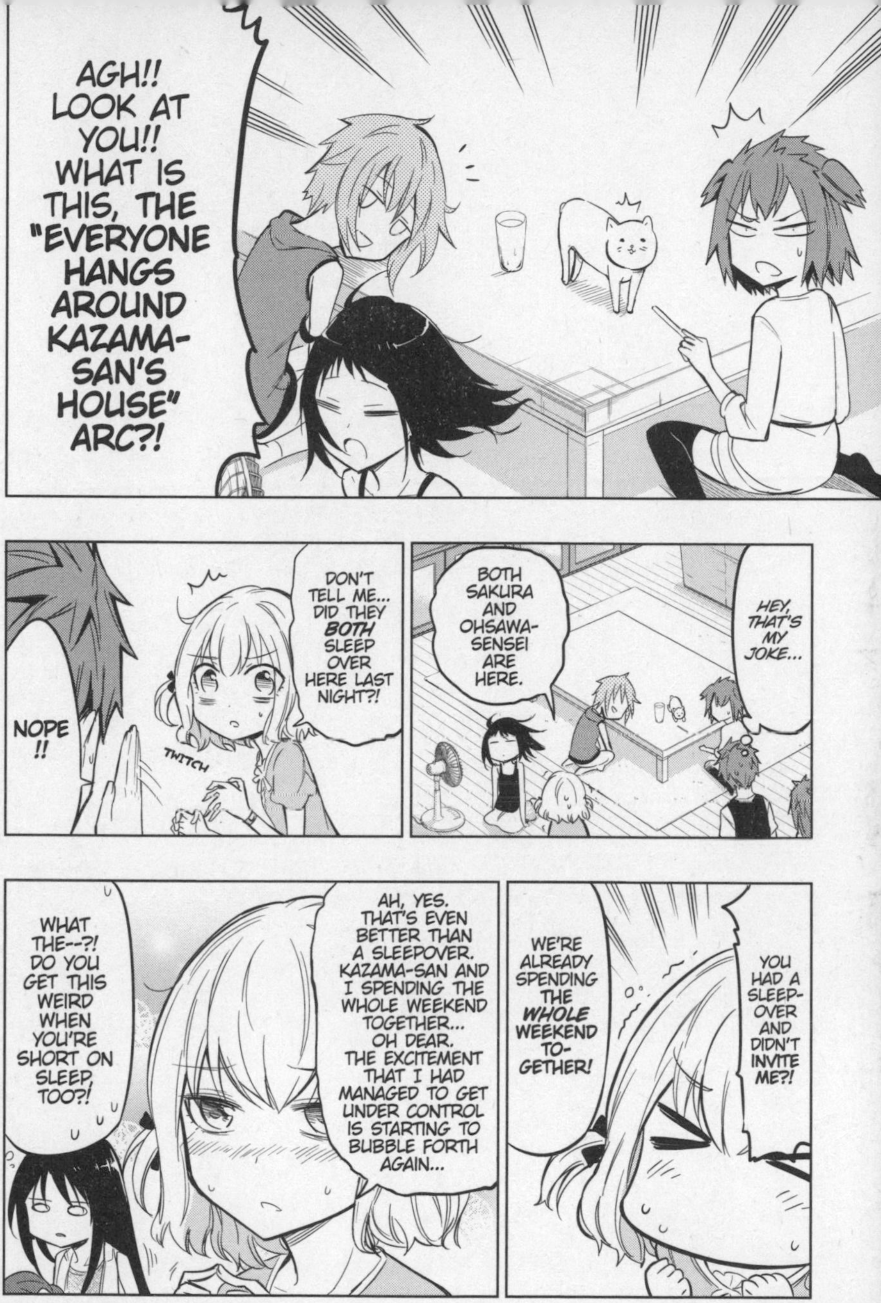
AGH!! LOOK AT YOU!! WHAT IS THIS, THE "EVERYONE HANGS AROUND KAZAMA-SAN'S HOUSE" ARC?!
HEY, THAT'S MY JOKE...
BOTH SAKURA AND OHSAWA-SENSEI ARE HERE.
DON'T TELL ME... DID THEY BOTH SLEEP OVER HERE LAST NIGHT?!
NOPE !!
TWITCH
YOU HAD A SLEEP-OVER AND DIDN'T INVITE ME?!
WE'RE ALREADY SPENDING THE WHOLE WEEKEND TO-GETHER!
AH, YES. THAT'S EVEN BETTER THAN A SLEEPOVER. KAZAMA-SAN AND I SPENDING THE WHOLE WEEKEND TOGETHER... OH DEAR. THE EXCITEMENT THAT I HAD MANAGED TO GET UNDER CONTROL IS STARTING TO BUBBLE FORTH AGAIN...
WHAT THE--?! DO YOU GET THIS WEIRD WHEN YOU'RE SHORT ON SLEEP, TOO?!

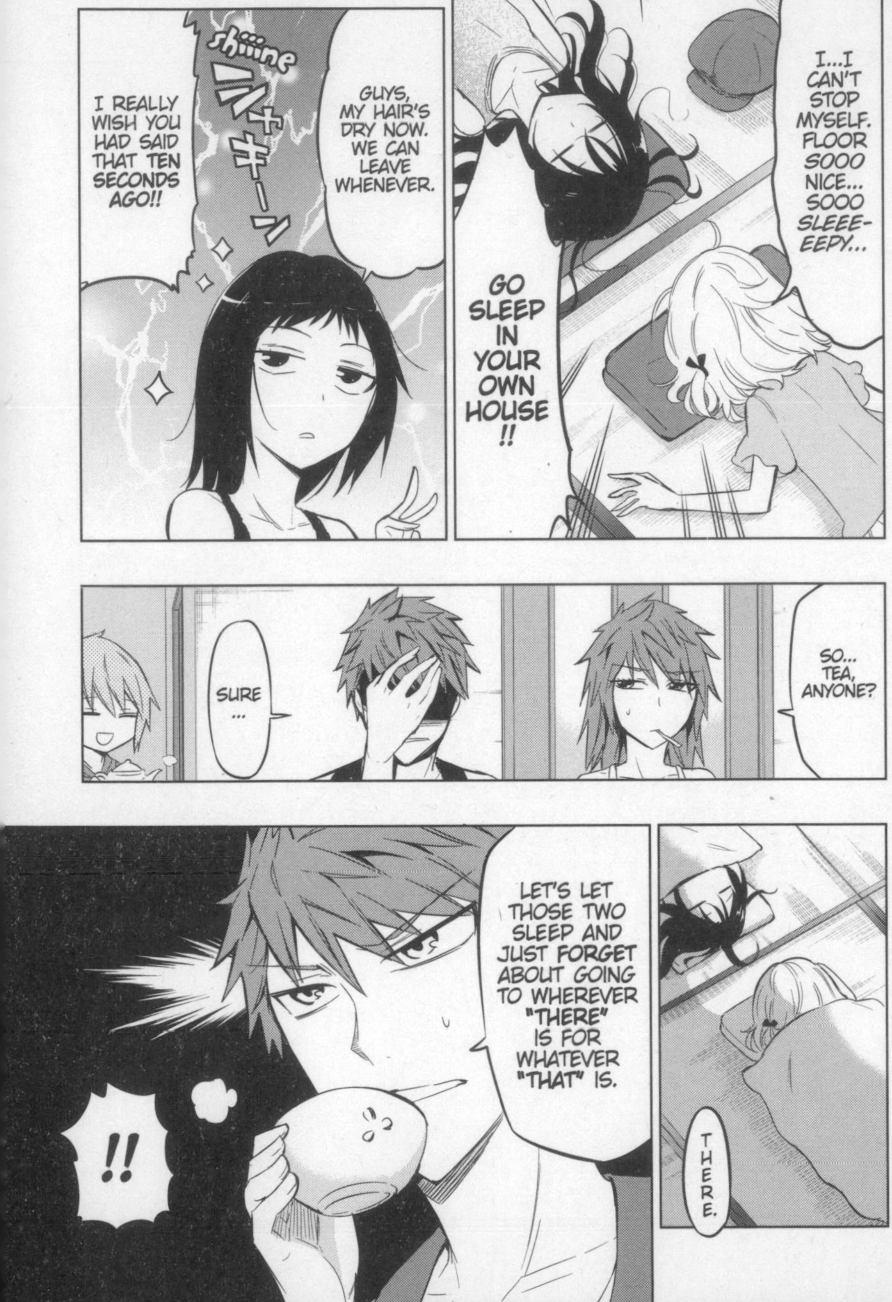
I...I CAN'T STOP MYSELF. FLOOR SOOO NICE... SOOO SLEEE-EEPY...
GO SLEEP IN YOUR OWN HOUSE !!
GUYS, MY HAIR'S DRY NOW. WE CAN LEAVE WHENEVER.
shiiine
I REALLY WISH YOU HAD SAID THAT TEN SECONDS AGO!!
SO... TEA, ANYONE?
SURE ...
THERE.
LET'S LET THOSE TWO SLEEP AND JUST FORGET ABOUT GOING TO WHEREVER "THERE" IS FOR WHATEVER "THAT" IS.
!!

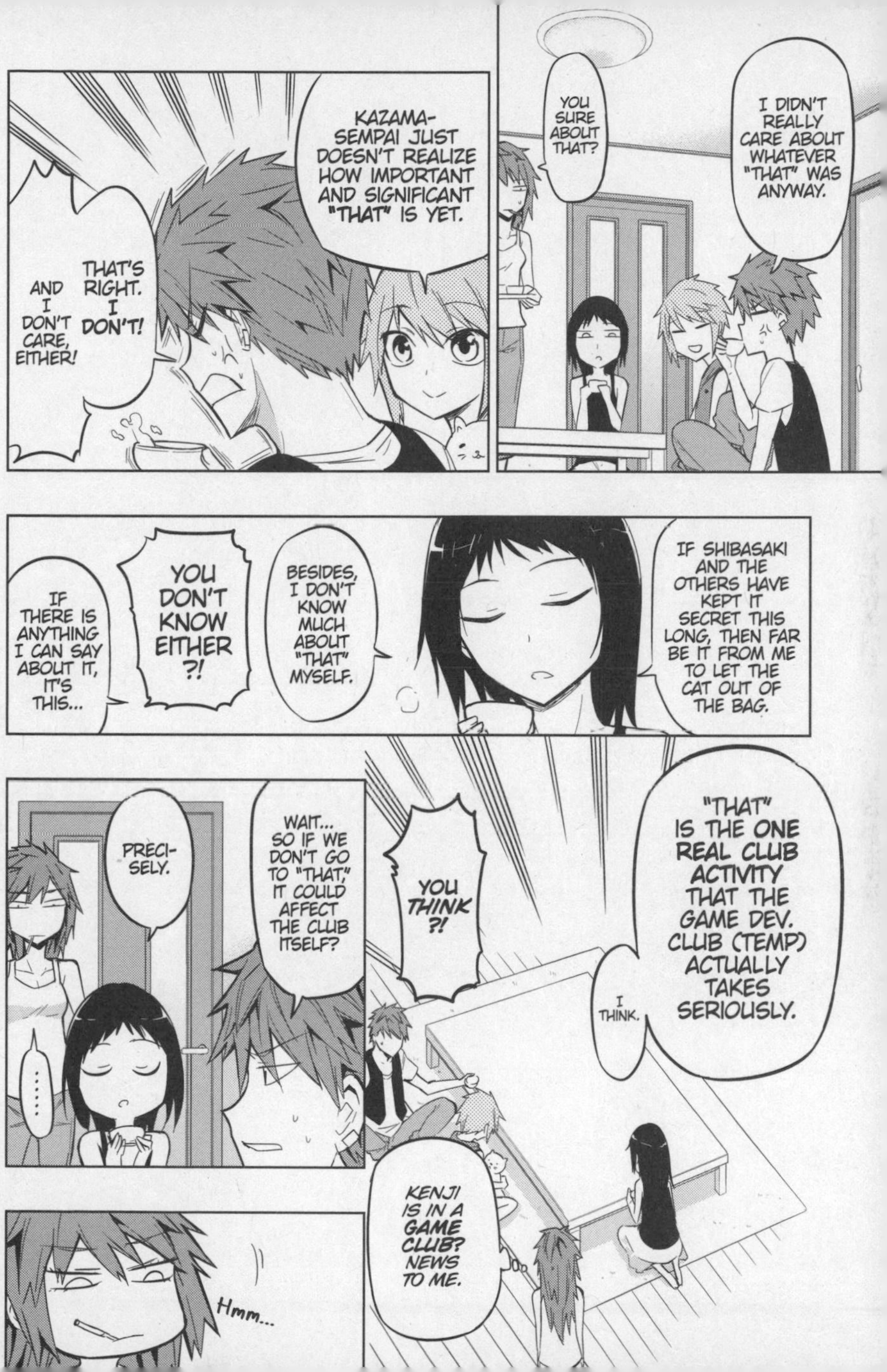
I DIDN'T REALLY CARE ABOUT WHATEVER "THAT" WAS ANYWAY.
YOU SURE ABOUT THAT?
KAZAMA-SEMPAI JUST DOESN'T REALIZE HOW IMPORTANT AND SIGNIFICANT "THAT" IS YET.
THAT'S RIGHT. I DON'T!
AND I DON'T CARE, EITHER!
IF SHIBASAKI AND THE OTHERS HAVE KEPT IT SECRET THIS LONG, THEN FAR BE IT FROM ME TO LET THE CAT OUT OF THE BAG.
BESIDES, I DON'T KNOW MUCH ABOUT "THAT" MYSELF.
YOU DON'T KNOW EITHER?!
IF THERE IS ANYTHING I CAN SAY ABOUT IT, IT'S THIS...
"THAT" IS THE ONE REAL CLUB ACTIVITY THAT THE GAME DEV. CLUB (TEMP) ACTUALLY TAKES SERIOUSLY.
I THINK.
YOU THINK?!
WAIT... SO IF WE DON'T GO TO "THAT," IT COULD AFFECT THE CLUB ITSELF?
PRECI-SELY.
......
KENJI IS IN A GAME CLUB? NEWS TO ME.
Hmm...

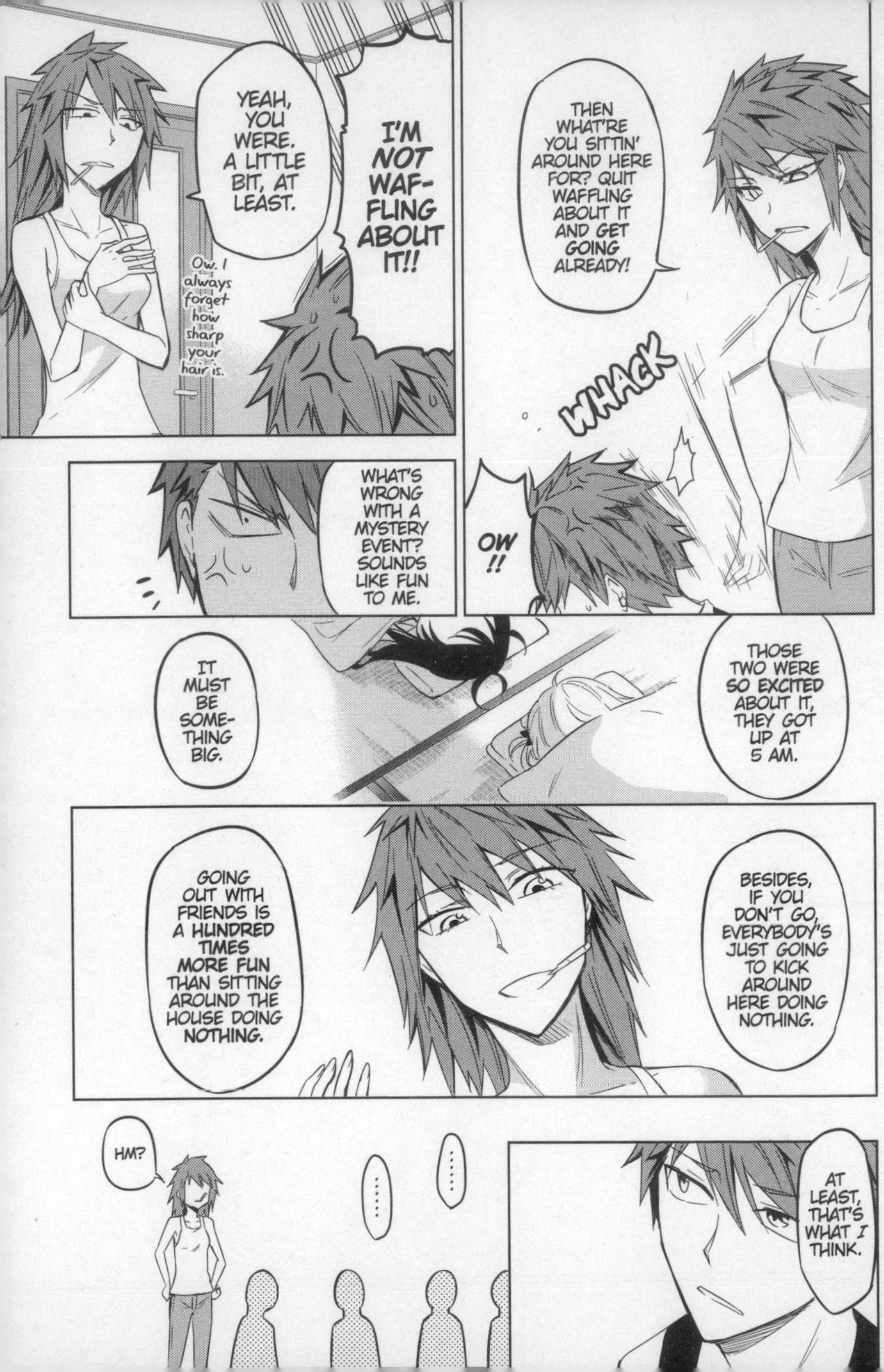
THEN WHAT'RE YOU SITTIN' AROUND HERE FOR? QUIT WAFFLING ABOUT IT AND GET GOING ALREADY!
WHACK
OW!!
I'M NOT WAF-FLING ABOUT IT!!
YEAH, YOU WERE. A LITTLE BIT, AT LEAST.
Ow. I always forget how sharp your hair is.
WHAT'S WRONG WITH A MYSTERY EVENT? SOUNDS LIKE FUN TO ME.
THOSE TWO WERE SO EXCITED ABOUT IT, THEY GOT UP AT 5 AM.
IT MUST BE SOME-THING BIG.
BESIDES, IF YOU DON'T GO, EVERYBODY'S JUST GOING TO KICK AROUND HERE DOING NOTHING.
GOING OUT WITH FRIENDS IS A HUNDRED TIMES MORE FUN THAN SITTING AROUND THE HOUSE DOING NOTHING.
AT LEAST, THAT'S WHAT I THINK.
......
......
HM?

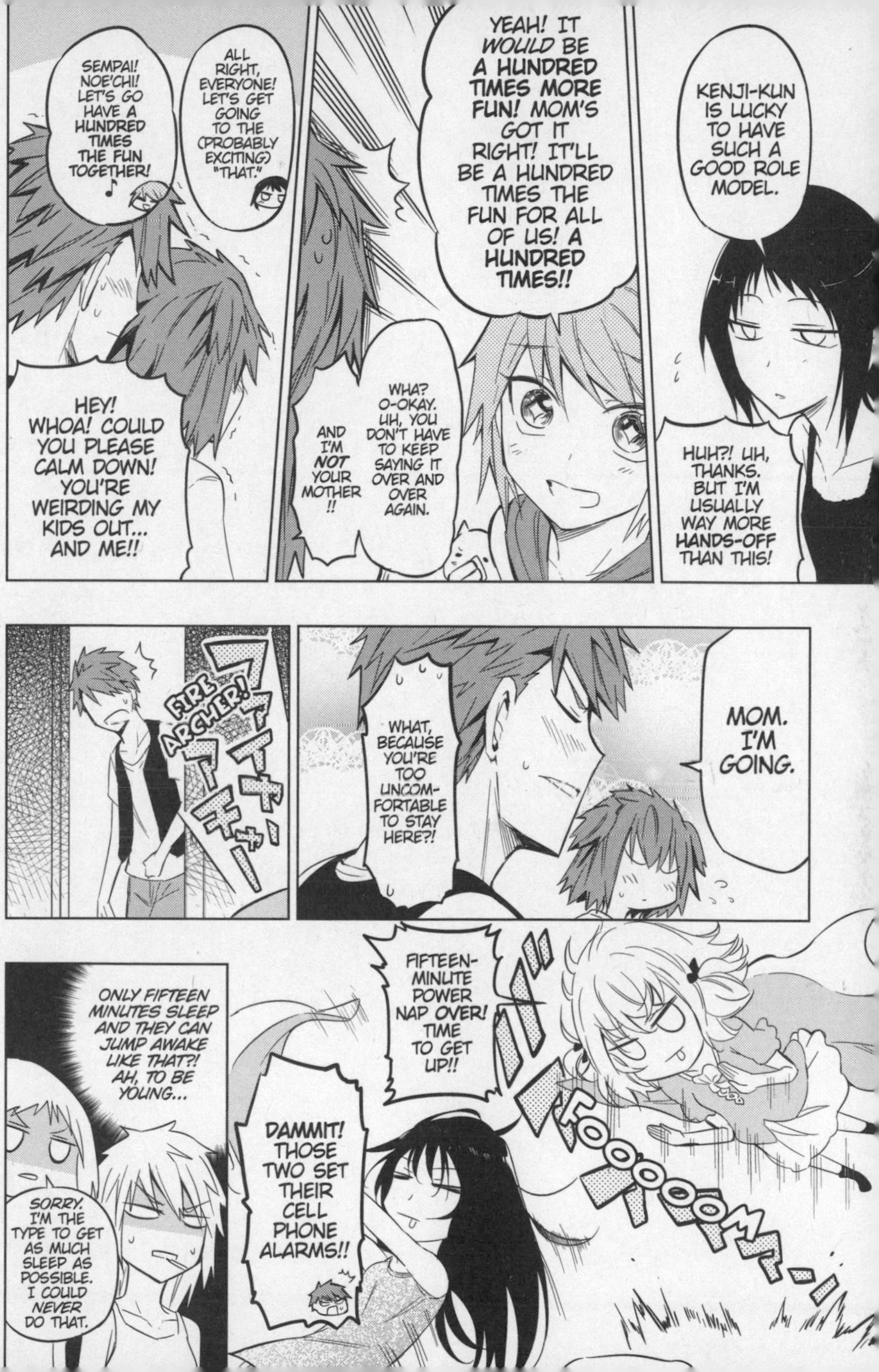
KENJI-KUN IS LUCKY TO HAVE SUCH A GOOD ROLE MODEL.
HUH?! UH, THANKS. BUT I'M USUALLY WAY MORE HANDS-OFF THAN THIS!
YEAH! IT *WOULD* BE A HUNDRED TIMES MORE FUN! MOM'S GOT IT RIGHT! IT'LL BE A HUNDRED TIMES THE FUN FOR ALL OF US! A HUNDRED TIMES!!
WHA? O-OKAY. UH, YOU DON'T HAVE TO KEEP SAYING IT OVER AND OVER AGAIN.
AND I'M *NOT* YOUR MOTHER!!
ALL RIGHT, EVERYONE! LET'S GET GOING TO THE (PROBABLY EXCITING) "THAT."
SEMPAI! NOE'CHI! LET'S GO HAVE A HUNDRED TIMES THE FUN TOGETHER! ♪
HEY! WHOA! COULD YOU PLEASE CALM DOWN! YOU'RE WEIRDING MY KIDS OUT... AND ME!!
MOM. I'M GOING.
WHAT, BECAUSE YOU'RE TOO UNCOMFORTABLE TO STAY HERE?!
FIRE ARCHER!
FOOOOOOM--!
FIFTEEN-MINUTE POWER NAP OVER! TIME TO GET UP!!
DAMMIT! THOSE TWO SET THEIR CELL PHONE ALARMS!!
ONLY FIFTEEN MINUTES SLEEP AND THEY CAN JUMP AWAKE LIKE THAT?! AH, TO BE YOUNG...
SORRY. I'M THE TYPE TO GET AS MUCH SLEEP AS POSSIBLE. I COULD NEVER DO THAT.

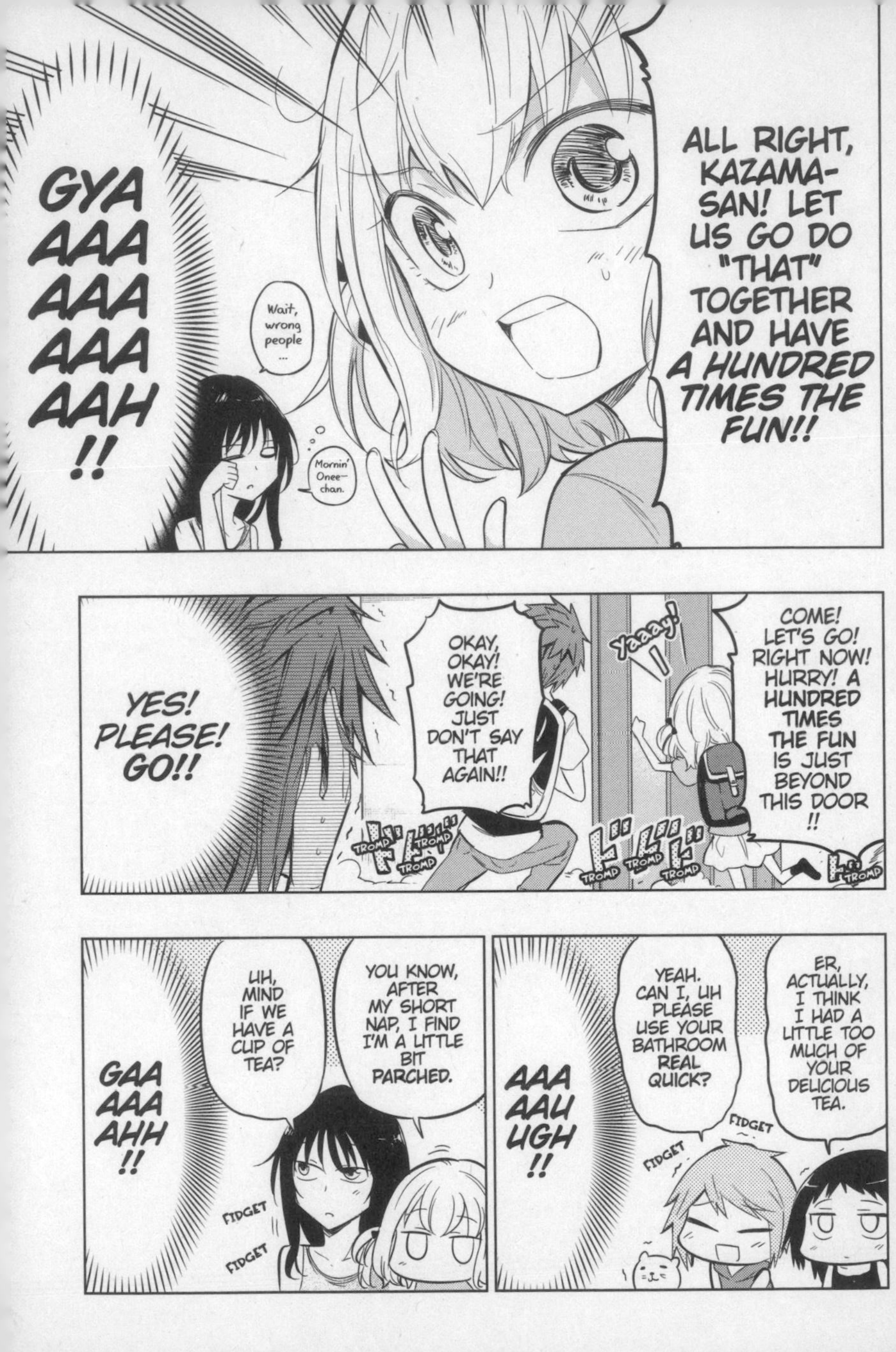
ALL RIGHT, KAZAMA-SAN! LET US GO DO "THAT" TOGETHER AND HAVE A HUNDRED TIMES THE FUN!!
Wait, wrong people ...
Mornin' Onee-chan.
GYAAAAAAAAAAAAAH!!
COME! LET'S GO! RIGHT NOW! HURRY! A HUNDRED TIMES THE FUN IS JUST BEYOND THIS DOOR!!
Yaaay!
OKAY, OKAY! WE'RE GOING! JUST DON'T SAY THAT AGAIN!!
YES! PLEASE! GO!!
TROMP TROMP TROMP TROMP
TROMP TROMP TROMP TROMP
ER, ACTUALLY, I THINK I HAD A LITTLE TOO MUCH OF YOUR DELICIOUS TEA.
YEAH. CAN I, UH PLEASE USE YOUR BATHROOM REAL QUICK?
FIDGET FIDGET
AAAAAUUGH!!
YOU KNOW, AFTER MY SHORT NAP, I FIND I'M A LITTLE BIT PARCHED.
UH, MIND IF WE HAVE A CUP OF TEA?
GAAAAAAHH!!
FIDGET FIDGET

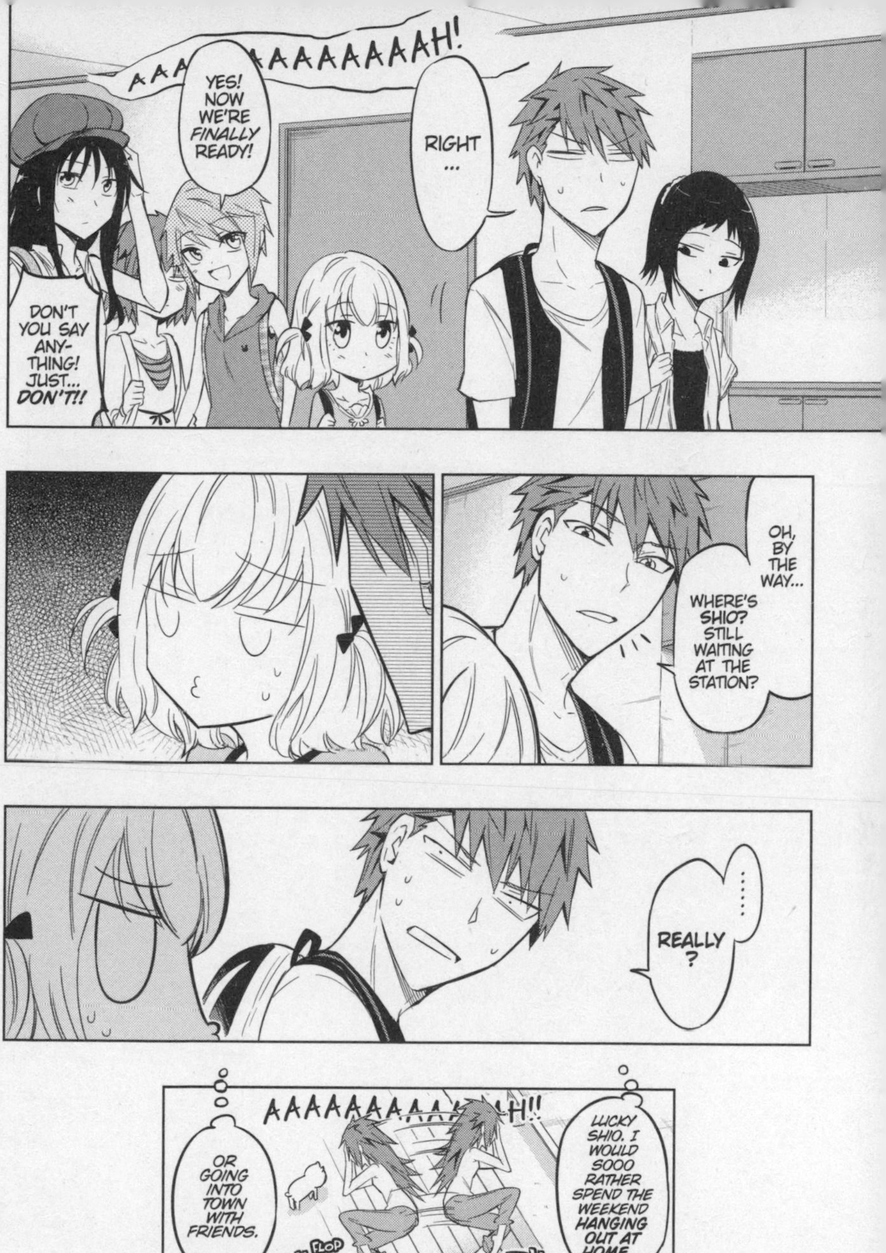
AAA AAAAAAAAAH!
RIGHT ...
YES! NOW WE'RE *FINALLY* READY!
DON'T YOU SAY ANY-THING! JUST... ***DON'T!!***
OH, BY THE WAY... WHERE'S SHIO? STILL WAITING AT THE STATION?
......
REALLY ?
LUCKY SHIO. I WOULD SOOO RATHER SPEND THE WEEKEND **HANGING OUT AT HOME...**
AAAAAAAAAH!!
FLOP
FLOP
OR GOING INTO TOWN WITH *FRIENDS.*

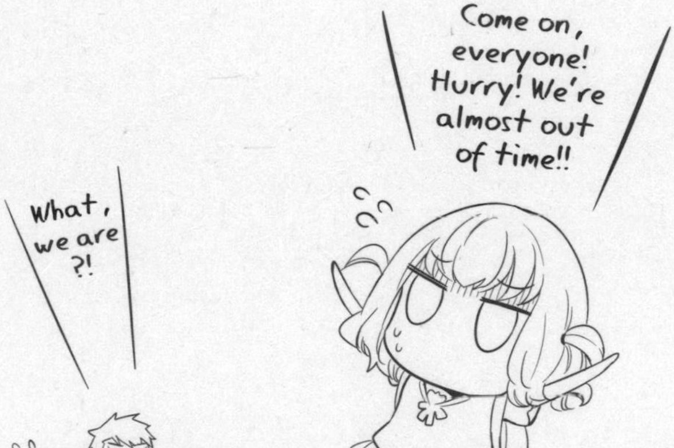
Come on, everyone! Hurry! We're almost out of time!!
What, we are?!

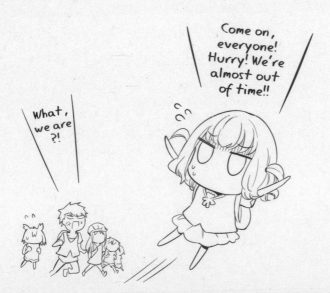

D-FRAGMENTS

ディーふらぐ!

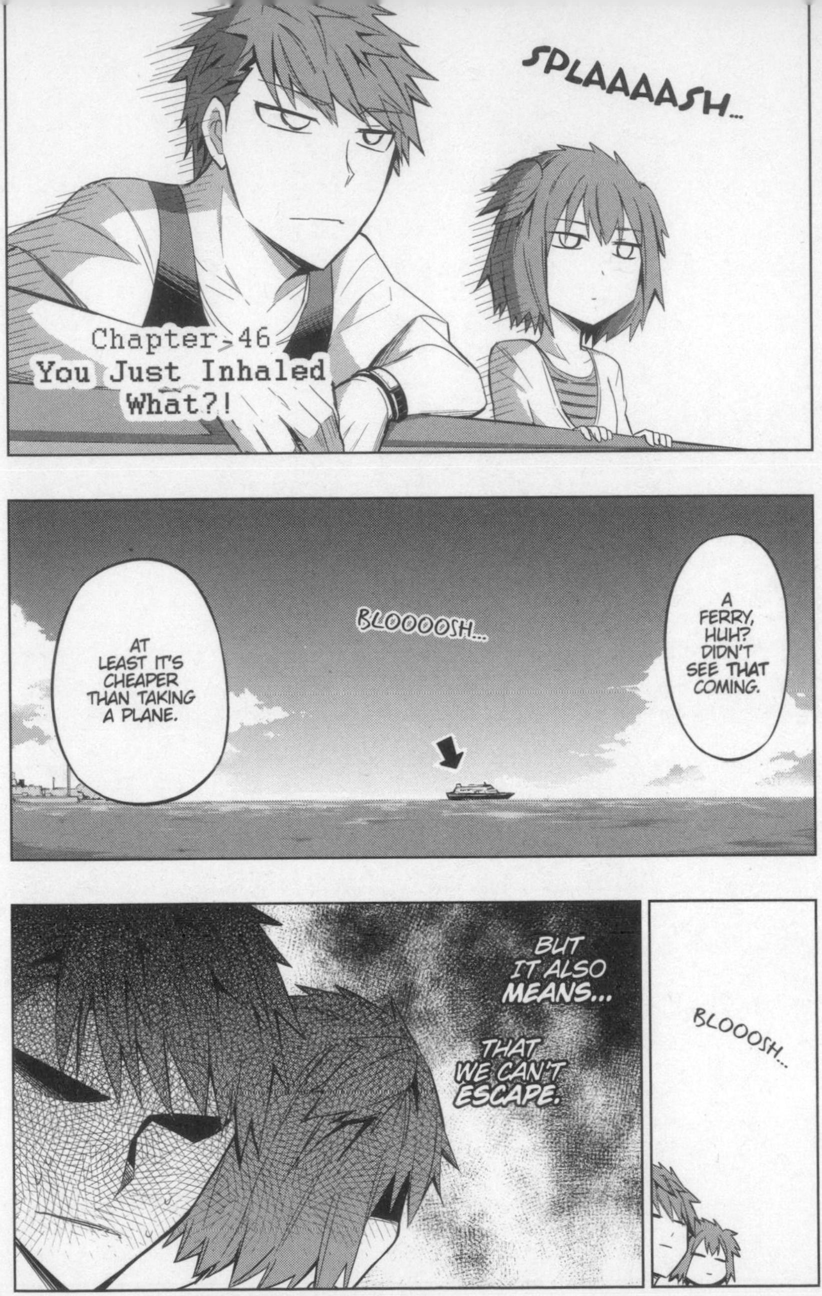
SPLAAAASH...
Chapter 46
You Just Inhaled What?!
A FERRY, HUH? DIDN'T SEE THAT COMING.
BLOOOOSH...
AT LEAST IT'S CHEAPER THAN TAKING A PLANE.
BLOOOSH...
BUT IT ALSO MEANS...
THAT WE CAN'T ESCAPE.

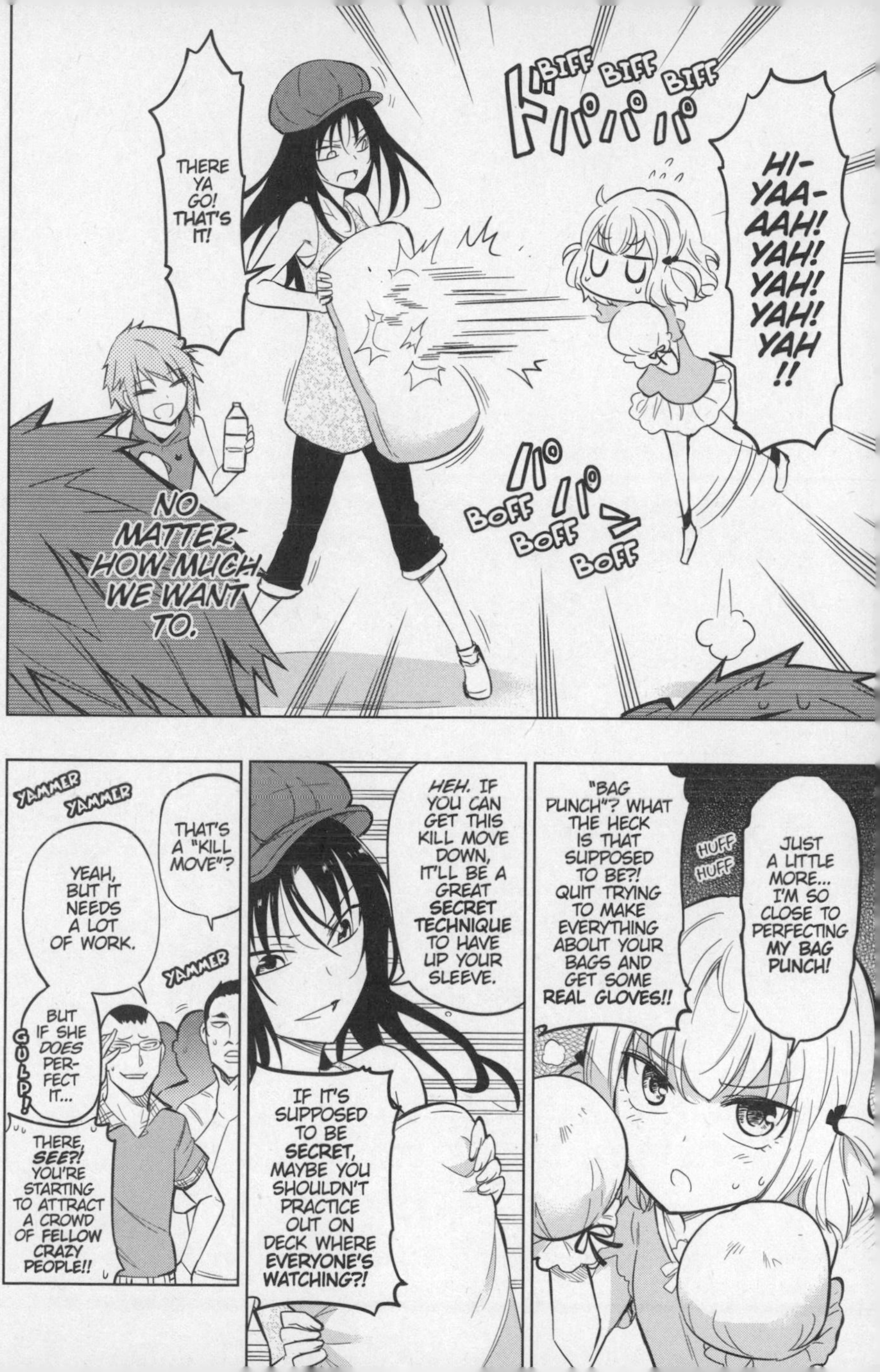
BIFF BIFF BIFF
HI-YAA-AAH! YAH! YAH! YAH! YAH!!
THERE YA GO! THAT'S IT!
BOFF BOFF BOFF
NO MATTER HOW MUCH WE WANT TO.
HUFF HUFF
JUST A LITTLE MORE... I'M SO CLOSE TO PERFECTING MY BAG PUNCH!
"BAG PUNCH"? WHAT THE HECK IS THAT SUPPOSED TO BE?! QUIT TRYING TO MAKE EVERYTHING ABOUT YOUR BAGS AND GET SOME REAL GLOVES!!
HEH. IF YOU CAN GET THIS KILL MOVE DOWN, IT'LL BE A GREAT SECRET TECHNIQUE TO HAVE UP YOUR SLEEVE.
IF IT'S SUPPOSED TO BE SECRET, MAYBE YOU SHOULDN'T PRACTICE OUT ON DECK WHERE EVERYONE'S WATCHING?!
YAMMER YAMMER
THAT'S A "KILL MOVE"?
YEAH, BUT IT NEEDS A LOT OF WORK.
YAMMER
BUT IF SHE DOES PERFECT IT...
GULP!
THERE, SEE?! YOU'RE STARTING TO ATTRACT A CROWD OF FELLOW CRAZY PEOPLE!!

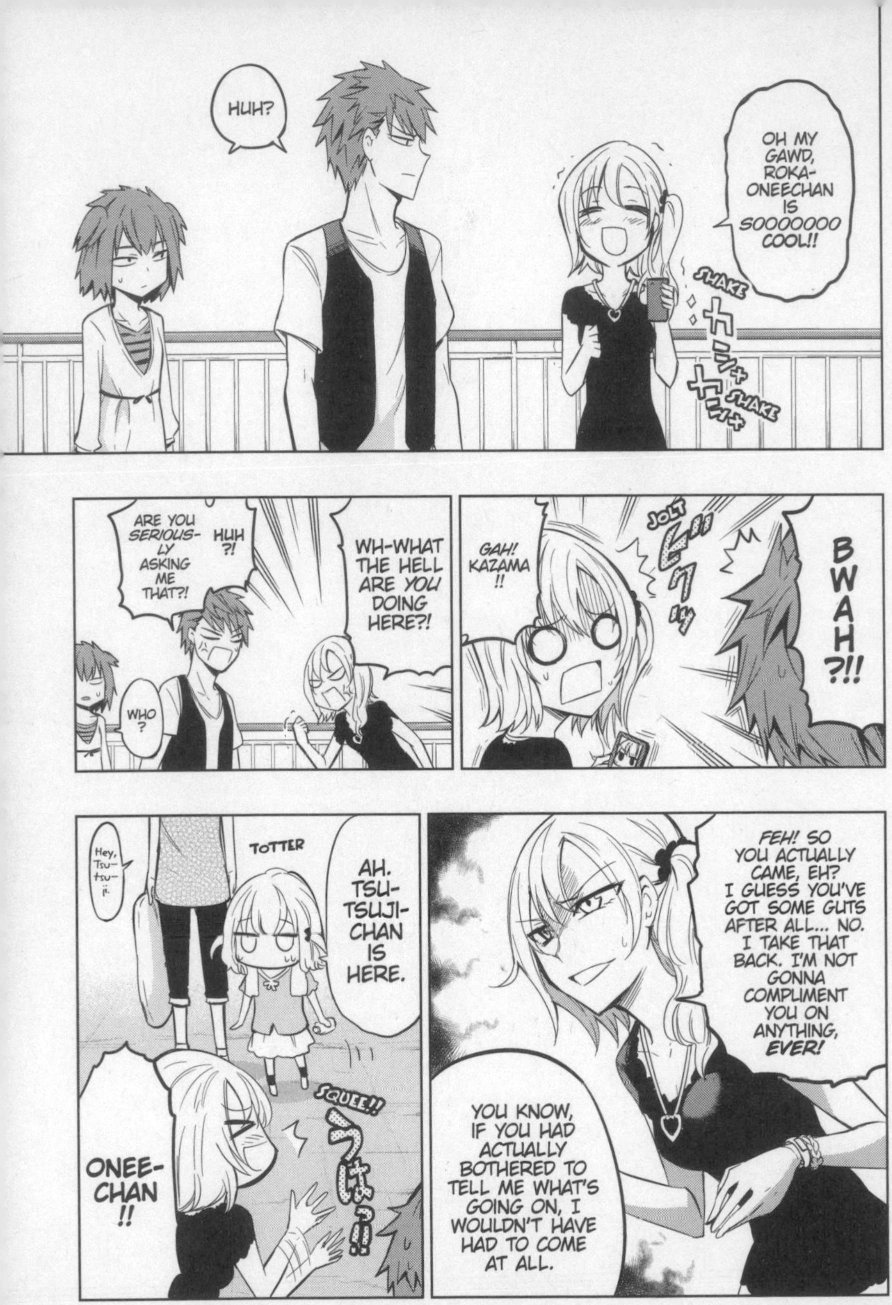
OH MY GAWD, ROKA-ONEECHAN IS SOOOOOOO COOL!!
SHAKE
SHAKE
HUH?
BWAH?!!
JOLT
GAH! KAZAMA!!
WH-WHAT THE HELL ARE YOU DOING HERE?!
HUH?!
ARE YOU SERIOUS-LY ASKING ME THAT?!
WHO?
FEH! SO YOU ACTUALLY CAME, EH? I GUESS YOU'VE GOT SOME GUTS AFTER ALL... NO. I TAKE THAT BACK. I'M NOT GONNA COMPLIMENT YOU ON ANYTHING, EVER!
YOU KNOW, IF YOU HAD ACTUALLY BOTHERED TO TELL ME WHAT'S GOING ON, I WOULDN'T HAVE HAD TO COME AT ALL.
AH. TSU-TSUJI-CHAN IS HERE.
TOTTER
Hey, Tsu-tsu-ji.
SQUEE!!
ONEE-CHAN!!

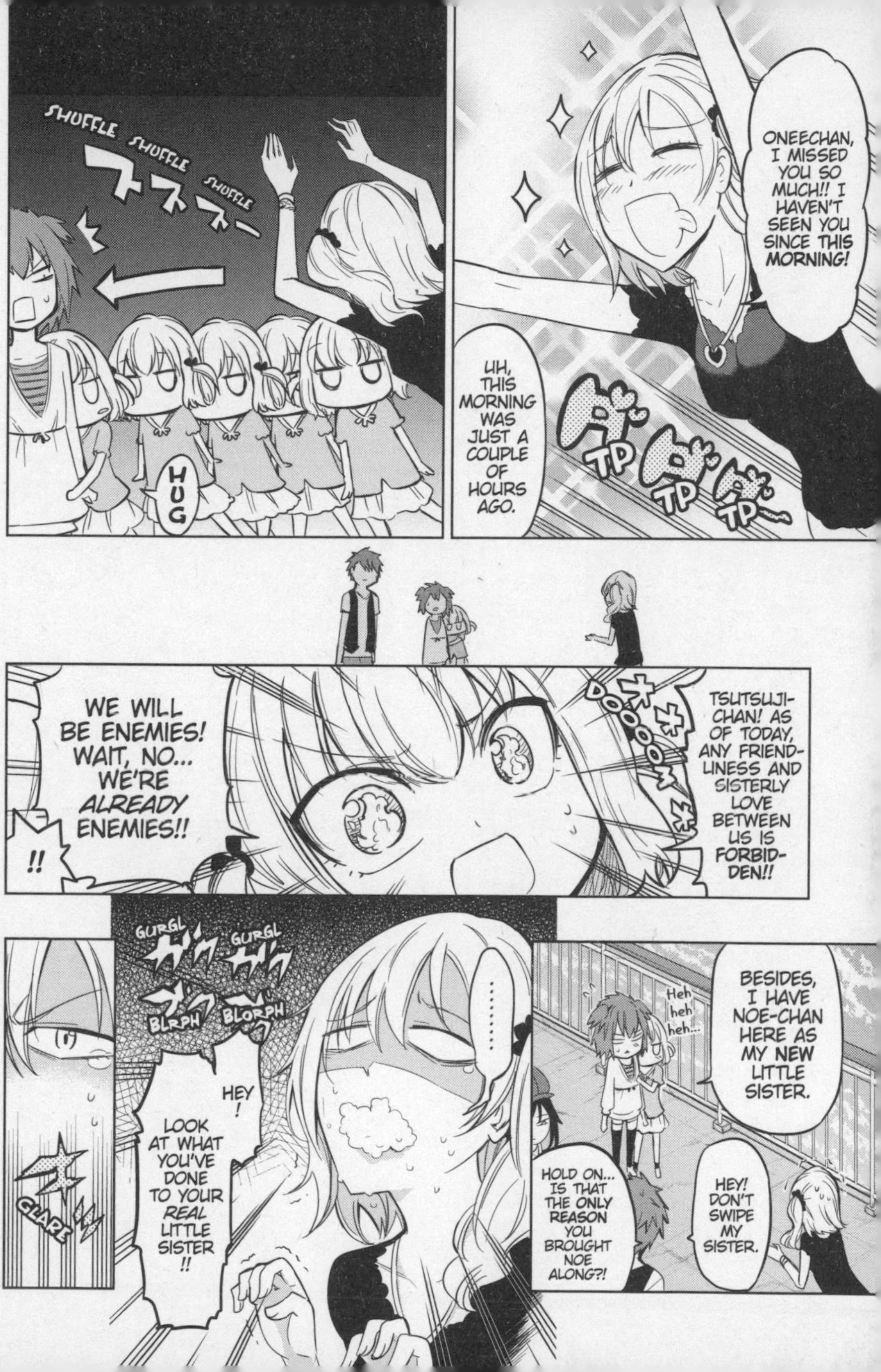
ONEECHAN, I MISSED YOU SO MUCH!! I HAVEN'T SEEN YOU SINCE THIS MORNING!
TP TP TP
UH, THIS MORNING WAS JUST A COUPLE OF HOURS AGO.
SHUFFLE SHUFFLE SHUFFLE
HUG
TSUTSUJI-CHAN! AS OF TODAY, ANY FRIEND-LINESS AND SISTERLY LOVE BETWEEN US IS FORBID-DEN!!
DOOOOOM
WE WILL BE ENEMIES! WAIT, NO... WE'RE *ALREADY* ENEMIES!!
!!
BESIDES, I HAVE NOE-CHAN HERE AS MY NEW LITTLE SISTER.
Heh heh heh...
HEY! DON'T SWIPE MY SISTER.
HOLD ON... IS THAT THE ONLY REASON YOU BROUGHT NOE ALONG?!
......
GURGL GURGL
BLRPH BLORPH
HEY!
LOOK AT WHAT YOU'VE DONE TO YOUR *REAL* LITTLE SISTER!!
GLARE

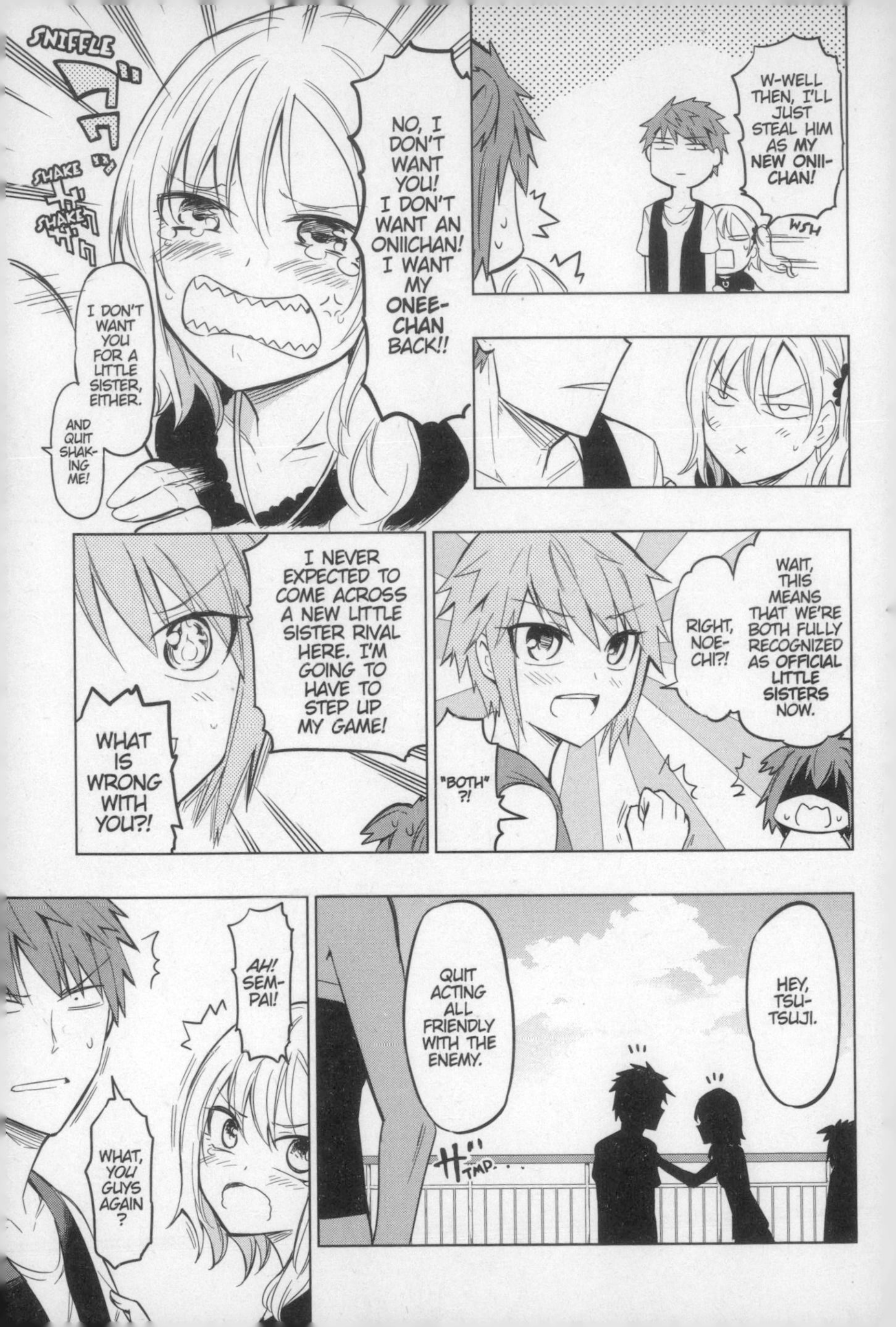
W-WELL THEN, I'LL JUST STEAL HIM AS MY NEW ONII-CHAN!
WSH
SNIFFLE
NO, I DON'T WANT YOU! I DON'T WANT AN ONIICHAN! I WANT MY ONEE-CHAN BACK!!
SHAKE
SHAKE
I DON'T WANT YOU FOR A LITTLE SISTER, EITHER.
AND QUIT SHAK-ING ME!
WAIT, THIS MEANS THAT WE'RE BOTH FULLY RECOGNIZED AS OFFICIAL LITTLE SISTERS NOW.
RIGHT, NOE-CHI?!
"BOTH"?!
I NEVER EXPECTED TO COME ACROSS A NEW LITTLE SISTER RIVAL HERE. I'M GOING TO HAVE TO STEP UP MY GAME!
WHAT IS WRONG WITH YOU?!
HEY, TSU-TSUJI.
QUIT ACTING ALL FRIENDLY WITH THE ENEMY.
TMP...
AH! SEM-PAI!
WHAT, YOU GUYS AGAIN?

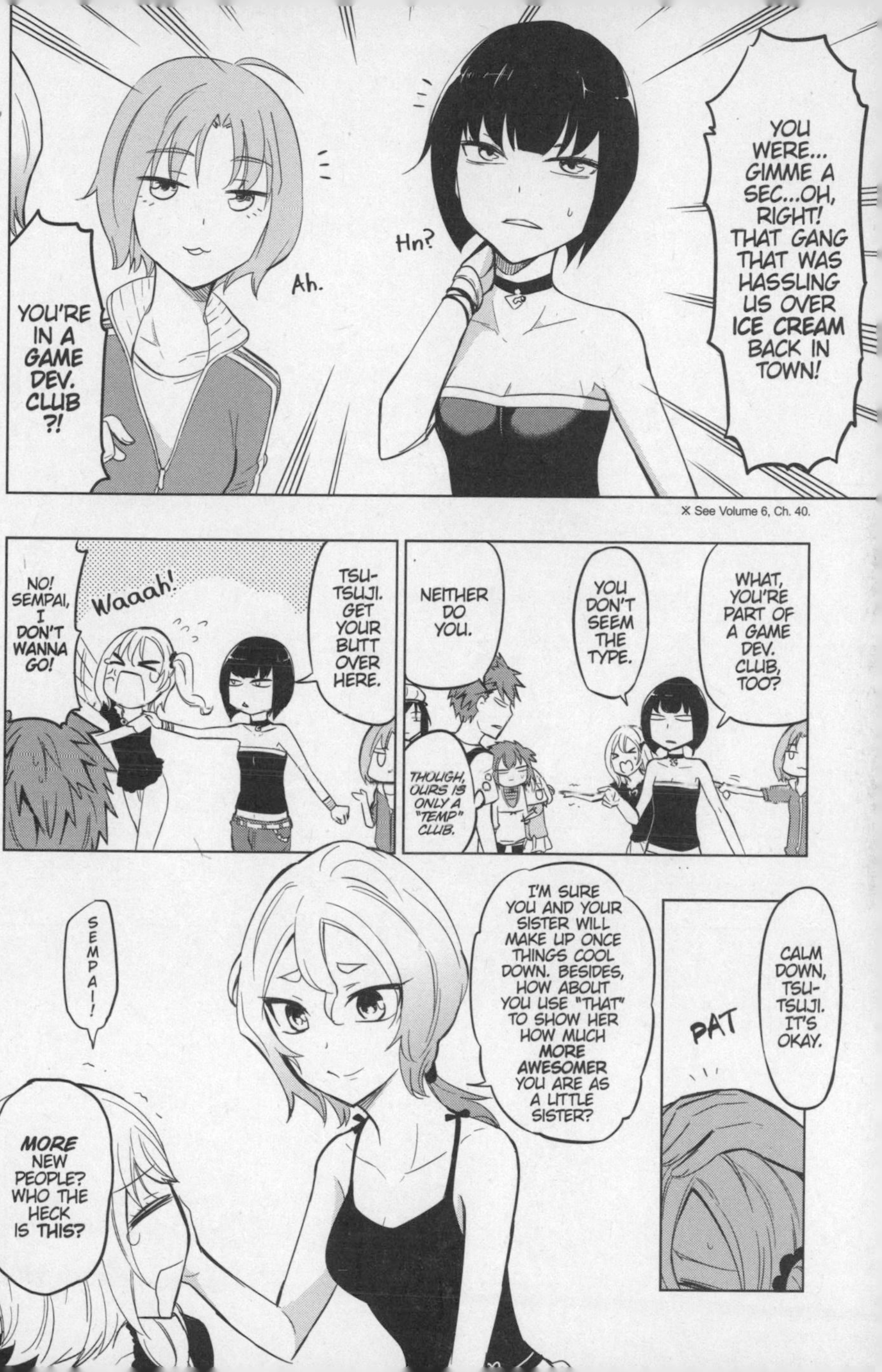
YOU WERE... GIMME A SEC...OH, RIGHT! THAT GANG THAT WAS HASSLING US OVER ICE CREAM BACK IN TOWN!
Hn?
Ah.
YOU'RE IN A GAME DEV. CLUB ?!
WHAT, YOU'RE PART OF A GAME DEV. CLUB, TOO?
YOU DON'T SEEM THE TYPE.
NEITHER DO YOU.
THOUGH, OURS IS ONLY A "TEMP" CLUB.
TSU-TSUJI. GET YOUR BUTT OVER HERE.
Waaah!
NO! SEMPAI, I DON'T WANNA GO!
CALM DOWN, TSU-TSUJI. IT'S OKAY.
PAT
I'M SURE YOU AND YOUR SISTER WILL MAKE UP ONCE THINGS COOL DOWN. BESIDES, HOW ABOUT YOU USE "THAT" TO SHOW HER HOW MUCH MORE AWESOMER YOU ARE AS A LITTLE SISTER?
SEMPAI!
MORE NEW PEOPLE? WHO THE HECK IS THIS?

※ See Volume 6, Ch. 40.

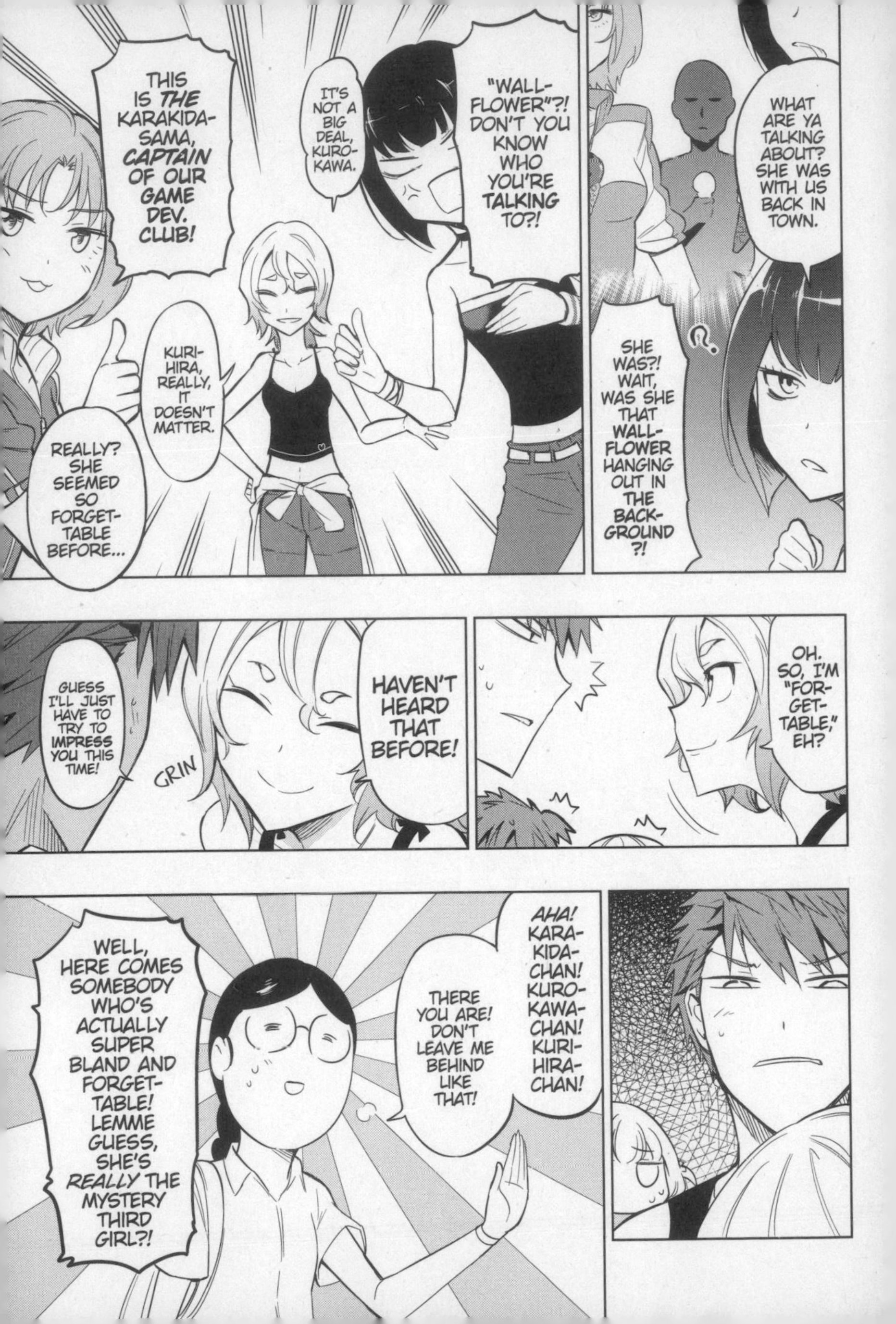
WHAT ARE YA TALKING ABOUT? SHE WAS WITH US BACK IN TOWN.
SHE WAS?! WAIT, WAS SHE THAT WALLFLOWER HANGING OUT IN THE BACKGROUND?!
"WALLFLOWER"?! DON'T YOU KNOW WHO YOU'RE TALKING TO?!
IT'S NOT A BIG DEAL, KUROKAWA.
THIS IS *THE* KARAKIDA-SAMA, *CAPTAIN* OF OUR GAME DEV. CLUB!
KURIHIRA, REALLY, IT DOESN'T MATTER.
REALLY? SHE SEEMED SO FORGETTABLE BEFORE...
OH. SO, I'M "FORGETTABLE," EH?
HAVEN'T HEARD THAT BEFORE!
GUESS I'LL JUST HAVE TO TRY TO IMPRESS YOU THIS TIME!
GRIN
AHA! KARAKIDA-CHAN! KUROKAWA-CHAN! KURIHIRA-CHAN!
THERE YOU ARE! DON'T LEAVE ME BEHIND LIKE THAT!
WELL, HERE COMES SOMEBODY WHO'S ACTUALLY SUPER BLAND AND FORGETTABLE! LEMME GUESS, SHE'S *REALLY* THE MYSTERY THIRD GIRL?!

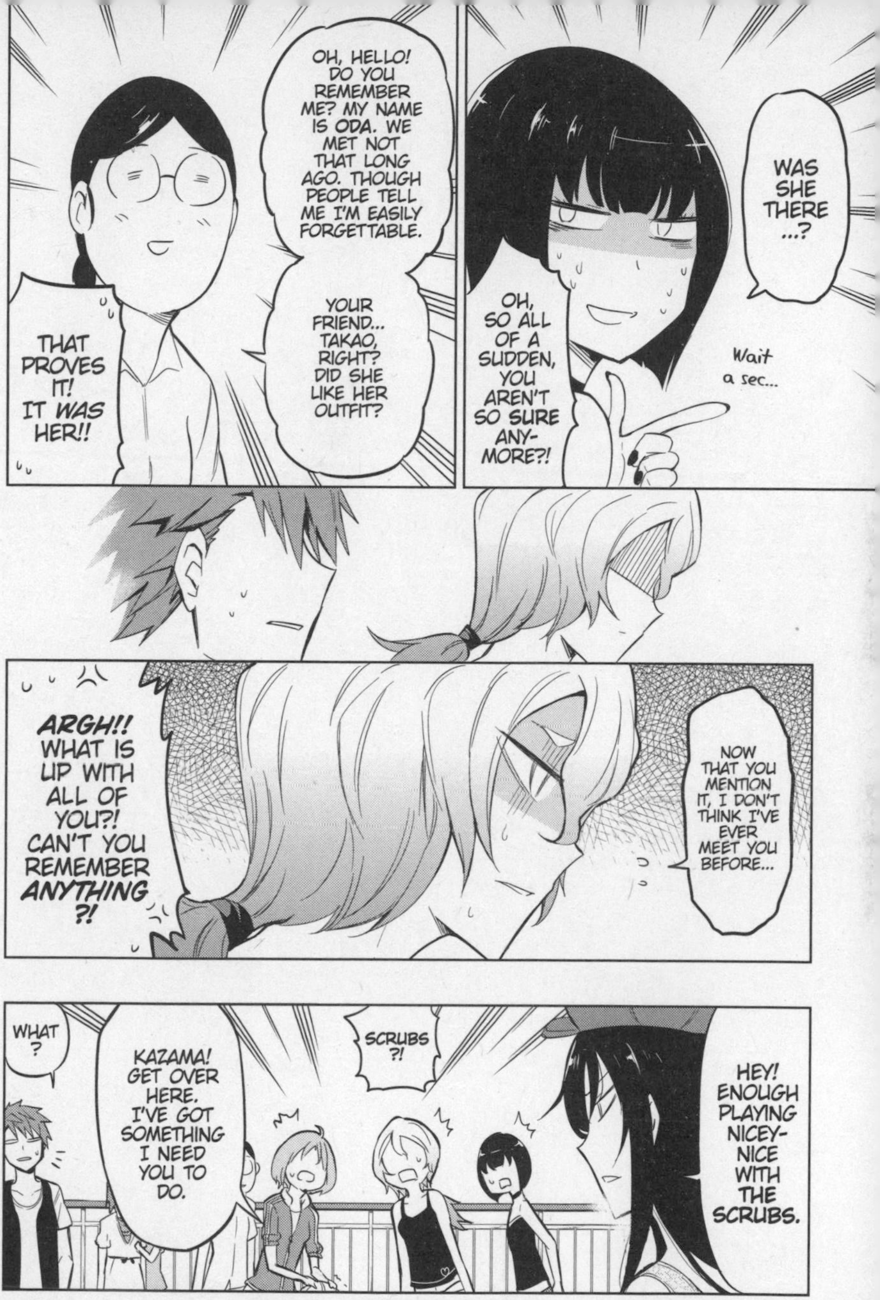
WAS SHE THERE ...?
OH, SO ALL OF A SUDDEN, YOU AREN'T SO SURE ANYMORE?!
Wait a sec...
OH, HELLO! DO YOU REMEMBER ME? MY NAME IS ODA. WE MET NOT THAT LONG AGO. THOUGH PEOPLE TELL ME I'M EASILY FORGETTABLE.
YOUR FRIEND... TAKAO, RIGHT? DID SHE LIKE HER OUTFIT?
THAT PROVES IT! IT WAS HER!!
NOW THAT YOU MENTION IT, I DON'T THINK I'VE EVER MEET YOU BEFORE...
ARGH!! WHAT IS UP WITH ALL OF YOU?! CAN'T YOU REMEMBER ANYTHING ?!
HEY! ENOUGH PLAYING NICEY-NICE WITH THE SCRUBS.
SCRUBS ?!
KAZAMA! GET OVER HERE. I'VE GOT SOMETHING I NEED YOU TO DO.
WHAT ?

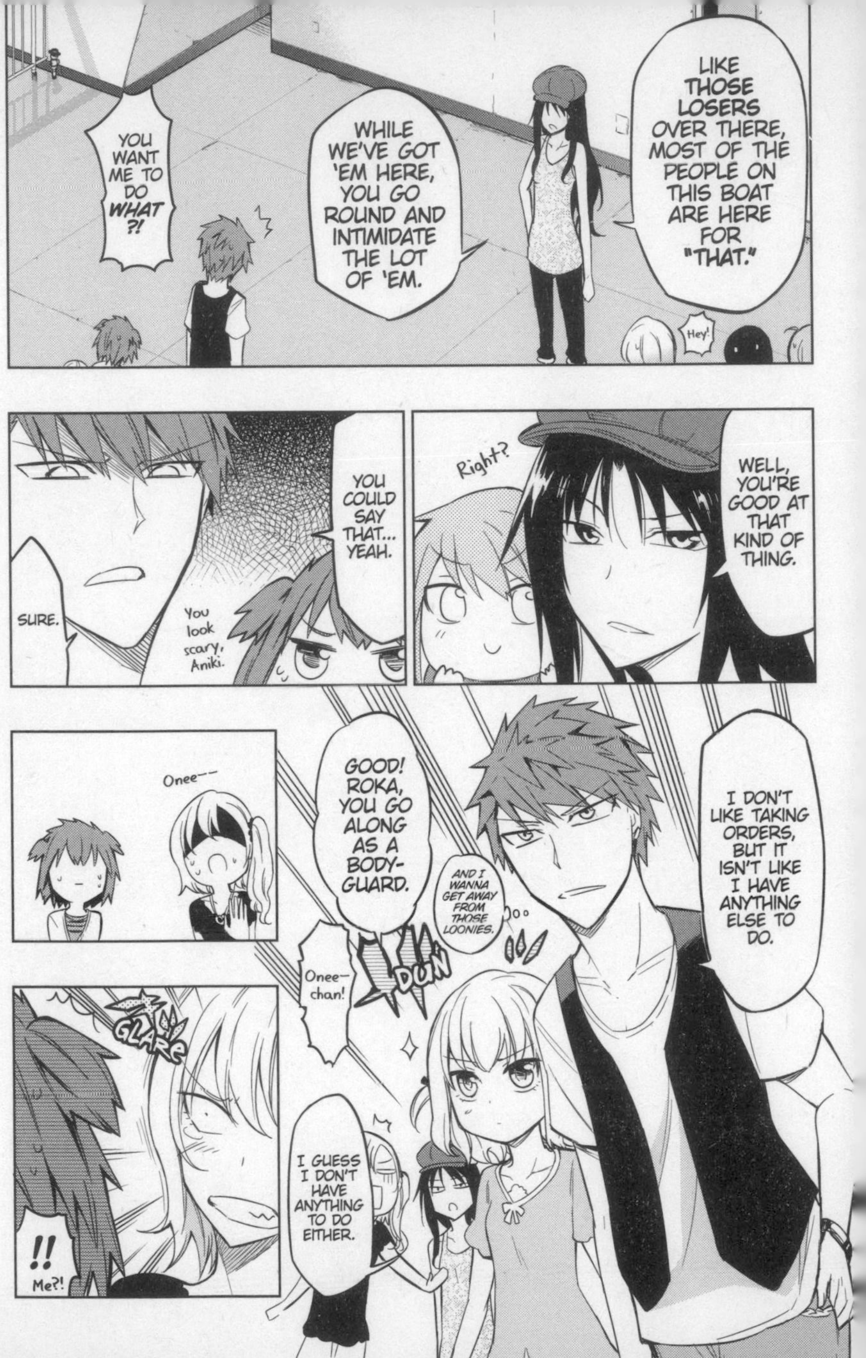
LIKE THOSE LOSERS OVER THERE, MOST OF THE PEOPLE ON THIS BOAT ARE HERE FOR "THAT."
Hey!
WHILE WE'VE GOT 'EM HERE, YOU GO ROUND AND INTIMIDATE THE LOT OF 'EM.
YOU WANT ME TO DO WHAT?!
WELL, YOU'RE GOOD AT THAT KIND OF THING.
Right?
YOU COULD SAY THAT... YEAH.
You look scary, Aniki.
SURE.
I DON'T LIKE TAKING ORDERS, BUT IT ISN'T LIKE I HAVE ANYTHING ELSE TO DO.
GOOD! ROKA, YOU GO ALONG AS A BODYGUARD.
AND I WANNA GET AWAY FROM THOSE LOONIES.
DUN
Onee-chan!
I GUESS I DON'T HAVE ANYTHING TO DO EITHER.
Onee--
GLARE
!!
Me?!

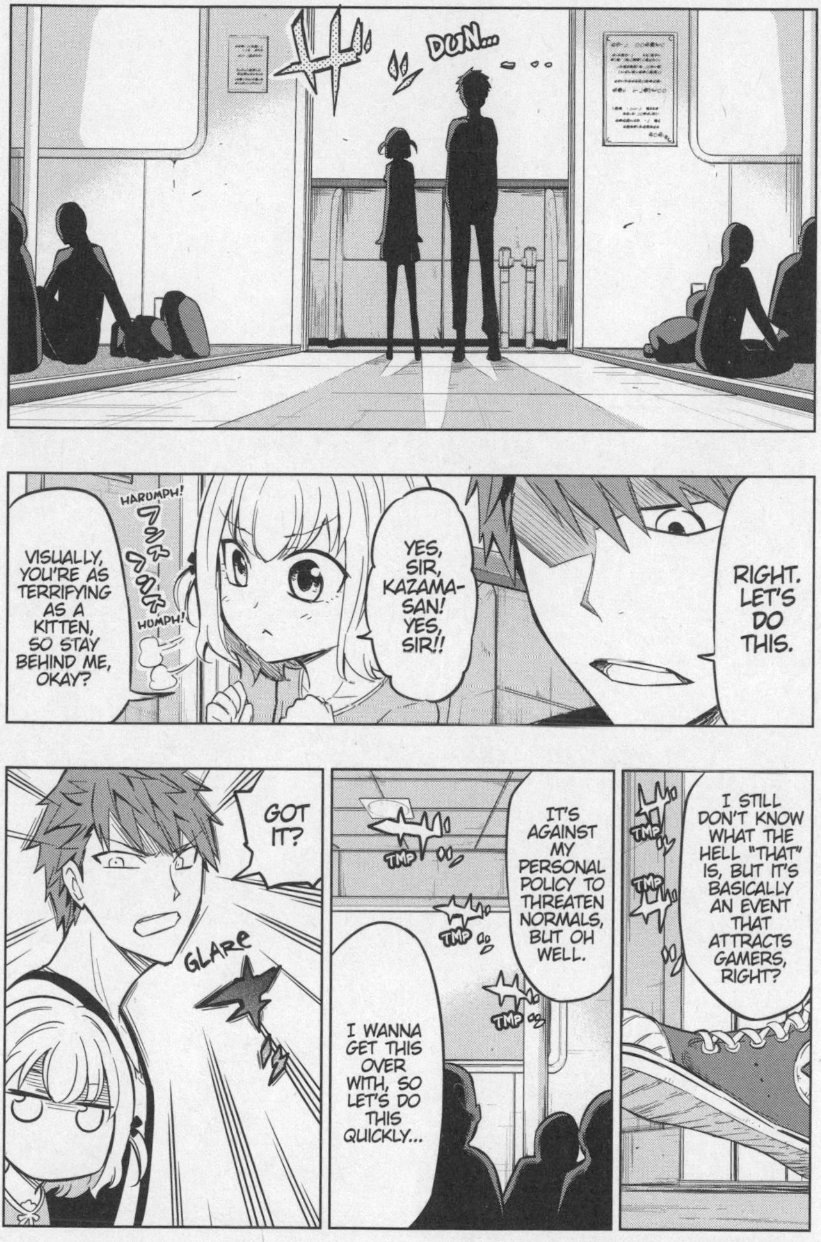
DUN...
RIGHT. LET'S DO THIS.
YES, SIR, KAZAMA-SAN! YES, SIR!!
HARUMPH!
HUMPH!
VISUALLY, YOU'RE AS TERRIFYING AS A KITTEN, SO STAY BEHIND ME, OKAY?
TMP
TMP
I STILL DON'T KNOW WHAT THE HELL "THAT" IS, BUT IT'S BASICALLY AN EVENT THAT ATTRACTS GAMERS, RIGHT?
TMP
TMP
TMP
IT'S AGAINST MY PERSONAL POLICY TO THREATEN NORMALS, BUT OH WELL.
I WANNA GET THIS OVER WITH, SO LET'S DO THIS QUICKLY...
GOT IT?
GLARE

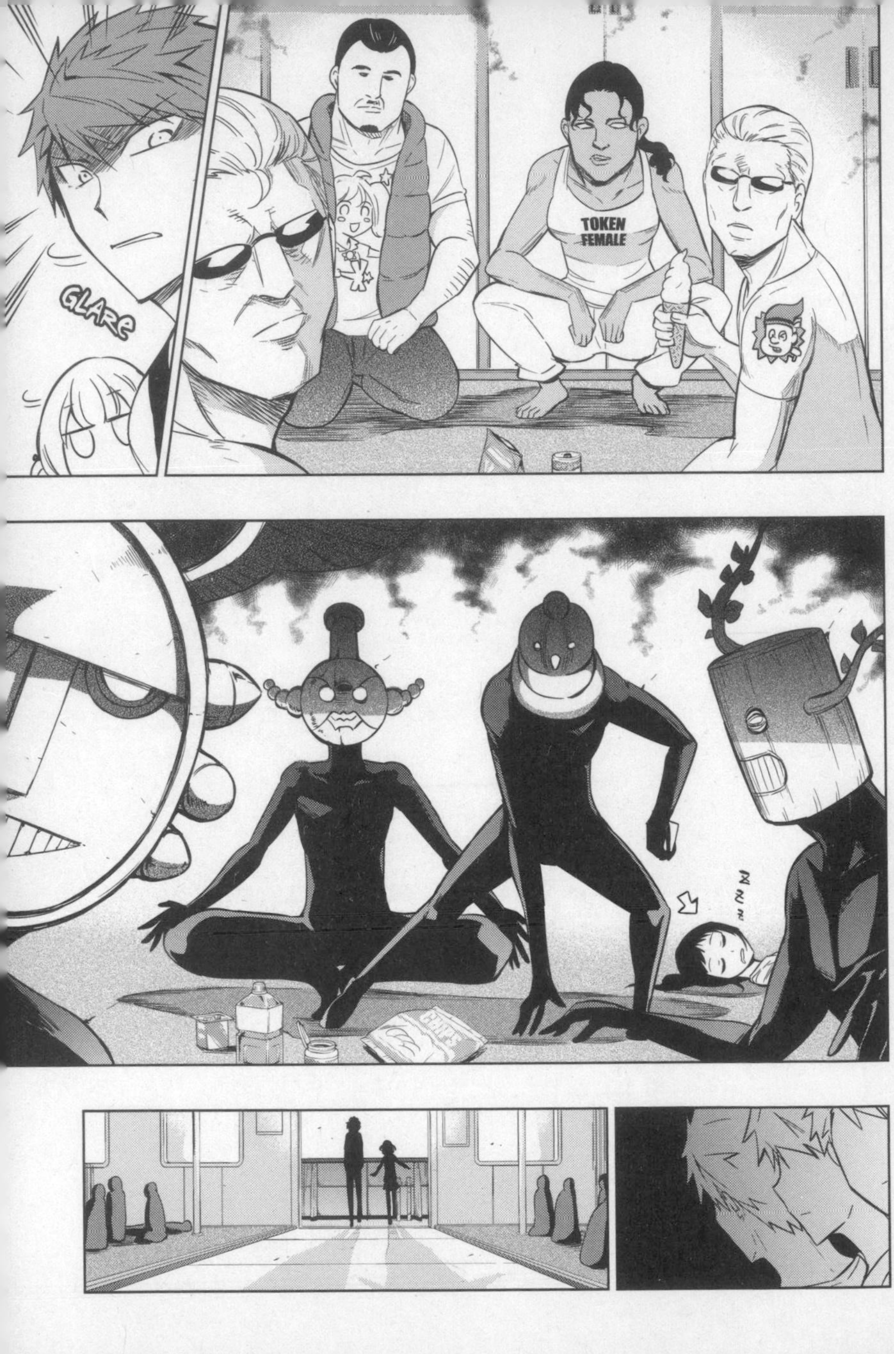
TOKEN
FEMALE
GLARE
CHIPS
Z Z Z

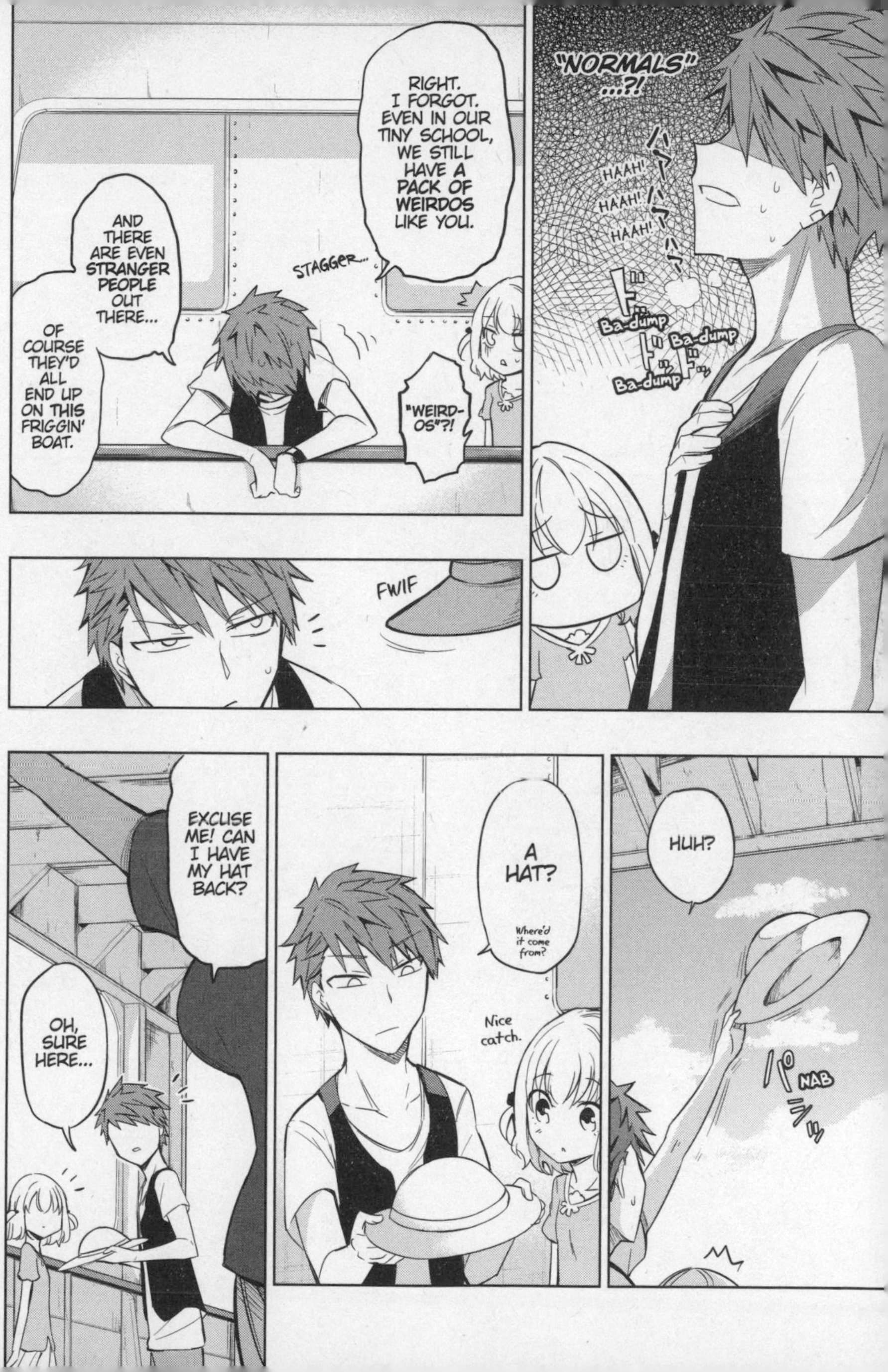
"NORMALS" ...?!
HAAH! HAAH! HAAH!
Ba-dump Ba-dump Ba-dump
RIGHT. I FORGOT. EVEN IN OUR TINY SCHOOL, WE STILL HAVE A PACK OF WEIRDOS LIKE YOU.
STAGGER...
AND THERE ARE EVEN STRANGER PEOPLE OUT THERE...
"WEIRD-OS"?!
OF COURSE THEY'D ALL END UP ON THIS FRIGGIN' BOAT.
FWIF
HUH?
NAB
A HAT?
Where'd it come from?
Nice catch.
EXCUSE ME! CAN I HAVE MY HAT BACK?
OH, SURE HERE...

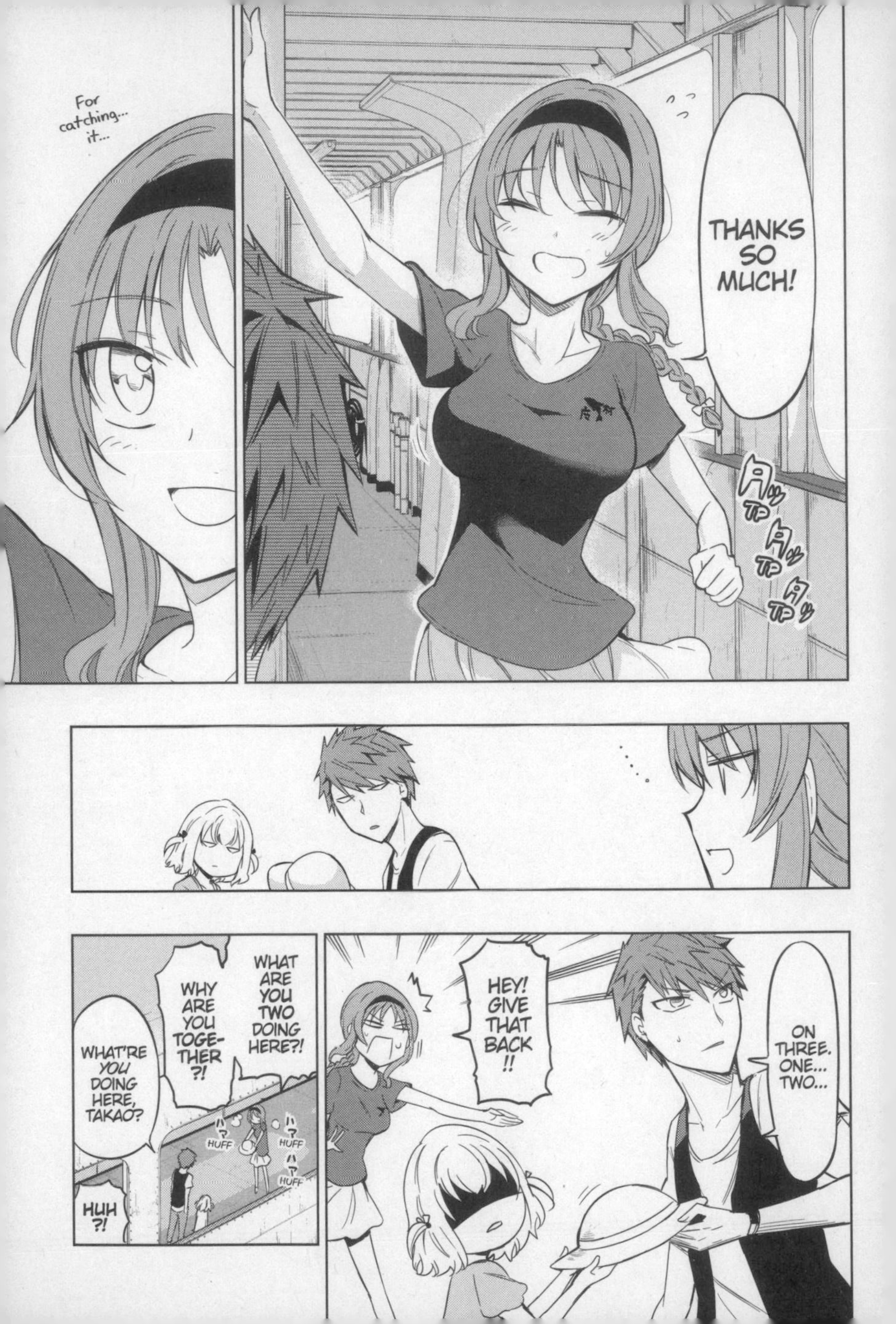
THANKS SO MUCH!
タッ TP
タッ TP
タッ TP
For catching... it...
.....
ON THREE. ONE... TWO...
HEY! GIVE THAT BACK!!
ハァ HUFF
ハァ HUFF
ハァ HUFF
WHAT ARE YOU TWO DOING HERE?!
WHY ARE YOU TOGE-THER?!
WHAT'RE YOU DOING HERE, TAKAO?
HUH?!

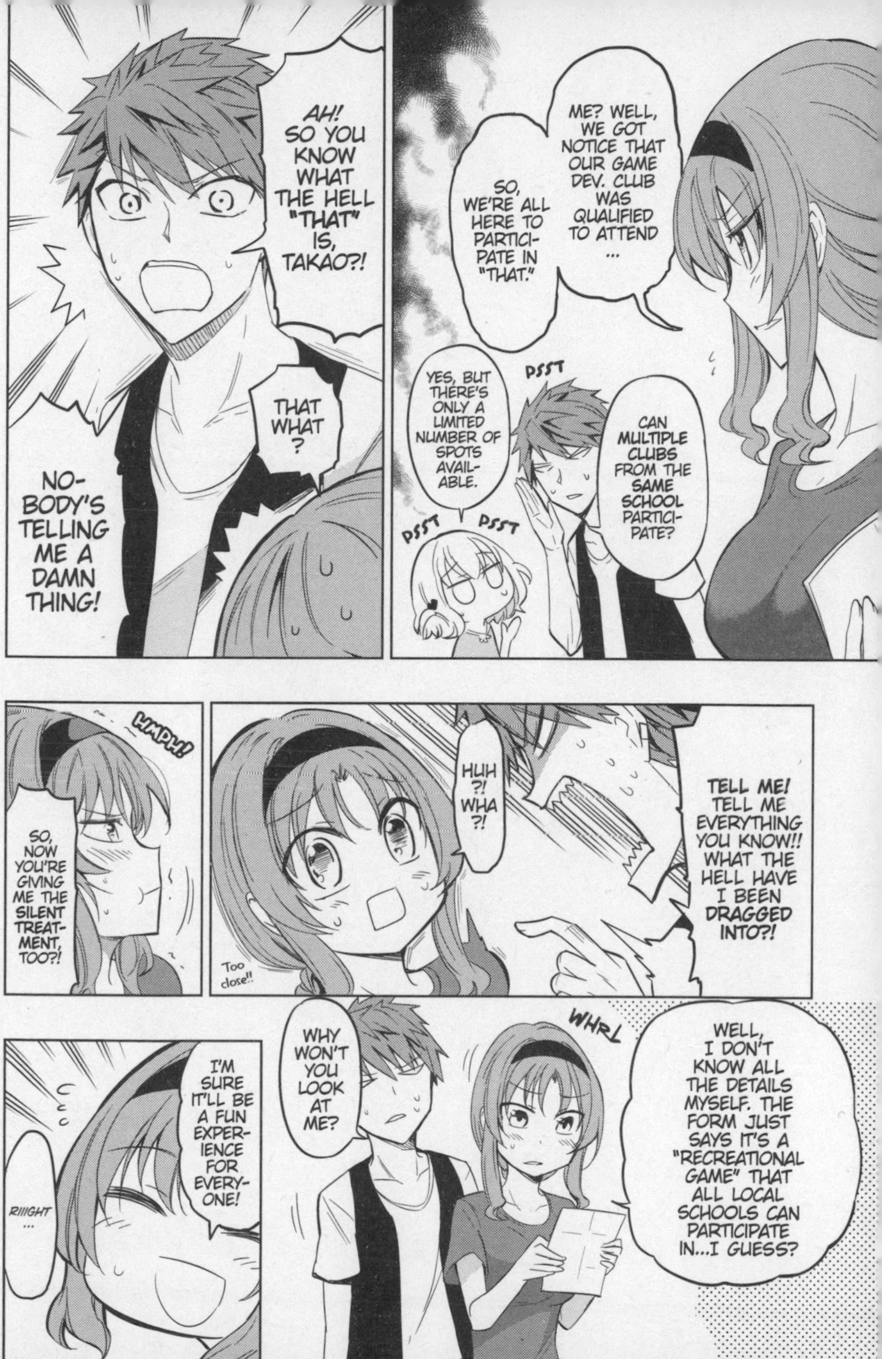
ME? WELL, WE GOT NOTICE THAT OUR GAME DEV. CLUB WAS QUALIFIED TO ATTEND ...
SO, WE'RE ALL HERE TO PARTICIPATE IN "THAT."
PSST
CAN MULTIPLE CLUBS FROM THE SAME SCHOOL PARTICIPATE?
YES, BUT THERE'S ONLY A LIMITED NUMBER OF SPOTS AVAILABLE.
PSST PSST
AH! SO YOU KNOW WHAT THE HELL "THAT" IS, TAKAO?!
THAT WHAT?
NOBODY'S TELLING ME A DAMN THING!
TELL ME! TELL ME EVERYTHING YOU KNOW!! WHAT THE HELL HAVE I BEEN DRAGGED INTO?!
HUH?! WHA?!
Too close!!
HMPH!
SO, NOW YOU'RE GIVING ME THE SILENT TREATMENT, TOO?!
WHRL
WELL, I DON'T KNOW ALL THE DETAILS MYSELF. THE FORM JUST SAYS IT'S A "RECREATIONAL GAME" THAT ALL LOCAL SCHOOLS CAN PARTICIPATE IN...I GUESS?
WHY WON'T YOU LOOK AT ME?
I'M SURE IT'LL BE A FUN EXPERIENCE FOR EVERYONE!
RIIIGHT ...

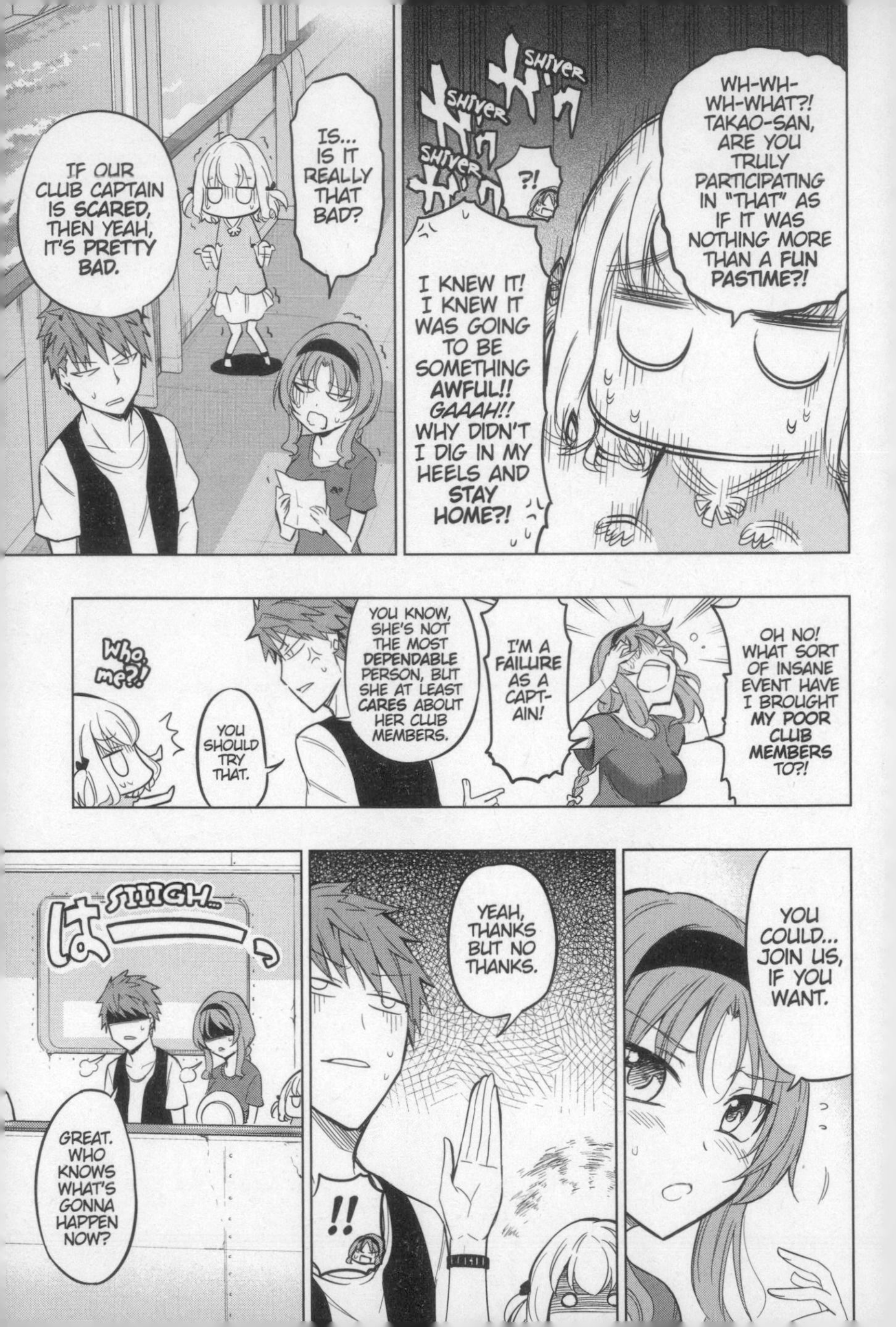
WH-WH-WH-WHAT?! TAKAO-SAN, ARE YOU TRULY PARTICIPATING IN "THAT" AS IF IT WAS NOTHING MORE THAN A FUN PASTIME?!
SHIVER
SHIVER
SHIVER
?!
I KNEW IT! I KNEW IT WAS GOING TO BE SOMETHING AWFUL!! GAAAH!! WHY DIDN'T I DIG IN MY HEELS AND STAY HOME?!
IS... IS IT REALLY THAT BAD?
IF OUR CLUB CAPTAIN IS SCARED, THEN YEAH, IT'S PRETTY BAD.
OH NO! WHAT SORT OF INSANE EVENT HAVE I BROUGHT MY POOR CLUB MEMBERS TO?!
I'M A FAILURE AS A CAPT-AIN!
YOU KNOW, SHE'S NOT THE MOST DEPENDABLE PERSON, BUT SHE AT LEAST CARES ABOUT HER CLUB MEMBERS.
YOU SHOULD TRY THAT.
Who, me?!
YOU COULD... JOIN US, IF YOU WANT.
YEAH, THANKS BUT NO THANKS.
!!
SIIIGH...
は——っ
GREAT. WHO KNOWS WHAT'S GONNA HAPPEN NOW?

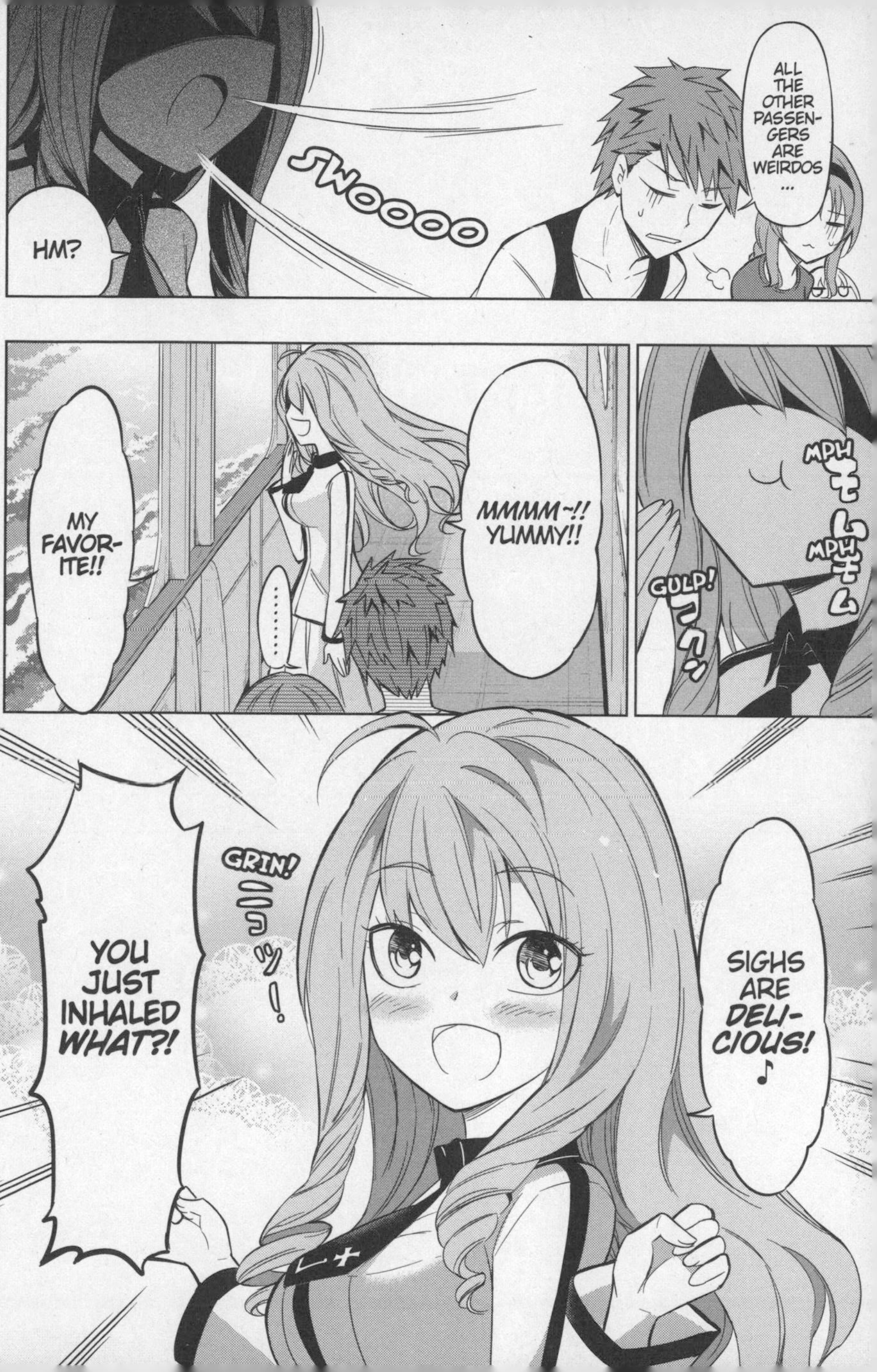
ALL THE OTHER PASSEN-GERS ARE WEIRDOS ...
SWOOOOO
HM?
MPH
モム
MPH
モム
GULP!
ゴクッ
MMMM~!! YUMMY!!
......
MY FAVOR-ITE!!
SIGHS ARE DELI-CIOUS! ♪
GRIN!
ニコッ!
YOU JUST INHALED WHAT?!

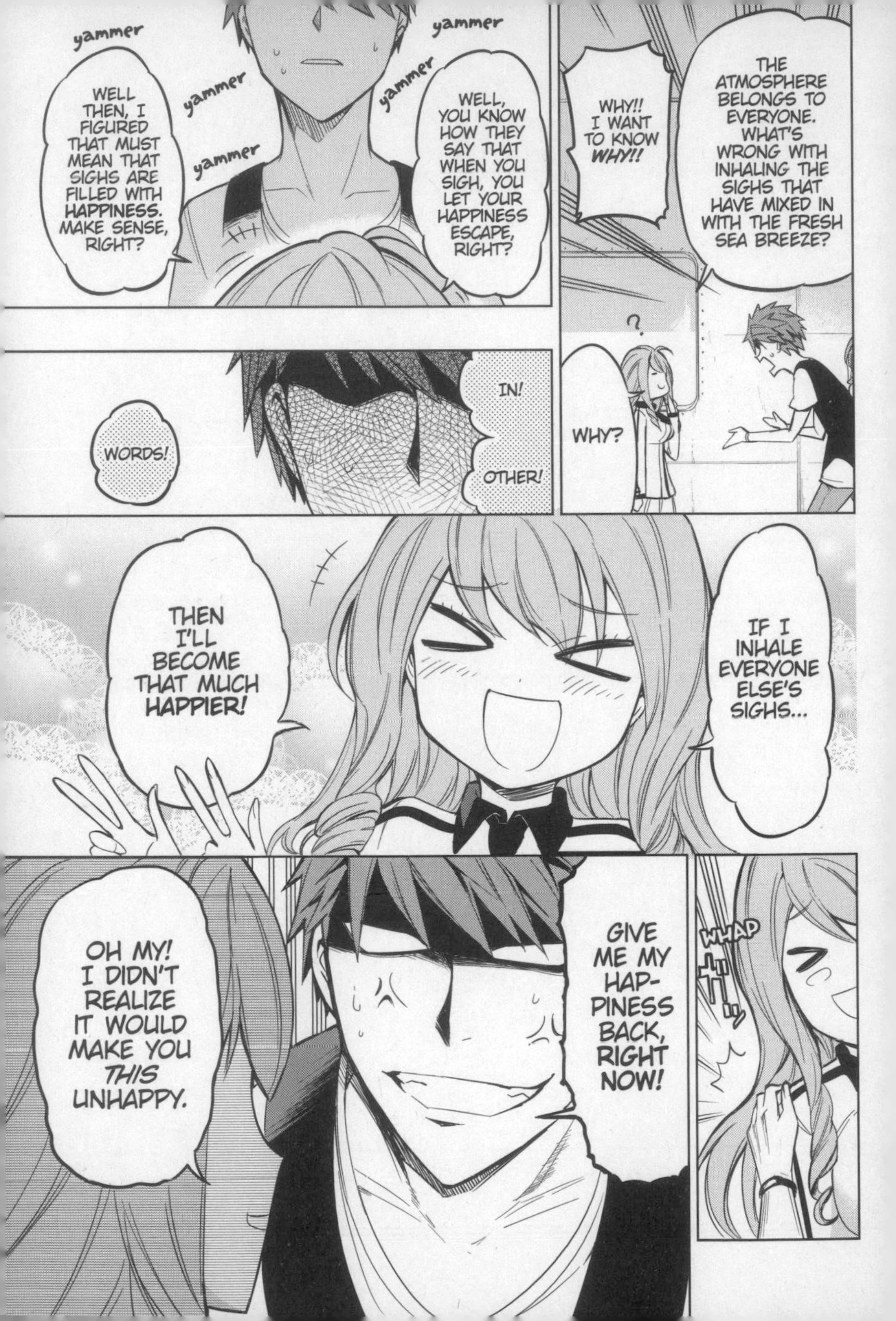
THE ATMOSPHERE BELONGS TO EVERYONE. WHAT'S WRONG WITH INHALING THE SIGHS THAT HAVE MIXED IN WITH THE FRESH SEA BREEZE?
WHY!! I WANT TO KNOW WHY!!
?
WHY?
yammer
yammer
WELL, YOU KNOW HOW THEY SAY THAT WHEN YOU SIGH, YOU LET YOUR HAPPINESS ESCAPE, RIGHT?
yammer
yammer
WELL THEN, I FIGURED THAT MUST MEAN THAT SIGHS ARE FILLED WITH HAPPINESS. MAKE SENSE, RIGHT?
IN!
OTHER!
WORDS!
IF I INHALE EVERYONE ELSE'S SIGHS...
THEN I'LL BECOME THAT MUCH HAPPIER!
WHAP
GIVE ME MY HAP-PINESS BACK, RIGHT NOW!
OH MY! I DIDN'T REALIZE IT WOULD MAKE YOU THIS UNHAPPY.

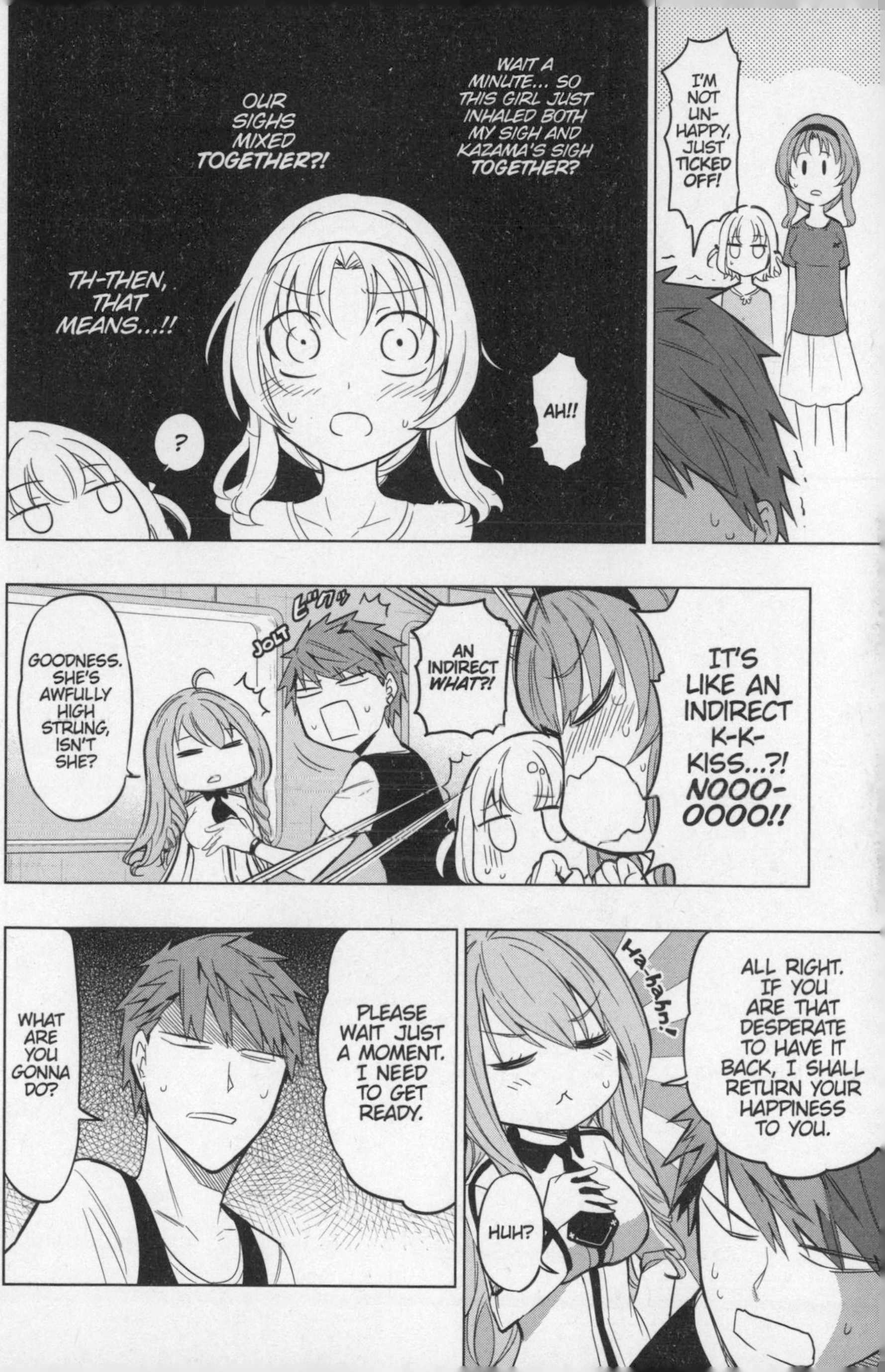
I'M NOT UN-HAPPY, JUST TICKED OFF!
WAIT A MINUTE... SO THIS GIRL JUST INHALED BOTH MY SIGH AND KAZAMA'S SIGH TOGETHER?
OUR SIGHS MIXED TOGETHER?!
AH!!
TH-THEN, THAT MEANS...!!
?
IT'S LIKE AN INDIRECT K-K-KISS...?! NOOO-OOOO!!
AN INDIRECT WHAT?!
JOLT
GOODNESS. SHE'S AWFULLY HIGH STRUNG, ISN'T SHE?
ALL RIGHT. IF YOU ARE THAT DESPERATE TO HAVE IT BACK, I SHALL RETURN YOUR HAPPINESS TO YOU.
Ha-hahn!
HUH?
PLEASE WAIT JUST A MOMENT. I NEED TO GET READY.
WHAT ARE YOU GONNA DO?

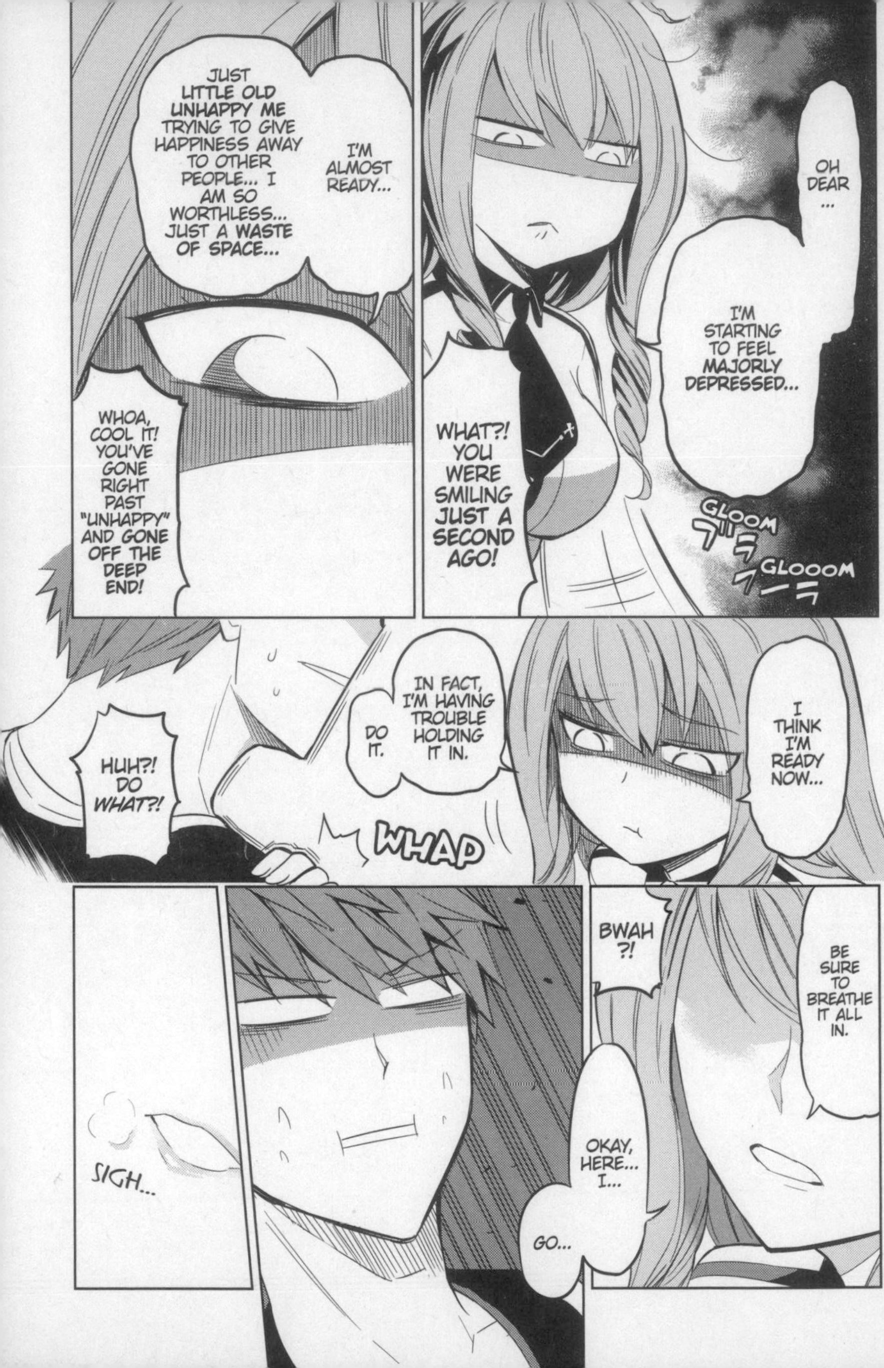
OH DEAR ...
I'M STARTING TO FEEL MAJORLY DEPRESSED...
GLOOOM
GLOOOM
WHAT?! YOU WERE SMILING JUST A SECOND AGO!
I'M ALMOST READY...
JUST LITTLE OLD UNHAPPY ME TRYING TO GIVE HAPPINESS AWAY TO OTHER PEOPLE... I AM SO WORTHLESS... JUST A WASTE OF SPACE...
WHOA, COOL IT! YOU'VE GONE RIGHT PAST "UNHAPPY" AND GONE OFF THE DEEP END!
I THINK I'M READY NOW...
IN FACT, I'M HAVING TROUBLE HOLDING IT IN.
DO IT.
WHAP
HUH?! DO WHAT?!
BE SURE TO BREATHE IT ALL IN.
BWAH ?!
OKAY, HERE... I...
GO...
SIGH...

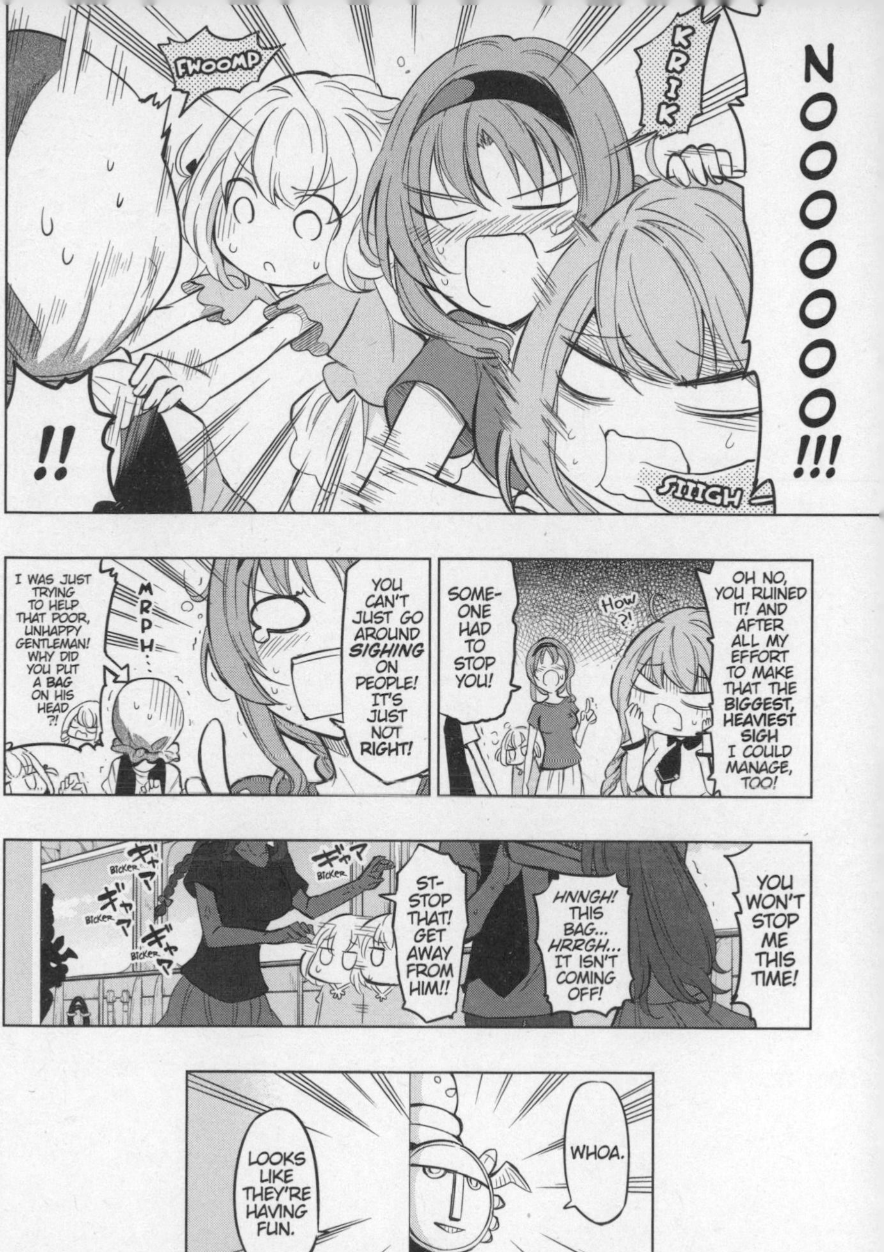
NOOOOOOOO!!!
KRIK
FWOOMP
STIIGH
!!
OH NO, YOU RUINED IT! AND AFTER ALL MY EFFORT TO MAKE THAT THE BIGGEST, HEAVIEST SIGH I COULD MANAGE, TOO!
How ?!
SOME-ONE HAD TO STOP YOU!
YOU CAN'T JUST GO AROUND SIGHING ON PEOPLE! IT'S JUST NOT RIGHT!
MRPH...
I WAS JUST TRYING TO HELP THAT POOR, UNHAPPY GENTLEMAN! WHY DID YOU PUT A BAG ON HIS HEAD ?!
YOU WON'T STOP ME THIS TIME!
HNNGH! THIS BAG... HRRGH... IT ISN'T COMING OFF!
ST-STOP THAT! GET AWAY FROM HIM!!
ギャア BICKER
ギャア BICKER
ギャア BICKER
ギャア BICKER
WHOA.
LOOKS LIKE THEY'RE HAVING FUN.

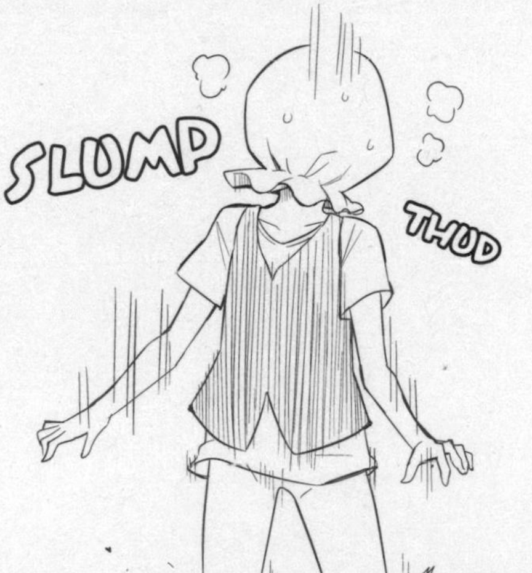
SLUMP
THUD

D-FRAGMENTS
ディーフラグメンツ！

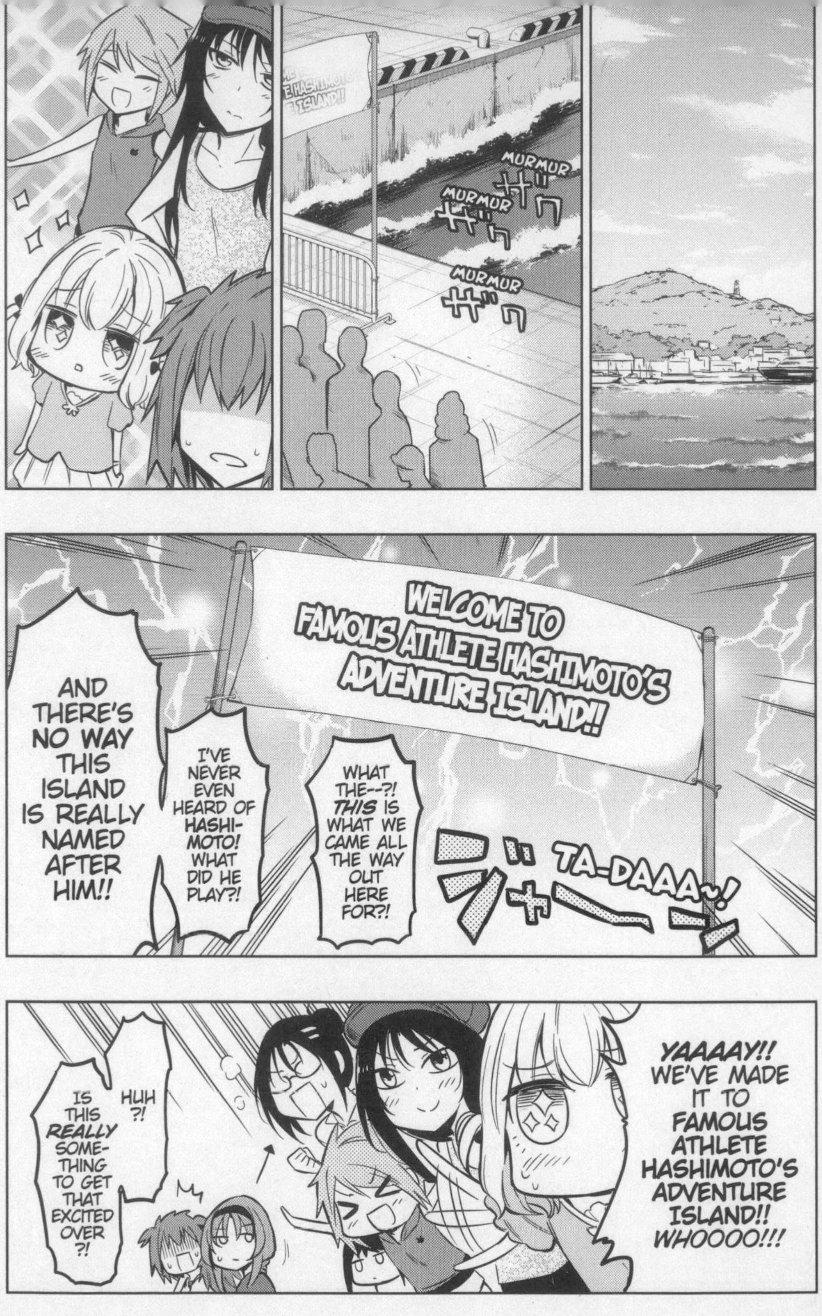
MURMUR
MURMUR
MURMUR
WELCOME TO FAMOUS ATHLETE HASHIMOTO'S ADVENTURE ISLAND!!
TA-DAAA~!
WHAT THE--?! THIS IS WHAT WE CAME ALL THE WAY OUT HERE FOR?!
I'VE NEVER EVEN HEARD OF HASHIMOTO! WHAT DID HE PLAY?!
AND THERE'S NO WAY THIS ISLAND IS REALLY NAMED AFTER HIM!!
YAAAAY!! WE'VE MADE IT TO FAMOUS ATHLETE HASHIMOTO'S ADVENTURE ISLAND!! WHOOOO!!!
HUH?!
IS THIS REALLY SOMETHING TO GET THAT EXCITED OVER?!

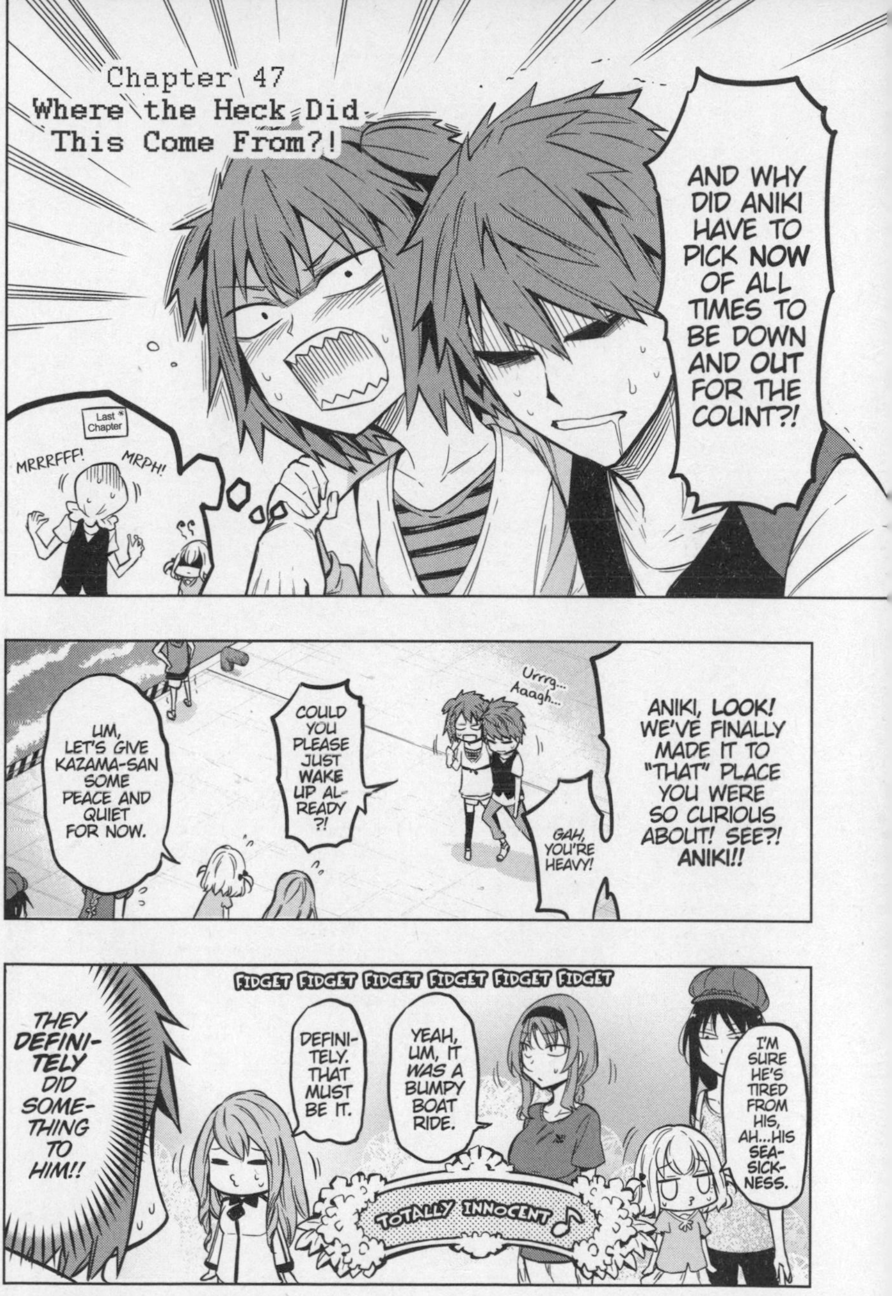
Chapter 47
Where the Heck Did This Come From?!
AND WHY DID ANIKI HAVE TO PICK NOW OF ALL TIMES TO BE DOWN AND OUT FOR THE COUNT?!
Last * Chapter
MRPH!
MRRRFFF!
ANIKI, LOOK! WE'VE FINALLY MADE IT TO "THAT" PLACE YOU WERE SO CURIOUS ABOUT! SEE?! ANIKI!!
GAH, YOU'RE HEAVY!
Urrrg... Aaagh...
COULD YOU PLEASE JUST WAKE UP AL-READY?!
UM, LET'S GIVE KAZAMA-SAN SOME PEACE AND QUIET FOR NOW.
FIDGET FIDGET FIDGET FIDGET FIDGET FIDGET
I'M SURE HE'S TIRED FROM HIS, AH...HIS SEA-SICK-NESS.
YEAH, UM, IT WAS A BUMPY BOAT RIDE.
DEFINI-TELY. THAT MUST BE IT.
TOTALLY INNOCENT
THEY DEFINI-TELY DID SOME-THING TO HIM!!

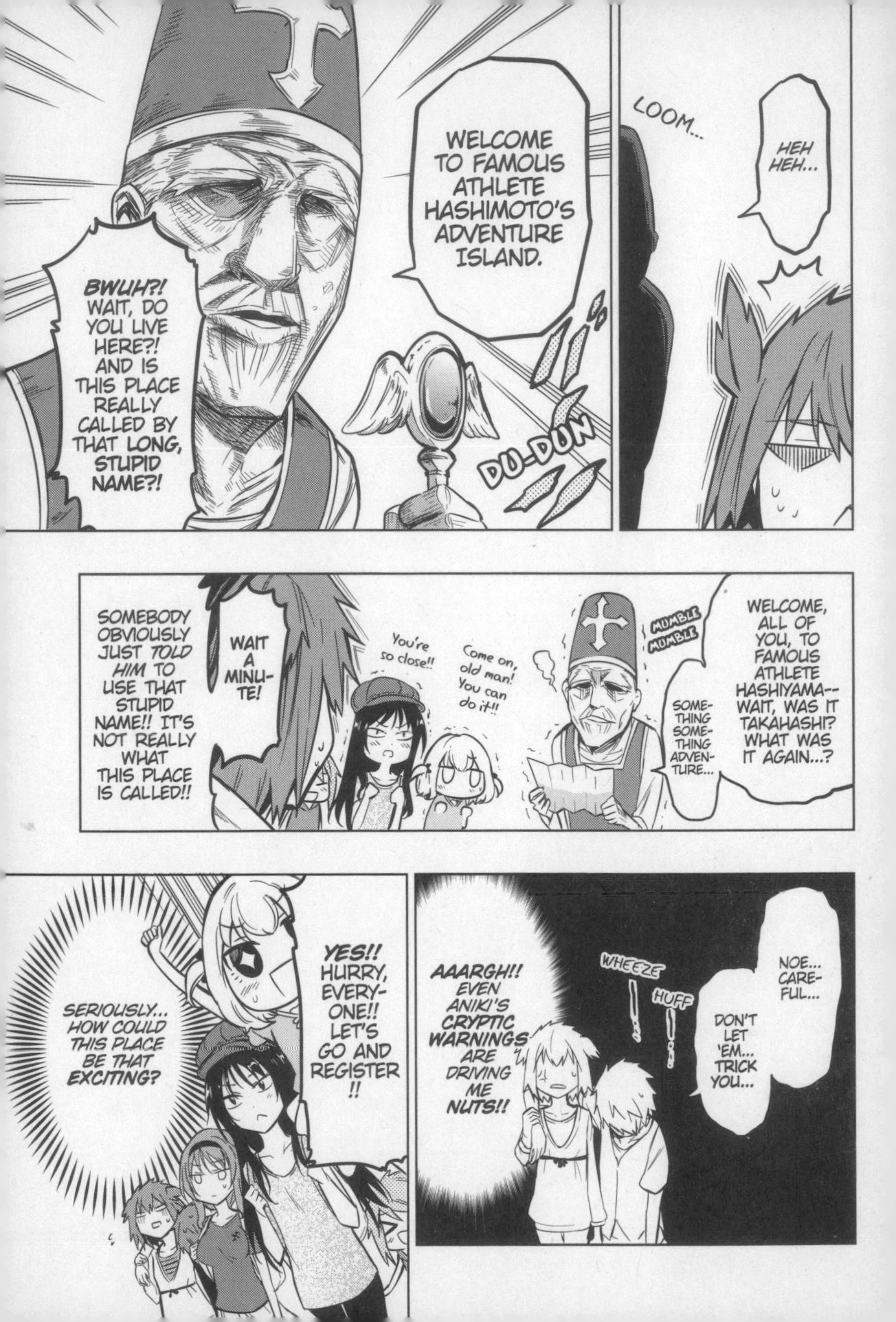
LOOM...
HEH HEH...
WELCOME TO FAMOUS ATHLETE HASHIMOTO'S ADVENTURE ISLAND.
DO-DUN
BWUH?! WAIT, DO YOU LIVE HERE?! AND IS THIS PLACE REALLY CALLED BY THAT LONG, STUPID NAME?!
WELCOME, ALL OF YOU, TO FAMOUS ATHLETE HASHIYAMA-- WAIT, WAS IT TAKAHASHI? WHAT WAS IT AGAIN...?
SOMETHING SOMETHING ADVENTURE...
MUMBLE MUMBLE
Come on, old man! You can do it!!
You're so close!!
WAIT A MINUTE!
SOMEBODY OBVIOUSLY JUST TOLD HIM TO USE THAT STUPID NAME!! IT'S NOT REALLY WHAT THIS PLACE IS CALLED!!
NOE... CAREFUL...
DON'T LET 'EM... TRICK YOU...
HUFF
WHEEZE
AAARGH!! EVEN ANIKI'S CRYPTIC WARNINGS ARE DRIVING ME NUTS!!
YES!! HURRY, EVERYONE!! LET'S GO AND REGISTER!!
SERIOUSLY... HOW COULD THIS PLACE BE THAT EXCITING?

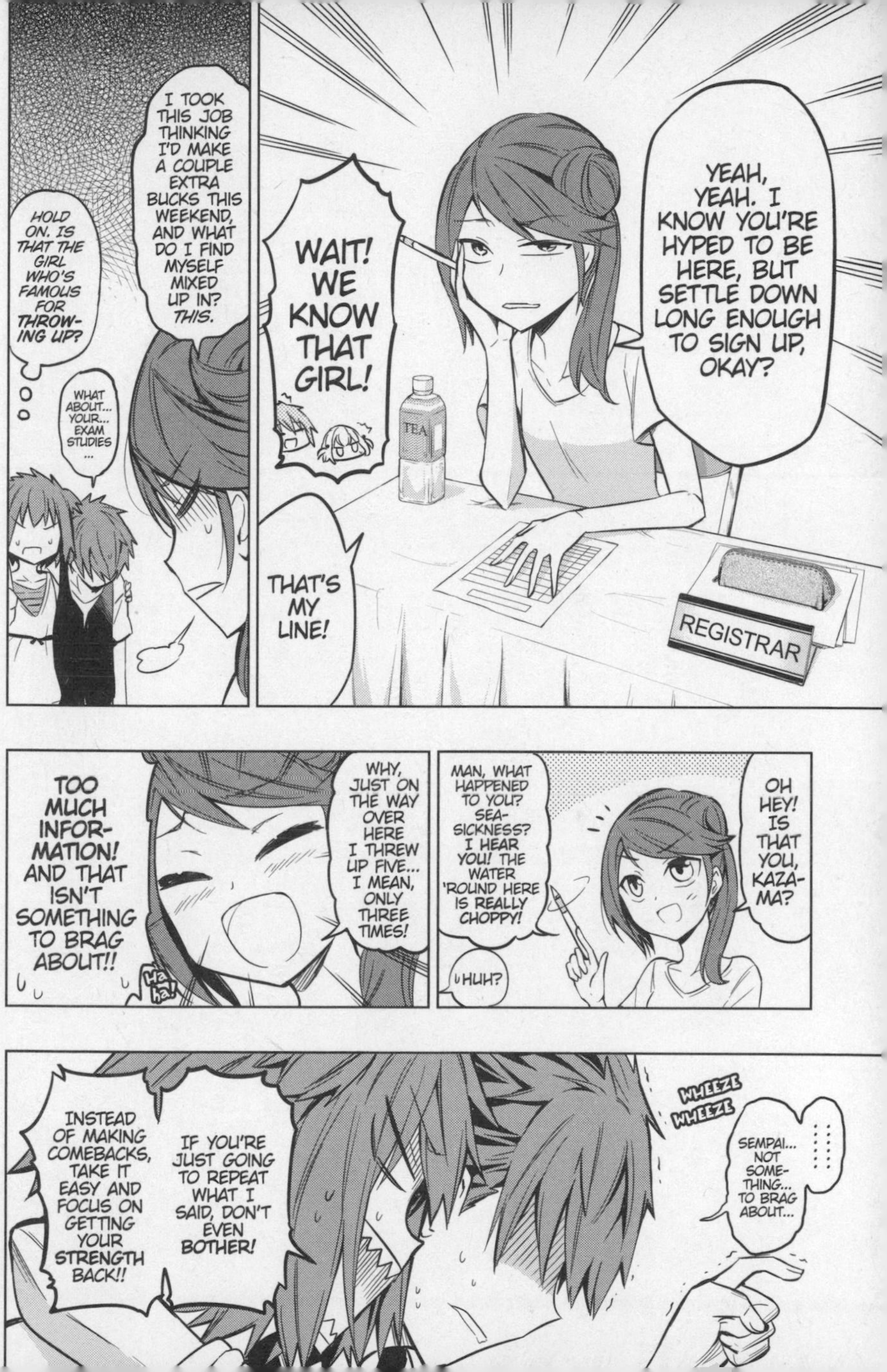
YEAH, YEAH. I KNOW YOU'RE HYPED TO BE HERE, BUT SETTLE DOWN LONG ENOUGH TO SIGN UP, OKAY?
WAIT! WE KNOW THAT GIRL!
TEA
REGISTRAR
THAT'S MY LINE!
I TOOK THIS JOB THINKING I'D MAKE A COUPLE EXTRA BUCKS THIS WEEKEND, AND WHAT DO I FIND MYSELF MIXED UP IN? THIS.
HOLD ON. IS THAT THE GIRL WHO'S FAMOUS FOR THROWING UP?
WHAT ABOUT... YOUR... EXAM STUDIES ...
OH HEY! IS THAT YOU, KAZAMA?
MAN, WHAT HAPPENED TO YOU? SEA-SICKNESS? I HEAR YOU! THE WATER 'ROUND HERE IS REALLY CHOPPY!
HUH?
WHY, JUST ON THE WAY OVER HERE I THREW UP FIVE... I MEAN, ONLY THREE TIMES!
TOO MUCH INFORMATION! AND THAT ISN'T SOMETHING TO BRAG ABOUT!!
Ha ha!
WHEEZE WHEEZE
......
SEMPAI... NOT SOMETHING... TO BRAG ABOUT...
IF YOU'RE JUST GOING TO REPEAT WHAT I SAID, DON'T EVEN BOTHER!
INSTEAD OF MAKING COMEBACKS, TAKE IT EASY AND FOCUS ON GETTING YOUR STRENGTH BACK!!

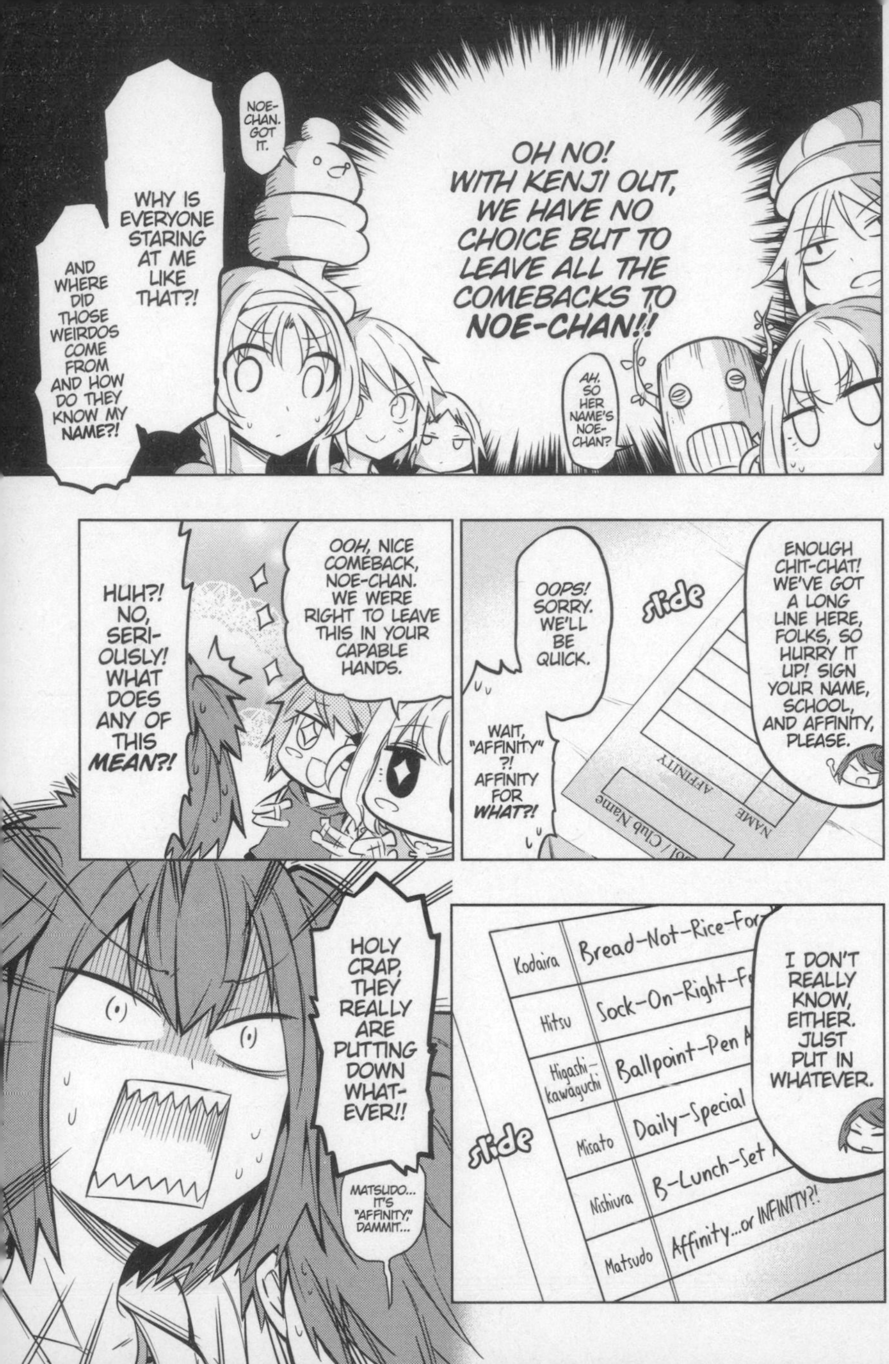
OH NO! WITH KENJI OUT, WE HAVE NO CHOICE BUT TO LEAVE ALL THE COMEBACKS TO NOE-CHAN!!
AH. SO HER NAME'S NOE-CHAN?
NOE-CHAN. GOT IT.
WHY IS EVERYONE STARING AT ME LIKE THAT?!
AND WHERE DID THOSE WEIRDOS COME FROM AND HOW DO THEY KNOW MY NAME?!
ENOUGH CHIT-CHAT! WE'VE GOT A LONG LINE HERE, FOLKS, SO HURRY IT UP! SIGN YOUR NAME, SCHOOL, AND AFFINITY, PLEASE.
slide
NAME
AFFINITY
OOPS! SORRY. WE'LL BE QUICK.
WAIT, "AFFINITY"?! AFFINITY FOR WHAT?!
OOH, NICE COMEBACK, NOE-CHAN. WE WERE RIGHT TO LEAVE THIS IN YOUR CAPABLE HANDS.
HUH?! NO, SERIOUSLY! WHAT DOES ANY OF THIS MEAN?!
I DON'T REALLY KNOW, EITHER. JUST PUT IN WHATEVER.
Kodaira Bread-Not-Rice-For
Hitsu Sock-On-Right-F
Higashi-kawaguchi Ballpoint-Pen
Misato Daily-Special
Nishiura B-Lunch-Set
Matsudo Affinity...or INFINITY?!
slide
HOLY CRAP, THEY REALLY ARE PUTTING DOWN WHATEVER!!
MATSUDO... IT'S "AFFINITY," DAMMIT...

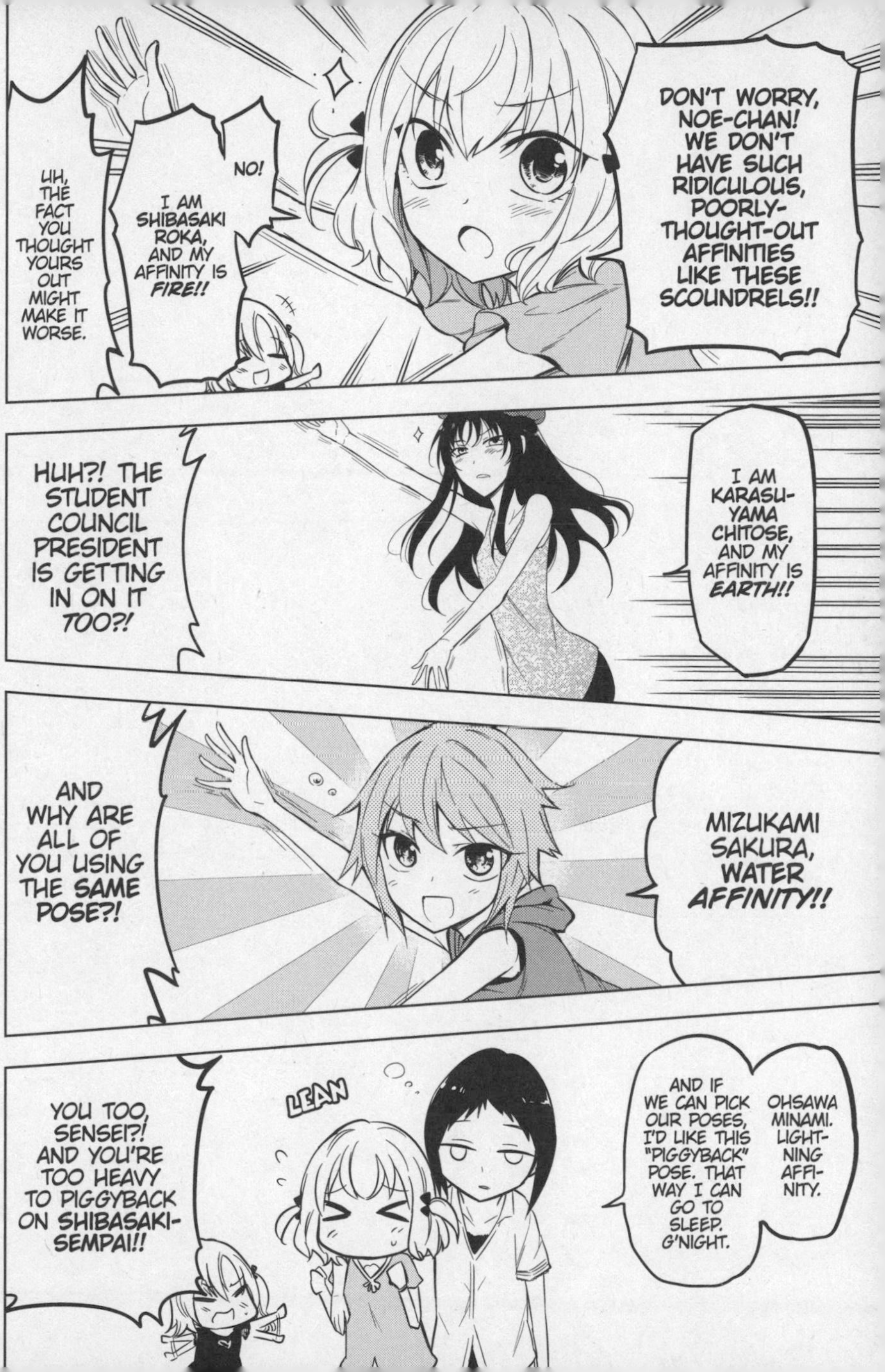
DON'T WORRY, NOE-CHAN! WE DON'T HAVE SUCH RIDICULOUS, POORLY-THOUGHT-OUT AFFINITIES LIKE THESE SCOUNDRELS!!
NO!
I AM SHIBASAKI ROKA, AND MY AFFINITY IS FIRE!!
UH, THE FACT YOU THOUGHT YOURS OUT MIGHT MAKE IT WORSE.
I AM KARASUYAMA CHITOSE, AND MY AFFINITY IS EARTH!!
HUH?! THE STUDENT COUNCIL PRESIDENT IS GETTING IN ON IT TOO?!
MIZUKAMI SAKURA, WATER AFFINITY!!
AND WHY ARE ALL OF YOU USING THE SAME POSE?!
OHSAWA MINAMI. LIGHTNING AFFINITY.
AND IF WE CAN PICK OUR POSES, I'D LIKE THIS "PIGGYBACK" POSE. THAT WAY I CAN GO TO SLEEP. G'NIGHT.
LEAN
YOU TOO, SENSEI?! AND YOU'RE TOO HEAVY TO PIGGYBACK ON SHIBASAKI-SEMPAI!!

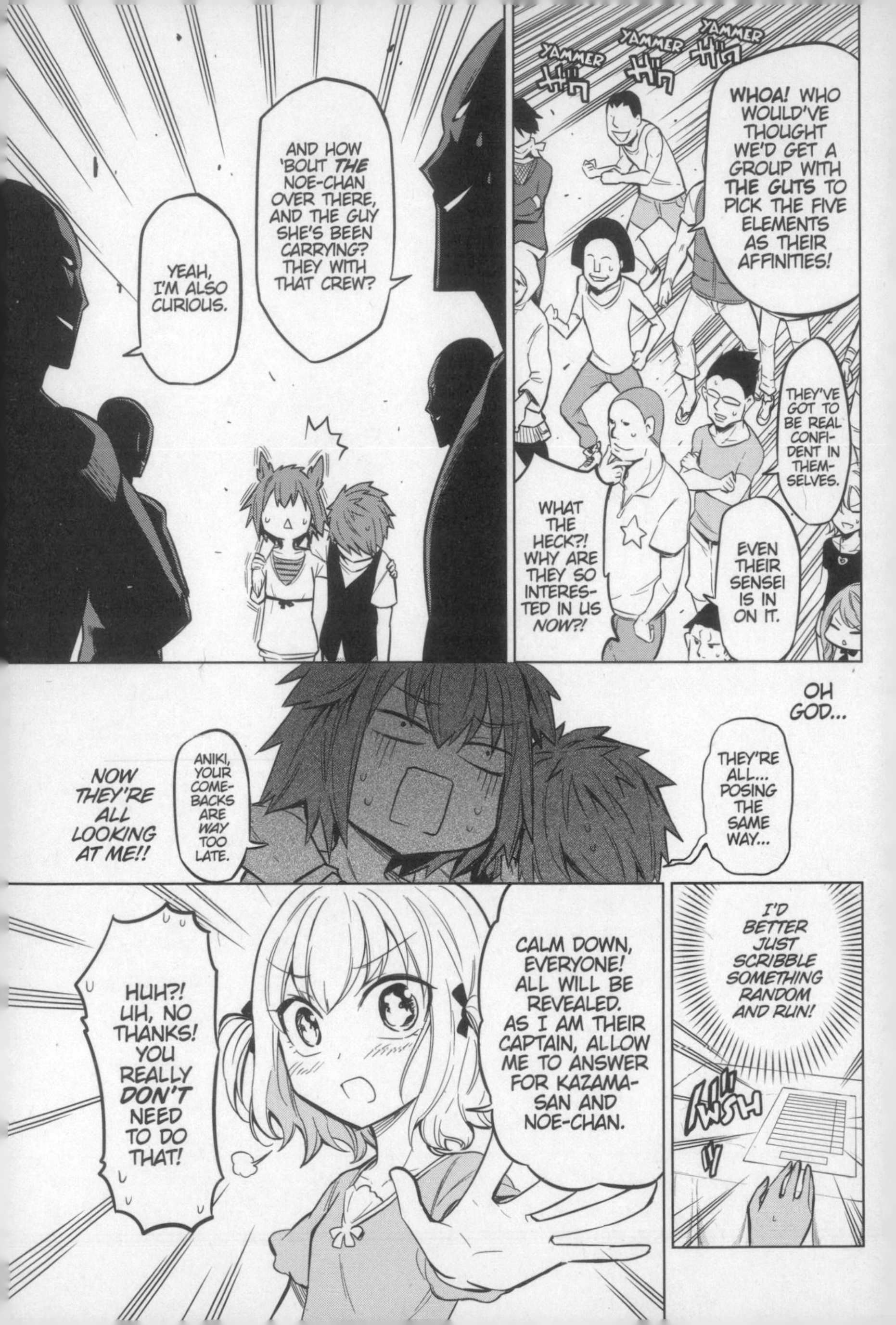
YAMMER
YAMMER
YAMMER
WHOA! WHO WOULD'VE THOUGHT WE'D GET A GROUP WITH THE GUTS TO PICK THE FIVE ELEMENTS AS THEIR AFFINITIES!
THEY'VE GOT TO BE REAL CONFIDENT IN THEMSELVES.
EVEN THEIR SENSEI IS IN ON IT.
WHAT THE HECK?! WHY ARE THEY SO INTERESTED IN US NOW?!
AND HOW 'BOUT THE NOE-CHAN OVER THERE, AND THE GUY SHE'S BEEN CARRYING? THEY WITH THAT CREW?
YEAH, I'M ALSO CURIOUS.
OH GOD...
THEY'RE ALL... POSING THE SAME WAY...
ANIKI, YOUR COMEBACKS ARE WAY TOO LATE.
NOW THEY'RE ALL LOOKING AT ME!!
I'D BETTER JUST SCRIBBLE SOMETHING RANDOM AND RUN!
WHSH
CALM DOWN, EVERYONE! ALL WILL BE REVEALED. AS I AM THEIR CAPTAIN, ALLOW ME TO ANSWER FOR KAZAMA-SAN AND NOE-CHAN.
HUH?! UH, NO THANKS! YOU REALLY DON'T NEED TO DO THAT!

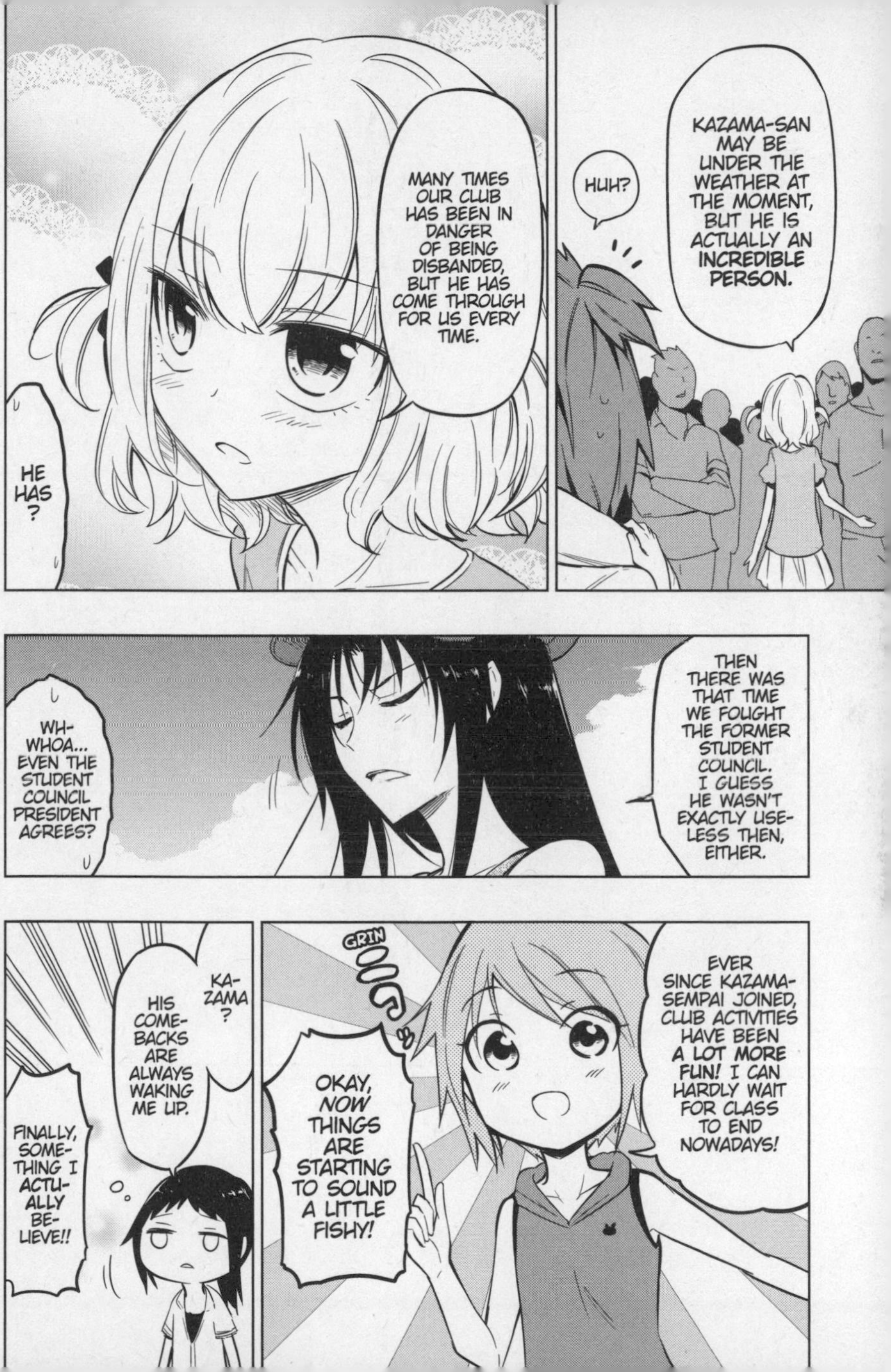
KAZAMA-SAN MAY BE UNDER THE WEATHER AT THE MOMENT, BUT HE IS ACTUALLY AN INCREDIBLE PERSON.
HUH?
MANY TIMES OUR CLUB HAS BEEN IN DANGER OF BEING DISBANDED, BUT HE HAS COME THROUGH FOR US EVERY TIME.
HE HAS?
THEN THERE WAS THAT TIME WE FOUGHT THE FORMER STUDENT COUNCIL. I GUESS HE WASN'T EXACTLY USELESS THEN, EITHER.
WH-WHOA... EVEN THE STUDENT COUNCIL PRESIDENT AGREES?
EVER SINCE KAZAMA-SEMPAI JOINED, CLUB ACTIVITIES HAVE BEEN A LOT MORE FUN! I CAN HARDLY WAIT FOR CLASS TO END NOWADAYS!
GRIN
OKAY, *NOW* THINGS ARE STARTING TO SOUND A LITTLE FISHY!
KA-ZAMA?
HIS COMEBACKS ARE ALWAYS WAKING ME UP.
FINALLY, SOMETHING I ACTUALLY BELIEVE!!

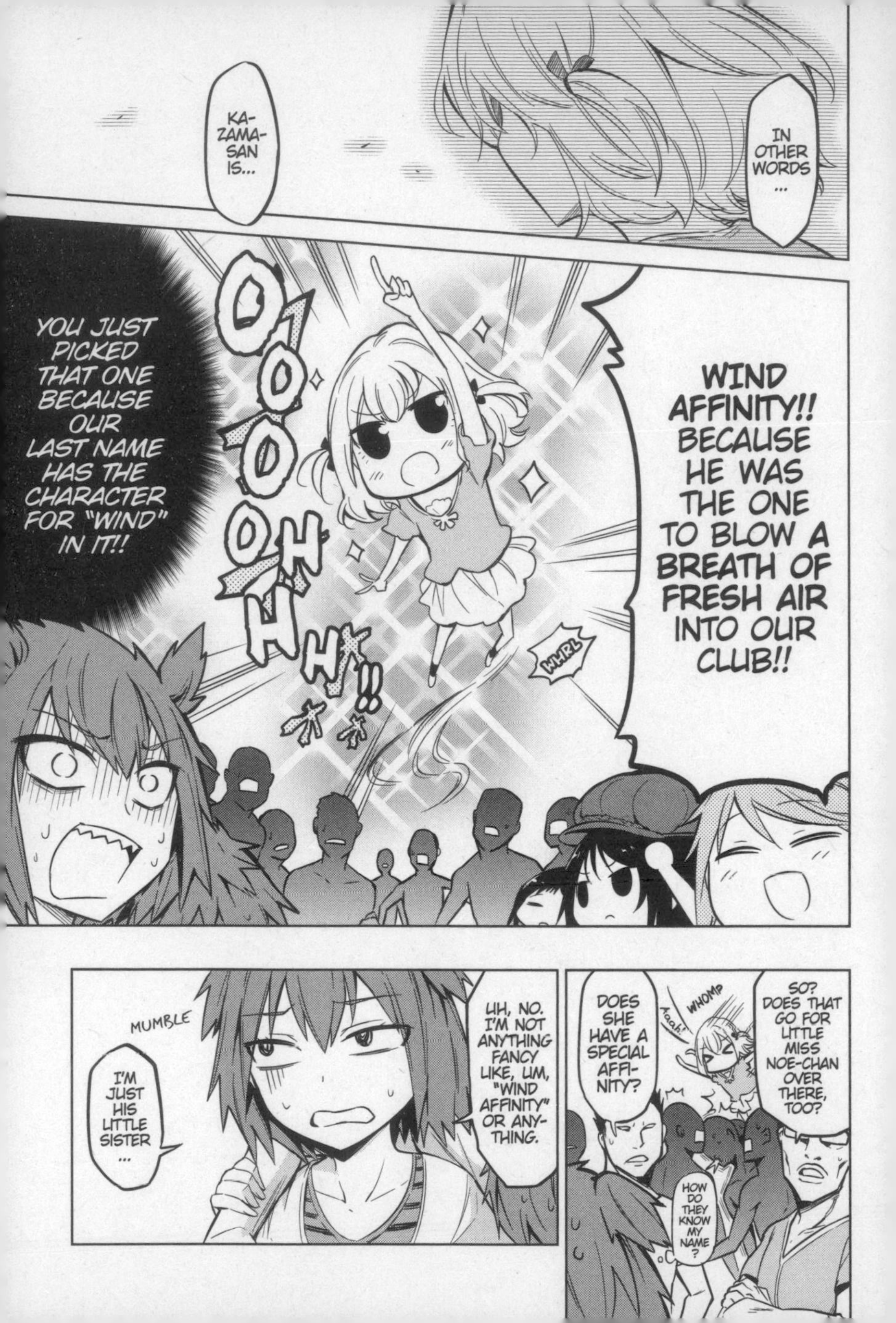
IN OTHER WORDS...
KA-ZAMA-SAN IS...
WIND AFFINITY!! BECAUSE HE WAS THE ONE TO BLOW A BREATH OF FRESH AIR INTO OUR CLUB!!
OOOOHHHH!!
WHRL
YOU JUST PICKED THAT ONE BECAUSE OUR LAST NAME HAS THE CHARACTER FOR "WIND" IN IT!!
SO? DOES THAT GO FOR LITTLE MISS NOE-CHAN OVER THERE, TOO?
WHOMP
Aaah!
DOES SHE HAVE A SPECIAL AFFI-NITY?
HOW DO THEY KNOW MY NAME?
UH, NO. I'M NOT ANYTHING FANCY LIKE, UM, "WIND AFFINITY" OR ANY-THING.
MUMBLE
I'M JUST HIS LITTLE SISTER...

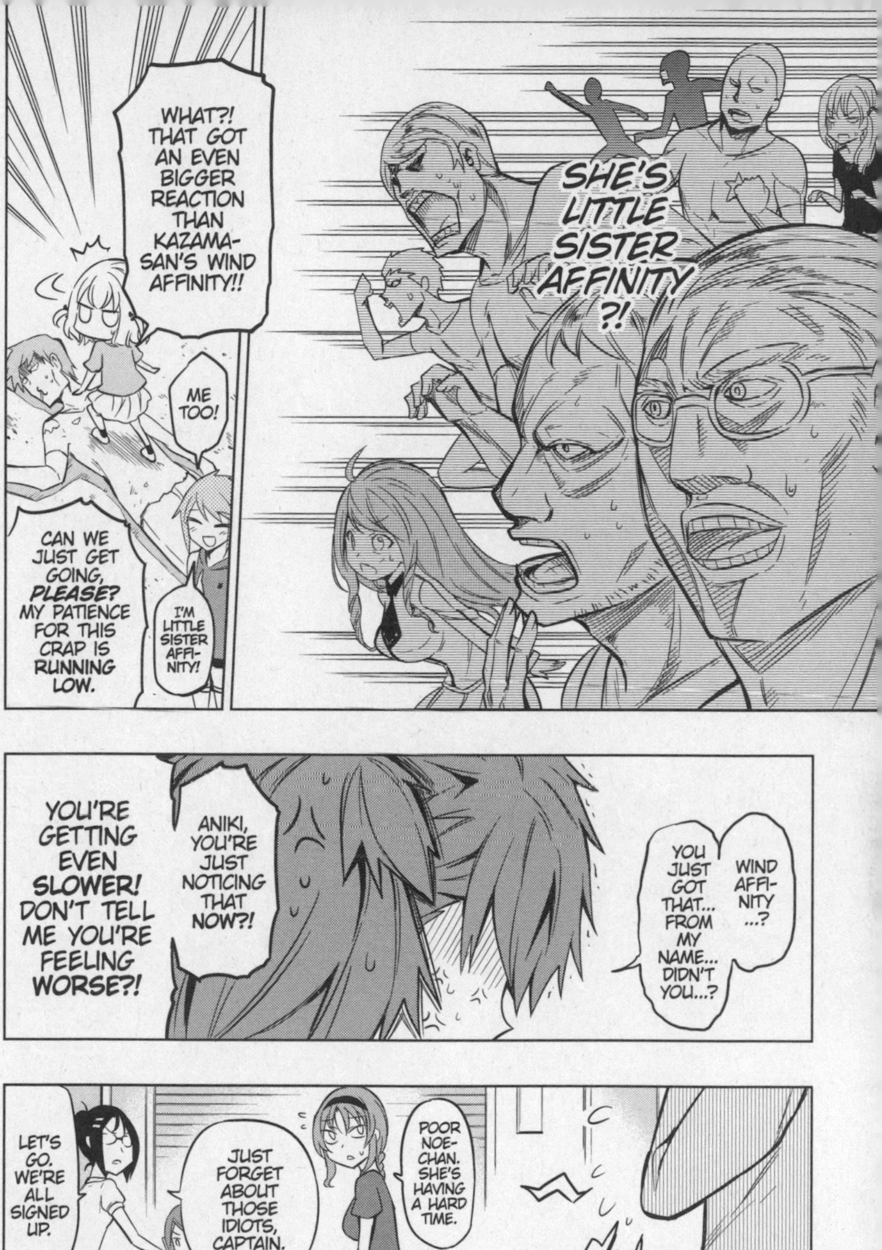
SHE'S LITTLE SISTER AFFINITY?!
WHAT?! THAT GOT AN EVEN BIGGER REACTION THAN KAZAMA-SAN'S WIND AFFINITY!!
ME TOO!
I'M LITTLE SISTER AFFI-NITY!
CAN WE JUST GET GOING, PLEASE? MY PATIENCE FOR THIS CRAP IS RUNNING LOW.
WIND AFFI-NITY ...?
YOU JUST GOT THAT... FROM MY NAME... DIDN'T YOU...?
ANIKI, YOU'RE JUST NOTICING THAT NOW?!
YOU'RE GETTING EVEN SLOWER! DON'T TELL ME YOU'RE FEELING WORSE?!
POOR NOE-CHAN. SHE'S HAVING A HARD TIME.
JUST FORGET ABOUT THOSE IDIOTS, CAPTAIN.
LET'S GO. WE'RE ALL SIGNED UP.

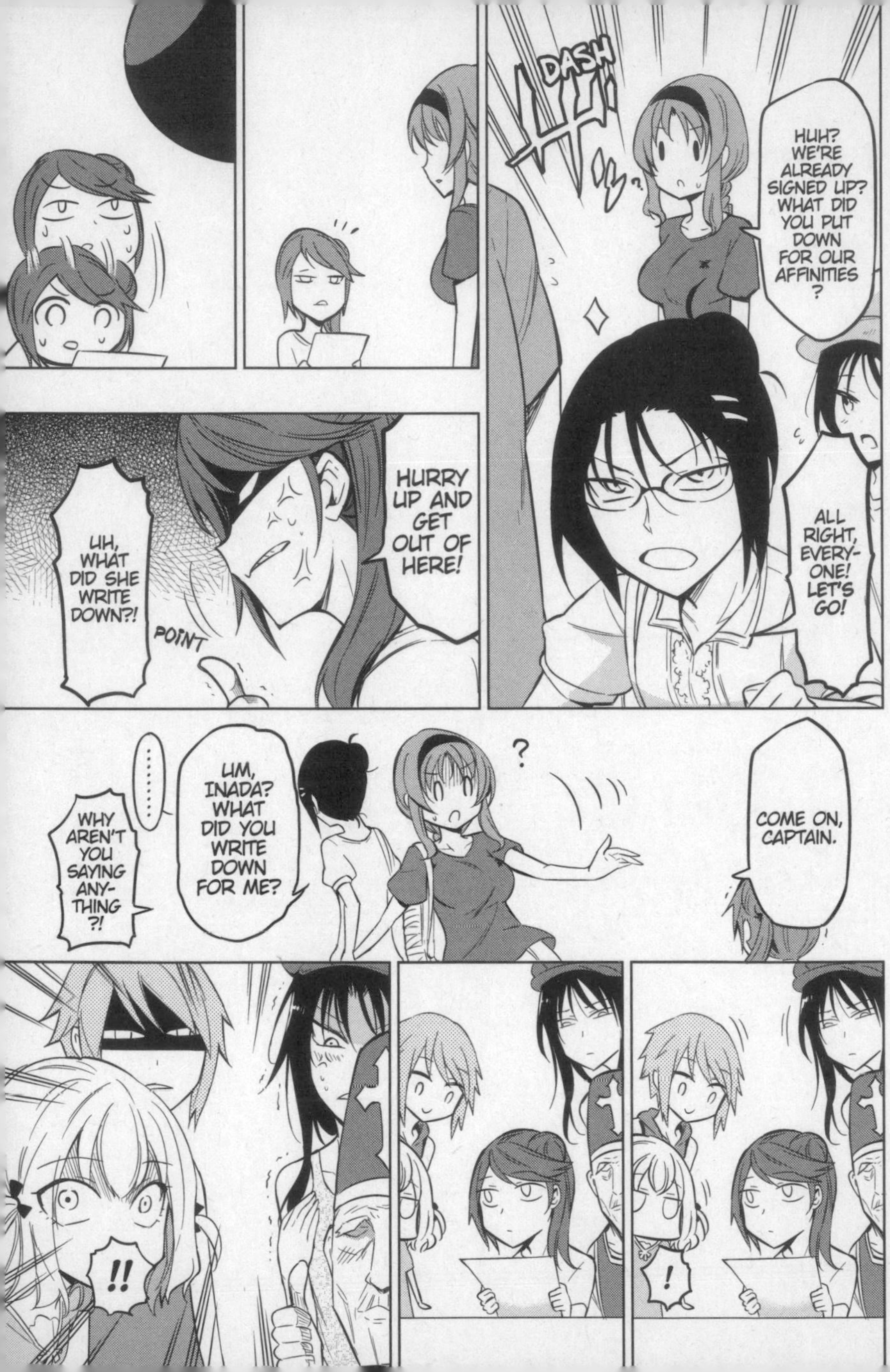
DASH
HUH? WE'RE ALREADY SIGNED UP? WHAT DID YOU PUT DOWN FOR OUR AFFINITIES?
ALL RIGHT, EVERYONE! LET'S GO!
HURRY UP AND GET OUT OF HERE!
UH, WHAT DID SHE WRITE DOWN?!
POINT
COME ON, CAPTAIN.
?
UM, INADA? WHAT DID YOU WRITE DOWN FOR ME?
......
WHY AREN'T YOU SAYING ANYTHING?!
!
!!

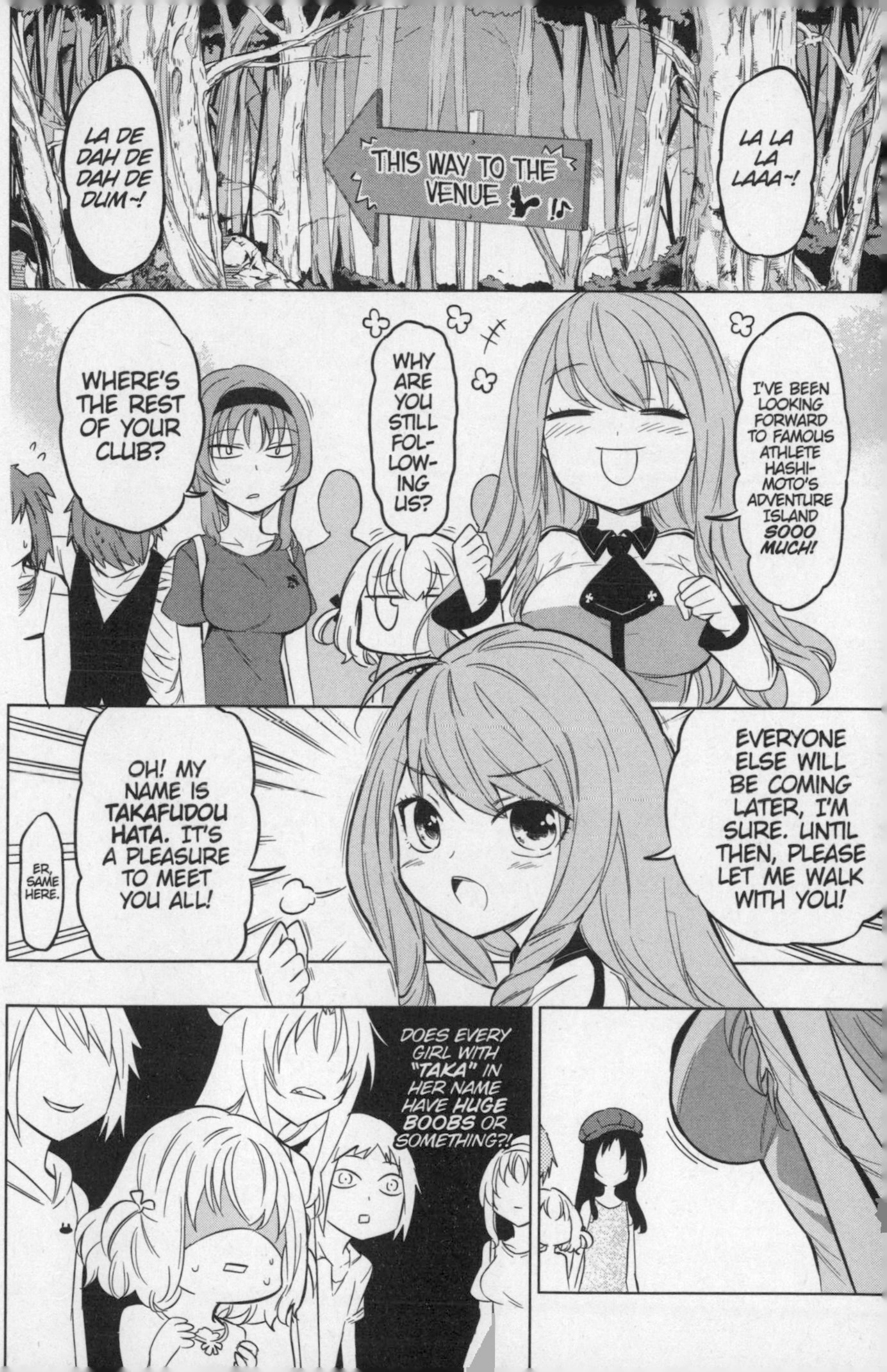
LA LA LA LAAA~!
THIS WAY TO THE VENUE !♪
LA DE DAH DE DAH DE DUM~!
I'VE BEEN LOOKING FORWARD TO FAMOUS ATHLETE HASHI-MOTO'S ADVENTURE ISLAND SOOO MUCH!
WHY ARE YOU STILL FOL-LOW-ING US?
WHERE'S THE REST OF YOUR CLUB?
EVERYONE ELSE WILL BE COMING LATER, I'M SURE. UNTIL THEN, PLEASE LET ME WALK WITH YOU!
OH! MY NAME IS TAKAFUDOU HATA. IT'S A PLEASURE TO MEET YOU ALL!
ER, SAME HERE.
DOES EVERY GIRL WITH "TAKA" IN HER NAME HAVE HUGE BOOBS OR SOMETHING?!

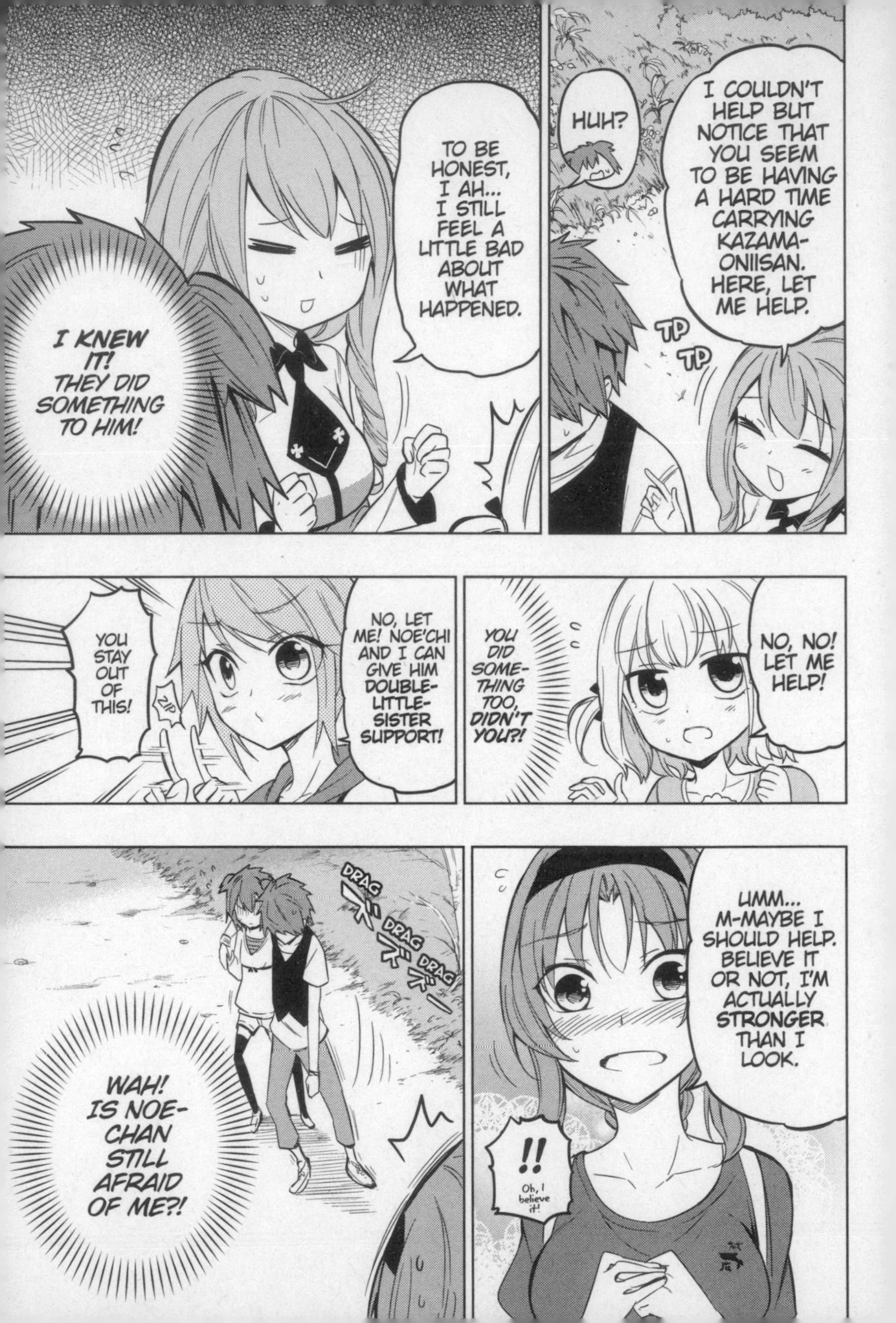
I COULDN'T HELP BUT NOTICE THAT YOU SEEM TO BE HAVING A HARD TIME CARRYING KAZAMA-ONIISAN. HERE, LET ME HELP.
HUH?
TP
TP
TO BE HONEST, I AH... I STILL FEEL A LITTLE BAD ABOUT WHAT HAPPENED.
I KNEW IT! THEY DID SOMETHING TO HIM!
NO, NO! LET ME HELP!
YOU DID SOME-THING TOO, DIDN'T YOU?!
NO, LET ME! NOE'CHI AND I CAN GIVE HIM DOUBLE-LITTLE-SISTER SUPPORT!
YOU STAY OUT OF THIS!
ZIP
UMM... M-MAYBE I SHOULD HELP. BELIEVE IT OR NOT, I'M ACTUALLY STRONGER THAN I LOOK.
!!
Oh, I believe it!
DRAG
DRAG
DRAG
WAH! IS NOE-CHAN STILL AFRAID OF ME?!

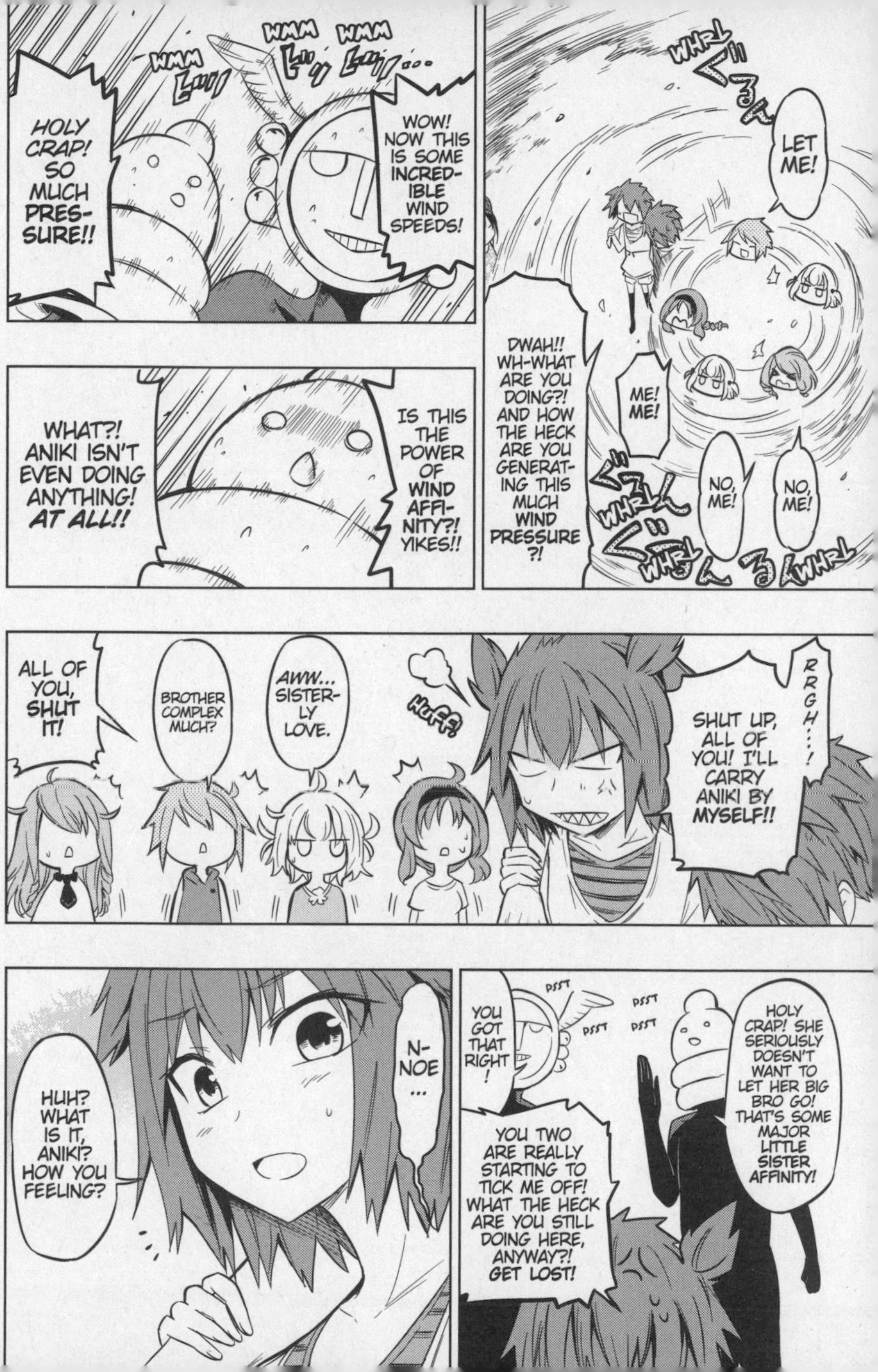
WHRL
LET ME!
ME! ME!
NO, ME!
NO, ME!
DWAH!! WH-WHAT ARE YOU DOING?! AND HOW THE HECK ARE YOU GENERATING THIS MUCH WIND PRESSURE?!
WHRL
WHRL
WHRL
WMM WMM
WMM
WOW! NOW THIS IS SOME INCREDIBLE WIND SPEEDS!
HOLY CRAP! SO MUCH PRESSURE!!
IS THIS THE POWER OF WIND AFFINITY?! YIKES!!
WHAT?! ANIKI ISN'T EVEN DOING ANYTHING! AT ALL!!
RRGH...!
SHUT UP, ALL OF YOU! I'LL CARRY ANIKI BY MYSELF!!
HUFF!
AWW... SISTERLY LOVE.
BROTHER COMPLEX MUCH?
ALL OF YOU, SHUT IT!
HOLY CRAP! SHE SERIOUSLY DOESN'T WANT TO LET HER BIG BRO GO! THAT'S SOME MAJOR LITTLE SISTER AFFINITY!
PSST PSST
PSST PSST
YOU GOT THAT RIGHT!
YOU TWO ARE REALLY STARTING TO TICK ME OFF! WHAT THE HECK ARE YOU STILL DOING HERE, ANYWAY?! GET LOST!
N-NOE...
HUH? WHAT IS IT, ANIKI? HOW YOU FEELING?

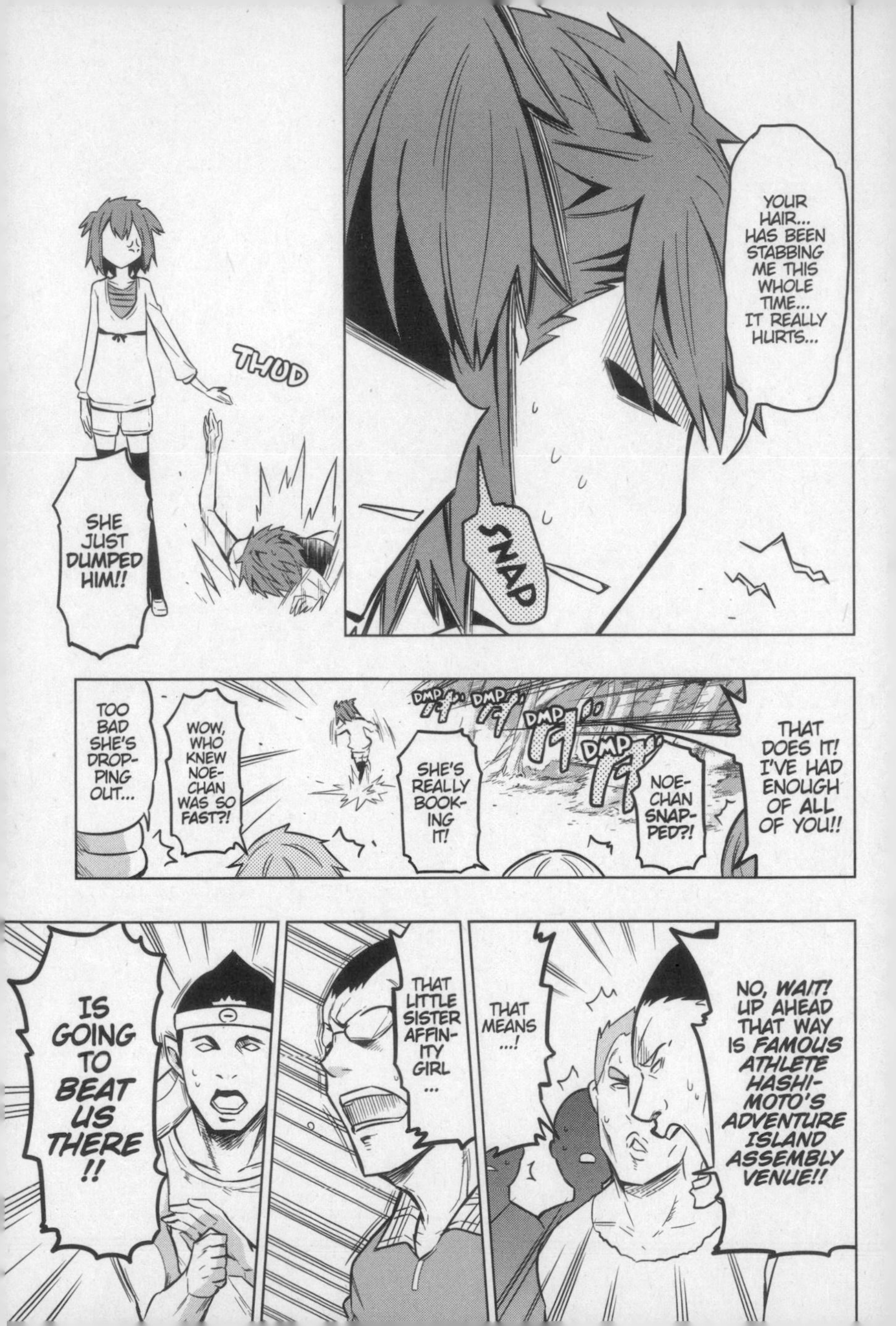
YOUR HAIR... HAS BEEN STABBING ME THIS WHOLE TIME... IT REALLY HURTS...
SNAP
THUD
SHE JUST DUMPED HIM!!
THAT DOES IT! I'VE HAD ENOUGH OF ALL OF YOU!!
DMP DMP DMP DMP
NOE-CHAN SNAPPED?!
SHE'S REALLY BOOKING IT!
WOW, WHO KNEW NOE-CHAN WAS SO FAST?!
TOO BAD SHE'S DROPPING OUT...
NO, WAIT! UP AHEAD THAT WAY IS FAMOUS ATHLETE HASHIMOTO'S ADVENTURE ISLAND ASSEMBLY VENUE!!
THAT MEANS ...!
THAT LITTLE SISTER AFFINITY GIRL ...
IS GOING TO BEAT US THERE!!

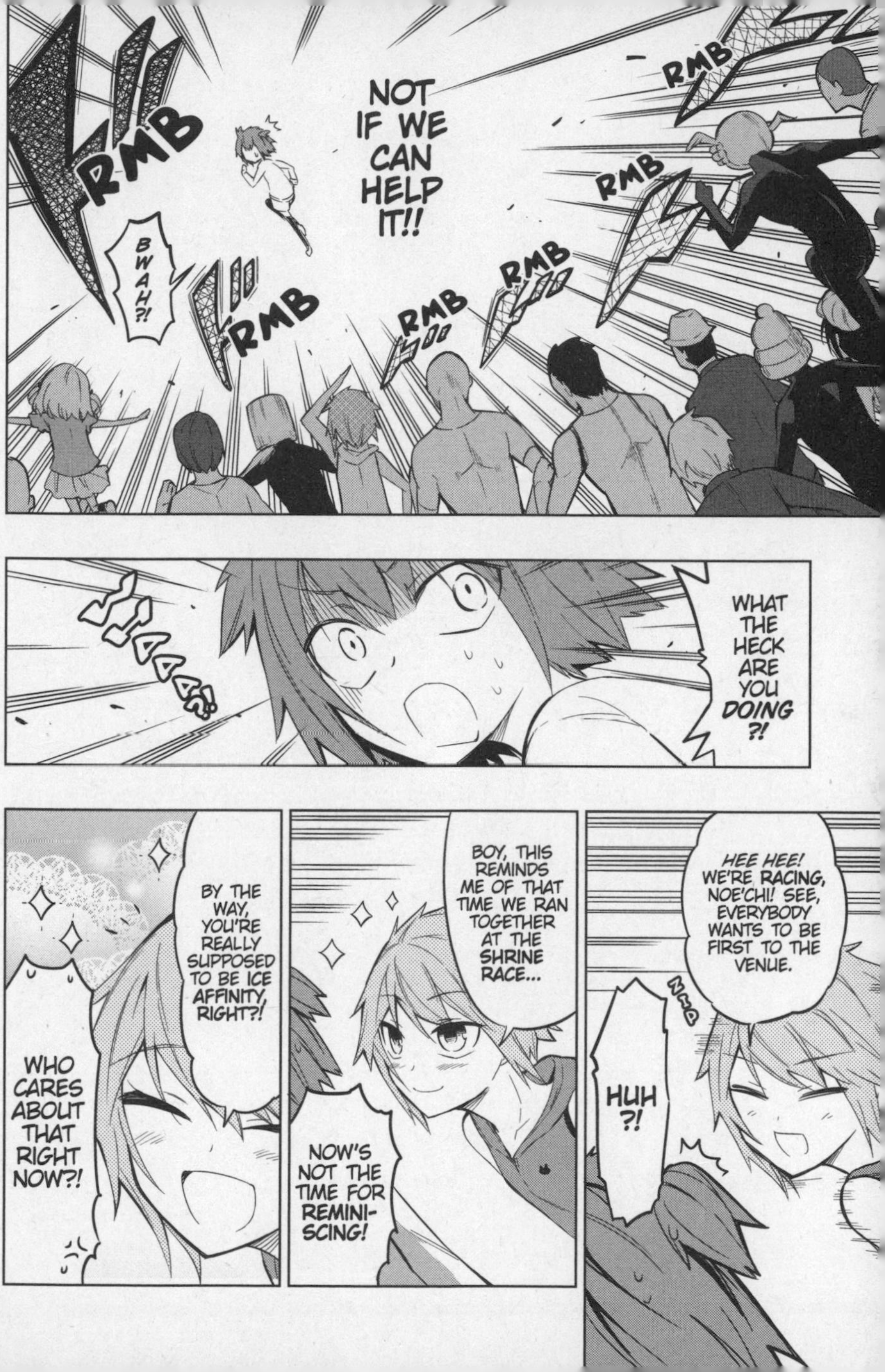
RMB
RMB
RMB
RMB
NOT IF WE CAN HELP IT!!
RMB
RMB
BWAH?!
RMB
WHAT THE HECK ARE YOU *DOING*?!
HEE HEE! WE'RE RACING, NOE'CHI! SEE, EVERYBODY WANTS TO BE FIRST TO THE VENUE.
HUH?!
BOY, THIS REMINDS ME OF THAT TIME WE RAN TOGETHER AT THE SHRINE RACE...
NOW'S NOT THE TIME FOR REMINI-SCING!
BY THE WAY, YOU'RE REALLY SUPPOSED TO BE ICE AFFINITY, RIGHT?!
WHO CARES ABOUT THAT RIGHT NOW?!

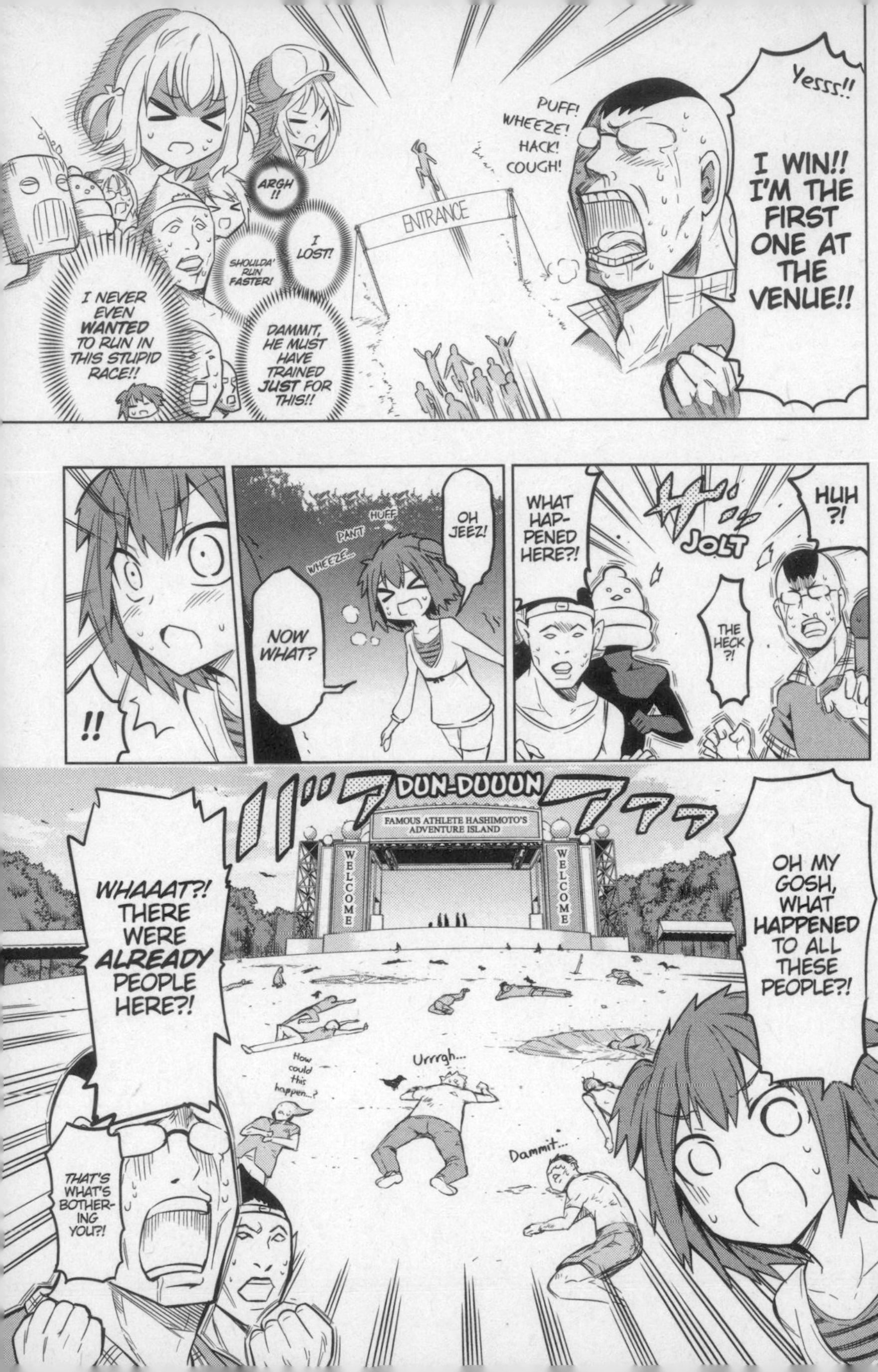
Yesss!!
I WIN!! I'M THE FIRST ONE AT THE VENUE!!
PUFF! WHEEZE! HACK! COUGH!
ENTRANCE
ARGH!!
I LOST!
SHOULDA' RUN FASTER!
DAMMIT, HE MUST HAVE TRAINED JUST FOR THIS!!
I NEVER EVEN WANTED TO RUN IN THIS STUPID RACE!!
HUH?!
JOLT
THE HECK?!
WHAT HAPPENED HERE?!
OH JEEZ!
HUFF
PANT
WHEEZE...
NOW WHAT?
!!
DUN-DUUUN
FAMOUS ATHLETE HASHIMOTO'S ADVENTURE ISLAND
WELCOME
WELCOME
OH MY GOSH, WHAT HAPPENED TO ALL THESE PEOPLE?!
WHAAAT?! THERE WERE ALREADY PEOPLE HERE?!
Urrrgh...
How could this happen...?
Dammit...
THAT'S WHAT'S BOTHERING YOU?!

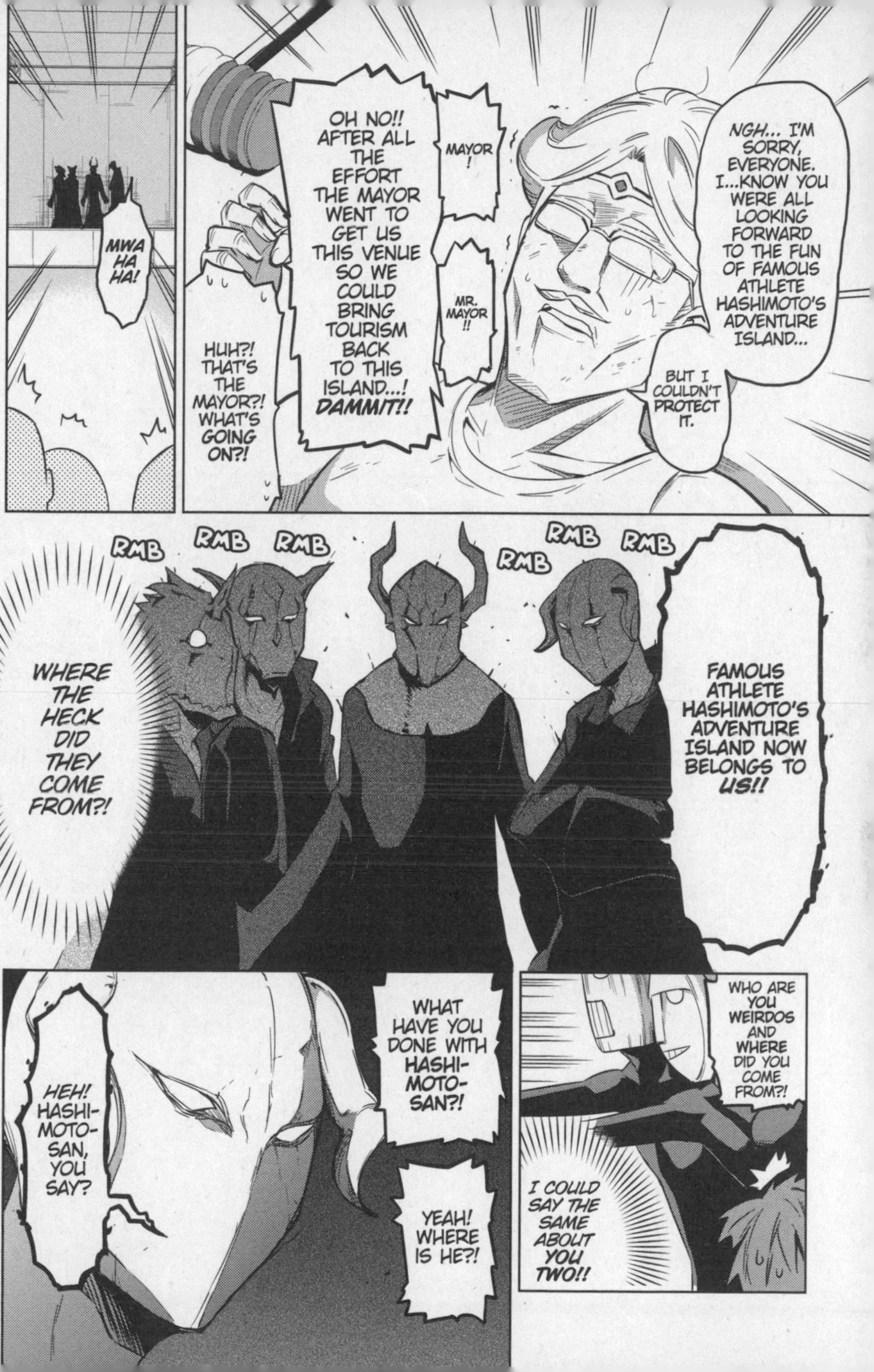
NGH... I'M SORRY, EVERYONE. I...KNOW YOU WERE ALL LOOKING FORWARD TO THE FUN OF FAMOUS ATHLETE HASHIMOTO'S ADVENTURE ISLAND...
BUT I COULDN'T PROTECT IT.
MAYOR!
MR. MAYOR!!
OH NO!! AFTER ALL THE EFFORT THE MAYOR WENT TO GET US THIS VENUE SO WE COULD BRING TOURISM BACK TO THIS ISLAND...! DAMMIT!!
HUH?! THAT'S THE MAYOR?! WHAT'S GOING ON?!
MWA HA HA!
RMB
RMB
RMB
RMB
RMB
RMB
FAMOUS ATHLETE HASHIMOTO'S ADVENTURE ISLAND NOW BELONGS TO US!!
WHERE THE HECK DID THEY COME FROM?!
WHO ARE YOU WEIRDOS AND WHERE DID YOU COME FROM?!
I COULD SAY THE SAME ABOUT YOU TWO!!
WHAT HAVE YOU DONE WITH HASHI-MOTO-SAN?!
YEAH! WHERE IS HE?!
HEH! HASHI-MOTO-SAN, YOU SAY?

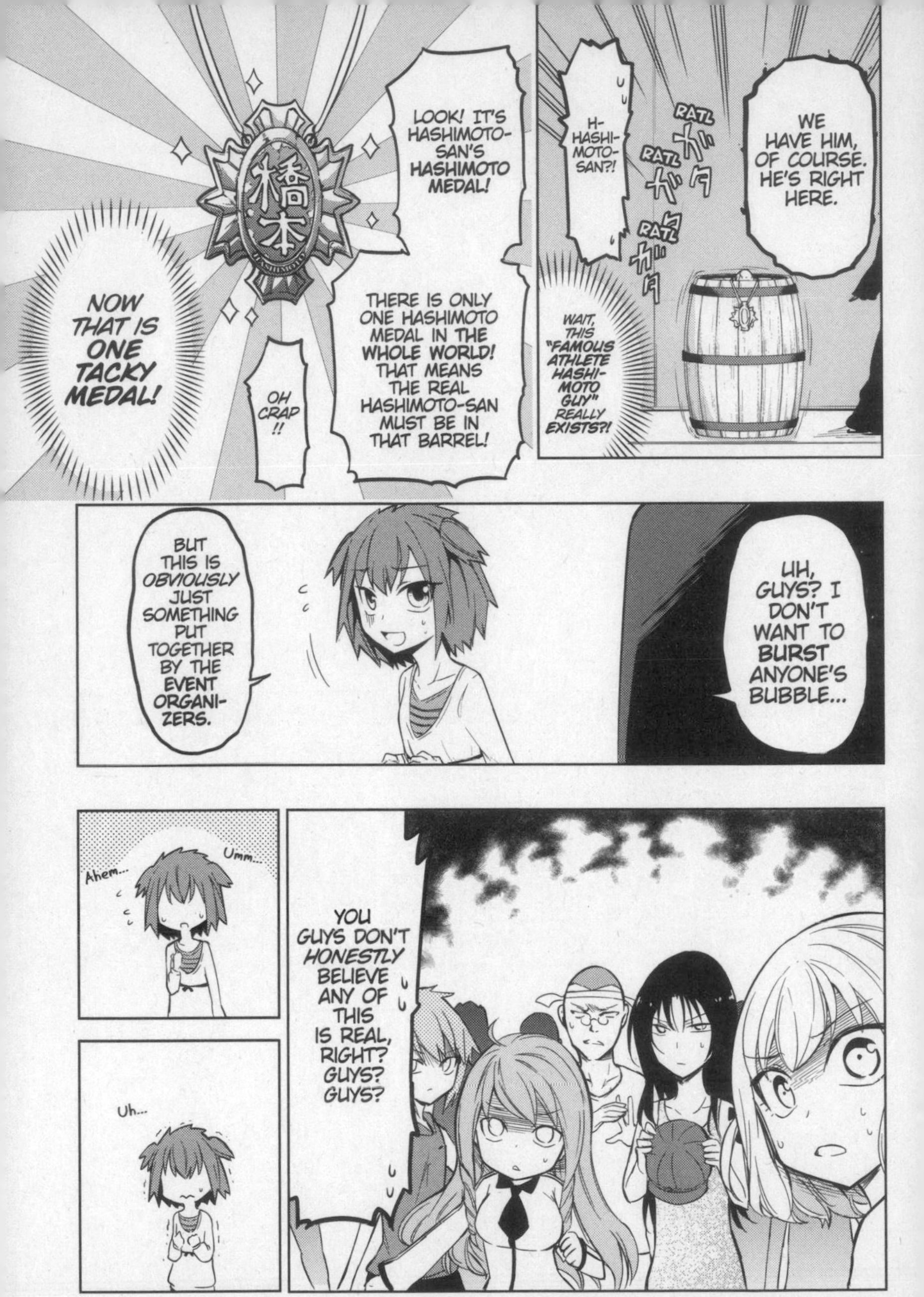
WE HAVE HIM, OF COURSE. HE'S RIGHT HERE.
H-HASHIMOTO-SAN?!
RATL
RATL
RATL
WAIT, THIS "FAMOUS ATHLETE HASHIMOTO GUY" REALLY EXISTS?!
LOOK! IT'S HASHIMOTO-SAN'S HASHIMOTO MEDAL!
THERE IS ONLY ONE HASHIMOTO MEDAL IN THE WHOLE WORLD! THAT MEANS THE REAL HASHIMOTO-SAN MUST BE IN THAT BARREL!
橋本
HASHIMOTO
OH CRAP!!
NOW THAT IS ONE TACKY MEDAL!
UH, GUYS? I DON'T WANT TO BURST ANYONE'S BUBBLE...
BUT THIS IS OBVIOUSLY JUST SOMETHING PUT TOGETHER BY THE EVENT ORGANIZERS.
YOU GUYS DON'T HONESTLY BELIEVE ANY OF THIS IS REAL, RIGHT? GUYS? GUYS?
Umm...
Ahem...
Uh...

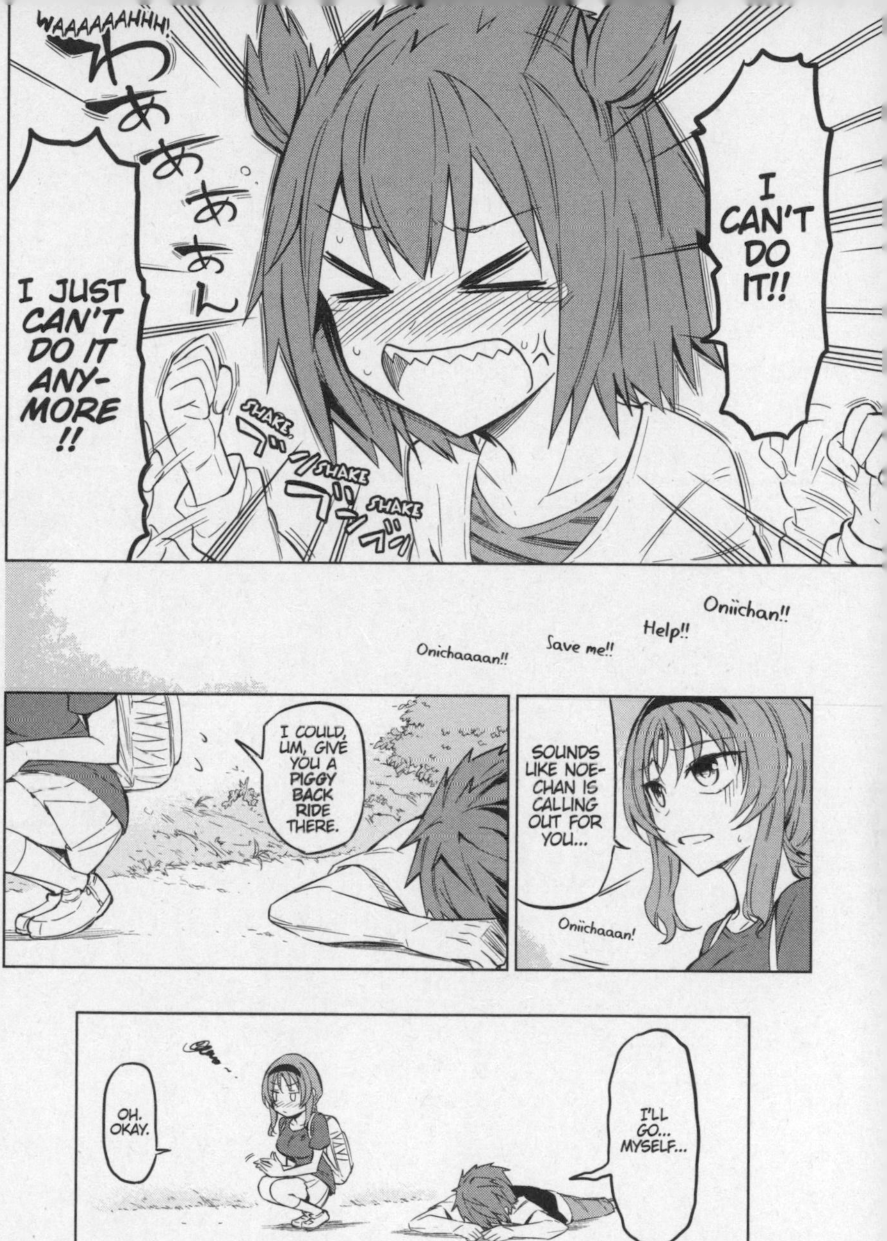
I CAN'T DO IT!!
WAAAAAAHHH!
わあああぁん
I JUST CAN'T DO IT ANYMORE!!
SHAKE,
SHAKE
SHAKE
Oniichan!!
Help!!
Save me!!
Onichaaaan!!
SOUNDS LIKE NOE-CHAN IS CALLING OUT FOR YOU...
Oniichaaan!
I COULD, UM, GIVE YOU A PIGGY BACK RIDE THERE.
I'LL GO... MYSELF...
OH. OKAY.

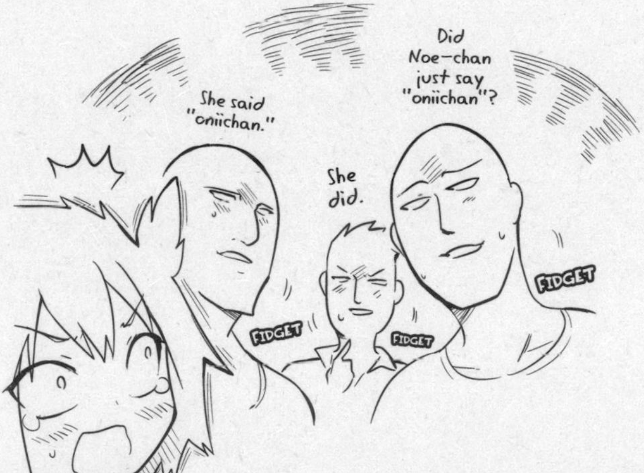
Did Noe-chan just say "oniichan"?
She said "oniichan."
She did.
FIDGET
FIDGET
FIDGET

D-FRAGMENTS

ディーふらぐ！

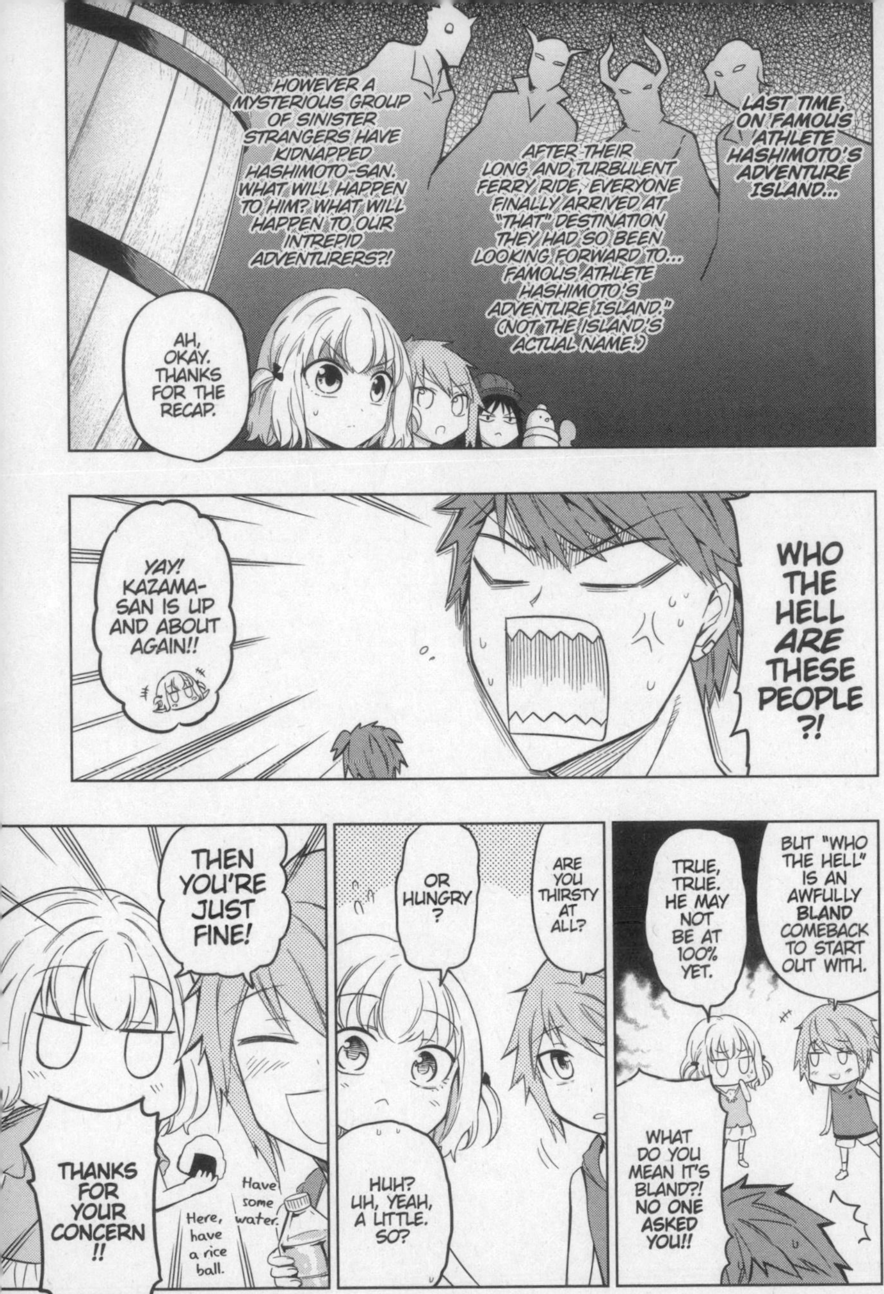
LAST TIME, ON FAMOUS ATHLETE HASHIMOTO'S ADVENTURE ISLAND...
AFTER THEIR LONG AND TURBULENT FERRY RIDE, EVERYONE FINALLY ARRIVED AT "THAT" DESTINATION THEY HAD SO BEEN LOOKING FORWARD TO... FAMOUS ATHLETE HASHIMOTO'S ADVENTURE ISLAND." (NOT THE ISLAND'S ACTUAL NAME.)
HOWEVER A MYSTERIOUS GROUP OF SINISTER STRANGERS HAVE KIDNAPPED HASHIMOTO-SAN. WHAT WILL HAPPEN TO HIM? WHAT WILL HAPPEN TO OUR INTREPID ADVENTURERS?!
AH, OKAY. THANKS FOR THE RECAP.
WHO THE HELL ARE THESE PEOPLE?!
YAY! KAZAMA-SAN IS UP AND ABOUT AGAIN!!
BUT "WHO THE HELL" IS AN AWFULLY BLAND COMEBACK TO START OUT WITH.
TRUE, TRUE. HE MAY NOT BE AT 100% YET.
WHAT DO YOU MEAN IT'S BLAND?! NO ONE ASKED YOU!!
ARE YOU THIRSTY AT ALL?
OR HUNGRY?
HUH? UH, YEAH, A LITTLE. SO?
THEN YOU'RE JUST FINE!
Have some water.
Here, have a rice ball.
THANKS FOR YOUR CONCERN!!

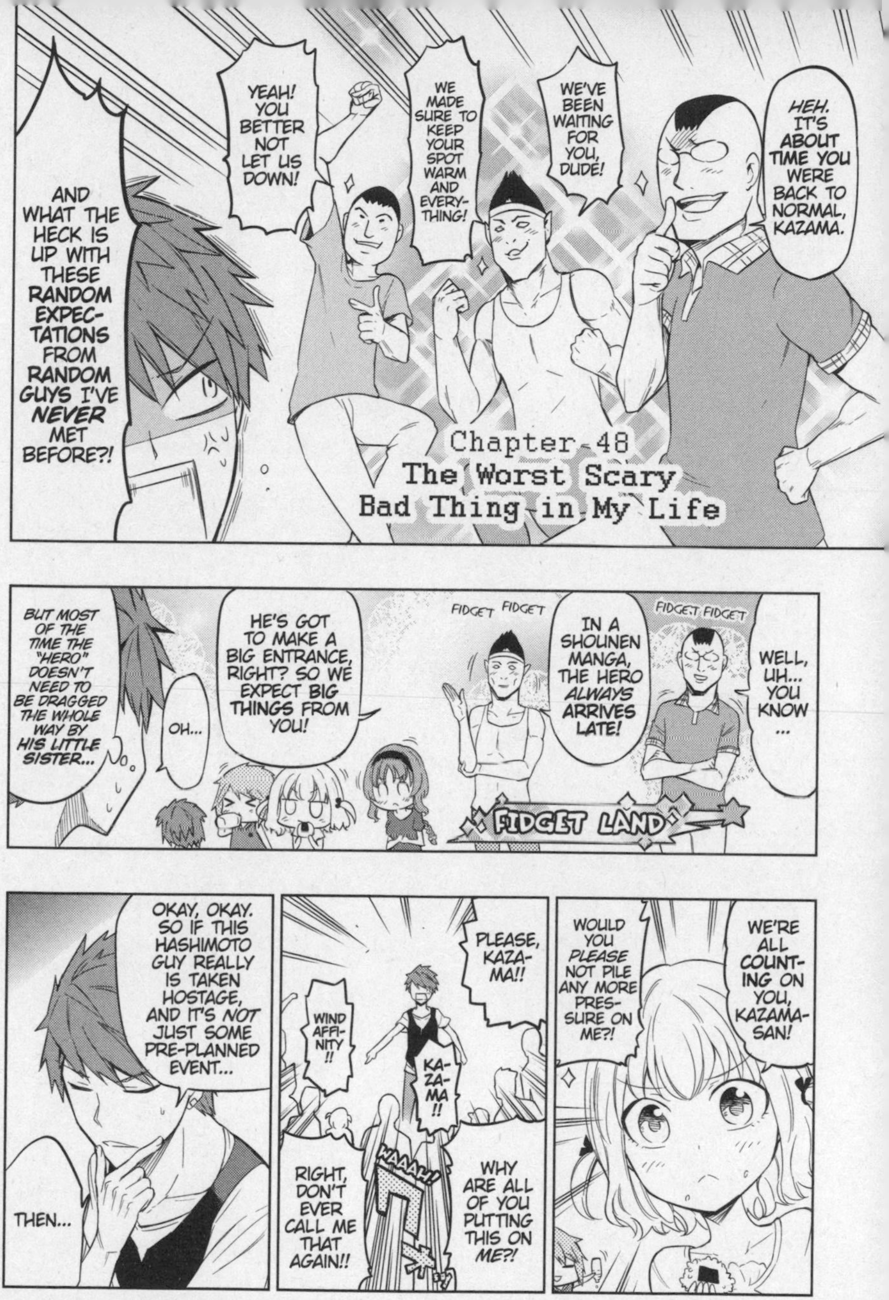
HEH. IT'S ABOUT TIME YOU WERE BACK TO NORMAL, KAZAMA.
WE'VE BEEN WAITING FOR YOU, DUDE!
WE MADE SURE TO KEEP YOUR SPOT WARM AND EVERYTHING!
YEAH! YOU BETTER NOT LET US DOWN!
AND WHAT THE HECK IS UP WITH THESE RANDOM EXPECTATIONS FROM RANDOM GUYS I'VE NEVER MET BEFORE?!
Chapter 48
The Worst Scary Bad Thing in My Life
WELL, UH... YOU KNOW...
FIDGET FIDGET
IN A SHOUNEN MANGA, THE HERO ALWAYS ARRIVES LATE!
FIDGET FIDGET
HE'S GOT TO MAKE A BIG ENTRANCE, RIGHT? SO WE EXPECT BIG THINGS FROM YOU!
OH...
BUT MOST OF THE TIME THE "HERO" DOESN'T NEED TO BE DRAGGED THE WHOLE WAY BY HIS LITTLE SISTER...
FIDGET LAND
WE'RE ALL COUNTING ON YOU, KAZAMA-SAN!
WOULD YOU PLEASE NOT PILE ANY MORE PRESSURE ON ME?!
PLEASE, KAZAMA!!
WIND AFFINITY!!
KAZAMA!!
KAAAH!
WHY ARE ALL OF YOU PUTTING THIS ON ME?!
RIGHT, DON'T EVER CALL ME THAT AGAIN!!
OKAY, OKAY. SO IF THIS HASHIMOTO GUY REALLY IS TAKEN HOSTAGE, AND IT'S NOT JUST SOME PRE-PLANNED EVENT...
THEN...

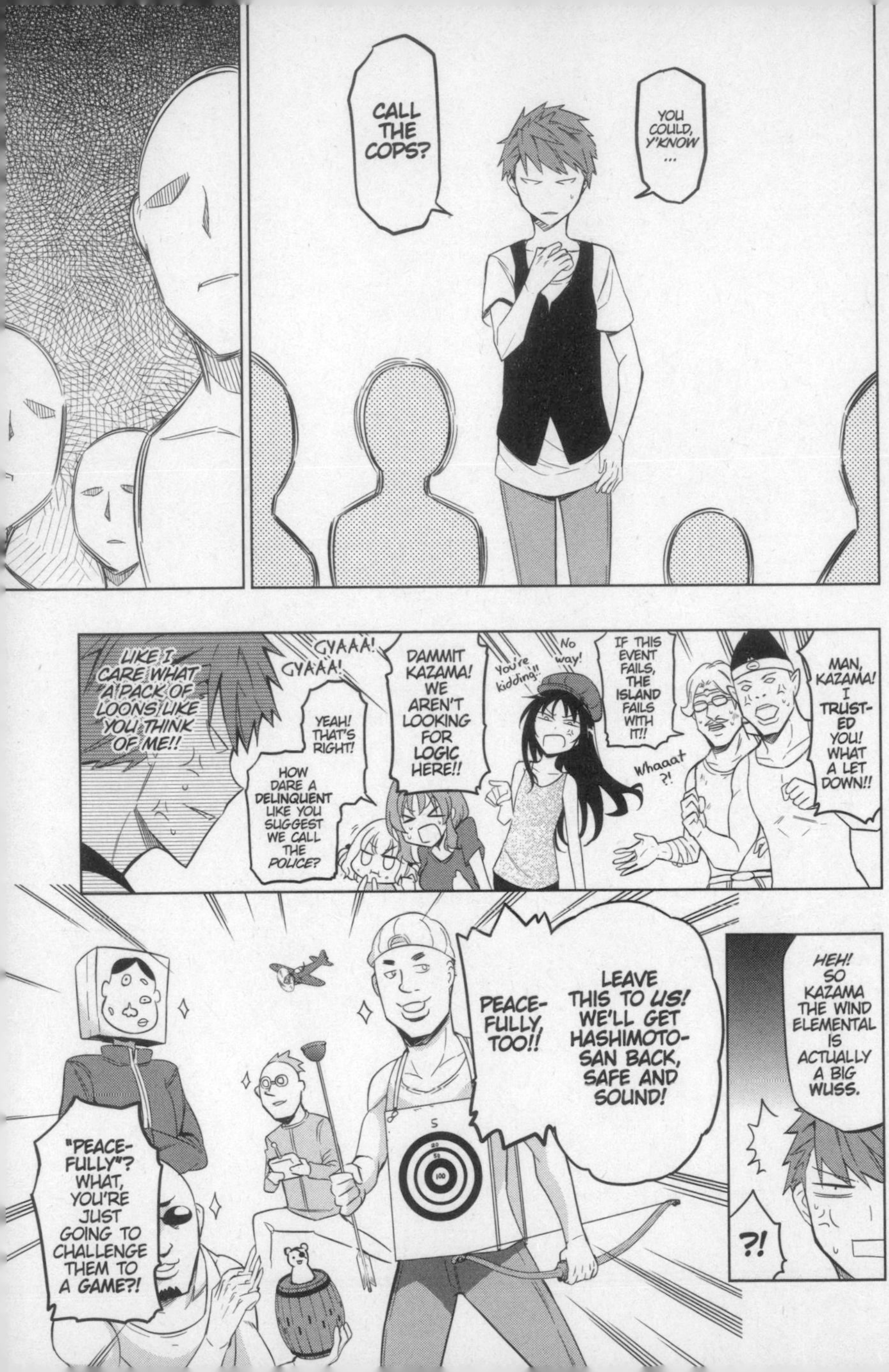
YOU COULD, Y'KNOW ...
CALL THE COPS?
MAN, KAZAMA! I TRUSTED YOU! WHAT A LET DOWN!!
IF THIS EVENT FAILS, THE ISLAND FAILS WITH IT!!
No way!
You're kidding!!
Whaaat?!
DAMMIT KAZAMA! WE AREN'T LOOKING FOR LOGIC HERE!!
GYAAA! GYAAA!
YEAH! THAT'S RIGHT!
HOW DARE A DELINQUENT LIKE YOU SUGGEST WE CALL THE *POLICE*?
LIKE I CARE WHAT A PACK OF LOONS LIKE YOU THINK OF ME!!
HEH! SO KAZAMA THE WIND ELEMENTAL IS ACTUALLY A BIG WUSS.
?!
LEAVE THIS TO *US*! WE'LL GET HASHIMOTO-SAN BACK, SAFE AND SOUND!
PEACE-FULLY TOO!!
"PEACE-FULLY"? WHAT, YOU'RE JUST GOING TO CHALLENGE THEM TO A GAME?!

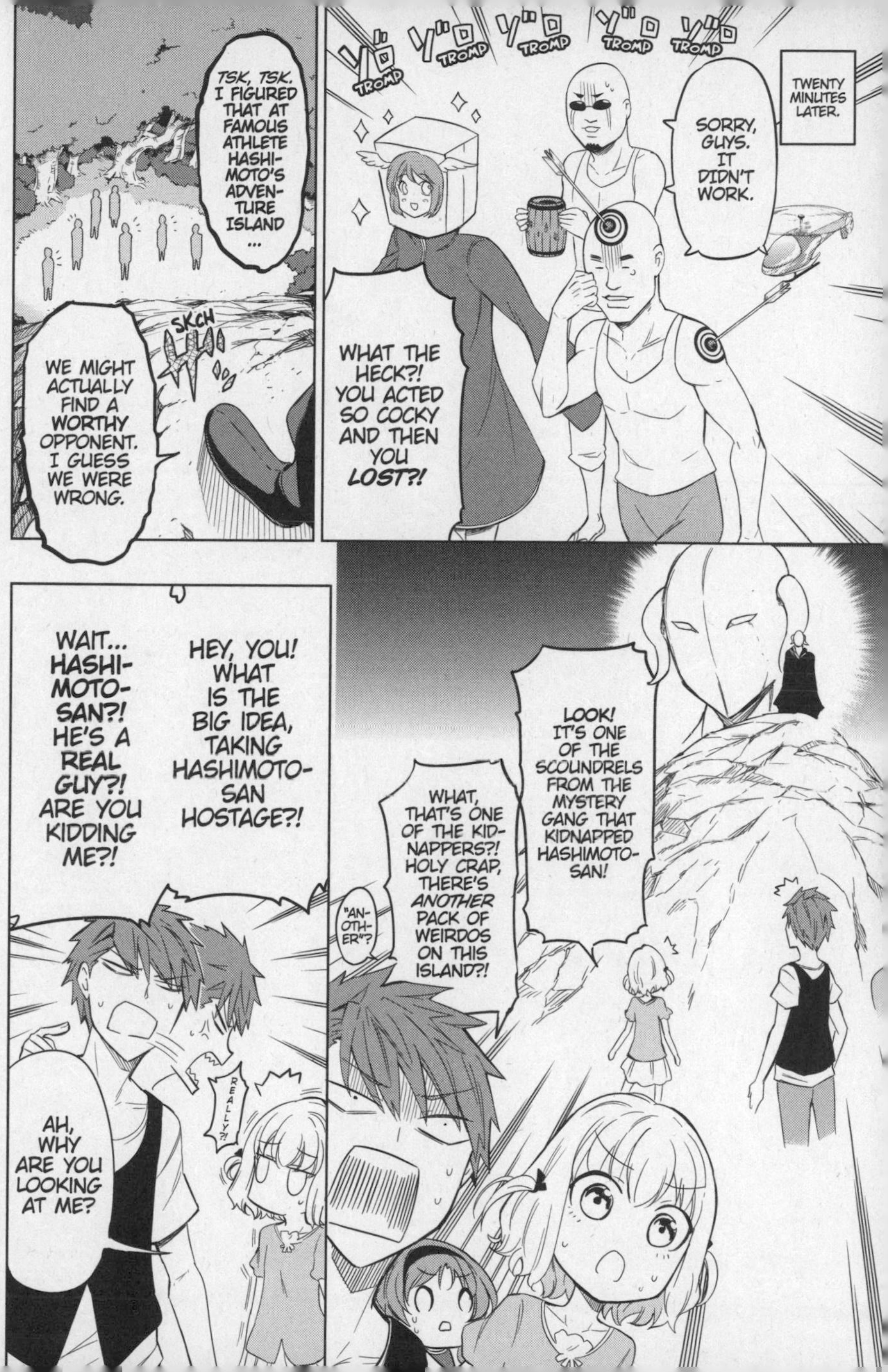
TWENTY MINUTES LATER.
ゾロ TROMP
ゾロ TROMP
ゾロ TROMP
ゾロ TROMP
ゾロ TROMP
SORRY, GUYS. IT DIDN'T WORK.
WHAT THE HECK?! YOU ACTED SO COCKY AND THEN YOU LOST?!
TSK, TSK. I FIGURED THAT AT FAMOUS ATHLETE HASHIMOTO'S ADVENTURE ISLAND ...
SKCH
WE MIGHT ACTUALLY FIND A WORTHY OPPONENT. I GUESS WE WERE WRONG.
LOOK! IT'S ONE OF THE SCOUNDRELS FROM THE MYSTERY GANG THAT KIDNAPPED HASHIMOTO-SAN!
WHAT, THAT'S ONE OF THE KIDNAPPERS?! HOLY CRAP, THERE'S ANOTHER PACK OF WEIRDOS ON THIS ISLAND?!
"AN-OTHER"?
HEY, YOU! WHAT IS THE BIG IDEA, TAKING HASHIMOTO-SAN HOSTAGE?!
WAIT... HASHI-MOTO-SAN?! HE'S A REAL GUY?! ARE YOU KIDDING ME?!
REALLY?!
AH, WHY ARE YOU LOOKING AT ME?

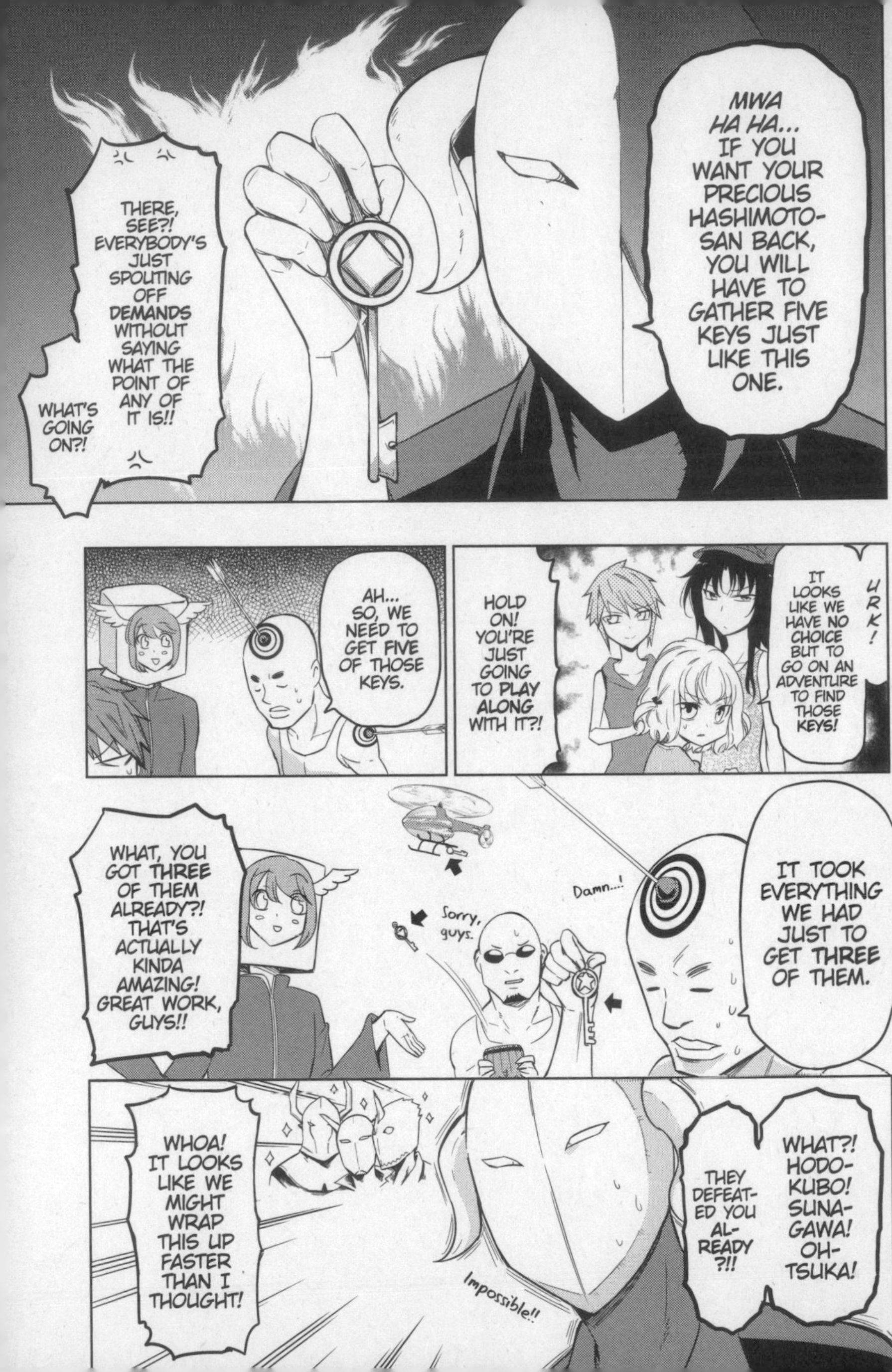
MWA HA HA... IF YOU WANT YOUR PRECIOUS HASHIMOTO-SAN BACK, YOU WILL HAVE TO GATHER FIVE KEYS JUST LIKE THIS ONE.
THERE, SEE?! EVERYBODY'S JUST SPOUTING OFF DEMANDS WITHOUT SAYING WHAT THE POINT OF ANY OF IT IS!!
WHAT'S GOING ON?!
URK!
IT LOOKS LIKE WE HAVE NO CHOICE BUT TO GO ON AN ADVENTURE TO FIND THOSE KEYS!
HOLD ON! YOU'RE JUST GOING TO PLAY ALONG WITH IT?!
AH... SO, WE NEED TO GET FIVE OF THOSE KEYS.
IT TOOK EVERYTHING WE HAD JUST TO GET THREE OF THEM.
Damn...!
Sorry, guys.
WHAT, YOU GOT THREE OF THEM ALREADY?! THAT'S ACTUALLY KINDA AMAZING! GREAT WORK, GUYS!!
WHAT?! HODO-KUBO! SUNA-GAWA! OH-TSUKA!
THEY DEFEAT-ED YOU AL-READY ?!!
Impossible!!
WHOA! IT LOOKS LIKE WE MIGHT WRAP THIS UP FASTER THAN I THOUGHT!

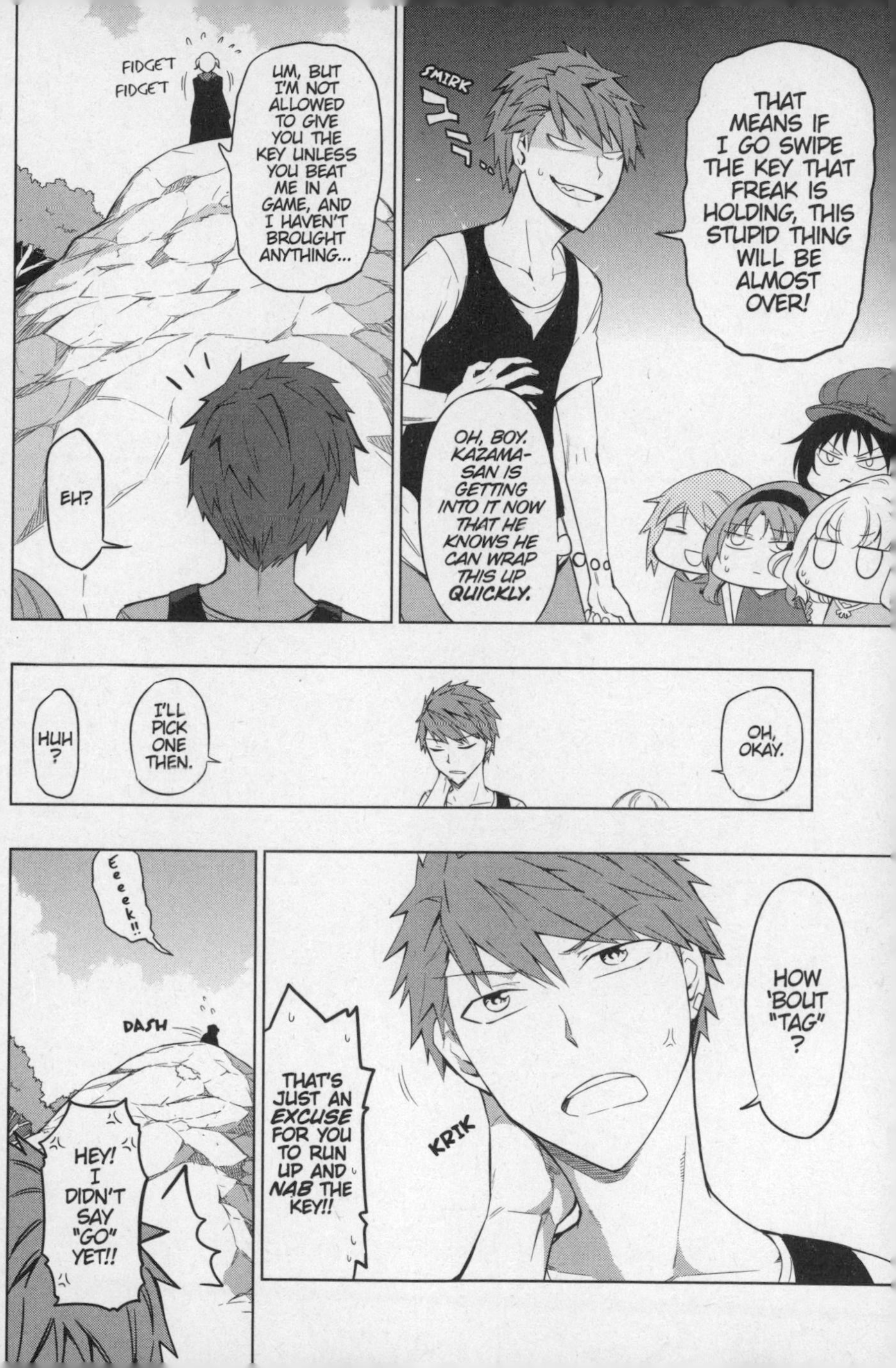
SMIRK
THAT MEANS IF I GO SWIPE THE KEY THAT FREAK IS HOLDING, THIS STUPID THING WILL BE ALMOST OVER!
OH, BOY. KAZAMA-SAN IS GETTING INTO IT NOW THAT HE KNOWS HE CAN WRAP THIS UP QUICKLY.
UM, BUT I'M NOT ALLOWED TO GIVE YOU THE KEY UNLESS YOU BEAT ME IN A GAME, AND I HAVEN'T BROUGHT ANYTHING...
FIDGET FIDGET
EH?
OH, OKAY.
I'LL PICK ONE THEN.
HUH?
HOW 'BOUT "TAG"?
KRIK
THAT'S JUST AN EXCUSE FOR YOU TO RUN UP AND NAB THE KEY!!
Eeeeek!!
DASH
HEY! I DIDN'T SAY "GO" YET!!

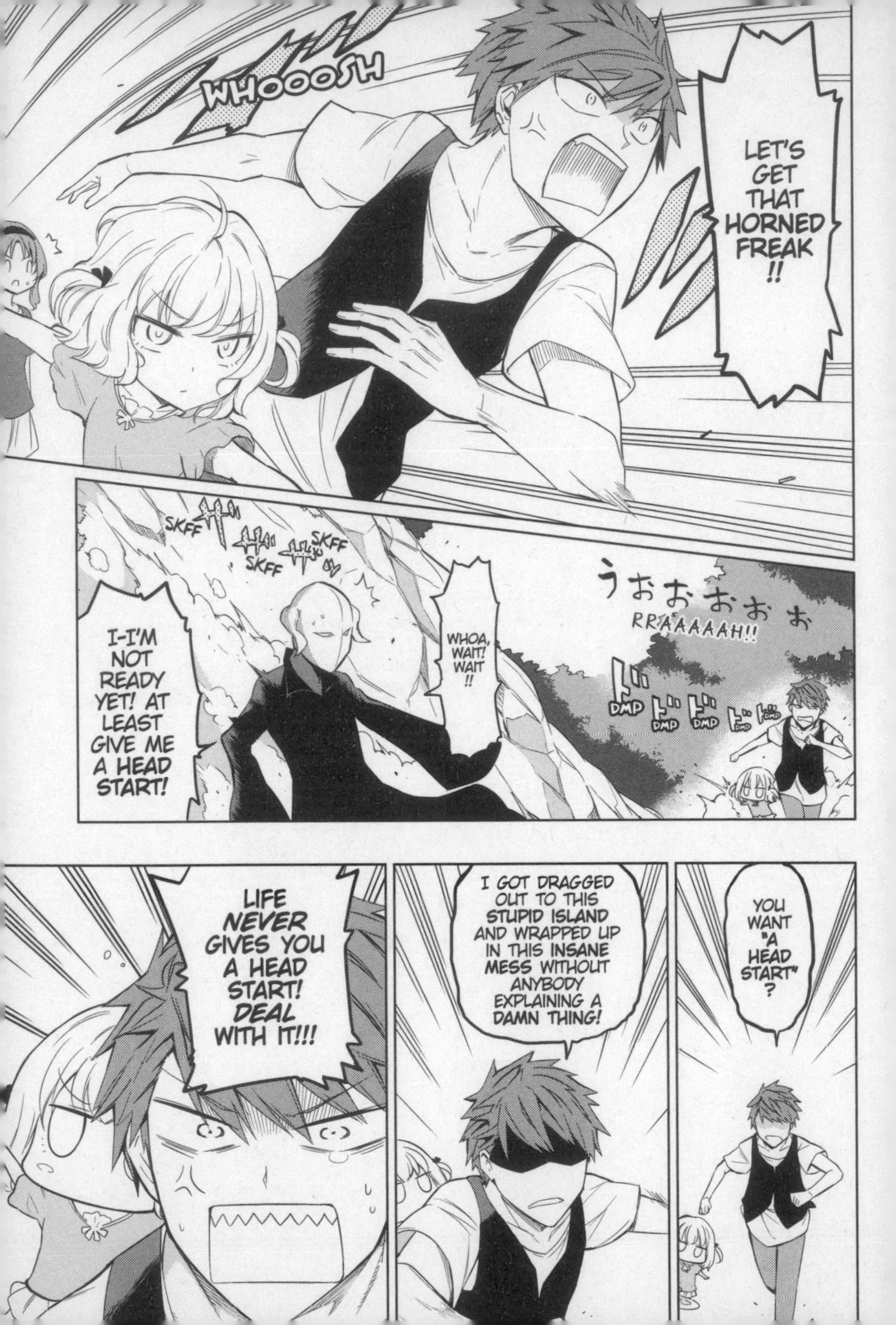
LET'S GET THAT HORNED FREAK!!
WHOOOSH
うおおおおお
RRAAAAAH!!
ドドドドド
DMP DMP DMP DMP DMP
WHOA, WAIT! WAIT!!
SKFF SKFF SKFF
I-I'M NOT READY YET! AT LEAST GIVE ME A HEAD START!
YOU WANT "A HEAD START"?
I GOT DRAGGED OUT TO THIS STUPID ISLAND AND WRAPPED UP IN THIS INSANE MESS WITHOUT ANYBODY EXPLAINING A DAMN THING!
LIFE *NEVER* GIVES YOU A HEAD START! *DEAL* WITH IT!!!

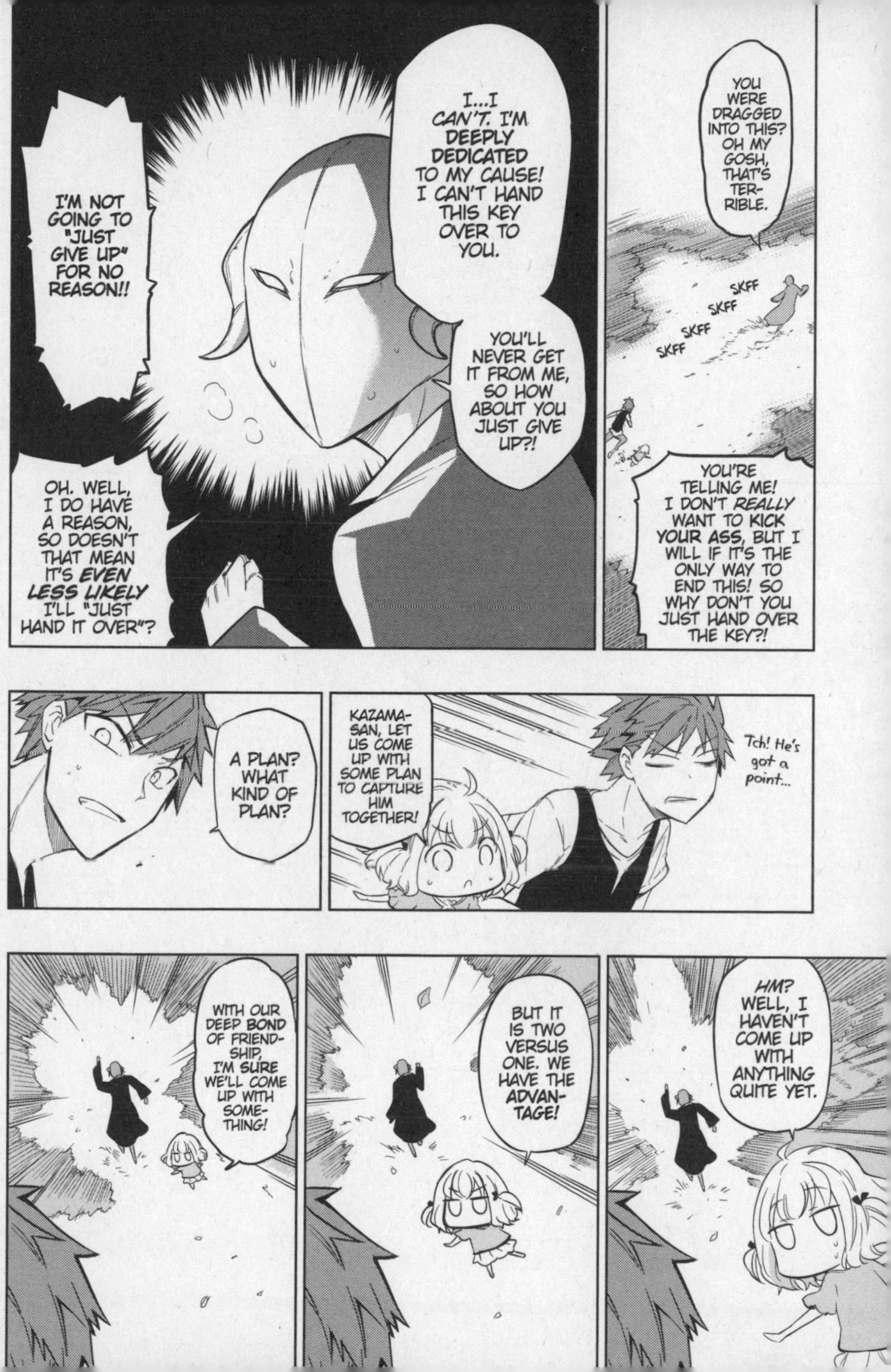
YOU WERE DRAGGED INTO THIS? OH MY GOSH, THAT'S TER-RIBLE.
SKFF SKFF SKFF SKFF
YOU'RE TELLING ME! I DON'T *REALLY* WANT TO KICK **YOUR ASS**, BUT I WILL IF IT'S THE ONLY WAY TO END THIS! SO WHY DON'T YOU JUST HAND OVER THE KEY?!
I...I *CAN'T*. I'M **DEEPLY DEDICATED** TO MY CAUSE! I CAN'T HAND THIS KEY OVER TO YOU.
YOU'LL NEVER GET IT FROM ME, SO HOW ABOUT YOU JUST GIVE UP?!
I'M NOT GOING TO "JUST GIVE UP" FOR NO REASON!!
OH. WELL, I DO HAVE A REASON, SO DOESN'T THAT MEAN IT'S ***EVEN LESS LIKELY*** I'LL "JUST HAND IT OVER"?
Tch! He's got a point...
KAZAMA-SAN, LET US COME UP WITH SOME PLAN TO CAPTURE HIM TOGETHER!
A PLAN? WHAT KIND OF PLAN?
HM? WELL, I HAVEN'T COME UP WITH ANYTHING QUITE YET.
BUT IT IS TWO VERSUS ONE. WE HAVE THE **ADVAN-TAGE!**
WITH OUR DEEP BOND OF FRIEND-SHIP, I'M SURE WE'LL COME UP WITH SOME-THING!

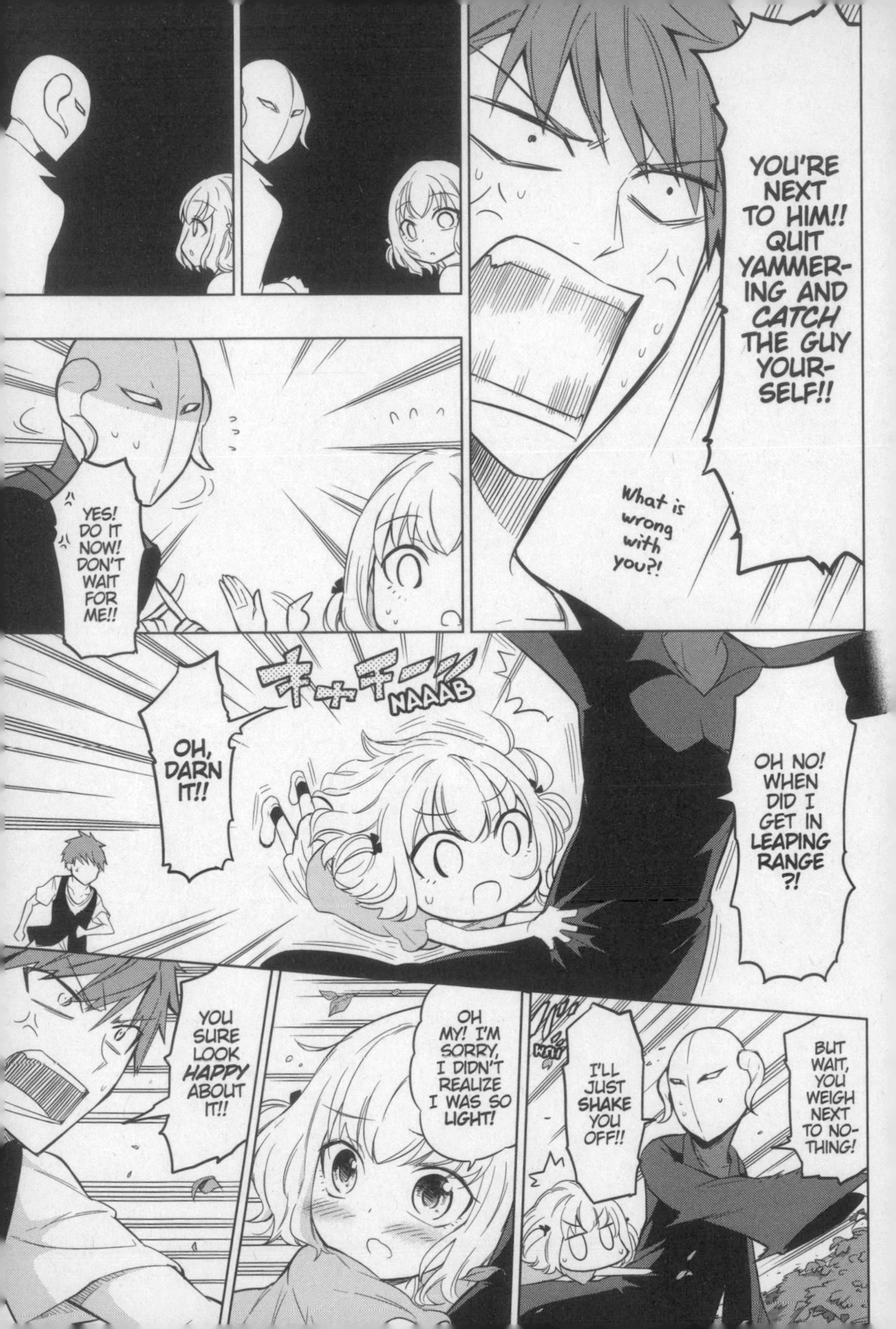
YOU'RE NEXT TO HIM!! QUIT YAMMERING AND *CATCH* THE GUY YOURSELF!!
What is wrong with you?!
YES! DO IT NOW! DON'T WAIT FOR ME!!
NAAAB
OH NO! WHEN DID I GET IN LEAPING RANGE?!
OH, DARN IT!!
BUT WAIT, YOU WEIGH NEXT TO NOTHING!
I'LL JUST SHAKE YOU OFF!!
OH MY! I'M SORRY, I DIDN'T REALIZE I WAS SO LIGHT!
YOU SURE LOOK *HAPPY* ABOUT IT!!

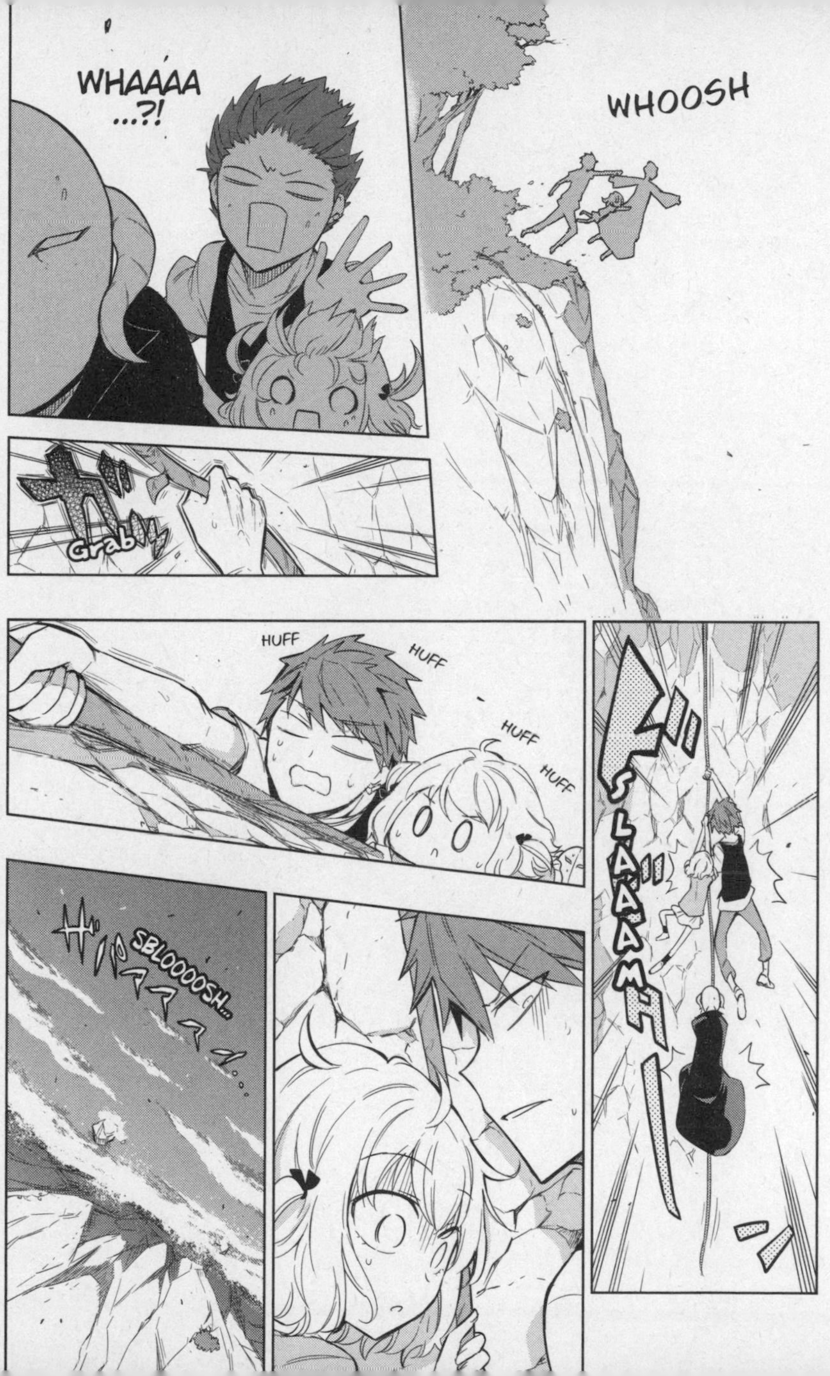
WHOOSH
WHAAAA ...?!
Grab
SLAAAMH
HUFF
HUFF
HUFF
HUFF
SBLOOOOSH...

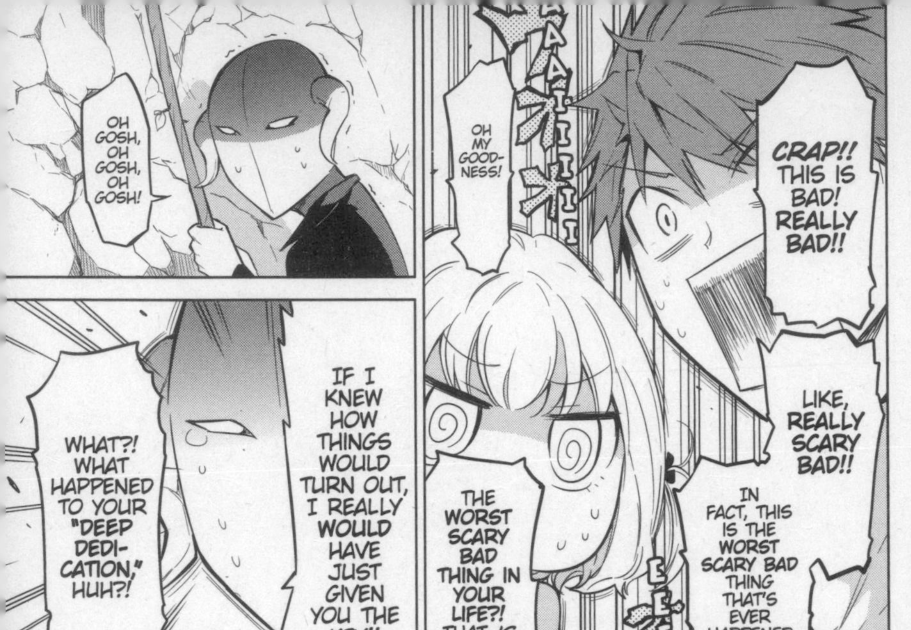
CRAP!! THIS IS BAD! REALLY BAD!!
LIKE, REALLY SCARY BAD!!
OH MY GOOD-NESS!
IN FACT, THIS IS THE WORST SCARY BAD THING THAT'S EVER HAPPENED TO ME!!
THE WORST SCARY BAD THING IN YOUR LIFE?! THAT IS SCARY BAD!!
OH GOSH, OH GOSH, OH GOSH!
IF I KNEW HOW THINGS WOULD TURN OUT, I REALLY WOULD HAVE JUST GIVEN YOU THE KEY!!
WHAT?! WHAT HAPPENED TO YOUR "DEEP DEDI-CATION," HUH?!
HEY, I KNOW! YOU STILL HAVE YOUR BAG, RIGHT?!
YOU CAN THROW IT, RIGHT?! SO HOW ABOUT YOU THROW IT AND HOOK IT ON A BRANCH OR SOMETHING!!
ZWIP
HUH? OH! YOU MEAN MY SPECIAL ROLLING CATCHER MOVE?
I DON'T GIVE A CRAP ABOUT WHAT IT'S CALLED, JUST DO IT!!

※See Volume 6, Chapter 43.

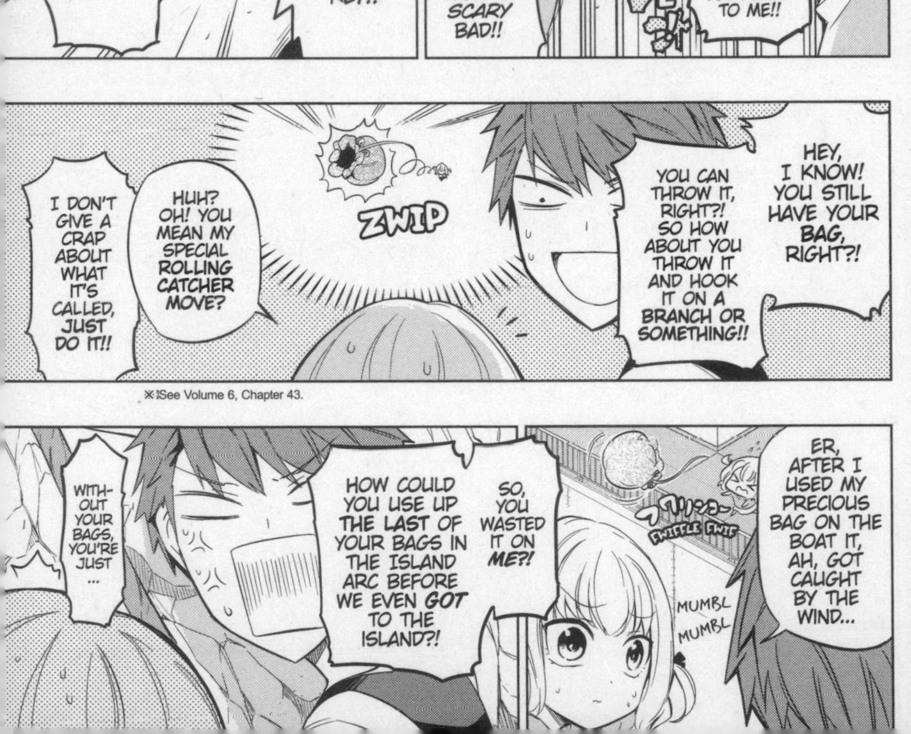
ER, AFTER I USED MY PRECIOUS BAG ON THE BOAT IT, AH, GOT CAUGHT BY THE WIND...
FWIFFLE FWIF
MUMBL MUMBL
SO, YOU WASTED IT ON ME?!
HOW COULD YOU USE UP THE LAST OF YOUR BAGS IN THE ISLAND ARC BEFORE WE EVEN GOT TO THE ISLAND?!
WITH-OUT YOUR BAGS, YOU'RE JUST ...

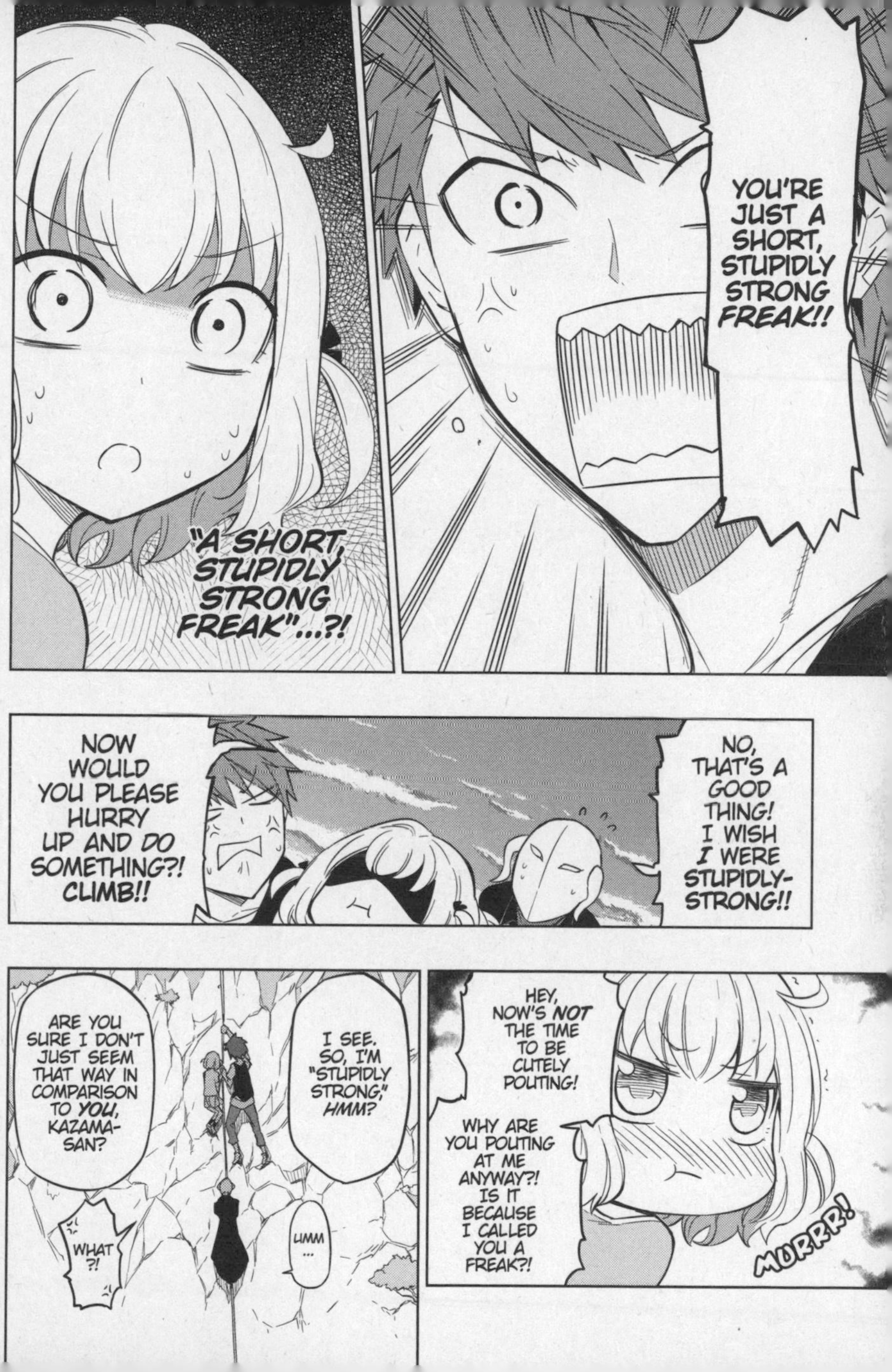
YOU'RE JUST A SHORT, STUPIDLY STRONG FREAK!!
"A SHORT, STUPIDLY STRONG FREAK"...?!
NO, THAT'S A GOOD THING! I WISH I WERE STUPIDLY-STRONG!!
NOW WOULD YOU PLEASE HURRY UP AND DO SOMETHING?! CLIMB!!
HEY, NOW'S NOT THE TIME TO BE CUTELY POUTING!
WHY ARE YOU POUTING AT ME ANYWAY?! IS IT BECAUSE I CALLED YOU A FREAK?!
MURRR!
I SEE. SO, I'M "STUPIDLY STRONG," HMM?
ARE YOU SURE I DON'T JUST SEEM THAT WAY IN COMPARISON TO YOU, KAZAMA-SAN?
UMM ...
WHAT ?!

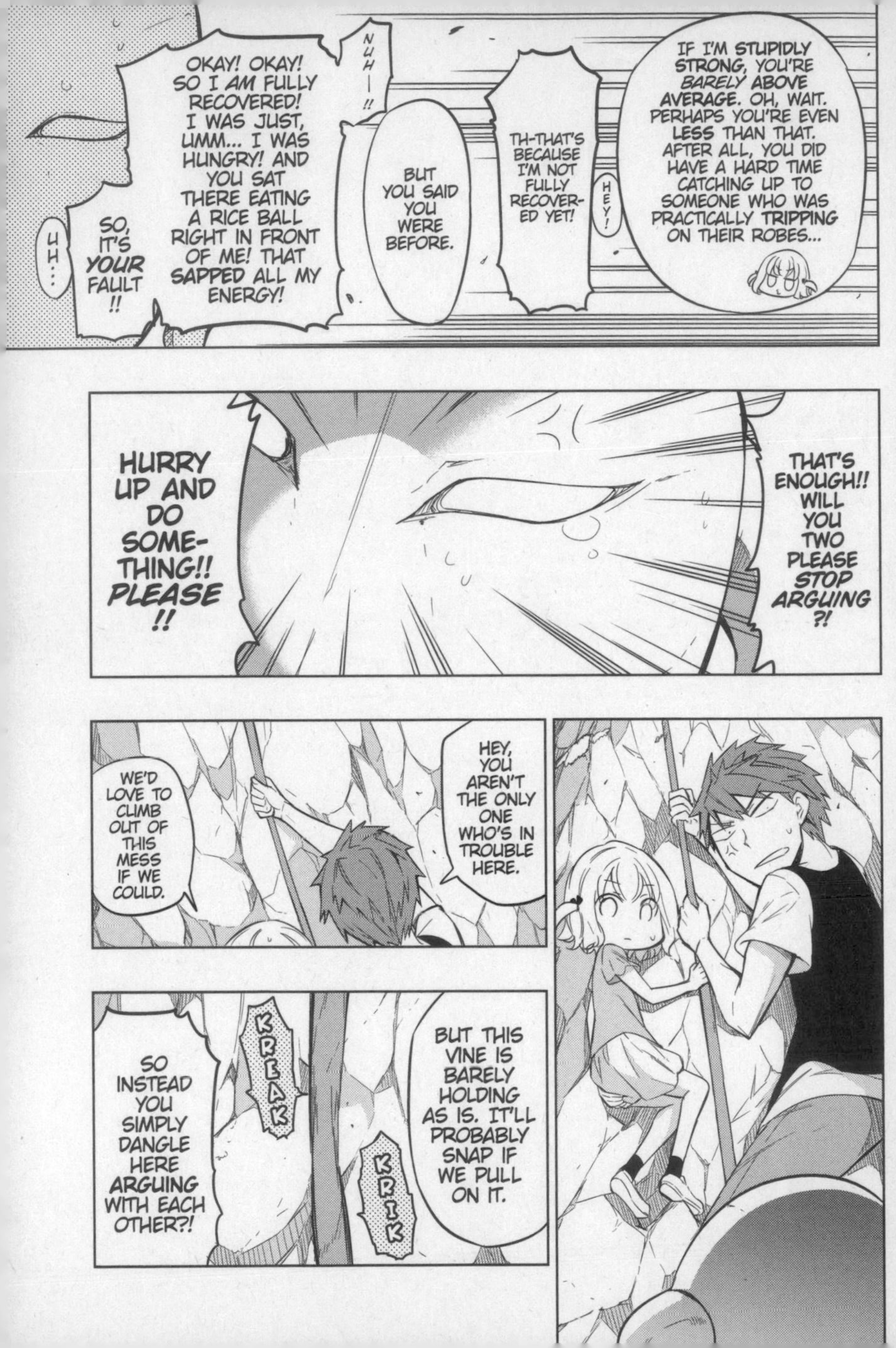
IF I'M STUPIDLY STRONG, YOU'RE BARELY ABOVE AVERAGE. OH, WAIT. PERHAPS YOU'RE EVEN LESS THAN THAT. AFTER ALL, YOU DID HAVE A HARD TIME CATCHING UP TO SOMEONE WHO WAS PRACTICALLY TRIPPING ON THEIR ROBES...
HEY!
TH-THAT'S BECAUSE I'M NOT FULLY RECOVER-ED YET!
BUT YOU SAID YOU WERE BEFORE.
NUH—!!
OKAY! OKAY! SO I AM FULLY RECOVERED! I WAS JUST, UMM... I WAS HUNGRY! AND YOU SAT THERE EATING A RICE BALL RIGHT IN FRONT OF ME! THAT SAPPED ALL MY ENERGY!
SO, IT'S YOUR FAULT!!
UH...
THAT'S ENOUGH!! WILL YOU TWO PLEASE STOP ARGUING?!
HURRY UP AND DO SOME-THING!! PLEASE!!
HEY, YOU AREN'T THE ONLY ONE WHO'S IN TROUBLE HERE.
WE'D LOVE TO CLIMB OUT OF THIS MESS IF WE COULD.
BUT THIS VINE IS BARELY HOLDING AS IS. IT'LL PROBABLY SNAP IF WE PULL ON IT.
KREAK
KRIK
SO INSTEAD YOU SIMPLY DANGLE HERE ARGUING WITH EACH OTHER?!

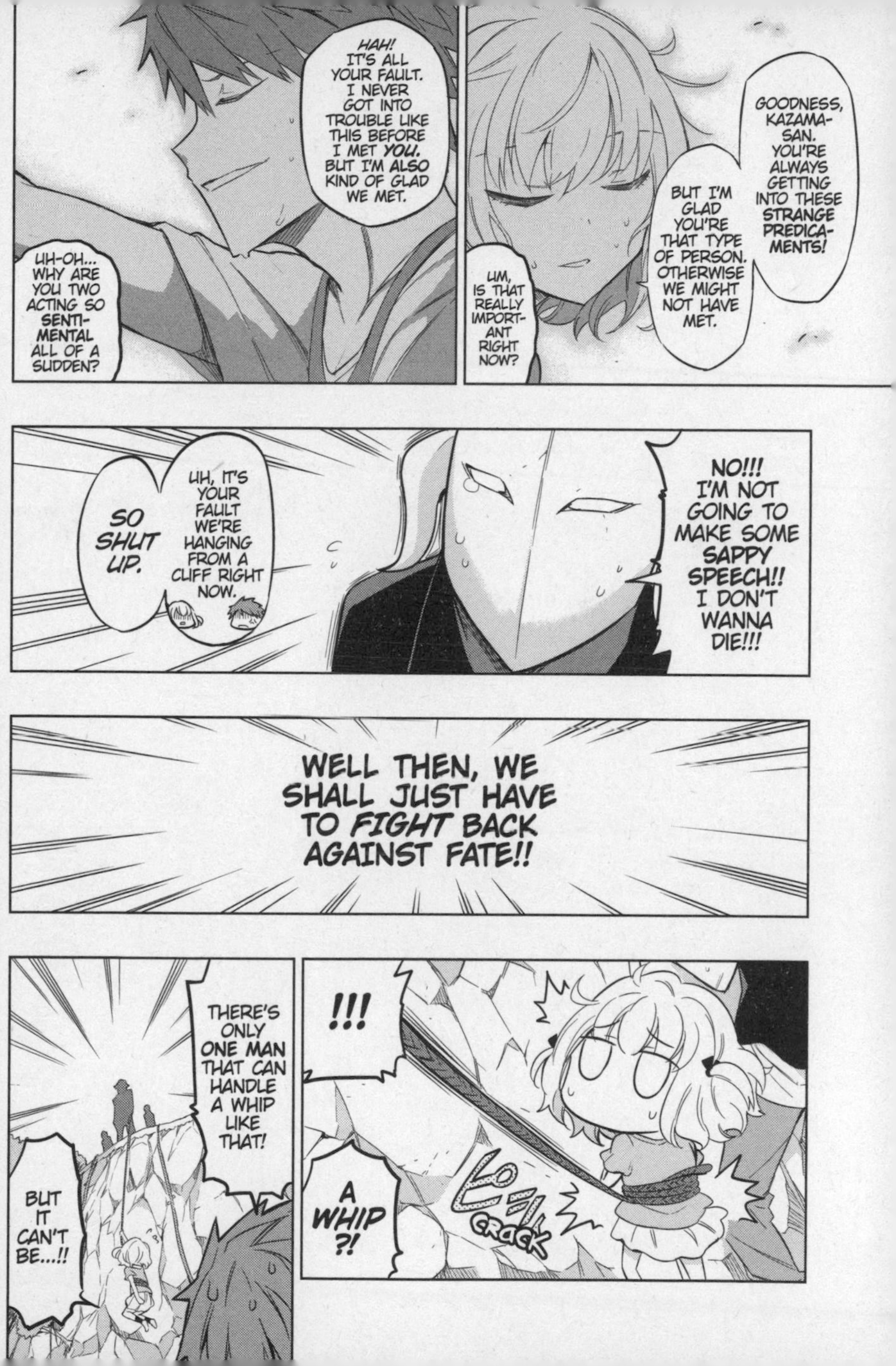
GOODNESS, KAZAMA-SAN. YOU'RE ALWAYS GETTING INTO THESE STRANGE PREDICAMENTS!
BUT I'M GLAD YOU'RE THAT TYPE OF PERSON. OTHERWISE WE MIGHT NOT HAVE MET.
UM, IS THAT REALLY IMPORTANT RIGHT NOW?
HAH! IT'S ALL YOUR FAULT. I NEVER GOT INTO TROUBLE LIKE THIS BEFORE I MET YOU. BUT I'M ALSO KIND OF GLAD WE MET.
UH-OH... WHY ARE YOU TWO ACTING SO SENTIMENTAL ALL OF A SUDDEN?
NO!!! I'M NOT GOING TO MAKE SOME SAPPY SPEECH!! I DON'T WANNA DIE!!!
UH, IT'S YOUR FAULT WE'RE HANGING FROM A CLIFF RIGHT NOW.
SO SHUT UP.
WELL THEN, WE SHALL JUST HAVE TO FIGHT BACK AGAINST FATE!!
!!!
CRACK
A WHIP?!
THERE'S ONLY ONE MAN THAT CAN HANDLE A WHIP LIKE THAT!
BUT IT CAN'T BE...!!

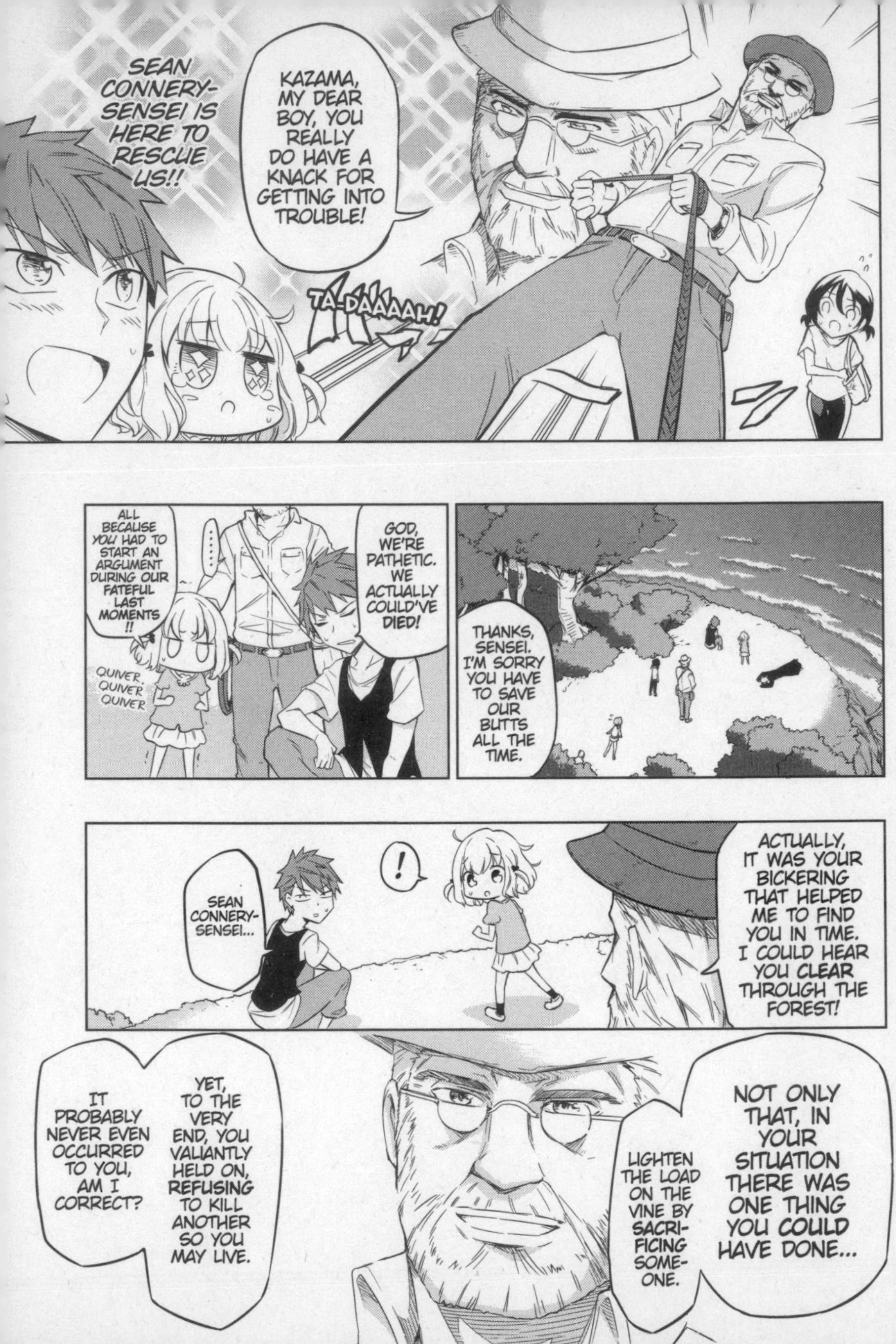
KAZAMA, MY DEAR BOY, YOU REALLY DO HAVE A KNACK FOR GETTING INTO TROUBLE!
SEAN CONNERY-SENSEI IS HERE TO RESCUE US!!
TA-DAAAAH!
THANKS, SENSEI. I'M SORRY YOU HAVE TO SAVE OUR BUTTS ALL THE TIME.
GOD, WE'RE PATHETIC. WE ACTUALLY COULD'VE DIED!
......
ALL BECAUSE YOU HAD TO START AN ARGUMENT DURING OUR FATEFUL LAST MOMENTS!!
QUIVER QUIVER QUIVER
ACTUALLY, IT WAS YOUR BICKERING THAT HELPED ME TO FIND YOU IN TIME. I COULD HEAR YOU CLEAR THROUGH THE FOREST!
!
SEAN CONNERY-SENSEI...
NOT ONLY THAT, IN YOUR SITUATION THERE WAS ONE THING YOU COULD HAVE DONE...
LIGHTEN THE LOAD ON THE VINE BY SACRIFICING SOMEONE.
YET, TO THE VERY END, YOU VALIANTLY HELD ON, REFUSING TO KILL ANOTHER SO YOU MAY LIVE.
IT PROBABLY NEVER EVEN OCCURRED TO YOU, AM I CORRECT?

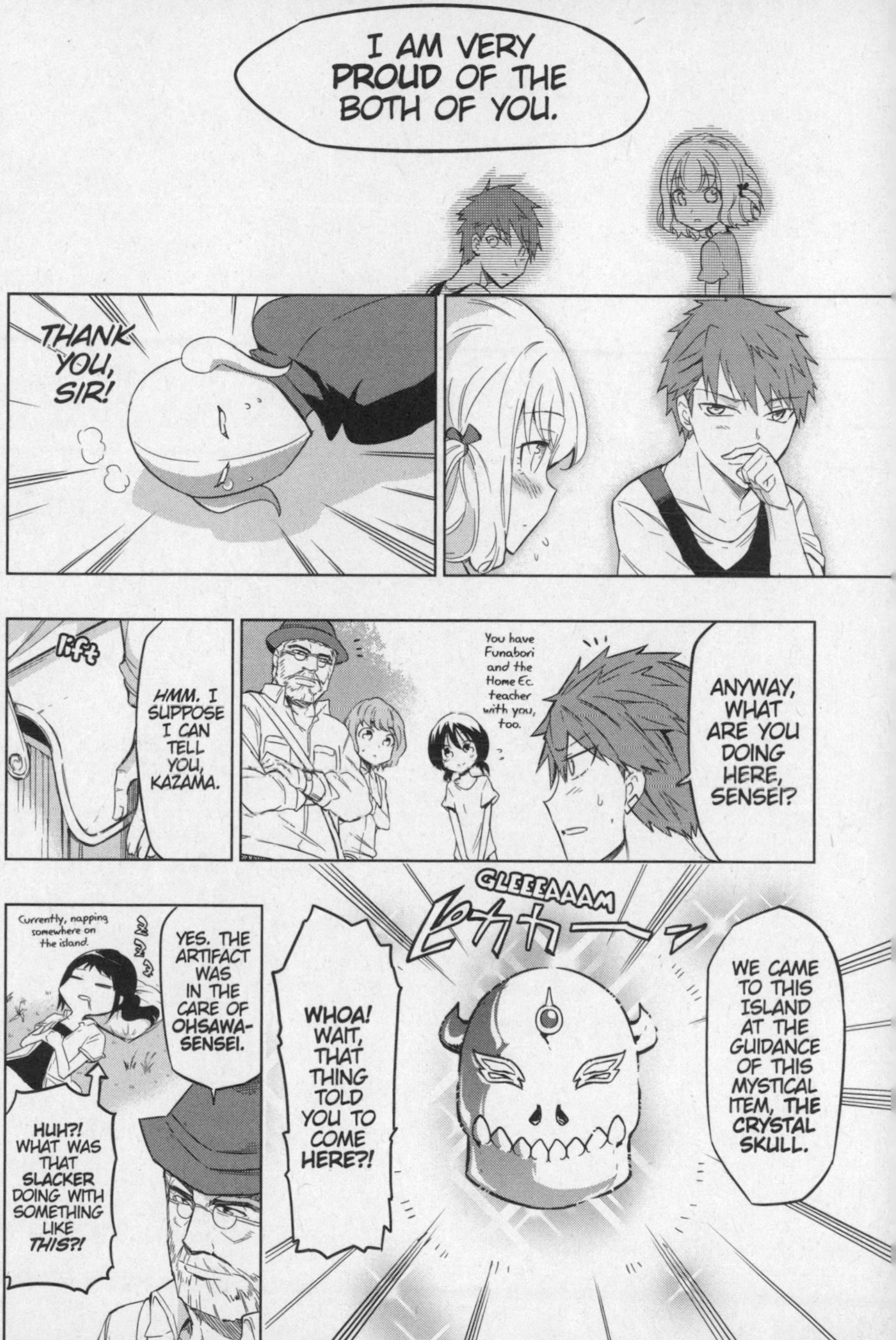
I AM VERY PROUD OF THE BOTH OF YOU.
THANK YOU, SIR!
ANYWAY, WHAT ARE YOU DOING HERE, SENSEI?
You have Funabori and the Home Ec. teacher with you, too.
lift
HMM. I SUPPOSE I CAN TELL YOU, KAZAMA.
GLEEEAAAM
WE CAME TO THIS ISLAND AT THE GUIDANCE OF THIS MYSTICAL ITEM, THE CRYSTAL SKULL.
WHOA! WAIT, THAT THING TOLD YOU TO COME HERE?!
YES. THE ARTIFACT WAS IN THE CARE OF OHSAWA-SENSEI.
Currently, napping somewhere on the island.
HUH?! WHAT WAS THAT SLACKER DOING WITH SOMETHING LIKE THIS?!

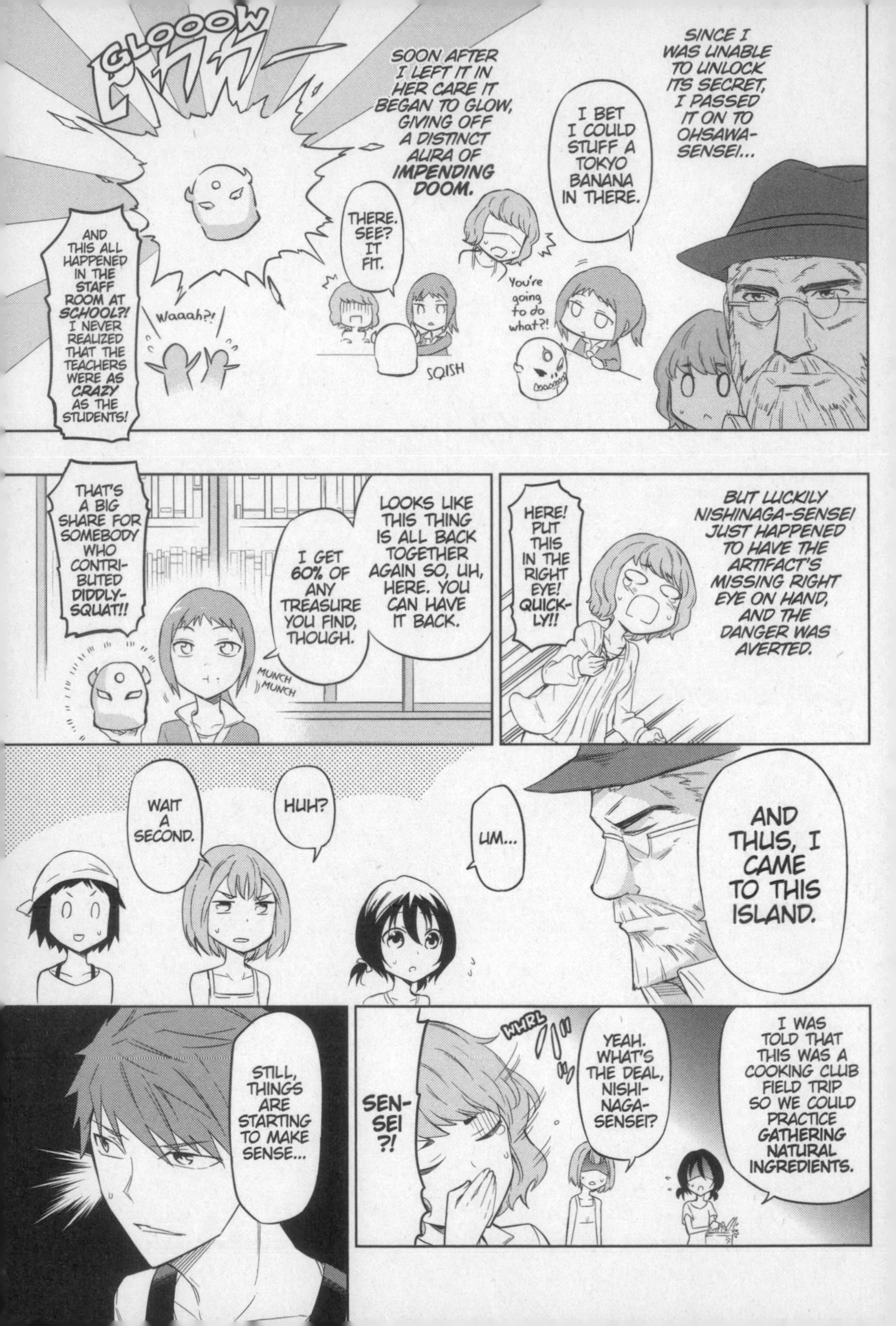
SINCE I WAS UNABLE TO UNLOCK ITS SECRET, I PASSED IT ON TO OHSAWA-SENSEI...
I BET I COULD STUFF A TOKYO BANANA IN THERE.
You're going to do what?!
SOON AFTER I LEFT IT IN HER CARE IT BEGAN TO GLOW, GIVING OFF A DISTINCT AURA OF IMPENDING DOOM.
THERE. SEE? IT FIT.
SQISH
GLOOOW
AND THIS ALL HAPPENED IN THE STAFF ROOM AT SCHOOL?! I NEVER REALIZED THAT THE TEACHERS WERE AS CRAZY AS THE STUDENTS!
Waaah?!
BUT LUCKILY NISHINAGA-SENSEI JUST HAPPENED TO HAVE THE ARTIFACT'S MISSING RIGHT EYE ON HAND, AND THE DANGER WAS AVERTED.
HERE! PUT THIS IN THE RIGHT EYE! QUICKLY!!
LOOKS LIKE THIS THING IS ALL BACK TOGETHER AGAIN SO, UH, HERE. YOU CAN HAVE IT BACK.
I GET 60% OF ANY TREASURE YOU FIND, THOUGH.
THAT'S A BIG SHARE FOR SOMEBODY WHO CONTRIBUTED DIDDLY-SQUAT!!
MUNCH MUNCH
AND THUS, I CAME TO THIS ISLAND.
UM...
HUH?
WAIT A SECOND.
I WAS TOLD THAT THIS WAS A COOKING CLUB FIELD TRIP SO WE COULD PRACTICE GATHERING NATURAL INGREDIENTS.
YEAH. WHAT'S THE DEAL, NISHINAGA-SENSEI?
WHRL
SENSEI?!
STILL, THINGS ARE STARTING TO MAKE SENSE...

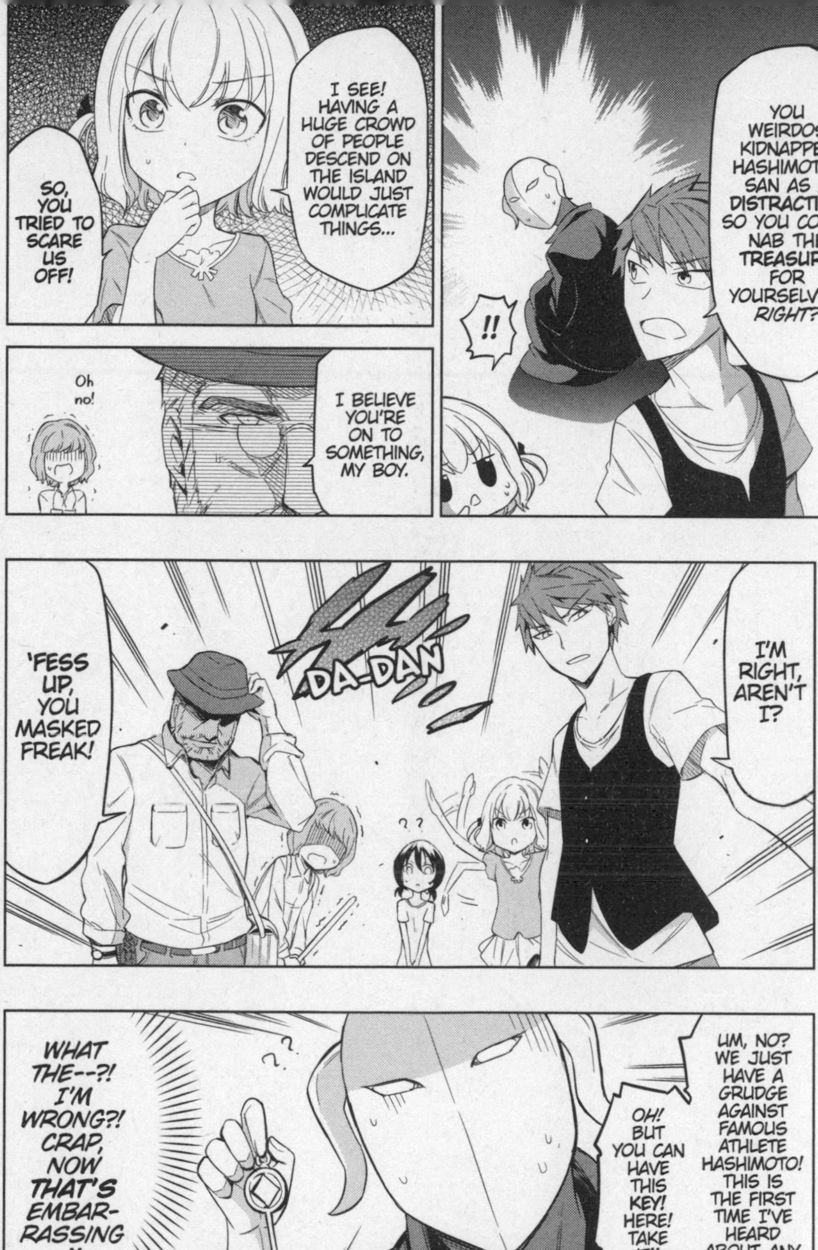
YOU WEIRDOS KIDNAPPED HASHIMOTO-SAN AS A DISTRACTION SO YOU COULD NAB THE TREASURE FOR YOURSELVES, RIGHT?
!!
I SEE! HAVING A HUGE CROWD OF PEOPLE DESCEND ON THE ISLAND WOULD JUST COMPLICATE THINGS...
SO, YOU TRIED TO SCARE US OFF!
I BELIEVE YOU'RE ON TO SOMETHING, MY BOY.
Oh no!
I'M RIGHT, AREN'T I?
DA-DAN
'FESS UP, YOU MASKED FREAK!
? ?
UM, NO? WE JUST HAVE A GRUDGE AGAINST FAMOUS ATHLETE HASHIMOTO! THIS IS THE FIRST TIME I'VE HEARD ABOUT ANY TREASURE!
OH! BUT YOU CAN HAVE THIS KEY! HERE! TAKE IT!!
WHAT THE--?! I'M WRONG?! CRAP, NOW THAT'S EMBARRASSING!!
? ?

D-FRAGMENTS

ディーふらぐ!

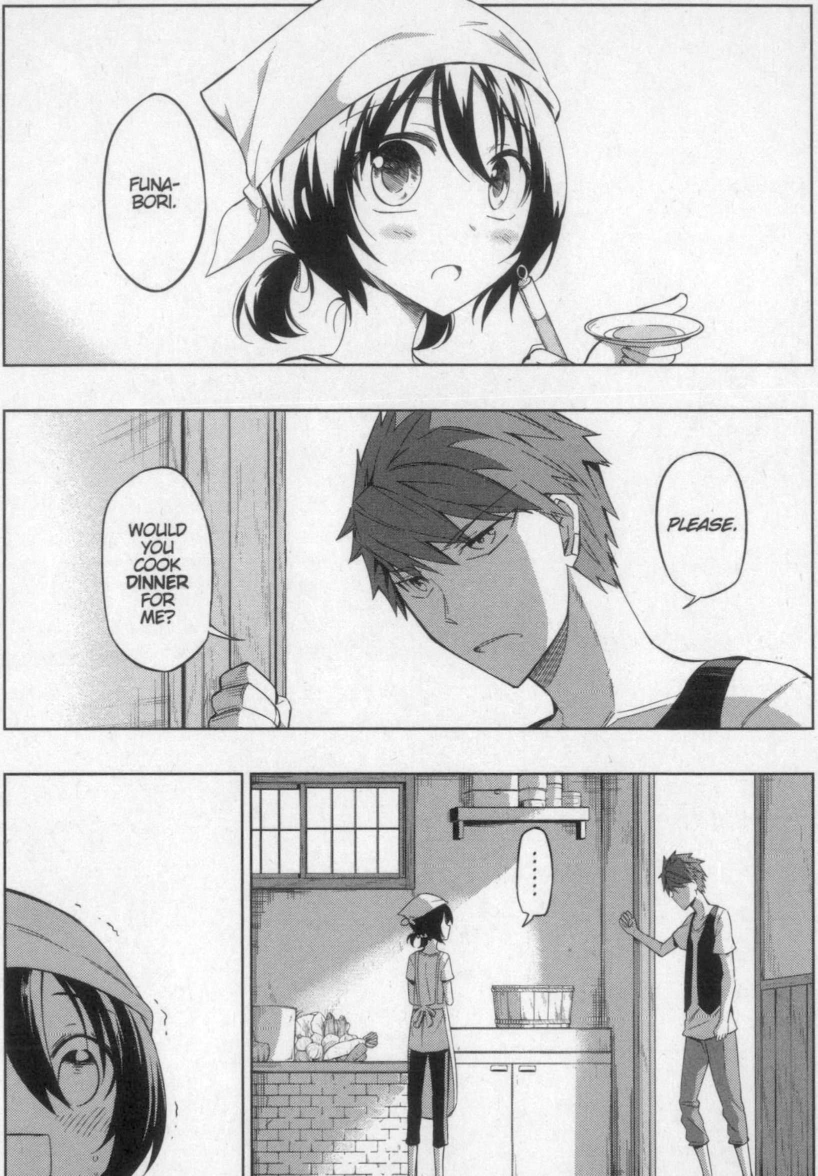
FUNA-BORI.
PLEASE.
WOULD YOU COOK DINNER FOR ME?
......

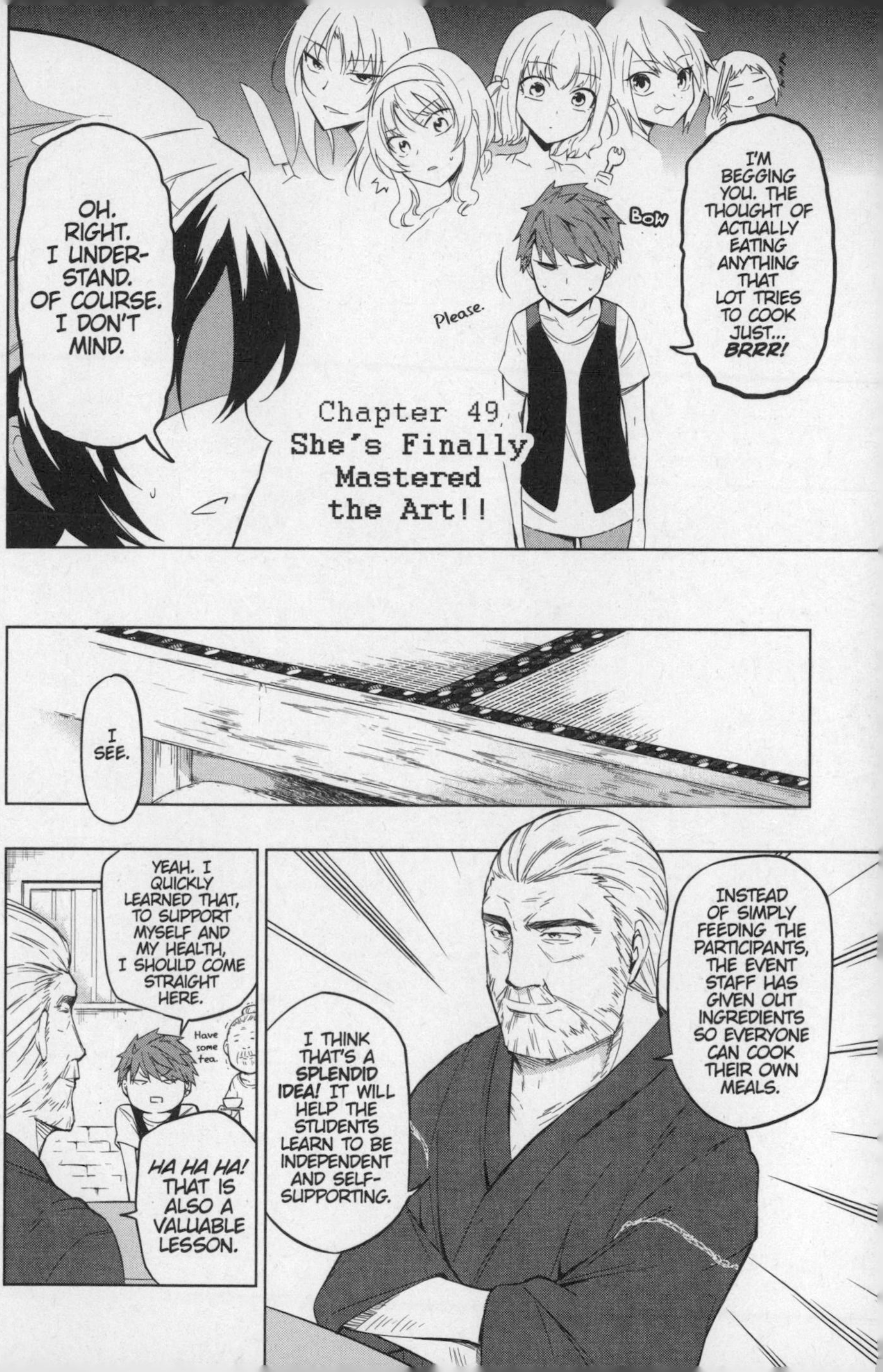
I'M BEGGING YOU. THE THOUGHT OF ACTUALLY EATING ANYTHING THAT LOT TRIES TO COOK JUST... BRRR!
BOW
Please.
OH. RIGHT. I UNDER-STAND. OF COURSE. I DON'T MIND.
Chapter 49
She's Finally Mastered the Art!!
I SEE.
INSTEAD OF SIMPLY FEEDING THE PARTICIPANTS, THE EVENT STAFF HAS GIVEN OUT INGREDIENTS SO EVERYONE CAN COOK THEIR OWN MEALS.
I THINK THAT'S A SPLENDID IDEA! IT WILL HELP THE STUDENTS LEARN TO BE INDEPENDENT AND SELF-SUPPORTING.
YEAH. I QUICKLY LEARNED THAT, TO SUPPORT MYSELF AND MY HEALTH, I SHOULD COME STRAIGHT HERE.
Have some tea.
HA HA HA! THAT IS ALSO A VALUABLE LESSON.

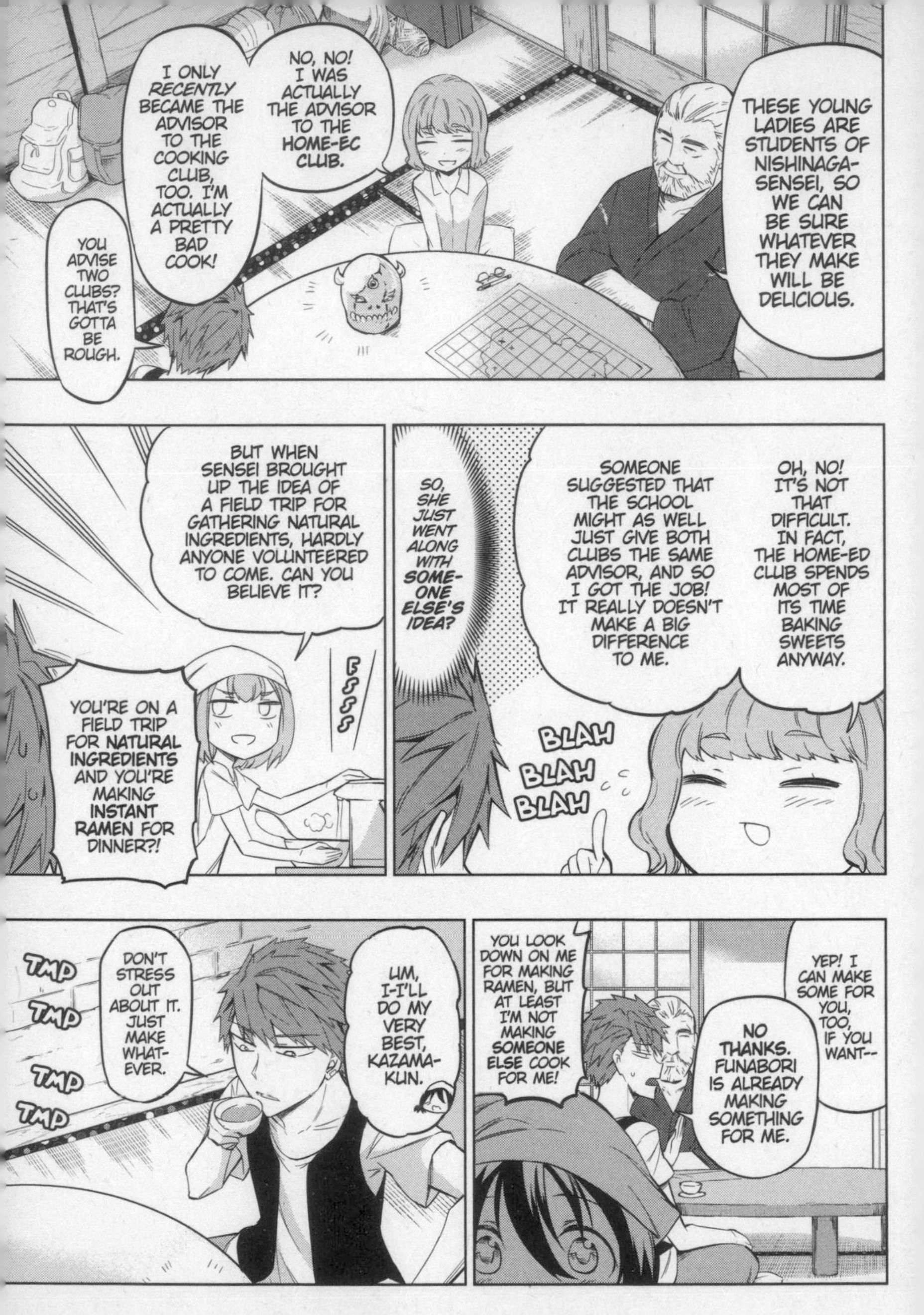
THESE YOUNG LADIES ARE STUDENTS OF NISHINAGA-SENSEI, SO WE CAN BE SURE WHATEVER THEY MAKE WILL BE DELICIOUS.
NO, NO! I WAS ACTUALLY THE ADVISOR TO THE HOME-EC CLUB.
I ONLY *RECENTLY* BECAME THE ADVISOR TO THE COOKING CLUB, TOO. I'M ACTUALLY A PRETTY BAD COOK!
YOU ADVISE TWO CLUBS? THAT'S GOTTA BE ROUGH.
OH, NO! IT'S NOT THAT DIFFICULT. IN FACT, THE HOME-ED CLUB SPENDS MOST OF ITS TIME BAKING SWEETS ANYWAY.
SOMEONE SUGGESTED THAT THE SCHOOL MIGHT AS WELL JUST GIVE BOTH CLUBS THE SAME ADVISOR, AND SO I GOT THE JOB! IT REALLY DOESN'T MAKE A BIG DIFFERENCE TO ME.
SO, SHE JUST WENT ALONG WITH **SOMEONE ELSE'S IDEA?**
BLAH
BLAH
BLAH
BUT WHEN SENSEI BROUGHT UP THE IDEA OF A FIELD TRIP FOR GATHERING NATURAL INGREDIENTS, HARDLY ANYONE VOLUNTEERED TO COME. CAN YOU BELIEVE IT?
FSSS
YOU'RE ON A FIELD TRIP FOR **NATURAL INGREDIENTS** AND YOU'RE MAKING **INSTANT** RAMEN FOR DINNER?!
YEP! I CAN MAKE SOME FOR YOU, TOO, IF YOU WANT--
NO THANKS. FUNABORI IS ALREADY MAKING SOMETHING FOR ME.
YOU LOOK DOWN ON ME FOR MAKING RAMEN, BUT AT LEAST I'M NOT MAKING SOMEONE ELSE COOK FOR ME!
UM, I-I'LL DO MY VERY BEST, KAZAMA-KUN.
DON'T STRESS OUT ABOUT IT. JUST MAKE WHAT-EVER.
TMP
TMP
TMP
TMP

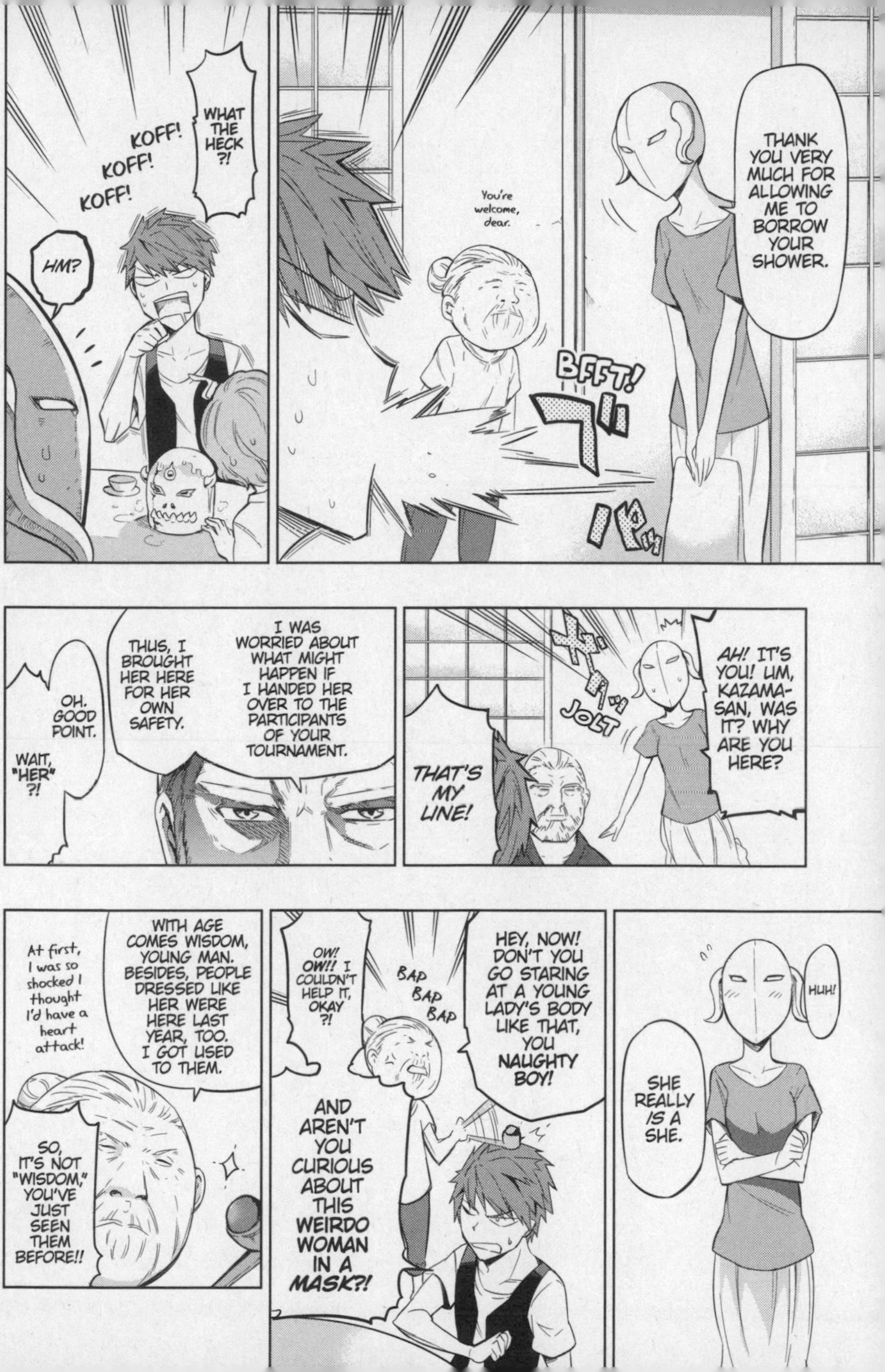
THANK YOU VERY MUCH FOR ALLOWING ME TO BORROW YOUR SHOWER.
You're welcome, dear.
BFFT!
WHAT THE HECK?!
KOFF! KOFF! KOFF!
HM?
AH! IT'S YOU! UM, KAZAMA-SAN, WAS IT? WHY ARE YOU HERE?
JOLT
THAT'S MY LINE!
I WAS WORRIED ABOUT WHAT MIGHT HAPPEN IF I HANDED HER OVER TO THE PARTICIPANTS OF YOUR TOURNAMENT.
THUS, I BROUGHT HER HERE FOR HER OWN SAFETY.
OH. GOOD POINT.
WAIT, "HER"?!
HUH!
SHE REALLY IS A SHE.
HEY, NOW! DON'T YOU GO STARING AT A YOUNG LADY'S BODY LIKE THAT, YOU NAUGHTY BOY!
BAP BAP BAP
OW! OW!! I COULDN'T HELP IT, OKAY?!
AND AREN'T YOU CURIOUS ABOUT THIS WEIRDO WOMAN IN A MASK?!
WITH AGE COMES WISDOM, YOUNG MAN. BESIDES, PEOPLE DRESSED LIKE HER WERE HERE LAST YEAR, TOO. I GOT USED TO THEM.
At first, I was so shocked I thought I'd have a heart attack!
SO, IT'S NOT "WISDOM," YOU'VE JUST SEEN THEM BEFORE!!

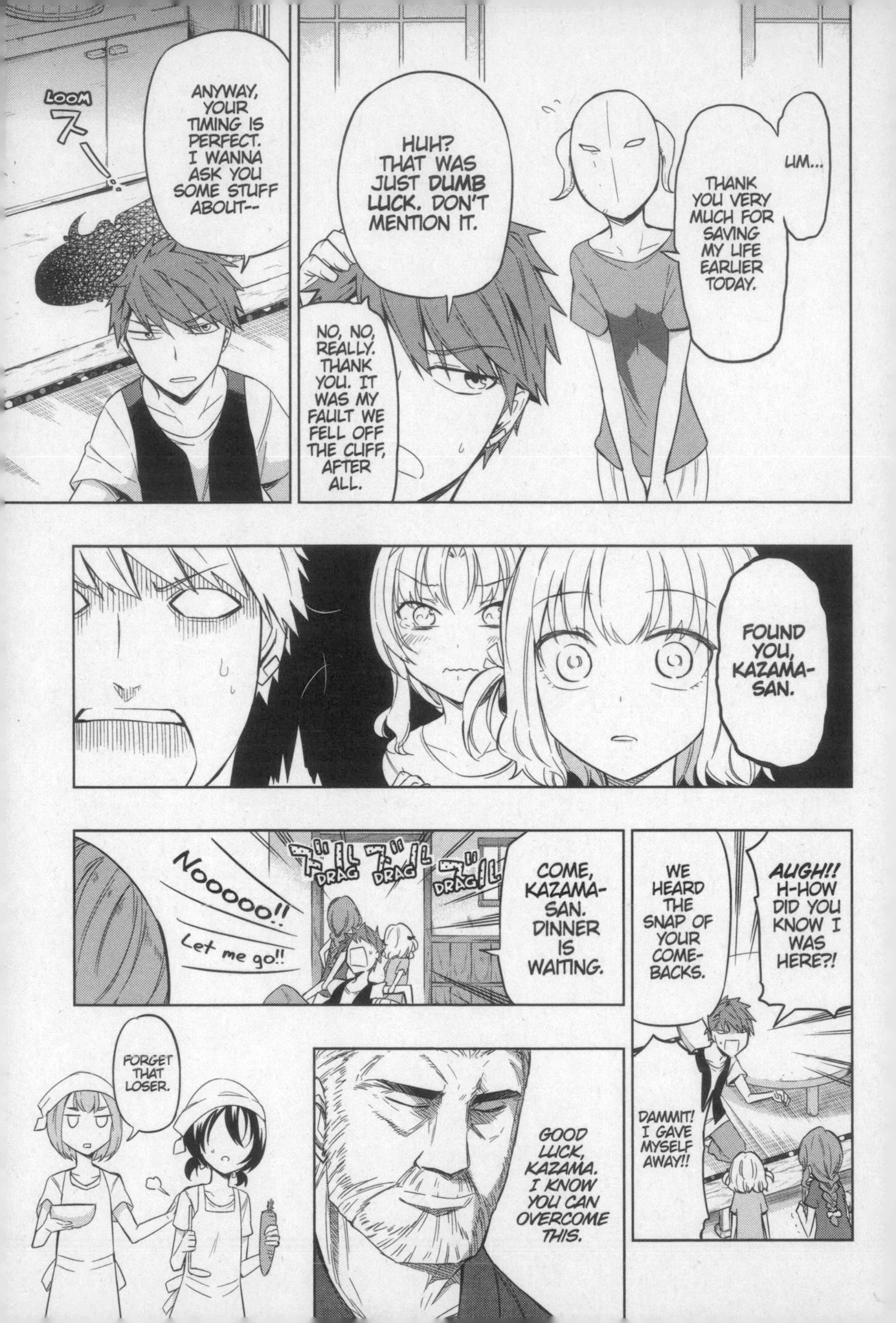
UM...
THANK YOU VERY MUCH FOR SAVING MY LIFE EARLIER TODAY.
HUH? THAT WAS JUST DUMB LUCK. DON'T MENTION IT.
NO, NO, REALLY. THANK YOU. IT WAS MY FAULT WE FELL OFF THE CLIFF, AFTER ALL.
LOOM
ANYWAY, YOUR TIMING IS PERFECT. I WANNA ASK YOU SOME STUFF ABOUT--
FOUND YOU, KAZAMA-SAN.
AUGH!! H-HOW DID YOU KNOW I WAS HERE?!
WE HEARD THE SNAP OF YOUR COMEBACKS.
DAMMIT! I GAVE MYSELF AWAY!!
COME, KAZAMA-SAN. DINNER IS WAITING.
DRAG
DRAG
DRAG
Noooooo!!
Let me go!!
GOOD LUCK, KAZAMA. I KNOW YOU CAN OVERCOME THIS.
FORGET THAT LOSER.

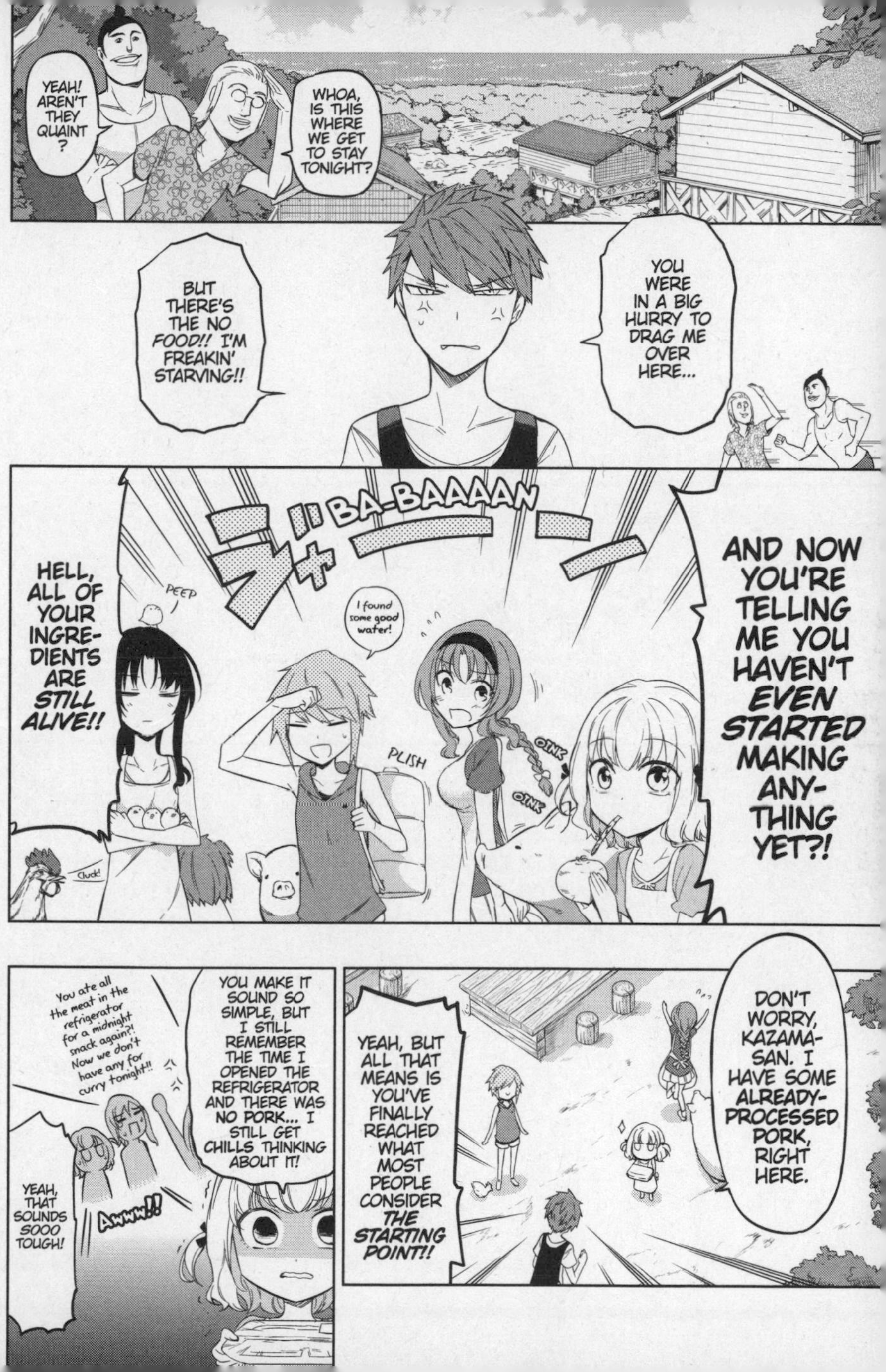
WHOA, IS THIS WHERE WE GET TO STAY TONIGHT?
YEAH! AREN'T THEY QUAINT?
YOU WERE IN A BIG HURRY TO DRAG ME OVER HERE...
BUT THERE'S THE NO FOOD!! I'M FREAKIN' STARVING!!
BA-BAAAAN
AND NOW YOU'RE TELLING ME YOU HAVEN'T EVEN STARTED MAKING ANY-THING YET?!
OINK
OINK
I found some good water!
PLISH
HELL, ALL OF YOUR INGRE-DIENTS ARE STILL ALIVE!!
PEEP
Cluck!
DON'T WORRY, KAZAMA-SAN. I HAVE SOME ALREADY-PROCESSED PORK, RIGHT HERE.
YEAH, BUT ALL THAT MEANS IS YOU'VE FINALLY REACHED WHAT MOST PEOPLE CONSIDER THE STARTING POINT!!
YOU MAKE IT SOUND SO SIMPLE, BUT I STILL REMEMBER THE TIME I OPENED THE REFRIGERATOR AND THERE WAS NO PORK... I STILL GET CHILLS THINKING ABOUT IT!
You ate all the meat in the refrigerator for a midnight snack again?! Now we don't have any for curry tonight!!
Awww!!
YEAH, THAT SOUNDS SOOO TOUGH!

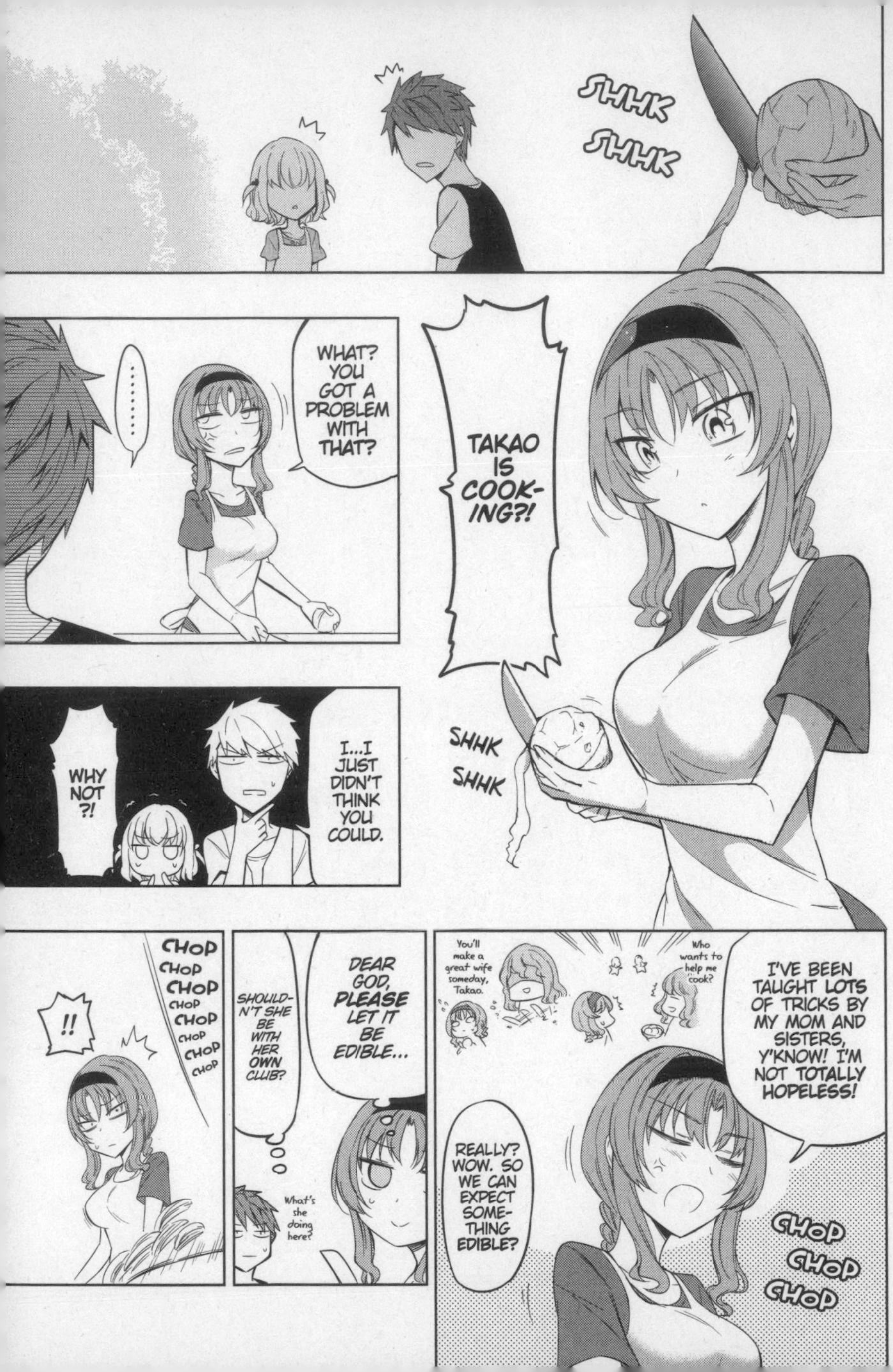
SHHK
SHHK
TAKAO IS COOKING?!
SHHK
SHHK
WHAT? YOU GOT A PROBLEM WITH THAT?
......
I...I JUST DIDN'T THINK YOU COULD.
WHY NOT?!
I'VE BEEN TAUGHT LOTS OF TRICKS BY MY MOM AND SISTERS, Y'KNOW! I'M NOT TOTALLY HOPELESS!
Who wants to help me cook?
You'll make a great wife someday, Takao.
REALLY? WOW. SO WE CAN EXPECT SOMETHING EDIBLE?
CHOP CHOP CHOP
DEAR GOD, PLEASE LET IT BE EDIBLE...
SHOULDN'T SHE BE WITH HER OWN CLUB?
What's she doing here?
CHOP CHOP CHOP CHOP CHOP CHOP CHOP CHOP
!!

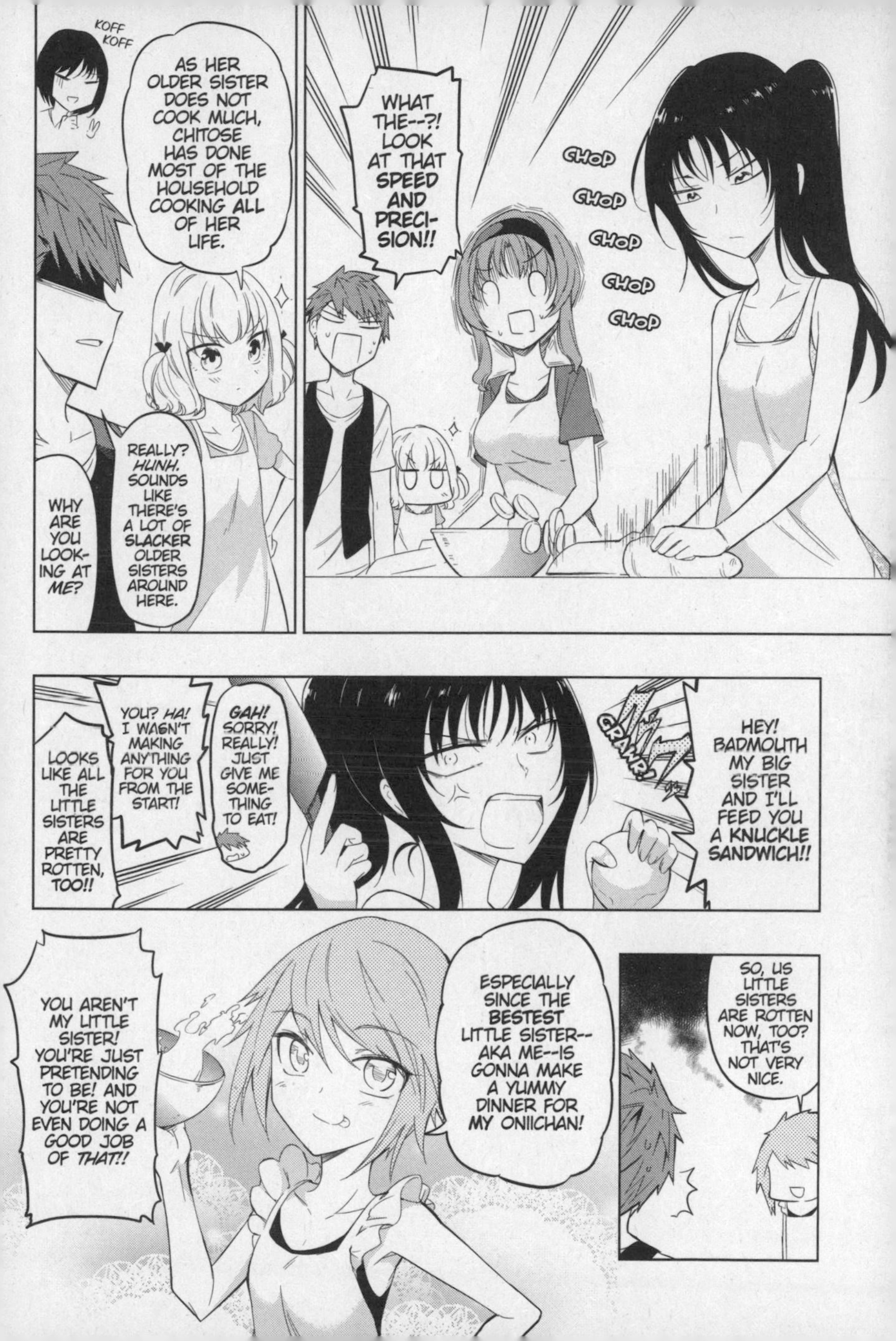
WHAT THE--?! LOOK AT THAT SPEED AND PRECISION!!
CHOP CHOP CHOP CHOP CHOP
KOFF KOFF
AS HER OLDER SISTER DOES NOT COOK MUCH, CHITOSE HAS DONE MOST OF THE HOUSEHOLD COOKING ALL OF HER LIFE.
REALLY? *HUNH.* SOUNDS LIKE THERE'S A LOT OF SLACKER OLDER SISTERS AROUND HERE.
WHY ARE YOU LOOKING AT *ME?*
HEY! BADMOUTH MY BIG SISTER AND I'LL FEED YOU A KNUCKLE SANDWICH!!
GRAWR!
GAH! SORRY! REALLY! JUST GIVE ME SOMETHING TO EAT!
YOU? *HA!* I WASN'T MAKING ANYTHING FOR YOU FROM THE START!
LOOKS LIKE ALL THE LITTLE SISTERS ARE PRETTY ROTTEN, TOO!!
SO, US LITTLE SISTERS ARE ROTTEN NOW, TOO? THAT'S NOT VERY NICE.
ESPECIALLY SINCE THE BESTEST LITTLE SISTER--AKA ME--IS GONNA MAKE A YUMMY DINNER FOR MY ONIICHAN!
YOU AREN'T MY LITTLE SISTER! YOU'RE JUST PRETENDING TO BE! AND YOU'RE NOT EVEN DOING A GOOD JOB OF *THAT!!*

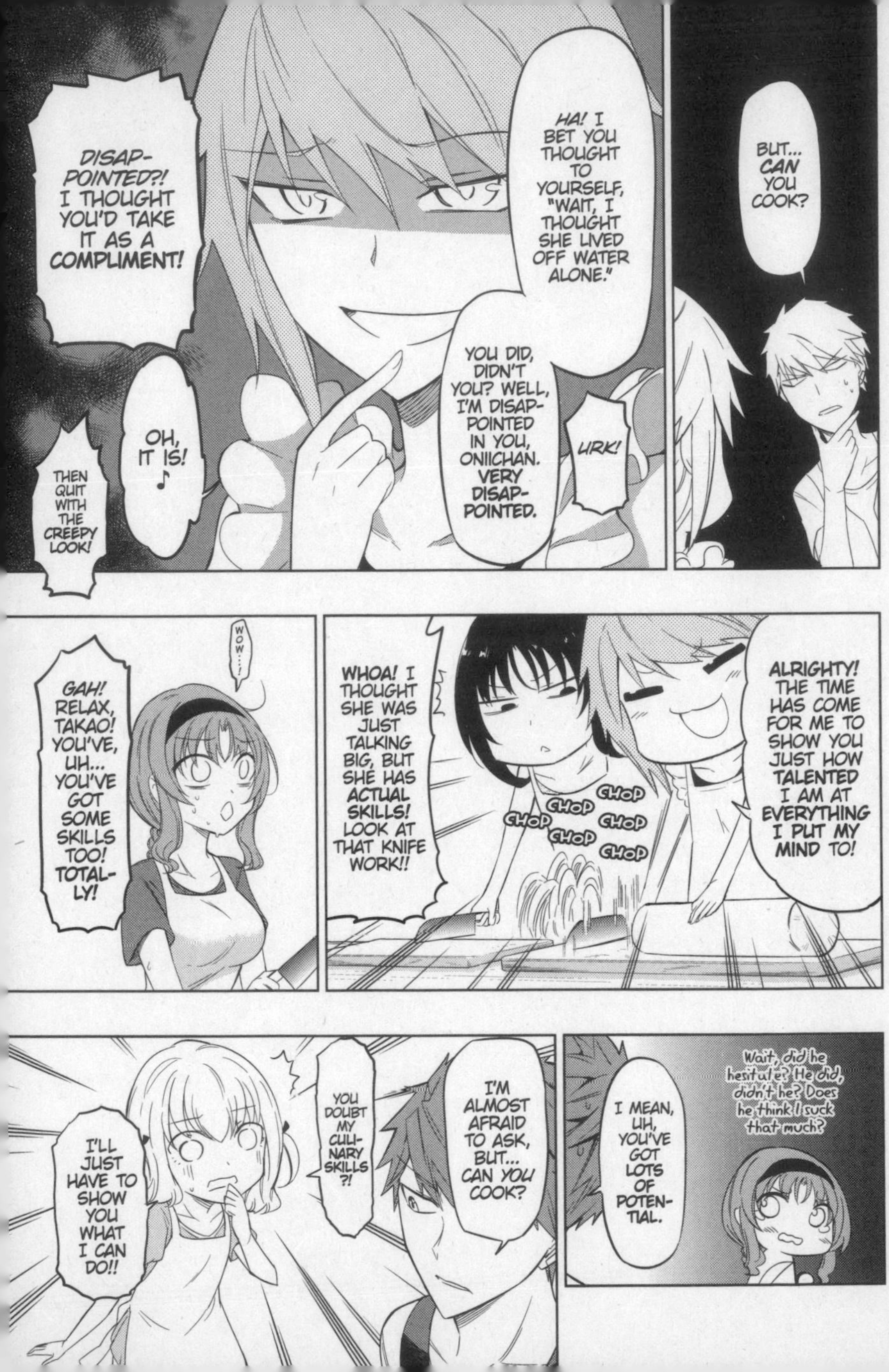
BUT... CAN YOU COOK?
HA! I BET YOU THOUGHT TO YOURSELF, "WAIT, I THOUGHT SHE LIVED OFF WATER ALONE."
YOU DID, DIDN'T YOU? WELL, I'M DISAP-POINTED IN YOU, ONIICHAN. VERY DISAP-POINTED.
URK!
DISAP-POINTED?! I THOUGHT YOU'D TAKE IT AS A COMPLIMENT!
OH, IT IS! ♪
THEN QUIT WITH THE CREEPY LOOK!
ALRIGHTY! THE TIME HAS COME FOR ME TO SHOW YOU JUST HOW TALENTED I AM AT EVERYTHING I PUT MY MIND TO!
CHOP CHOP CHOP CHOP CHOP CHOP
WHOA! I THOUGHT SHE WAS JUST TALKING BIG, BUT SHE HAS ACTUAL SKILLS! LOOK AT THAT KNIFE WORK!!
WOW...!
GAH! RELAX, TAKAO! YOU'VE, UH... YOU'VE GOT SOME SKILLS TOO! TOTAL-LY!
Wait, did he hesitate? He did, didn't he? Does he think I suck that much?
I MEAN, UH, YOU'VE GOT LOTS OF POTEN-TIAL.
I'M ALMOST AFRAID TO ASK, BUT... CAN YOU COOK?
YOU DOUBT MY CULI-NARY SKILLS?!
I'LL JUST HAVE TO SHOW YOU WHAT I CAN DO!!

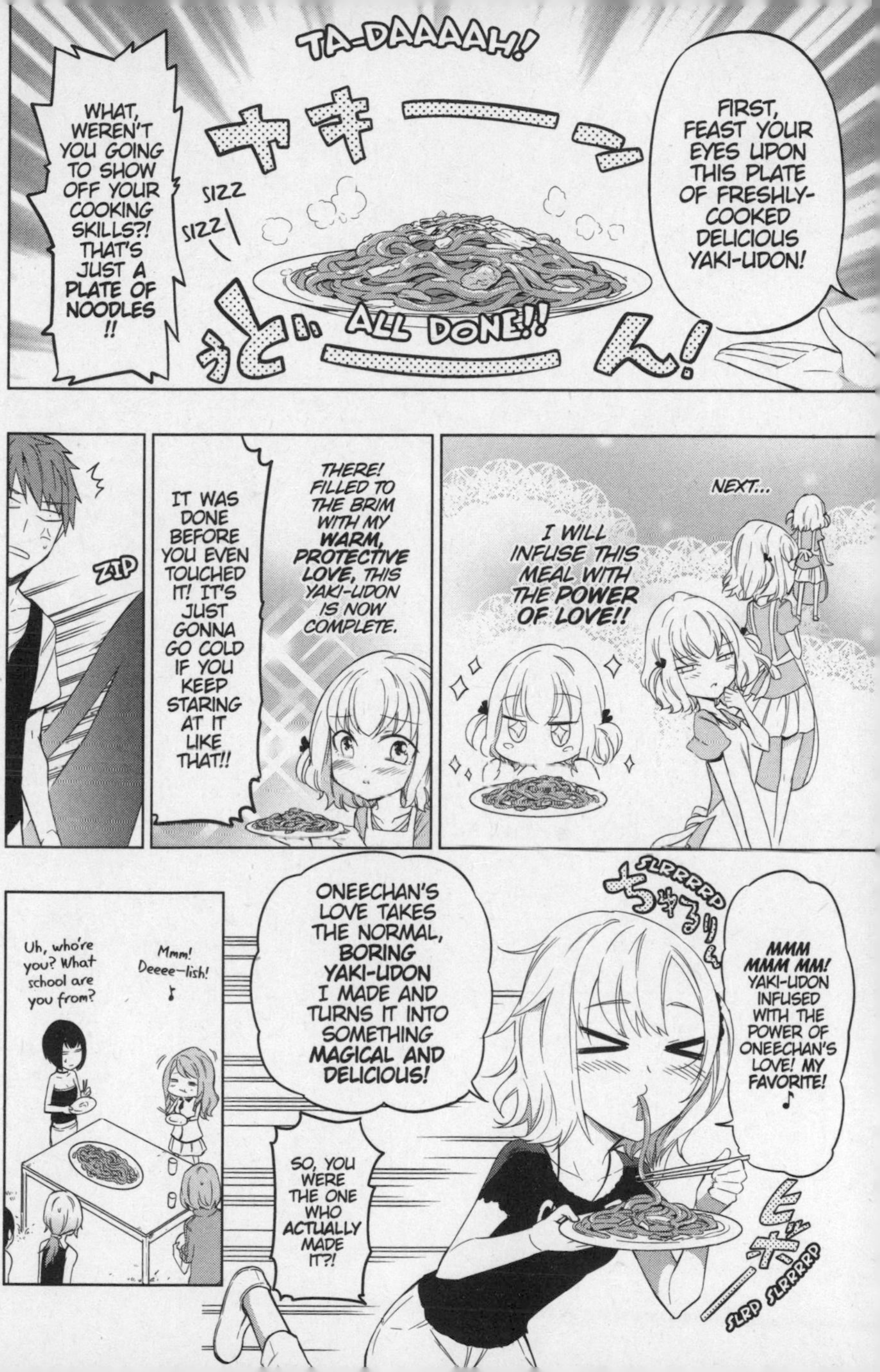
FIRST, FEAST YOUR EYES UPON THIS PLATE OF FRESHLY-COOKED DELICIOUS YAKI-UDON!
TA-DAAAAH!
ALL DONE!!
SIZZ SIZZ
WHAT, WEREN'T YOU GOING TO SHOW OFF YOUR COOKING SKILLS?! THAT'S JUST A PLATE OF NOODLES!!
NEXT...
I WILL INFUSE THIS MEAL WITH THE POWER OF LOVE!!
THERE! FILLED TO THE BRIM WITH MY WARM, PROTECTIVE LOVE, THIS YAKI-UDON IS NOW COMPLETE.
IT WAS DONE BEFORE YOU EVEN TOUCHED IT! IT'S JUST GONNA GO COLD IF YOU KEEP STARING AT IT LIKE THAT!!
ZIP
SLRRRRP
MMM MMM MM! YAKI-UDON INFUSED WITH THE POWER OF ONEECHAN'S LOVE! MY FAVORITE! ♪
ONEECHAN'S LOVE TAKES THE NORMAL, BORING YAKI-UDON I MADE AND TURNS IT INTO SOMETHING MAGICAL AND DELICIOUS!
SO, YOU WERE THE ONE WHO ACTUALLY MADE IT?!
SLRD SLRRRRP
Mmm! Deeee-lish! ♪
Uh, who're you? What school are you from?

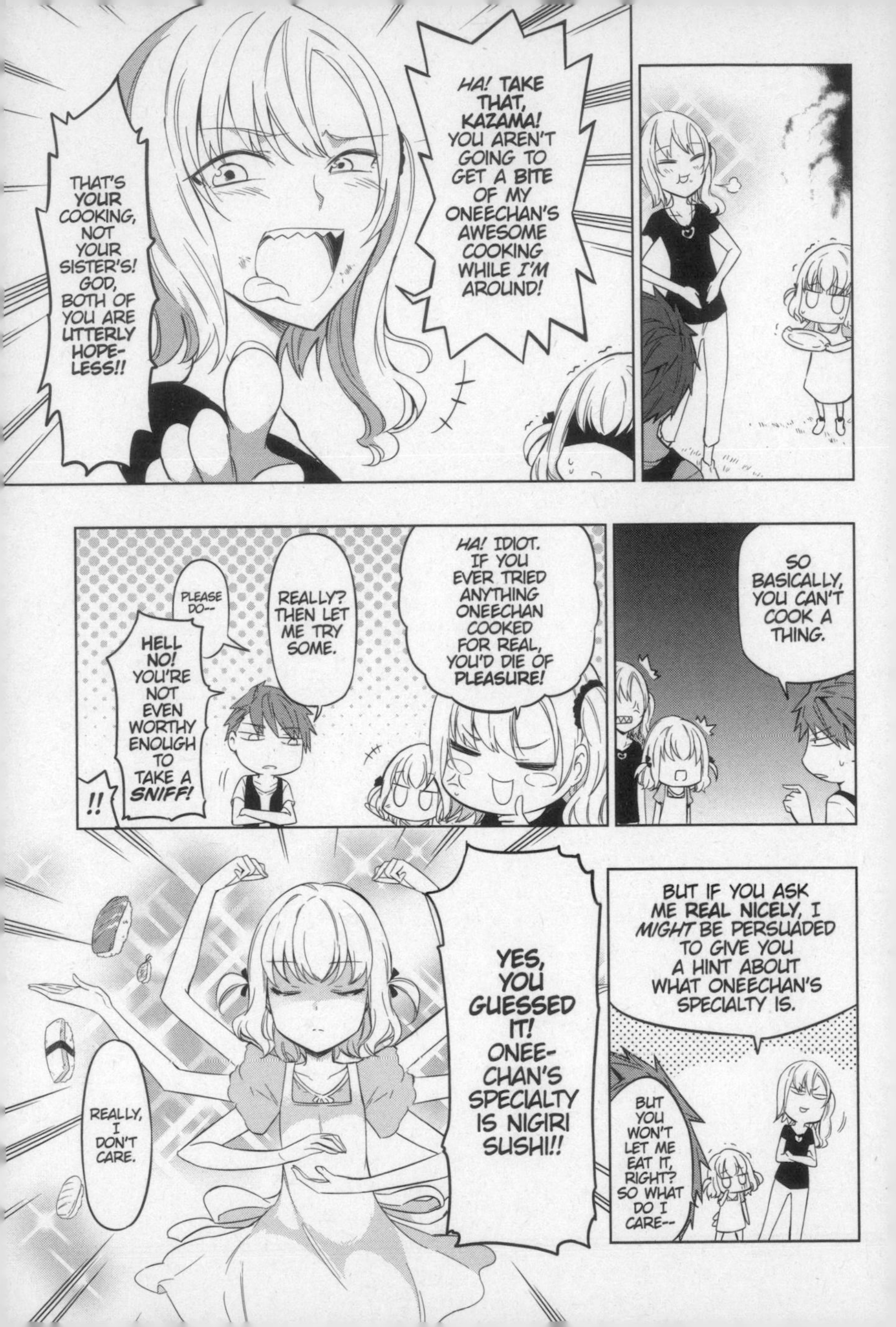
HA! TAKE THAT, KAZAMA! YOU AREN'T GOING TO GET A BITE OF MY ONEECHAN'S AWESOME COOKING WHILE I'M AROUND!
THAT'S YOUR COOKING, NOT YOUR SISTER'S! GOD, BOTH OF YOU ARE UTTERLY HOPE-LESS!!
SO BASICALLY, YOU CAN'T COOK A THING.
HA! IDIOT. IF YOU EVER TRIED ANYTHING ONEECHAN COOKED FOR REAL, YOU'D DIE OF PLEASURE!
REALLY? THEN LET ME TRY SOME.
PLEASE DO--
HELL NO! YOU'RE NOT EVEN WORTHY ENOUGH TO TAKE A SNIFF!
!!
BUT IF YOU ASK ME REAL NICELY, I MIGHT BE PERSUADED TO GIVE YOU A HINT ABOUT WHAT ONEECHAN'S SPECIALTY IS.
BUT YOU WON'T LET ME EAT IT, RIGHT? SO WHAT DO I CARE--
YES, YOU GUESSED IT! ONEE-CHAN'S SPECIALTY IS NIGIRI SUSHI!!
REALLY, I DON'T CARE.

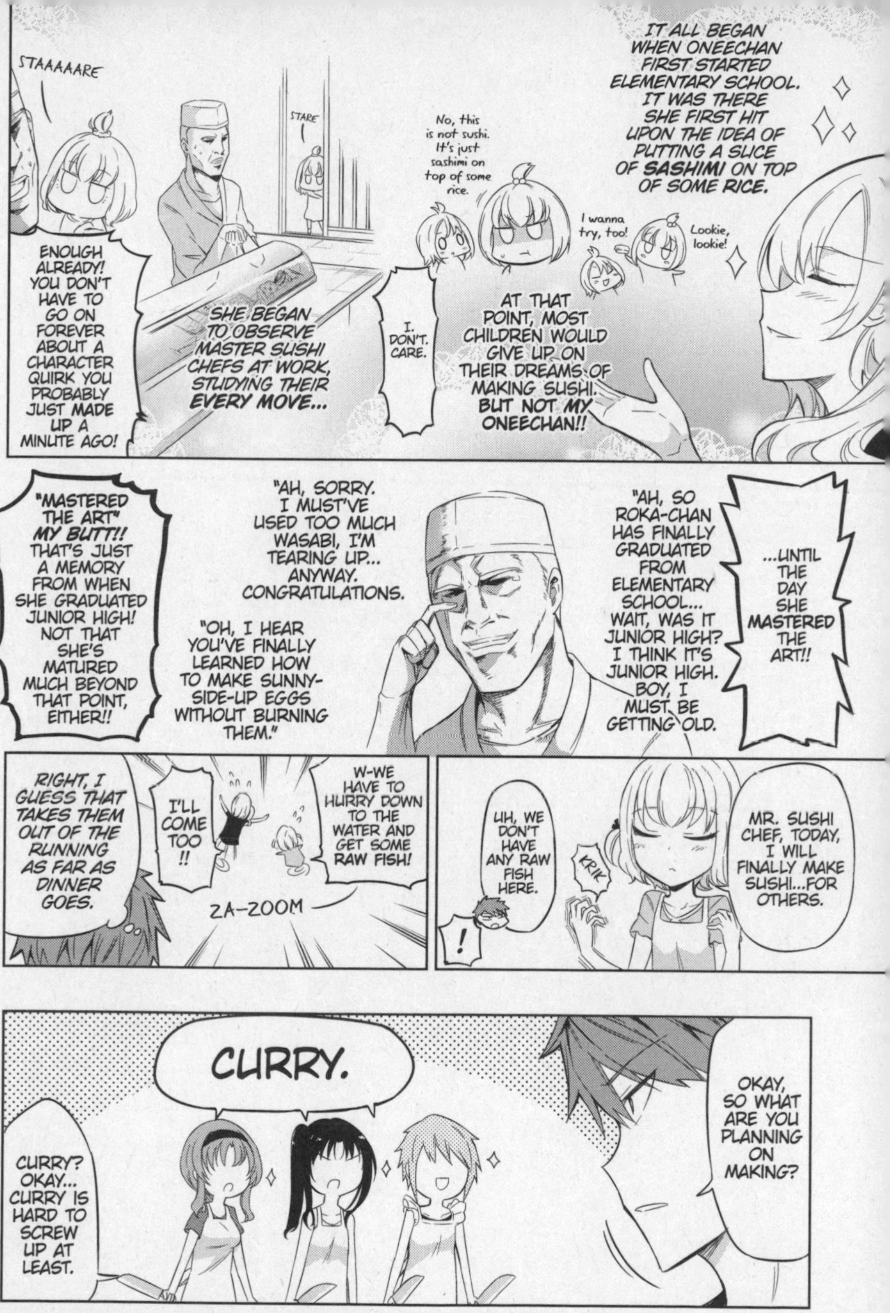
IT ALL BEGAN WHEN ONEECHAN FIRST STARTED ELEMENTARY SCHOOL. IT WAS THERE SHE FIRST HIT UPON THE IDEA OF PUTTING A SLICE OF SASHIMI ON TOP OF SOME RICE.
Lookie, lookie!
I wanna try, too!
No, this is not sushi. It's just sashimi on top of some rice.
AT THAT POINT, MOST CHILDREN WOULD GIVE UP ON THEIR DREAMS OF MAKING SUSHI. BUT NOT MY ONEECHAN!!
I. DON'T. CARE.
SHE BEGAN TO OBSERVE MASTER SUSHI CHEFS AT WORK, STUDYING THEIR EVERY MOVE...
STARE
STAAAAAARE
ENOUGH ALREADY! YOU DON'T HAVE TO GO ON FOREVER ABOUT A CHARACTER QUIRK YOU PROBABLY JUST MADE UP A MINUTE AGO!
...UNTIL THE DAY SHE MASTERED THE ART!!
"AH, SO ROKA-CHAN HAS FINALLY GRADUATED FROM ELEMENTARY SCHOOL... WAIT, WAS IT JUNIOR HIGH? I THINK IT'S JUNIOR HIGH. BOY, I MUST BE GETTING OLD.
"AH, SORRY. I MUST'VE USED TOO MUCH WASABI, I'M TEARING UP... ANYWAY. CONGRATULATIONS.
"OH, I HEAR YOU'VE FINALLY LEARNED HOW TO MAKE SUNNY-SIDE-UP EGGS WITHOUT BURNING THEM."
"MASTERED THE ART" MY BUTT!! THAT'S JUST A MEMORY FROM WHEN SHE GRADUATED JUNIOR HIGH! NOT THAT SHE'S MATURED MUCH BEYOND THAT POINT, EITHER!!
MR. SUSHI CHEF, TODAY, I WILL FINALLY MAKE SUSHI...FOR OTHERS.
KRIK
UH, WE DON'T HAVE ANY RAW FISH HERE.
!
W-WE HAVE TO HURRY DOWN TO THE WATER AND GET SOME RAW FISH!
I'LL COME TOO!!
ZA-ZOOM
RIGHT, I GUESS THAT TAKES THEM OUT OF THE RUNNING AS FAR AS DINNER GOES.
OKAY, SO WHAT ARE YOU PLANNING ON MAKING?
CURRY.
CURRY? OKAY... CURRY IS HARD TO SCREW UP AT LEAST.

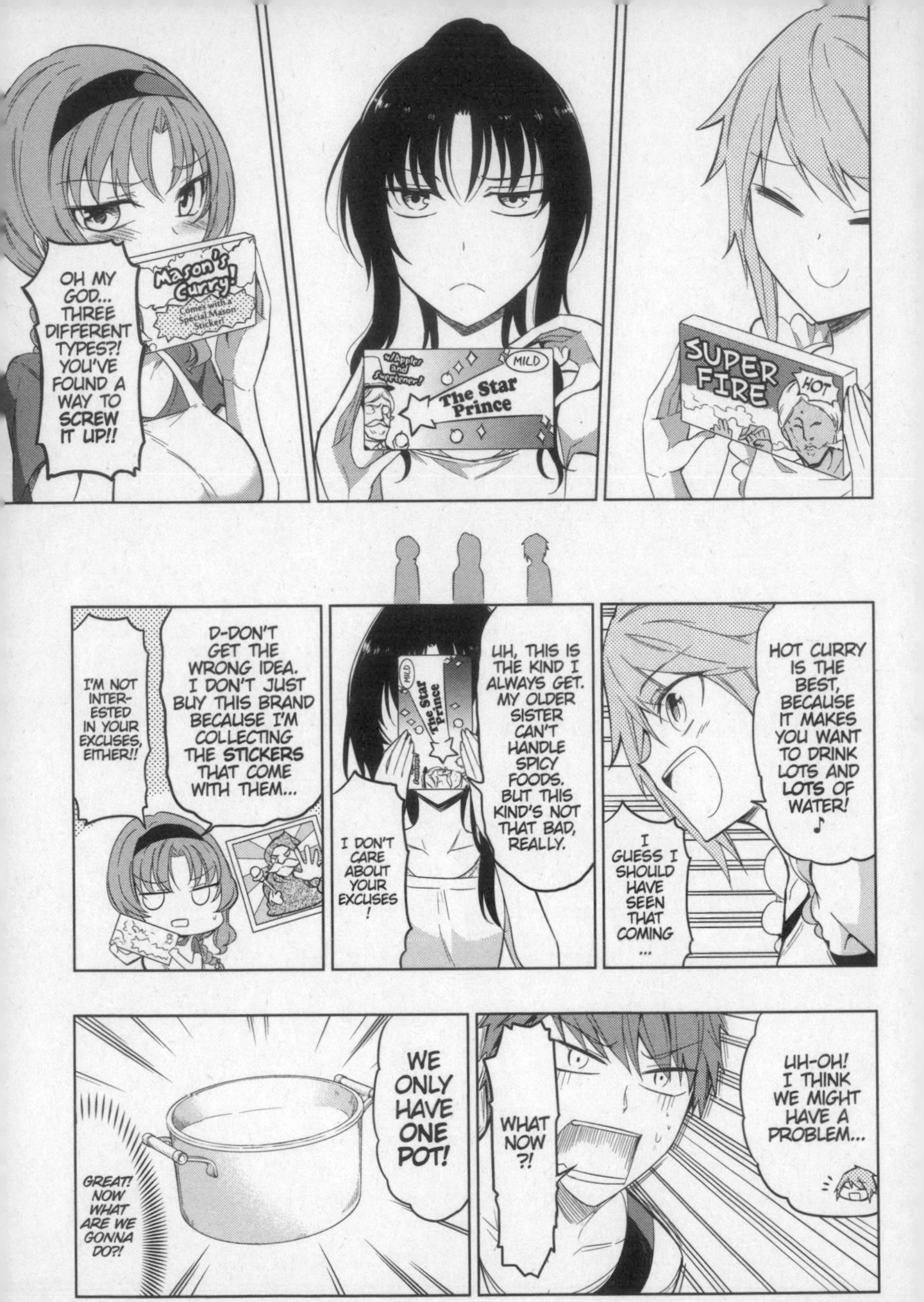
SUPER FIRE
HOT
MILD
w/Appler and Sweetener!
The Star Prince
Mason's Curry!
Comes with a Special Mason Sticker!
OH MY GOD... THREE DIFFERENT TYPES?! YOU'VE FOUND A WAY TO SCREW IT UP!!
HOT CURRY IS THE BEST, BECAUSE IT MAKES YOU WANT TO DRINK LOTS AND LOTS OF WATER! ♪
I GUESS I SHOULD HAVE SEEN THAT COMING...
MILD
The Star Prince
UH, THIS IS THE KIND I ALWAYS GET. MY OLDER SISTER CAN'T HANDLE SPICY FOODS. BUT THIS KIND'S NOT THAT BAD, REALLY.
I DON'T CARE ABOUT YOUR EXCUSES!
D-DON'T GET THE WRONG IDEA. I DON'T JUST BUY THIS BRAND BECAUSE I'M COLLECTING THE STICKERS THAT COME WITH THEM...
I'M NOT INTERESTED IN YOUR EXCUSES, EITHER!!
UH-OH! I THINK WE MIGHT HAVE A PROBLEM...
WHAT NOW?!
WE ONLY HAVE ONE POT!
GREAT! NOW WHAT ARE WE GONNA DO?!

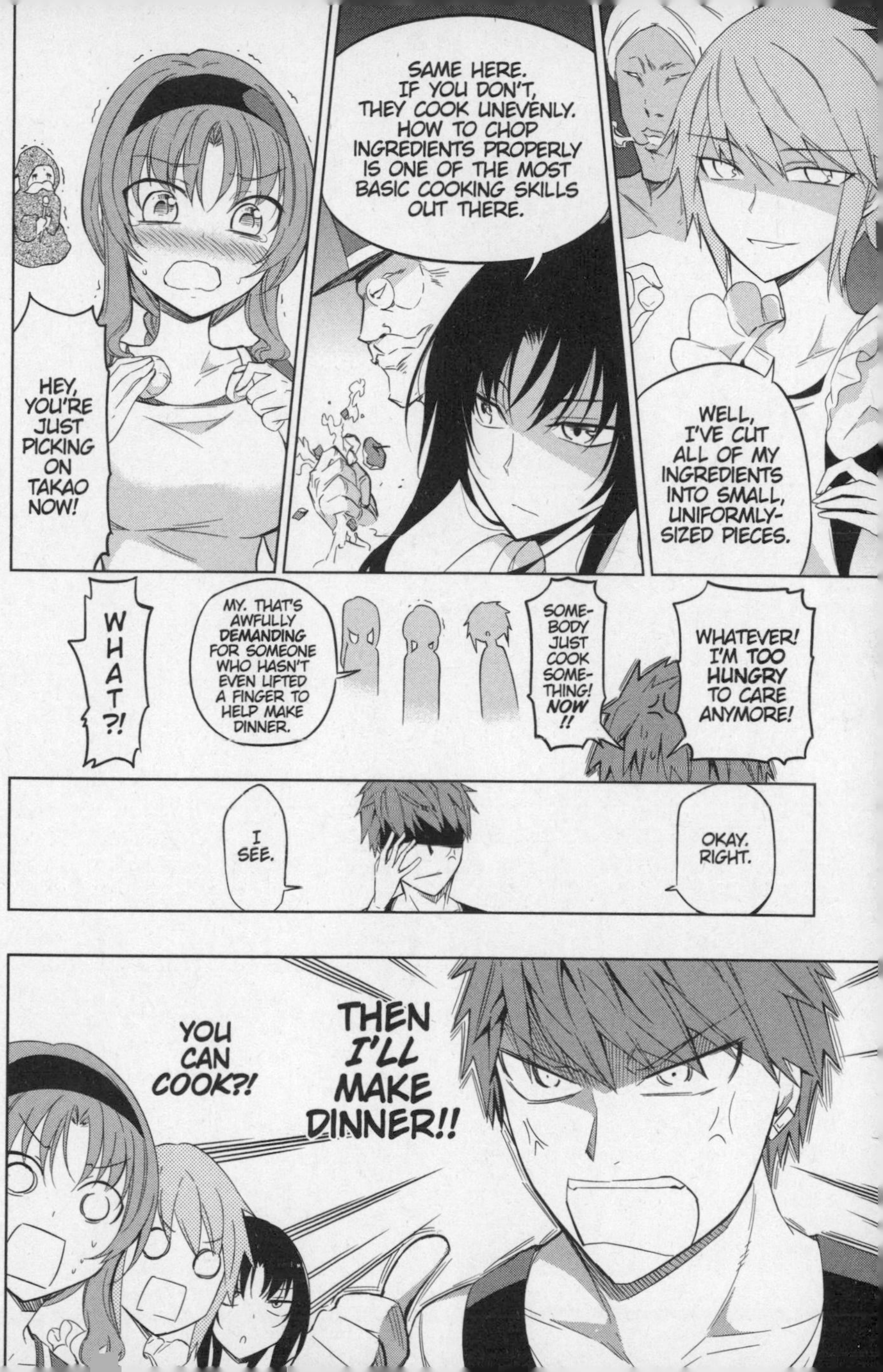
WELL, I'VE CUT ALL OF MY INGREDIENTS INTO SMALL, UNIFORMLY-SIZED PIECES.
SAME HERE. IF YOU DON'T, THEY COOK UNEVENLY. HOW TO CHOP INGREDIENTS PROPERLY IS ONE OF THE MOST BASIC COOKING SKILLS OUT THERE.
HEY, YOU'RE JUST PICKING ON TAKAO NOW!
WHATEVER! I'M TOO HUNGRY TO CARE ANYMORE!
SOMEBODY JUST COOK SOMETHING! NOW!!
MY. THAT'S AWFULLY DEMANDING FOR SOMEONE WHO HASN'T EVEN LIFTED A FINGER TO HELP MAKE DINNER.
WHAT?!
OKAY. RIGHT.
I SEE.
THEN I'LL MAKE DINNER!!
YOU CAN COOK?!

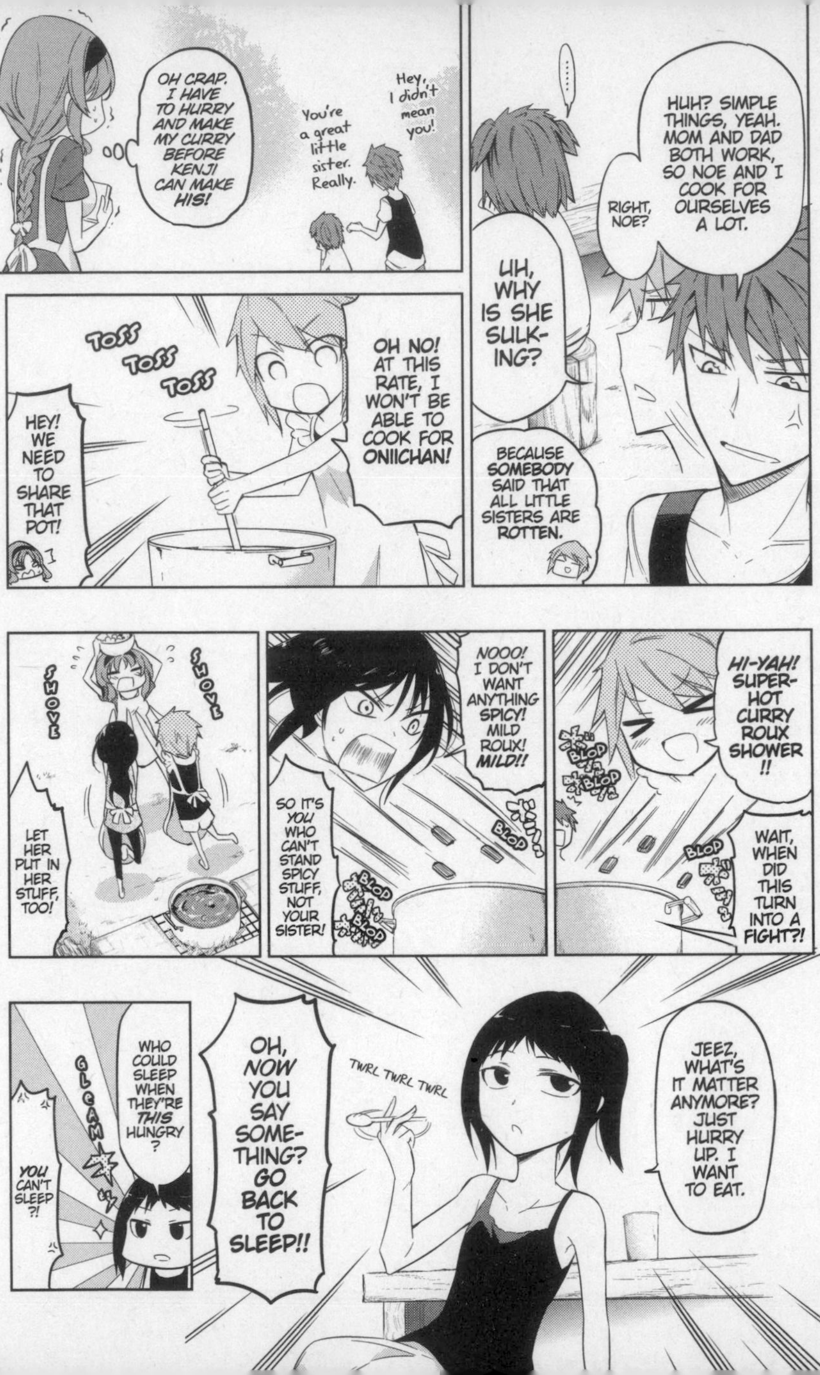
HUH? SIMPLE THINGS, YEAH. MOM AND DAD BOTH WORK, SO NOE AND I COOK FOR OURSELVES A LOT.
......
RIGHT, NOE?
UH, WHY IS SHE SULKING?
BECAUSE SOMEBODY SAID THAT ALL LITTLE SISTERS ARE ROTTEN.
Hey, I didn't mean you!
You're a great little sister. Really.
OH CRAP. I HAVE TO HURRY AND MAKE MY CURRY BEFORE KENJI CAN MAKE HIS!
TOSS TOSS TOSS
OH NO! AT THIS RATE, I WON'T BE ABLE TO COOK FOR ONIICHAN!
HEY! WE NEED TO SHARE THAT POT!
HI-YAH! SUPER-HOT CURRY ROUX SHOWER!!
BLOP BLOP BLOP
WAIT, WHEN DID THIS TURN INTO A FIGHT?!
NOOO! I DON'T WANT ANYTHING SPICY! MILD ROUX! MILD!!
SO IT'S YOU WHO CAN'T STAND SPICY STUFF, NOT YOUR SISTER!
BLOP BLOP
SHOVE SHOVE
LET HER PUT IN HER STUFF, TOO!
JEEZ, WHAT'S IT MATTER ANYMORE? JUST HURRY UP. I WANT TO EAT.
TWRL TWRL TWRL
OH, NOW YOU SAY SOME-THING? GO BACK TO SLEEP!!
WHO COULD SLEEP WHEN THEY'RE THIS HUNGRY?
GLEAM
YOU CAN'T SLEEP?!

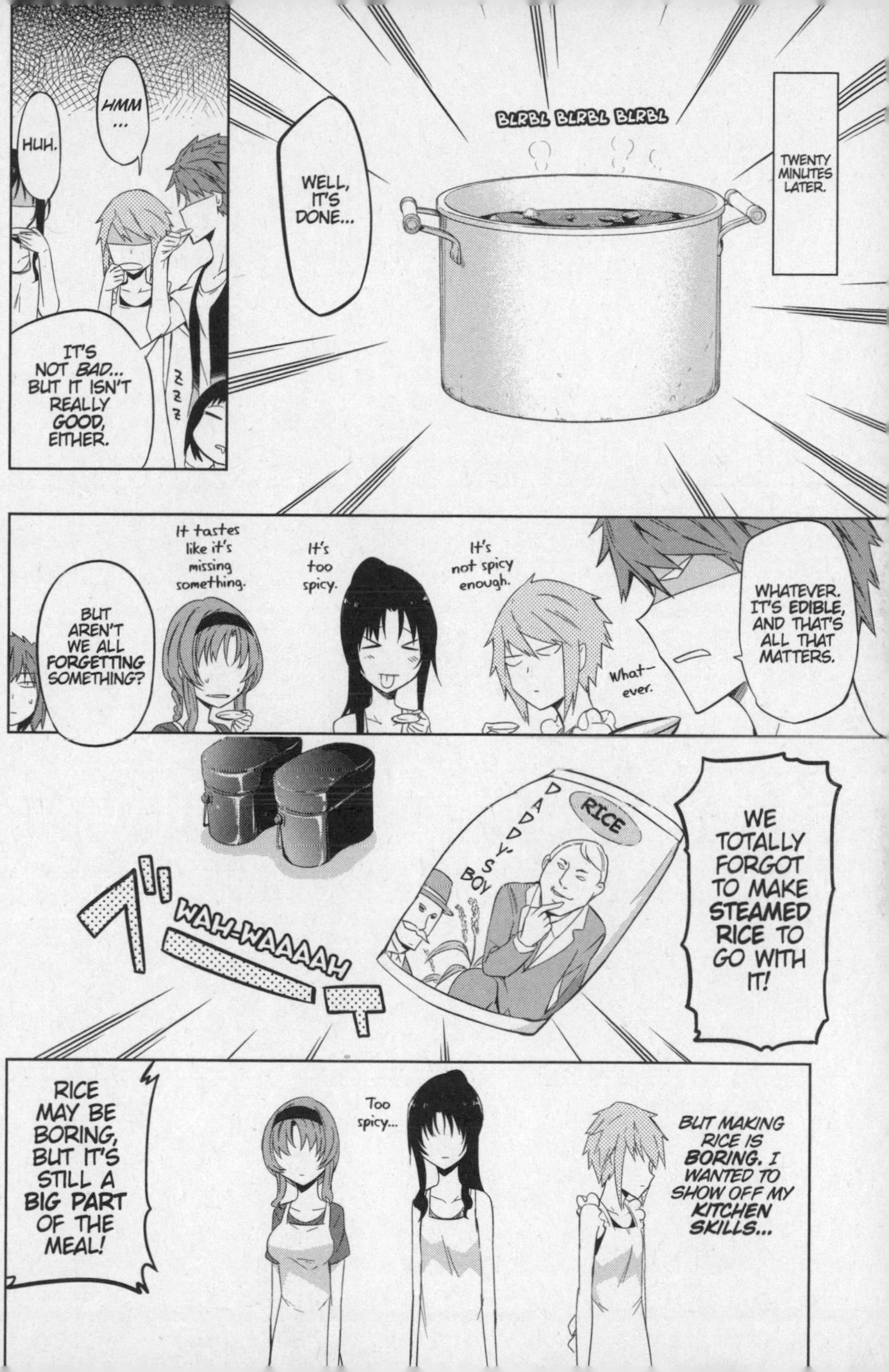
TWENTY MINUTES LATER.
BLRBL BLRBL BLRBL
WELL, IT'S DONE...
HMM ...
HUH.
IT'S NOT BAD... BUT IT ISN'T REALLY GOOD, EITHER.
Z Z Z
WHATEVER. IT'S EDIBLE, AND THAT'S ALL THAT MATTERS.
What-ever.
It's not spicy enough.
It's too spicy.
It tastes like it's missing something.
BUT AREN'T WE ALL FORGETTING SOMETHING?
WE TOTALLY FORGOT TO MAKE STEAMED RICE TO GO WITH IT!
RICE
DADDY'S BOY
WAH-WAAAAH
BUT MAKING RICE IS BORING. I WANTED TO SHOW OFF MY KITCHEN SKILLS...
Too spicy...
RICE MAY BE BORING, BUT IT'S STILL A BIG PART OF THE MEAL!

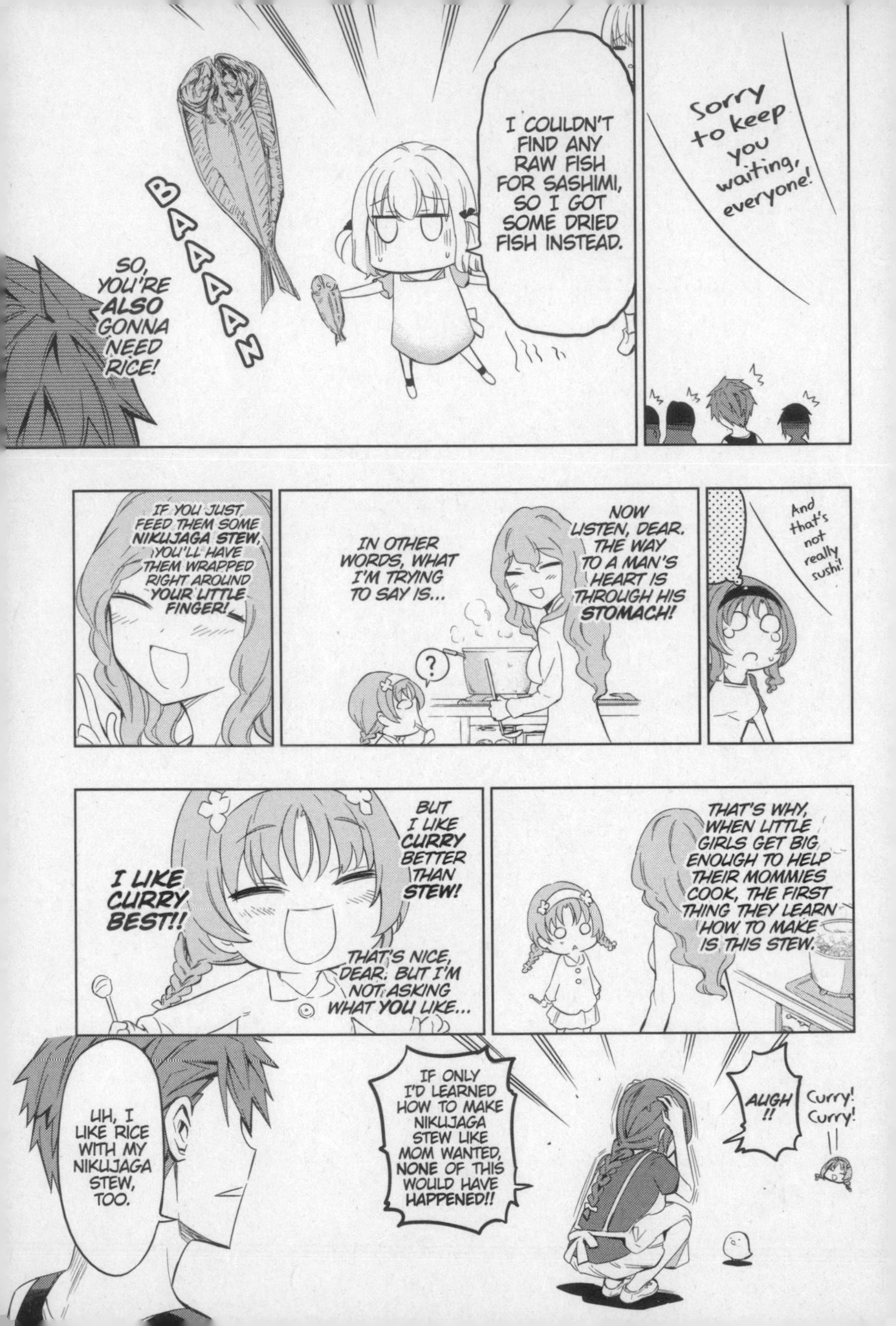
Sorry to keep you waiting, everyone!
I COULDN'T FIND ANY RAW FISH FOR SASHIMI, SO I GOT SOME DRIED FISH INSTEAD.
BAAAAAN
SO, YOU'RE ALSO GONNA NEED RICE!
And that's not really sushi!
NOW LISTEN, DEAR. THE WAY TO A MAN'S HEART IS THROUGH HIS STOMACH!
IN OTHER WORDS, WHAT I'M TRYING TO SAY IS...
?
IF YOU JUST FEED THEM SOME NIKUJAGA STEW, YOU'LL HAVE THEM WRAPPED RIGHT AROUND YOUR LITTLE FINGER!
THAT'S WHY, WHEN LITTLE GIRLS GET BIG ENOUGH TO HELP THEIR MOMMIES COOK, THE FIRST THING THEY LEARN HOW TO MAKE IS THIS STEW.
BUT I LIKE CURRY BETTER THAN STEW!
I LIKE CURRY BEST!!
THAT'S NICE, DEAR. BUT I'M NOT ASKING WHAT YOU LIKE...
Curry! Curry!
AUGH!!
IF ONLY I'D LEARNED HOW TO MAKE NIKUJAGA STEW LIKE MOM WANTED, NONE OF THIS WOULD HAVE HAPPENED!!
UH, I LIKE RICE WITH MY NIKUJAGA STEW, TOO.

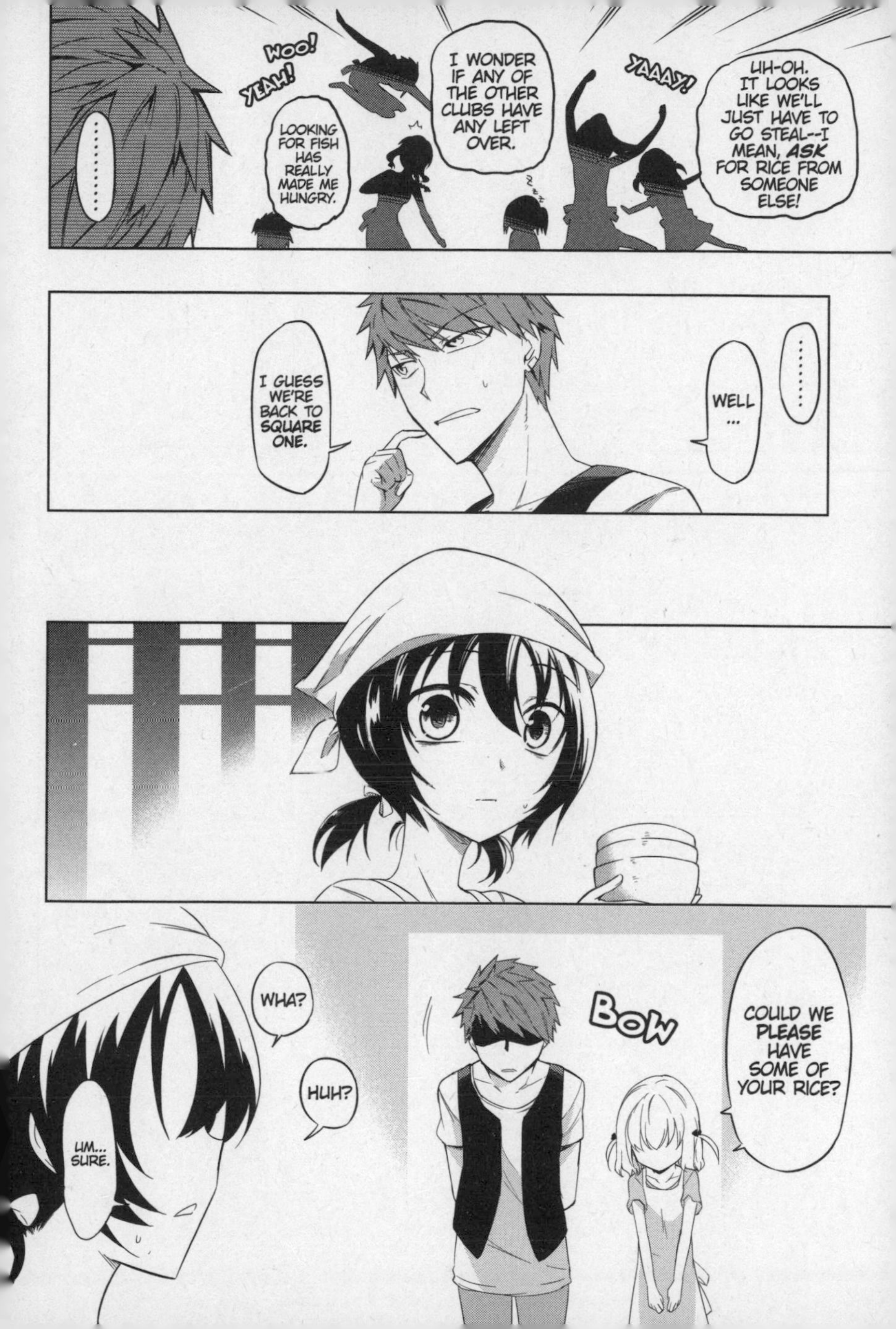
UH-OH. IT LOOKS LIKE WE'LL JUST HAVE TO GO STEAL--I MEAN, ASK FOR RICE FROM SOMEONE ELSE!
YAAAY!
I WONDER IF ANY OF THE OTHER CLUBS HAVE ANY LEFT OVER.
WOO! YEAH!
LOOKING FOR FISH HAS REALLY MADE ME HUNGRY.
......
......
WELL ...
I GUESS WE'RE BACK TO SQUARE ONE.
COULD WE PLEASE HAVE SOME OF YOUR RICE?
BOW
WHA?
HUH?
UM... SURE.

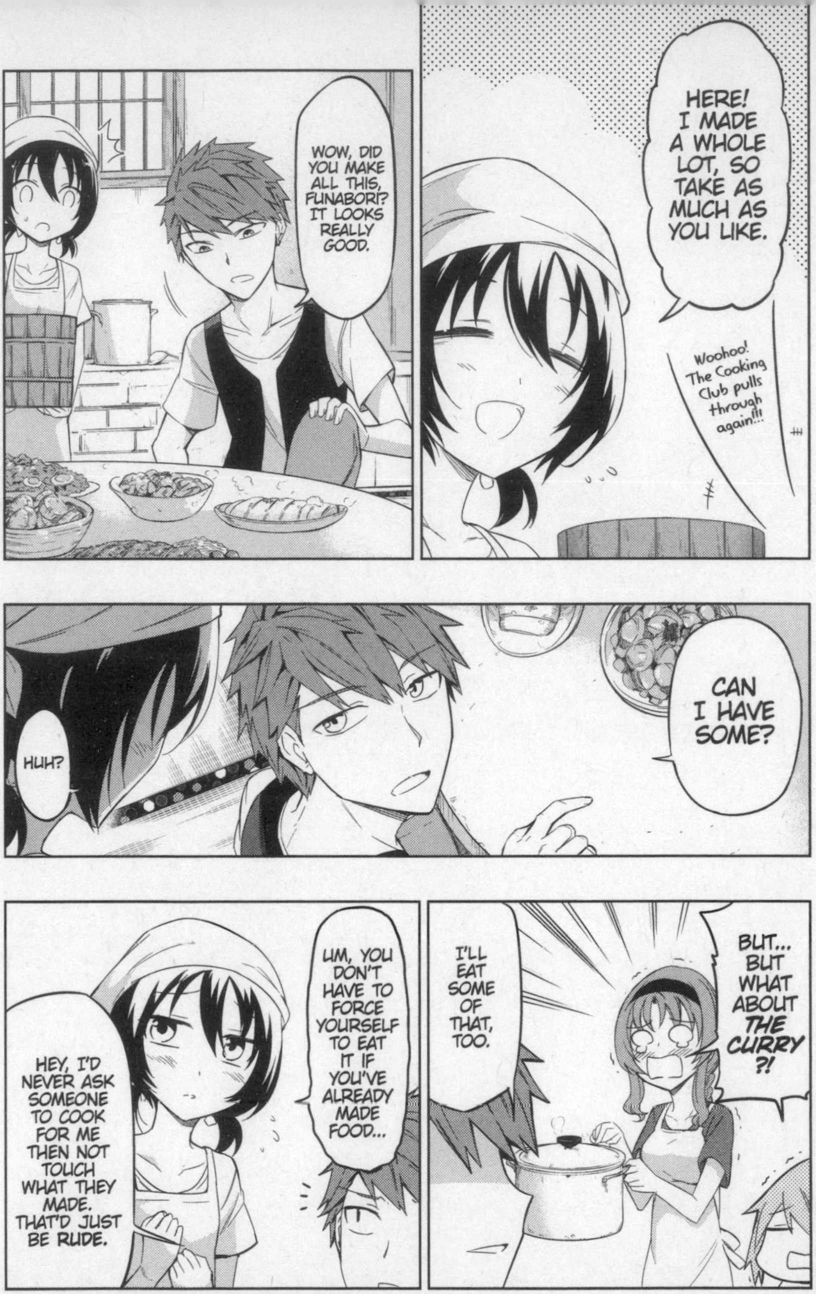
HERE! I MADE A WHOLE LOT, SO TAKE AS MUCH AS YOU LIKE.
Woohoo! The Cooking Club pulls through again!!!
WOW, DID YOU MAKE ALL THIS, FUNABORI? IT LOOKS REALLY GOOD.
CAN I HAVE SOME?
HUH?
BUT... BUT WHAT ABOUT *THE CURRY*?!
I'LL EAT SOME OF THAT, TOO.
UM, YOU DON'T HAVE TO FORCE YOURSELF TO EAT IT IF YOU'VE ALREADY MADE FOOD...
HEY, I'D NEVER ASK SOMEONE TO COOK FOR ME THEN NOT TOUCH WHAT THEY MADE. THAT'D JUST BE RUDE.

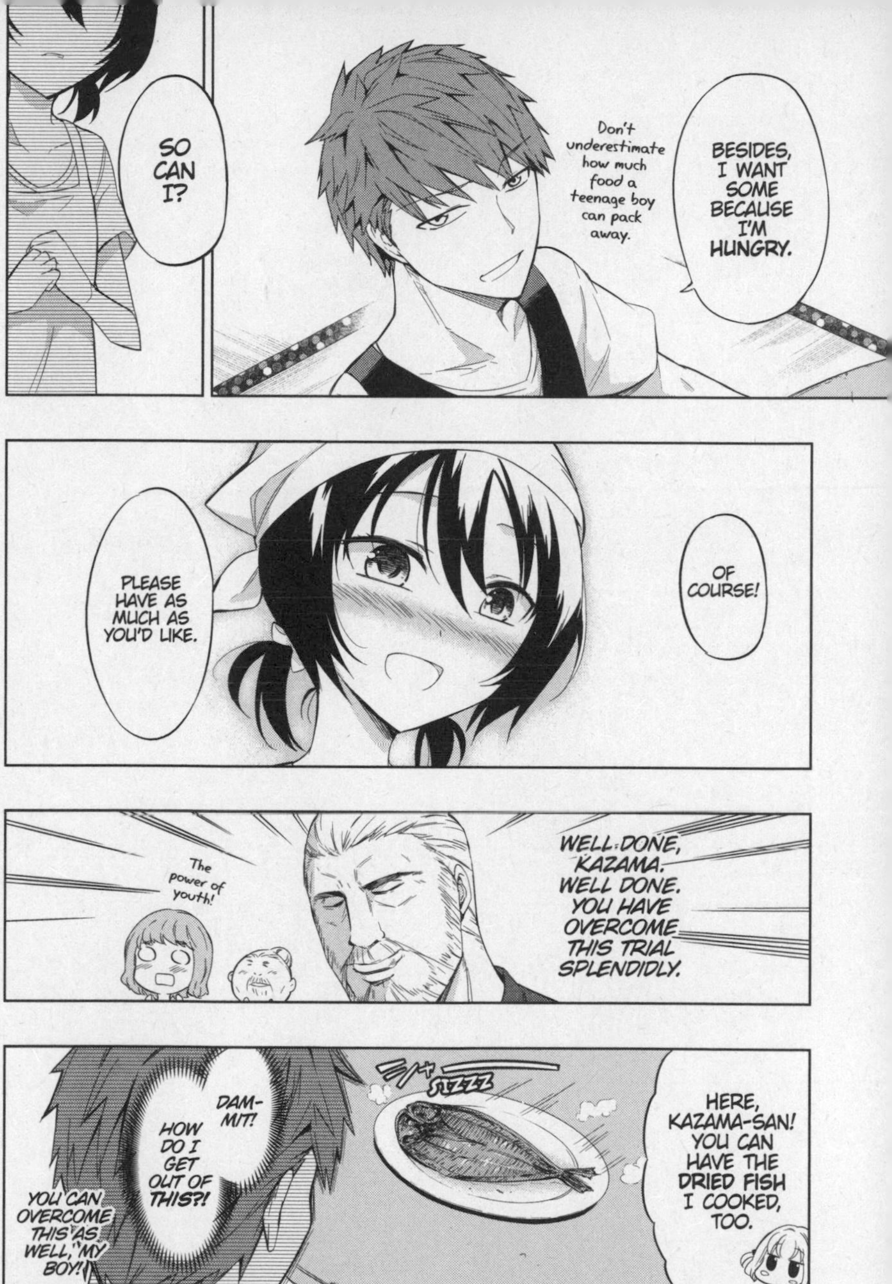
BESIDES, I WANT SOME BECAUSE I'M HUNGRY.
Don't underestimate how much food a teenage boy can pack away.
SO CAN I?
OF COURSE!
PLEASE HAVE AS MUCH AS YOU'D LIKE.
WELL DONE, KAZAMA. WELL DONE. YOU HAVE OVERCOME THIS TRIAL SPLENDIDLY.
The power of youth!
HERE, KAZAMA-SAN! YOU CAN HAVE THE DRIED FISH I COOKED, TOO.
SIZZZ
DAM-MIT!
HOW DO I GET OUT OF THIS?!
YOU CAN OVERCOME THIS AS WELL, MY BOY!

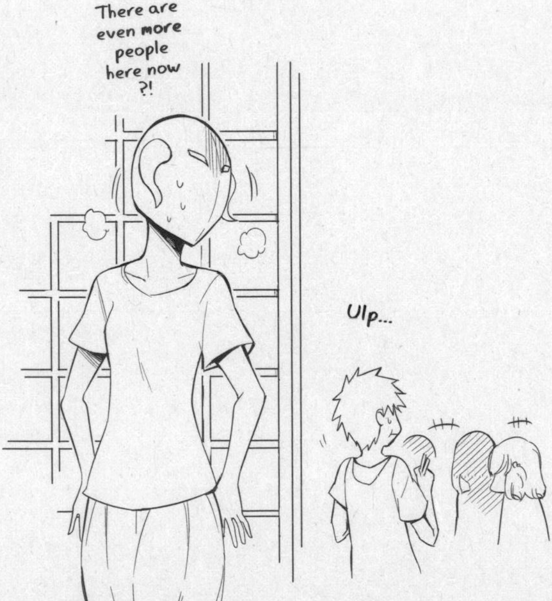
Ulp...
There are even more people here now ?!

D-FRAGMENTS

ディーふらぐ!

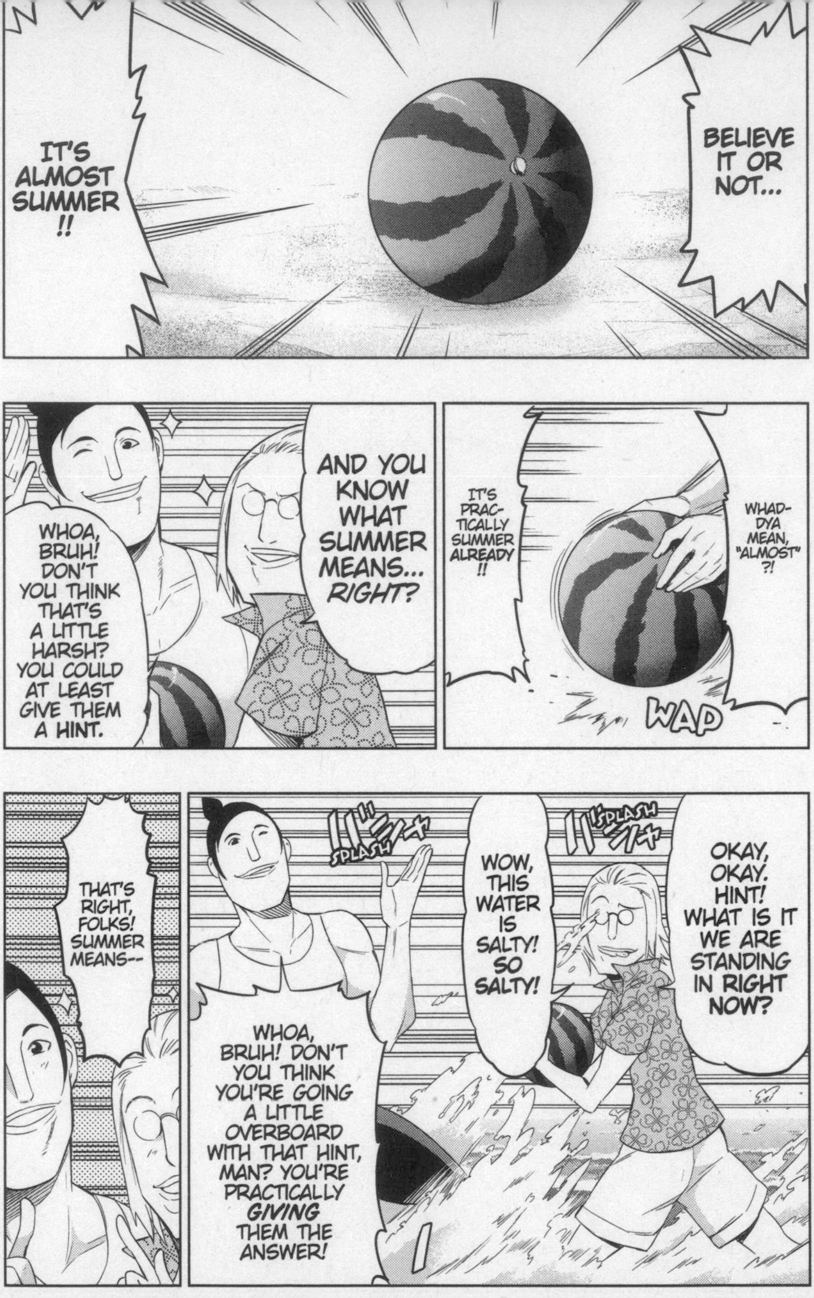
BELIEVE IT OR NOT...
IT'S ALMOST SUMMER !!
WHAD-DYA MEAN, "ALMOST" ?!
IT'S PRAC-TICALLY SUMMER ALREADY !!
WAP
AND YOU KNOW WHAT SUMMER MEANS... *RIGHT?*
WHOA, BRUH! DON'T YOU THINK THAT'S A LITTLE HARSH? YOU COULD AT LEAST GIVE THEM A HINT.
OKAY, OKAY. HINT! WHAT IS IT WE ARE STANDING IN RIGHT NOW?
SPLASH
WOW, THIS WATER IS SALTY! SO SALTY!
SPLASH
WHOA, BRUH! DON'T YOU THINK YOU'RE GOING A LITTLE OVERBOARD WITH THAT HINT, MAN? YOU'RE PRACTICALLY **GIVING** THEM THE ANSWER!
THAT'S RIGHT, FOLKS! SUMMER MEANS--

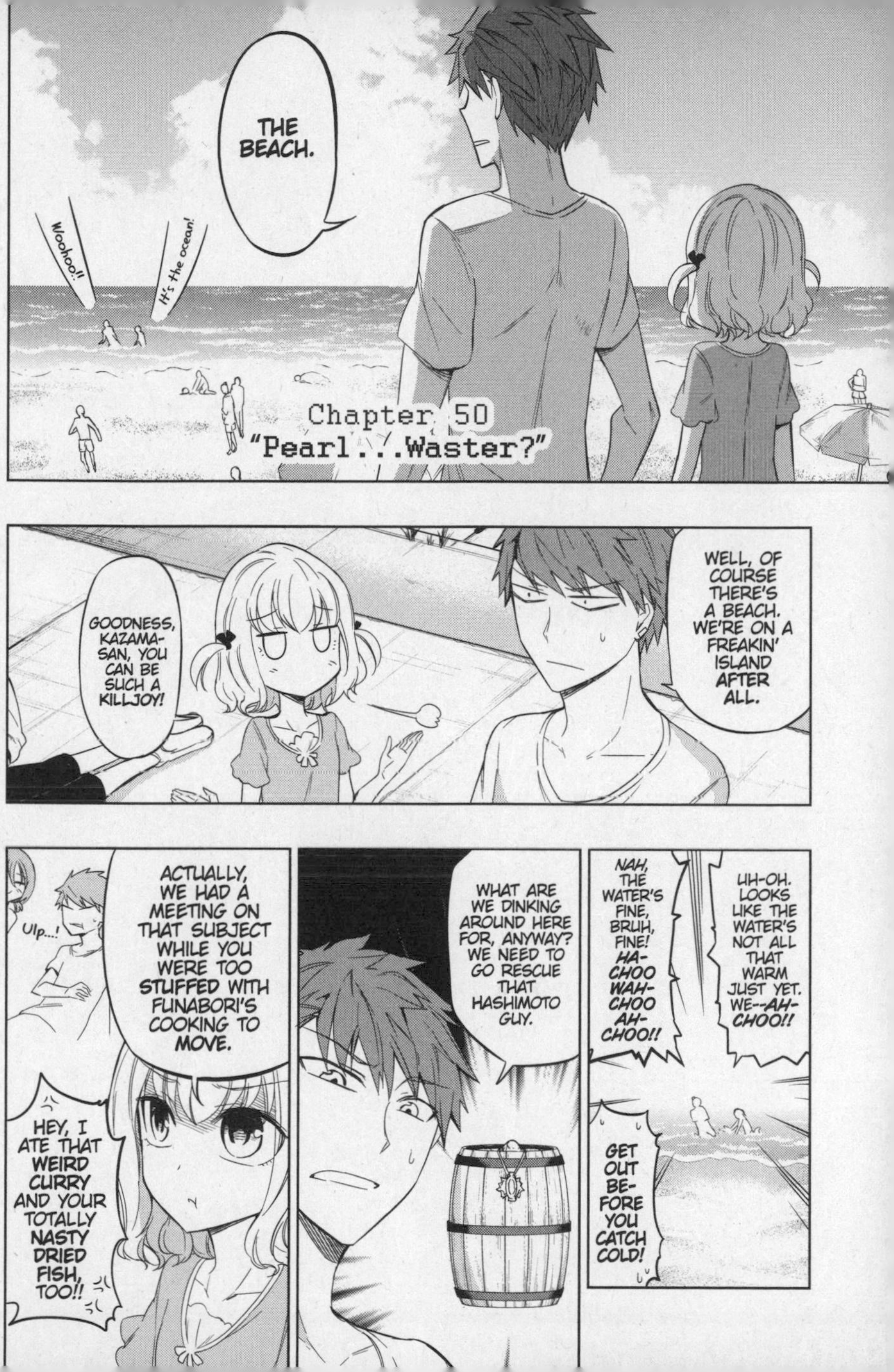
THE BEACH.
It's the ocean!
Woohoo!!
Chapter 50
"Pearl...Waster?"
WELL, OF COURSE THERE'S A BEACH. WE'RE ON A FREAKIN' ISLAND AFTER ALL.
GOODNESS, KAZAMA-SAN, YOU CAN BE SUCH A KILLJOY!
UH-OH. LOOKS LIKE THE WATER'S NOT ALL THAT WARM JUST YET. WE--AH-CHOO!!
NAH, THE WATER'S FINE, BRUH, FINE! HA-CHOO WAH-CHOO AH-CHOO!!
GET OUT BE-FORE YOU CATCH COLD!
WHAT ARE WE DINKING AROUND HERE FOR, ANYWAY? WE NEED TO GO RESCUE THAT HASHIMOTO GUY.
ACTUALLY, WE HAD A MEETING ON THAT SUBJECT WHILE YOU WERE TOO STUFFED WITH FUNABORI'S COOKING TO MOVE.
Ulp...!
HEY, I ATE THAT WEIRD CURRY AND YOUR TOTALLY NASTY DRIED FISH, TOO!!

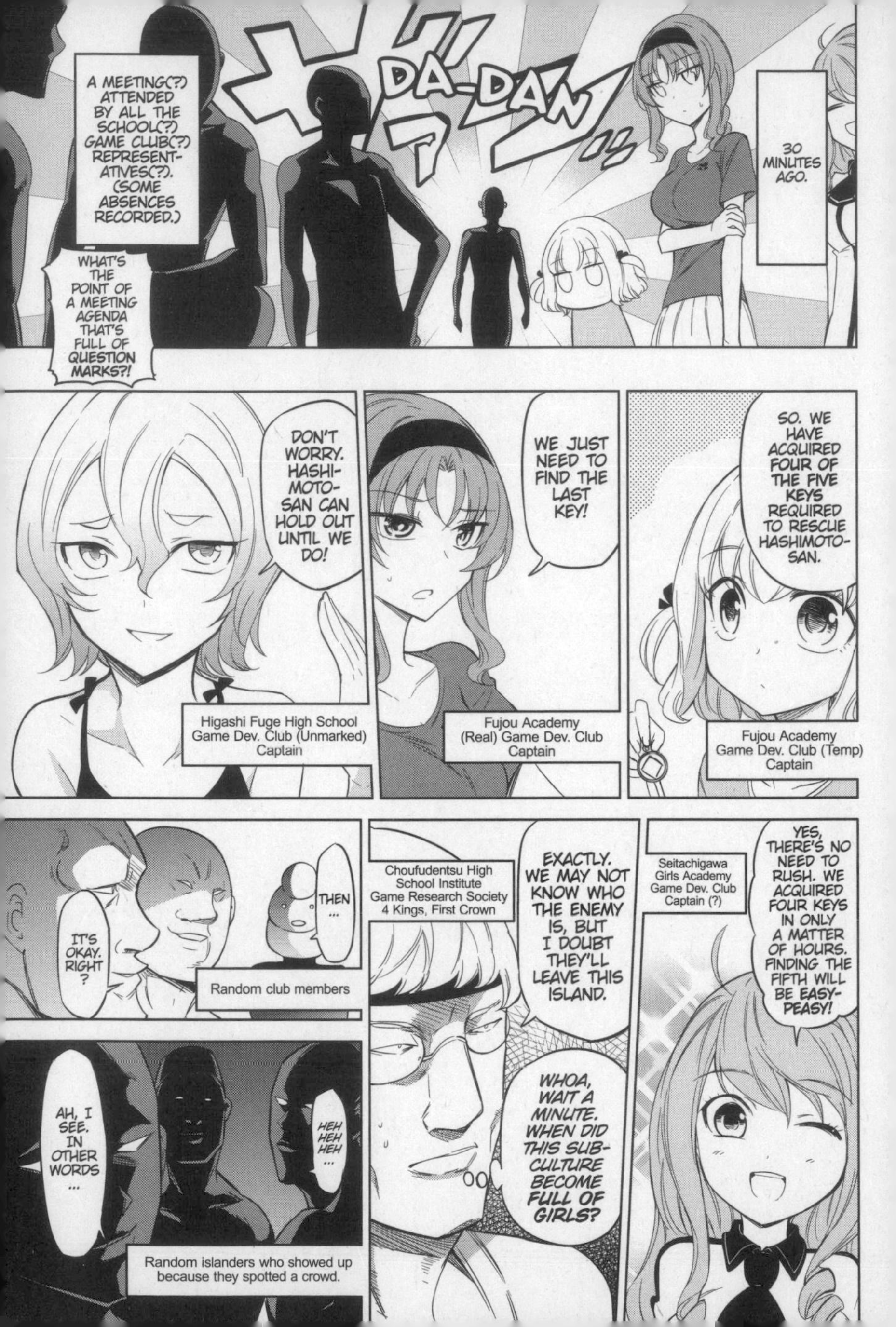
30 MINUTES AGO.
DA-DAN
A MEETING(?) ATTENDED BY ALL THE SCHOOL(?) GAME CLUB(?) REPRESENT-ATIVES(?). (SOME ABSENCES RECORDED.)
WHAT'S THE POINT OF A MEETING AGENDA THAT'S FULL OF QUESTION MARKS?!
SO. WE HAVE ACQUIRED FOUR OF THE FIVE KEYS REQUIRED TO RESCUE HASHIMOTO-SAN.
Fujou Academy Game Dev. Club (Temp) Captain
WE JUST NEED TO FIND THE LAST KEY!
Fujou Academy (Real) Game Dev. Club Captain
DON'T WORRY. HASHI-MOTO-SAN CAN HOLD OUT UNTIL WE DO!
Higashi Fuge High School Game Dev. Club (Unmarked) Captain
Seitachigawa Girls Academy Game Dev. Club Captain (?)
YES, THERE'S NO NEED TO RUSH. WE ACQUIRED FOUR KEYS IN ONLY A MATTER OF HOURS. FINDING THE FIFTH WILL BE EASY-PEASY!
Choufudentsu High School Institute Game Research Society 4 Kings, First Crown
EXACTLY. WE MAY NOT KNOW WHO THE ENEMY IS, BUT I DOUBT THEY'LL LEAVE THIS ISLAND.
WHOA, WAIT A MINUTE. WHEN DID THIS SUB-CULTURE BECOME FULL OF GIRLS?
THEN ...
IT'S OKAY. RIGHT?
Random club members
HEH HEH HEH ...
AH, I SEE. IN OTHER WORDS ...
Random islanders who showed up because they spotted a crowd.

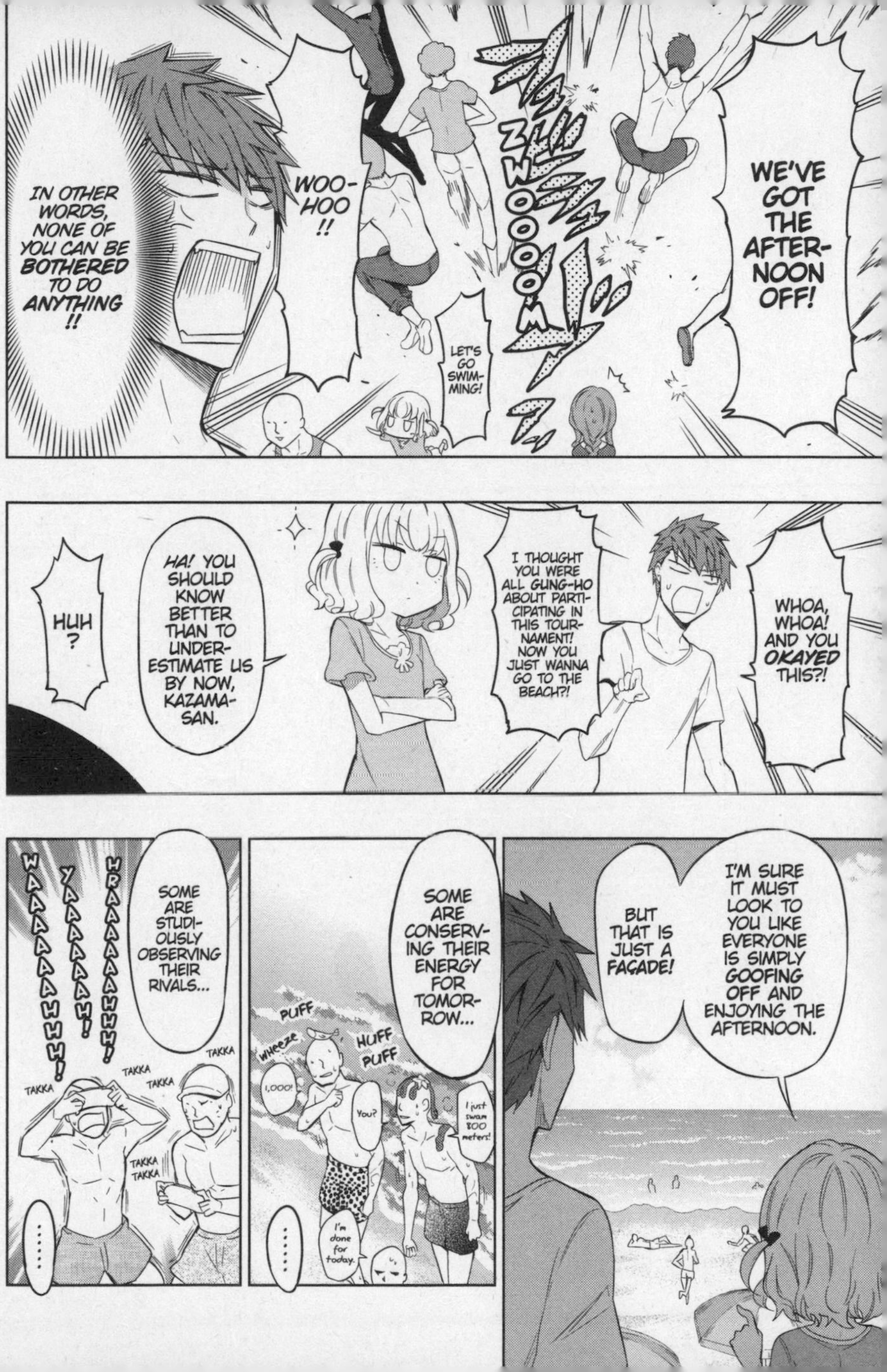
WE'VE GOT THE AFTERNOON OFF!
ZWOOOOM
WOO-HOO!!
LET'S GO SWIMMING!
IN OTHER WORDS, NONE OF YOU CAN BE BOTHERED TO DO ANYTHING!!
WHOA, WHOA! AND YOU OKAYED THIS?!
I THOUGHT YOU WERE ALL GUNG-HO ABOUT PARTICIPATING IN THIS TOURNAMENT! NOW YOU JUST WANNA GO TO THE BEACH?!
HA! YOU SHOULD KNOW BETTER THAN TO UNDERESTIMATE US BY NOW, KAZAMA-SAN.
HUH?
I'M SURE IT MUST LOOK TO YOU LIKE EVERYONE IS SIMPLY GOOFING OFF AND ENJOYING THE AFTERNOON.
BUT THAT IS JUST A FAÇADE!
SOME ARE CONSERVING THEIR ENERGY FOR TOMORROW...
PUFF
HUFF PUFF
wheeze
1,000!
You?
I just swam 800 meters!
I'm done for today.
......
SOME ARE STUDIOUSLY OBSERVING THEIR RIVALS...
HRAAAAAAAHHH!
YAAAAAAAH!
WAAAAAAAHHH!
TAKKA
TAKKA
TAKKA
TAKKA
TAKKA TAKKA
......

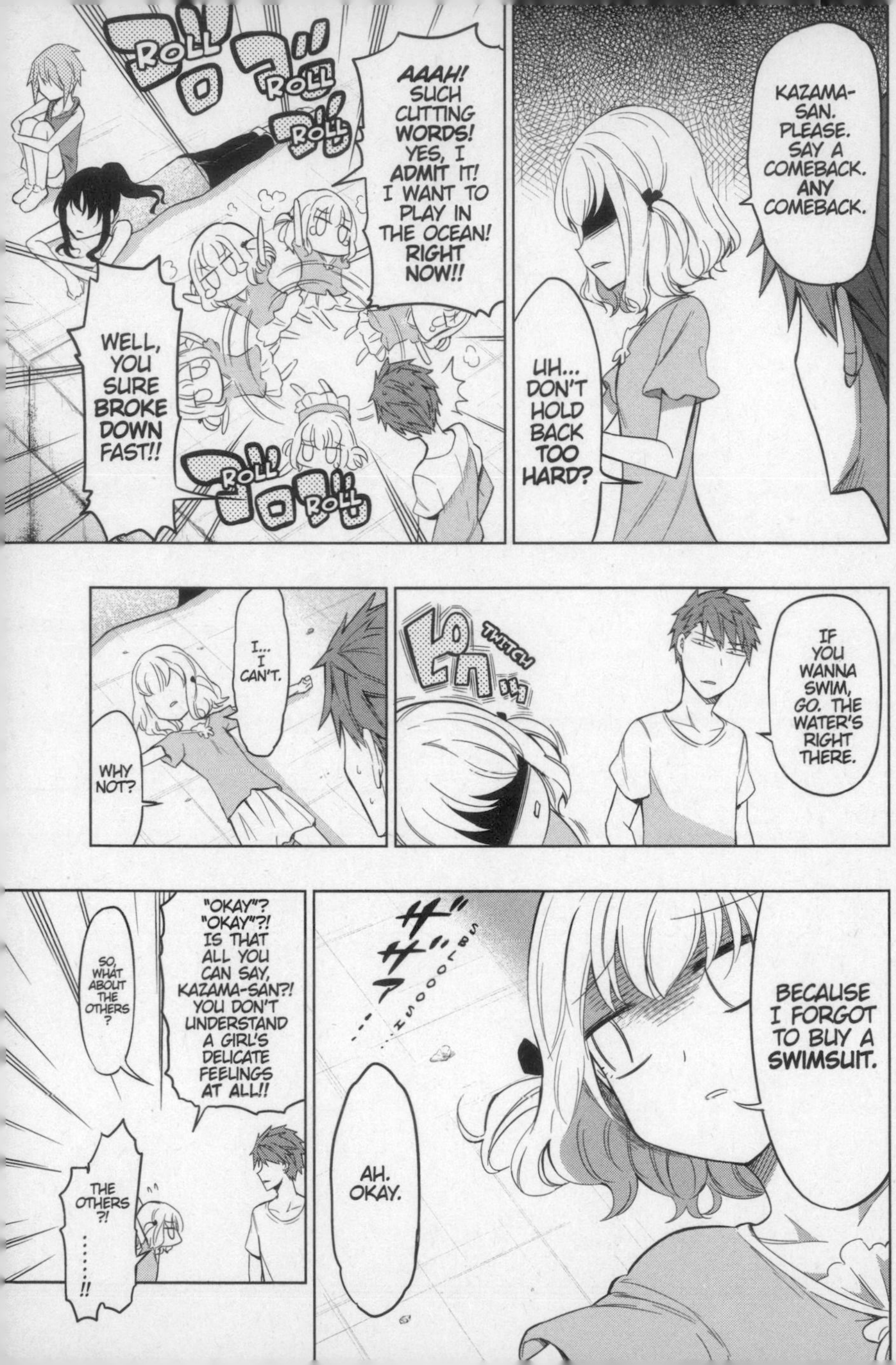
KAZAMA-SAN. PLEASE. SAY A COMEBACK. ANY COMEBACK.
UH... DON'T HOLD BACK TOO HARD?
AAAH! SUCH CUTTING WORDS! YES, I ADMIT IT! I WANT TO PLAY IN THE OCEAN! RIGHT NOW!!
ROLL ROLL ROLL
WELL, YOU SURE BROKE DOWN FAST!!
ROLL ROLL
IF YOU WANNA SWIM, GO. THE WATER'S RIGHT THERE.
TWITCH
I... I CAN'T.
WHY NOT?
BECAUSE I FORGOT TO BUY A SWIMSUIT.
SLOOOOSH...
AH. OKAY.
"OKAY"? "OKAY"?! IS THAT ALL YOU CAN SAY, KAZAMA-SAN?! YOU DON'T UNDERSTAND A GIRL'S DELICATE FEELINGS AT ALL!!
SO, WHAT ABOUT THE OTHERS?
THE OTHERS?!
......!!

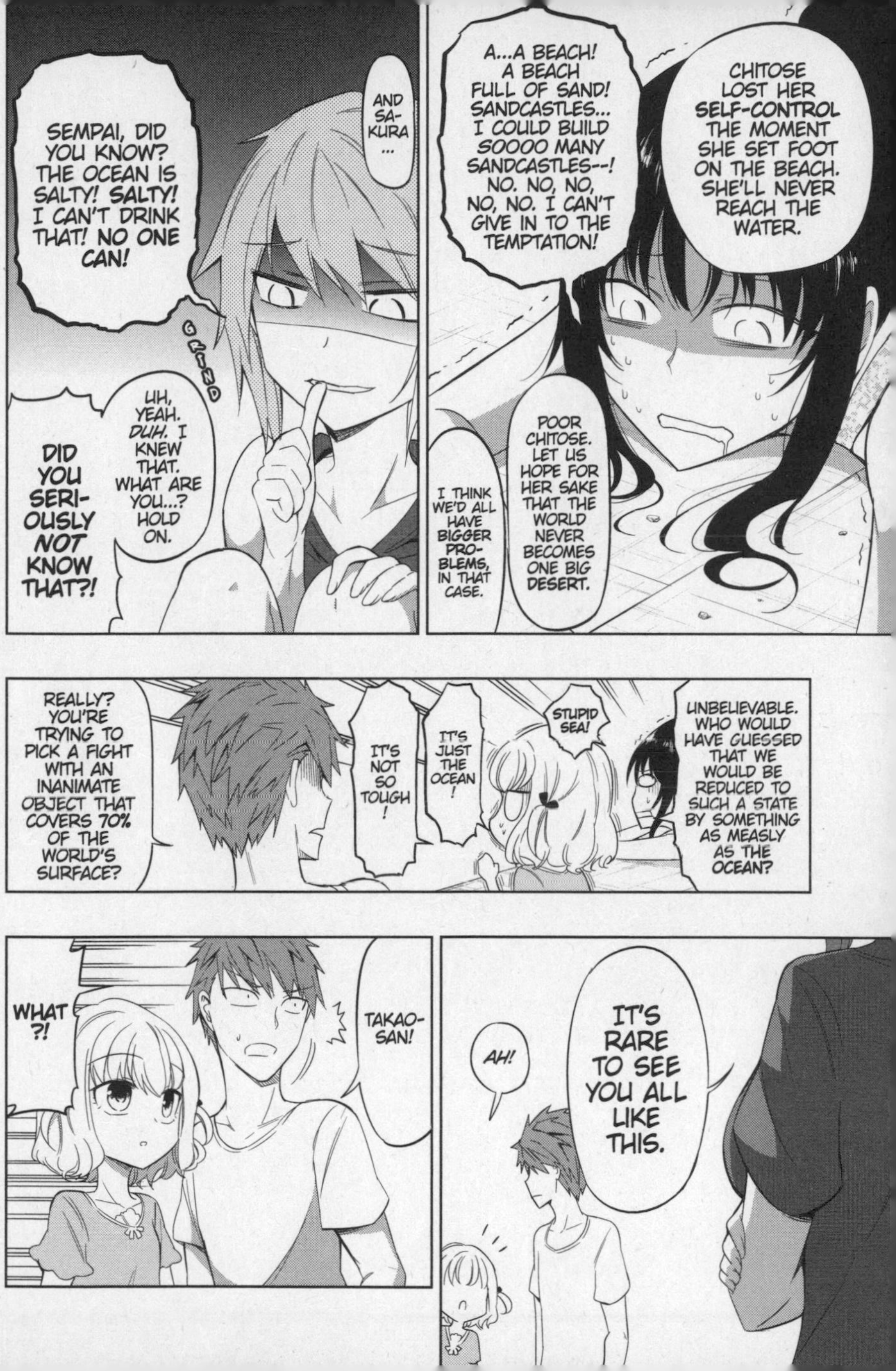
CHITOSE LOST HER SELF-CONTROL THE MOMENT SHE SET FOOT ON THE BEACH. SHE'LL NEVER REACH THE WATER.
A...A BEACH! A BEACH FULL OF SAND! SANDCASTLES... I COULD BUILD SOOOO MANY SANDCASTLES--! NO. NO, NO, NO, NO. I CAN'T GIVE IN TO THE TEMPTATION!
POOR CHITOSE. LET US HOPE FOR HER SAKE THAT THE WORLD NEVER BECOMES ONE BIG DESERT.
I THINK WE'D ALL HAVE BIGGER PROBLEMS, IN THAT CASE.
AND SAKURA...
SEMPAI, DID YOU KNOW? THE OCEAN IS SALTY! SALTY! I CAN'T DRINK THAT! NO ONE CAN!
GRIND
UH, YEAH. DUH. I KNEW THAT. WHAT ARE YOU...? HOLD ON.
DID YOU SERIOUSLY NOT KNOW THAT?!
UNBELIEVABLE. WHO WOULD HAVE GUESSED THAT WE WOULD BE REDUCED TO SUCH A STATE BY SOMETHING AS MEASLY AS THE OCEAN?
STUPID SEA!
IT'S JUST THE OCEAN!
IT'S NOT SO TOUGH!
REALLY? YOU'RE TRYING TO PICK A FIGHT WITH AN INANIMATE OBJECT THAT COVERS 70% OF THE WORLD'S SURFACE?
IT'S RARE TO SEE YOU ALL LIKE THIS.
AH!
TAKAO-SAN!
WHAT?!

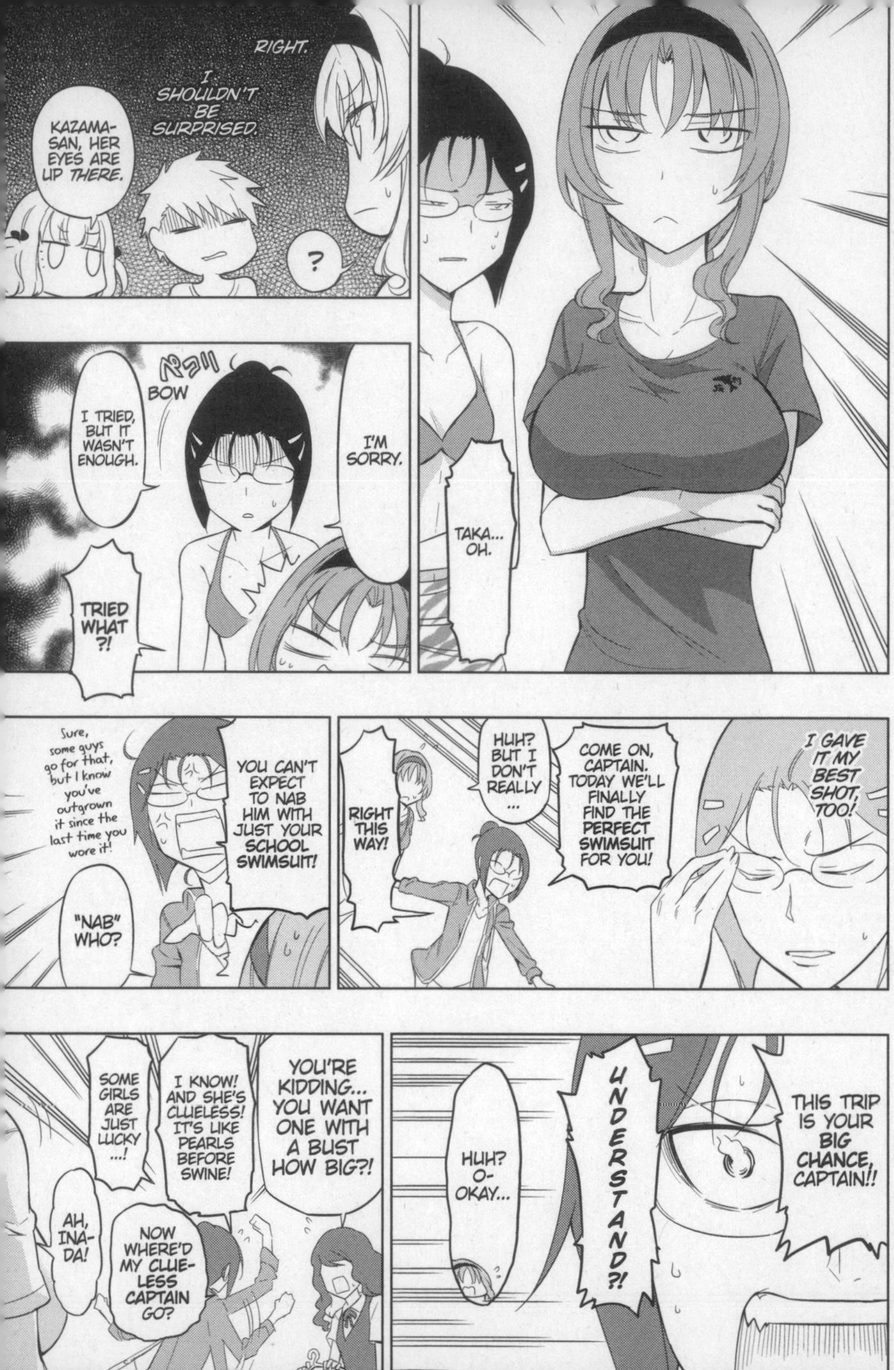
TAKA... OH.
RIGHT.
I SHOULDN'T BE SURPRISED.
?
KAZAMA-SAN, HER EYES ARE UP THERE.
I'M SORRY.
ペコリ BOW
I TRIED, BUT IT WASN'T ENOUGH.
TRIED WHAT?!
I GAVE IT MY BEST SHOT, TOO!
COME ON, CAPTAIN. TODAY WE'LL FINALLY FIND THE PERFECT SWIMSUIT FOR YOU!
HUH? BUT I DON'T REALLY ...
RIGHT THIS WAY!
YOU CAN'T EXPECT TO NAB HIM WITH JUST YOUR SCHOOL SWIMSUIT!
Sure, some guys go for that, but I know you've outgrown it since the last time you wore it!
"NAB" WHO?
THIS TRIP IS YOUR BIG CHANCE, CAPTAIN!!
UNDERSTAND?!
HUH? O-OKAY...
YOU'RE KIDDING... YOU WANT ONE WITH A BUST HOW BIG?!
I KNOW! AND SHE'S CLUELESS! IT'S LIKE PEARLS BEFORE SWINE!
SOME GIRLS ARE JUST LUCKY ...!
NOW WHERE'D MY CLUE-LESS CAPTAIN GO?
AH, INADA!

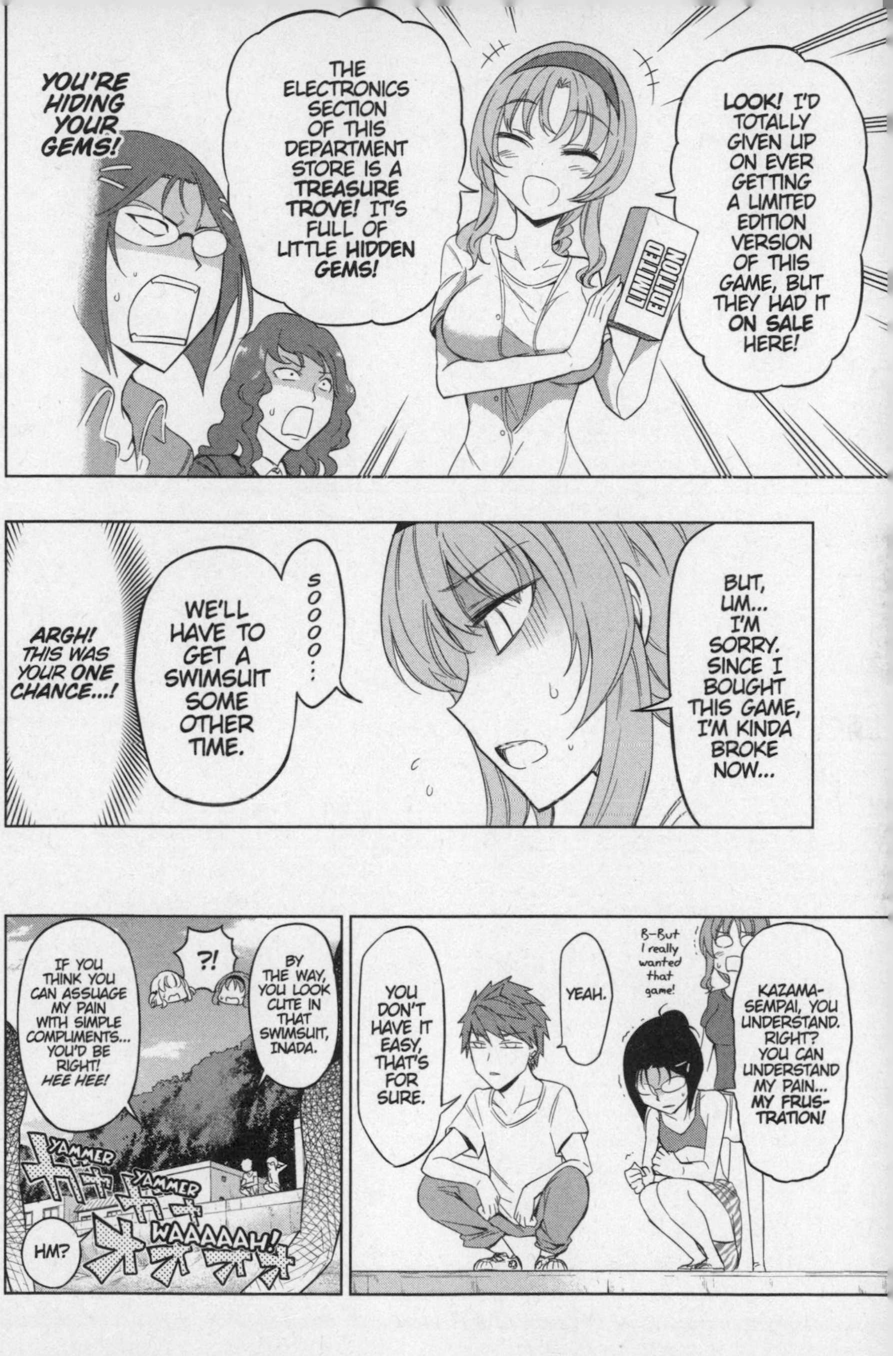
LOOK! I'D TOTALLY GIVEN UP ON EVER GETTING A LIMITED EDITION VERSION OF THIS GAME, BUT THEY HAD IT ON SALE HERE!
LIMITED EDITION
THE ELECTRONICS SECTION OF THIS DEPARTMENT STORE IS A TREASURE TROVE! IT'S FULL OF LITTLE HIDDEN GEMS!
YOU'RE HIDING YOUR GEMS!
BUT, UM... I'M SORRY. SINCE I BOUGHT THIS GAME, I'M KINDA BROKE NOW...
SOOOOO...
WE'LL HAVE TO GET A SWIMSUIT SOME OTHER TIME.
ARGH! THIS WAS YOUR ONE CHANCE...!
KAZAMA-SEMPAI, YOU UNDERSTAND. RIGHT? YOU CAN UNDERSTAND MY PAIN... MY FRUS-TRATION!
B-But I really wanted that game!
YEAH.
YOU DON'T HAVE IT EASY, THAT'S FOR SURE.
BY THE WAY, YOU LOOK CUTE IN THAT SWIMSUIT, INADA.
?!
IF YOU THINK YOU CAN ASSUAGE MY PAIN WITH SIMPLE COMPLIMENTS... YOU'D BE RIGHT! HEE HEE!
YAMMER
YAMMER
WAAAAAH!
HM?

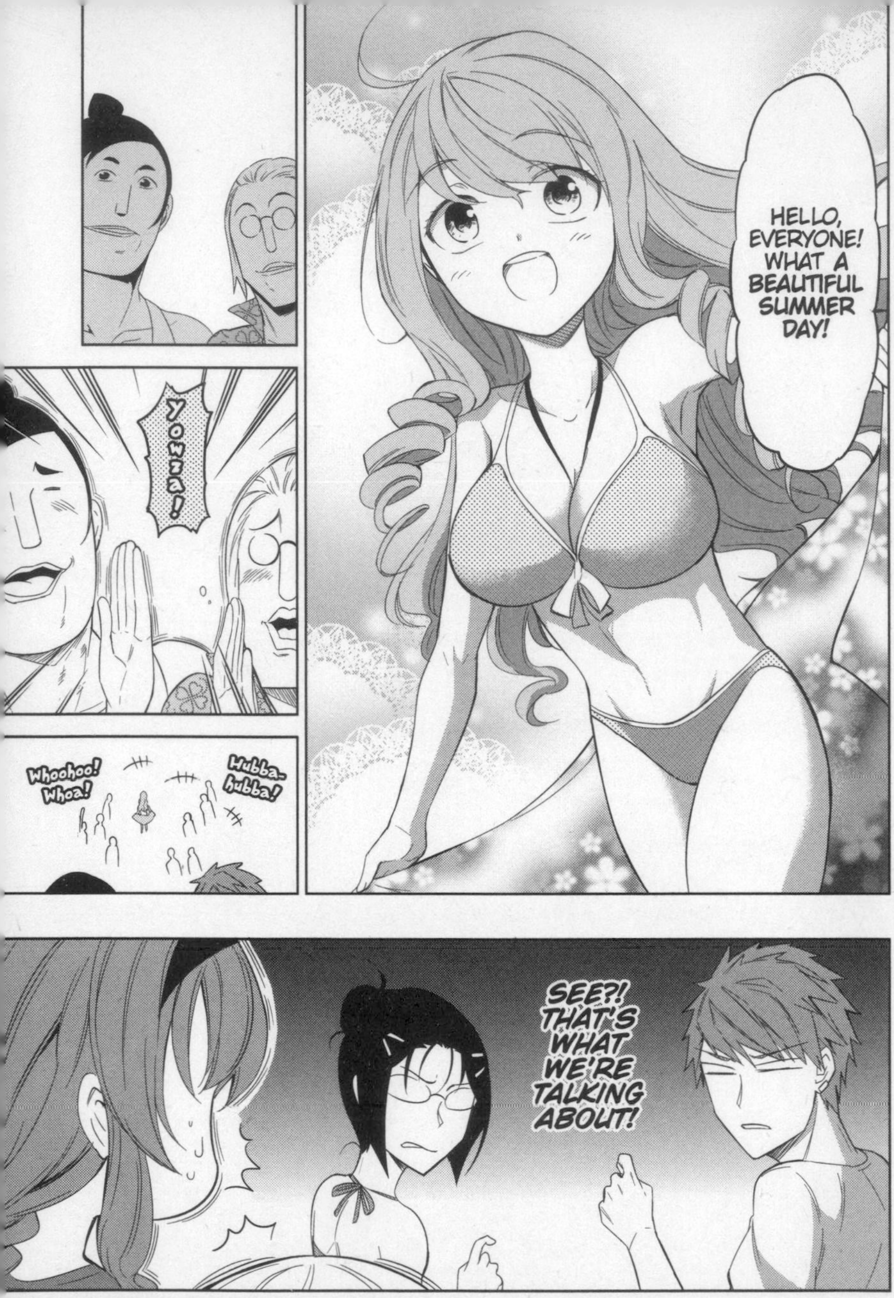
HELLO, EVERYONE! WHAT A BEAUTIFUL SUMMER DAY!
Yowza!
Hubba-hubba!
Whoohoo! Whoa!
SEE?! THAT'S WHAT WE'RE TALKING ABOUT!

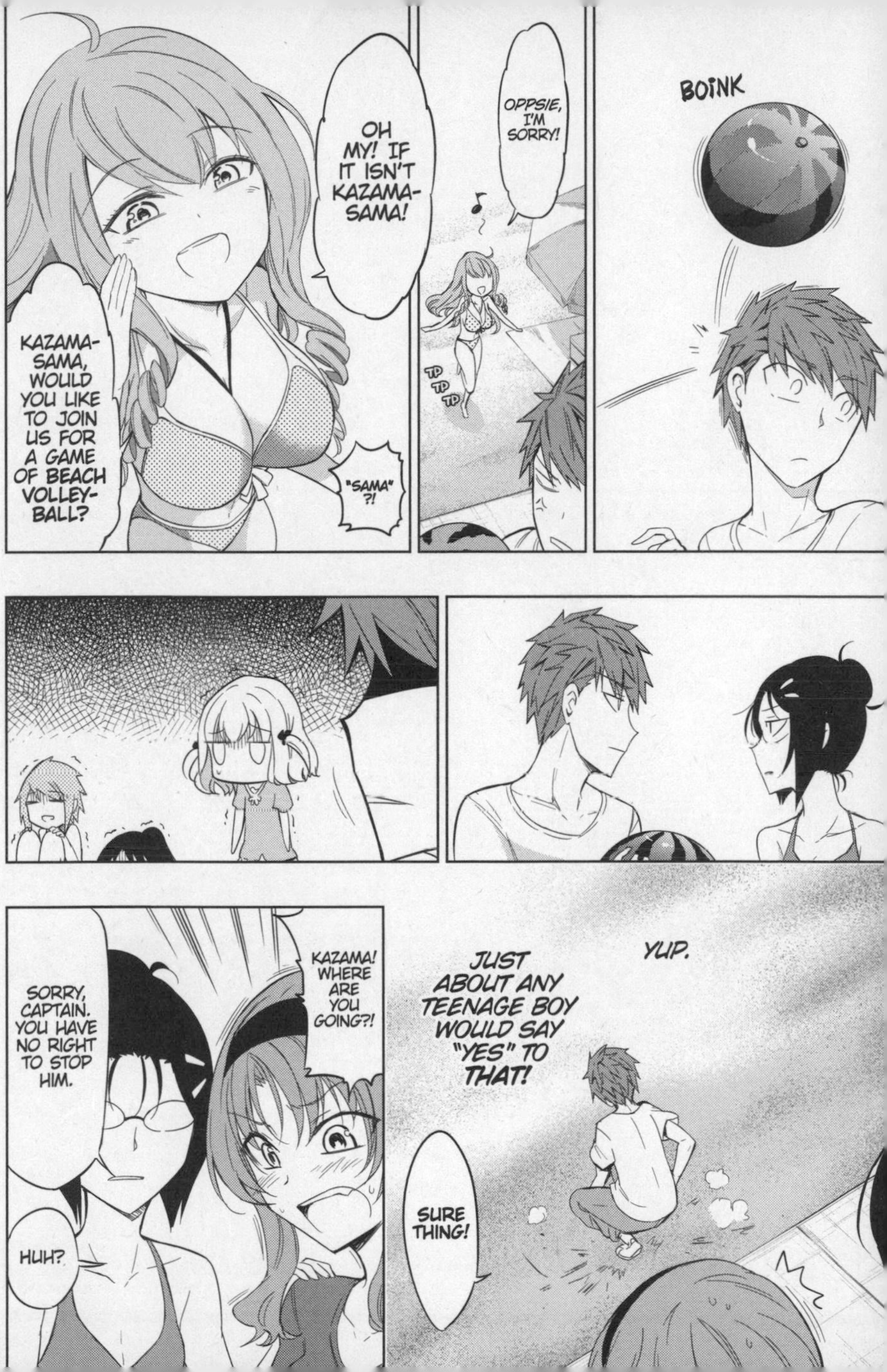
BOINK
OPPSIE, I'M SORRY!
TP TP TP
OH MY! IF IT ISN'T KAZAMA-SAMA!
KAZAMA-SAMA, WOULD YOU LIKE TO JOIN US FOR A GAME OF BEACH VOLLEY-BALL?
"SAMA"?!
YUP.
JUST ABOUT ANY TEENAGE BOY WOULD SAY "YES" TO THAT!
SURE THING!
KAZAMA! WHERE ARE YOU GOING?!
SORRY, CAPTAIN. YOU HAVE NO RIGHT TO STOP HIM.
HUH?

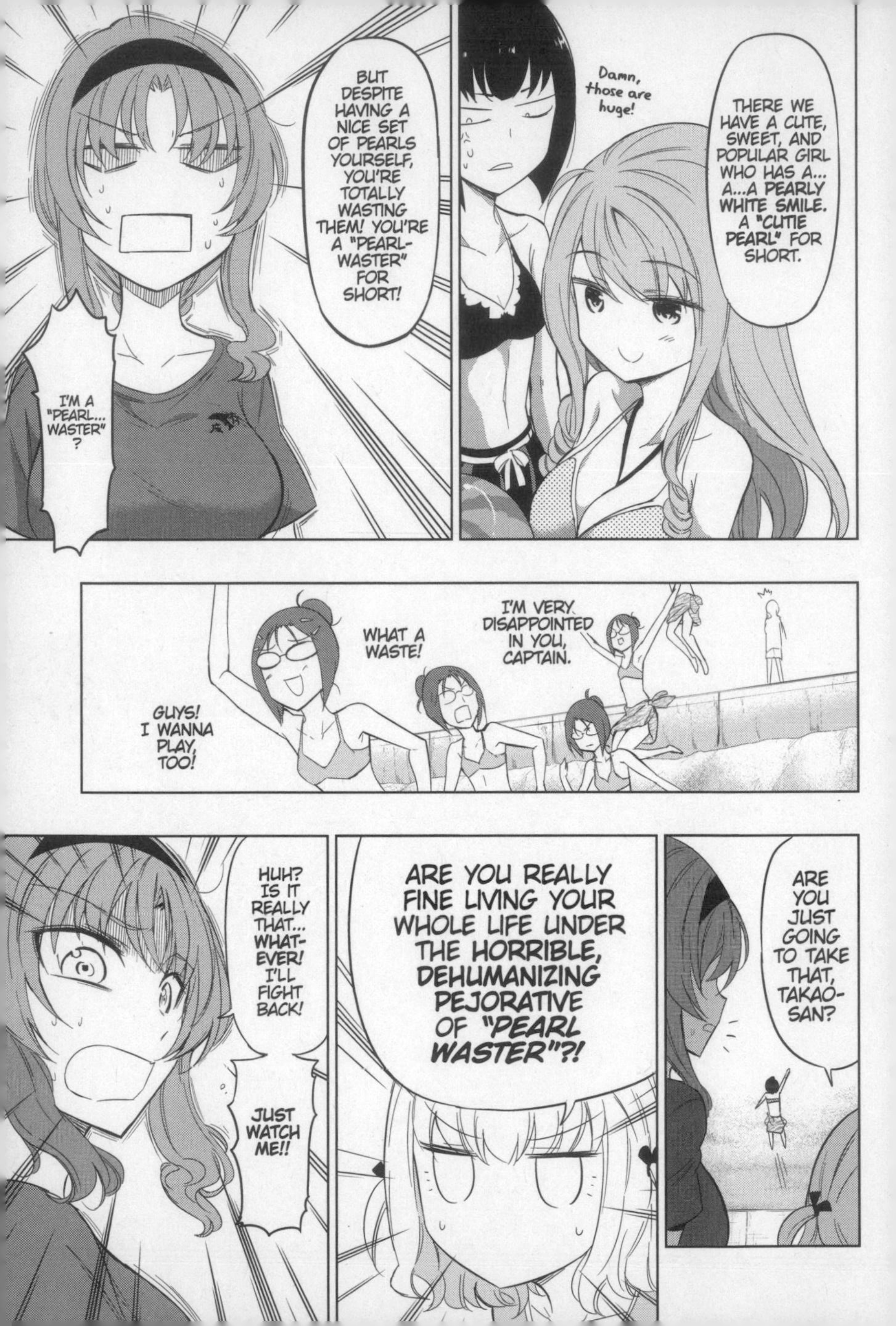
THERE WE HAVE A CUTE, SWEET, AND POPULAR GIRL WHO HAS A... A...A PEARLY WHITE SMILE. A "CUTIE PEARL" FOR SHORT.
Damn, those are huge!
BUT DESPITE HAVING A NICE SET OF PEARLS YOURSELF, YOU'RE TOTALLY WASTING THEM! YOU'RE A "PEARL-WASTER" FOR SHORT!
I'M A "PEARL... WASTER"?
I'M VERY DISAPPOINTED IN YOU, CAPTAIN.
WHAT A WASTE!
GUYS! I WANNA PLAY, TOO!
ARE YOU JUST GOING TO TAKE THAT, TAKAO-SAN?
ARE YOU REALLY FINE LIVING YOUR WHOLE LIFE UNDER THE HORRIBLE, DEHUMANIZING PEJORATIVE OF "PEARL WASTER"?!
HUH? IS IT REALLY THAT... WHATEVER! I'LL FIGHT BACK!
JUST WATCH ME!!

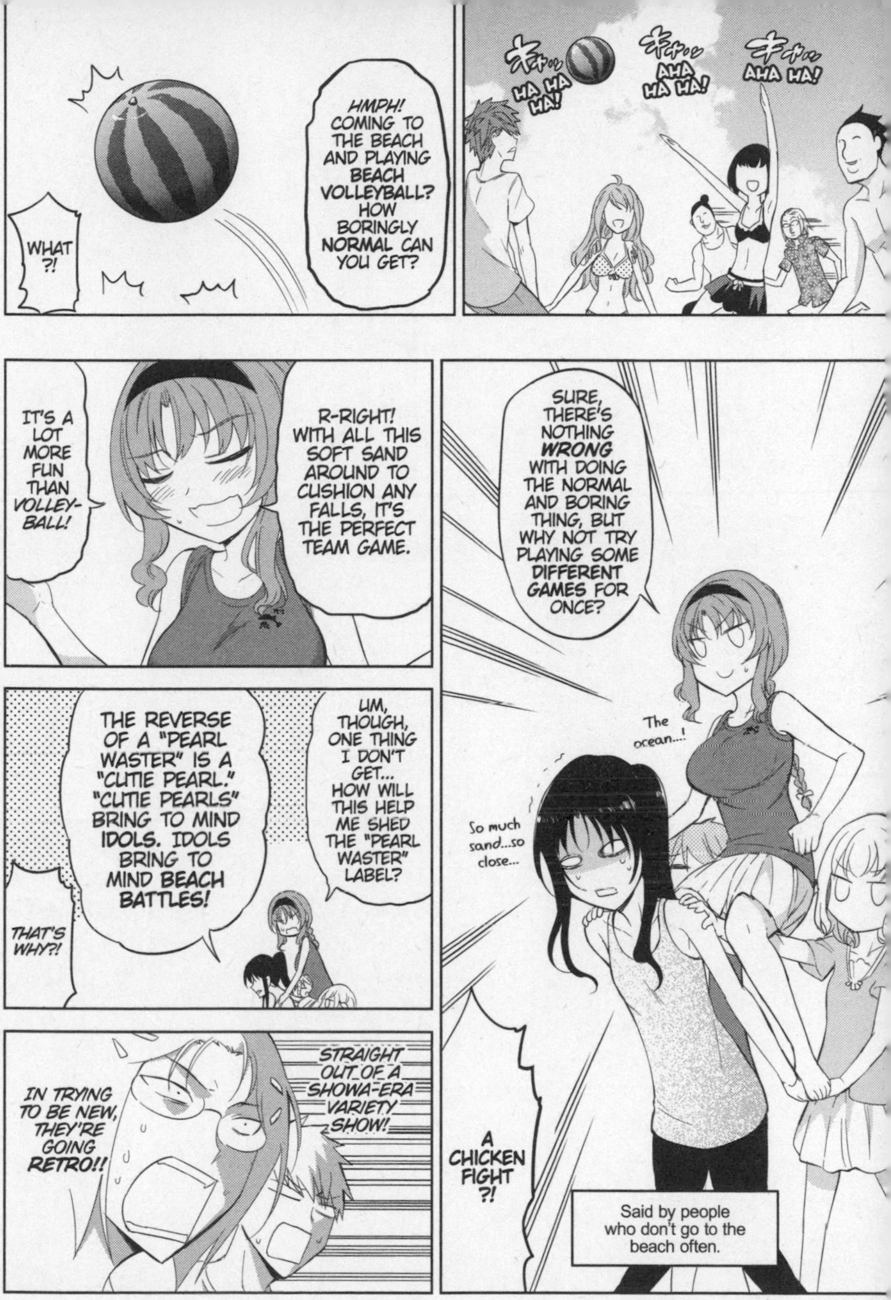
AHA HA!
AHA HA HA!
HA HA HA!
HMPH! COMING TO THE BEACH AND PLAYING BEACH VOLLEYBALL? HOW BORINGLY NORMAL CAN YOU GET?
WHAT?!
SURE, THERE'S NOTHING WRONG WITH DOING THE NORMAL AND BORING THING, BUT WHY NOT TRY PLAYING SOME DIFFERENT GAMES FOR ONCE?
The ocean...!
So much sand...so close...
A CHICKEN FIGHT?!
Said by people who don't go to the beach often.
R-RIGHT! WITH ALL THIS SOFT SAND AROUND TO CUSHION ANY FALLS, IT'S THE PERFECT TEAM GAME.
IT'S A LOT MORE FUN THAN VOLLEY-BALL!
UM, THOUGH, ONE THING I DON'T GET... HOW WILL THIS HELP ME SHED THE "PEARL WASTER" LABEL?
THE REVERSE OF A "PEARL WASTER" IS A "CUTIE PEARL." "CUTIE PEARLS" BRING TO MIND IDOLS. IDOLS BRING TO MIND BEACH BATTLES!
THAT'S WHY?!
STRAIGHT OUT OF A SHOWA-ERA VARIETY SHOW!
IN TRYING TO BE NEW, THEY'RE GOING RETRO!!

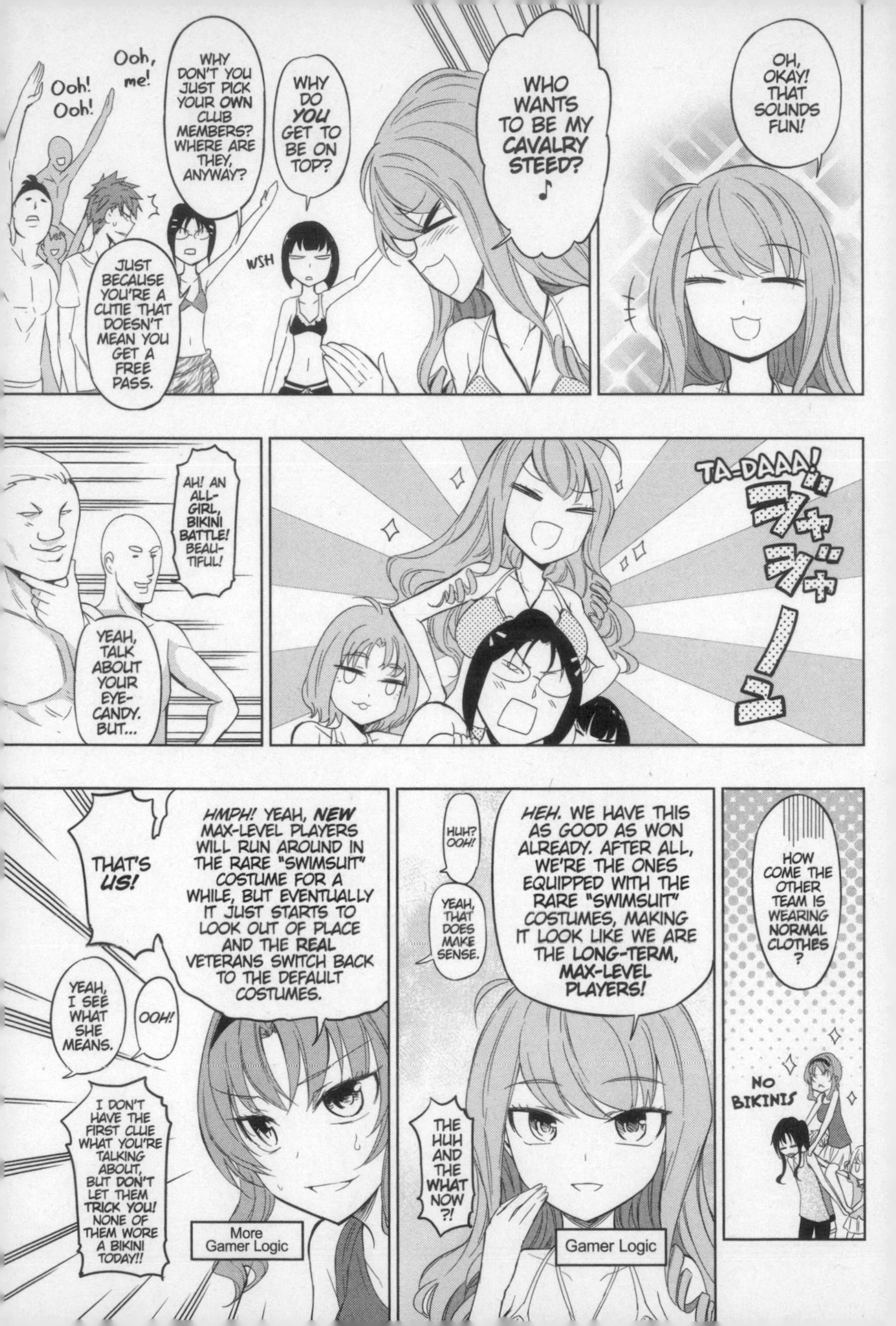
OH, OKAY! THAT SOUNDS FUN!
WHO WANTS TO BE MY CAVALRY STEED? ♪
WHY DO YOU GET TO BE ON TOP?
WHY DON'T YOU JUST PICK YOUR OWN CLUB MEMBERS? WHERE ARE THEY, ANYWAY?
Ooh, me!
Ooh! Ooh!
WSH
JUST BECAUSE YOU'RE A CUTIE THAT DOESN'T MEAN YOU GET A FREE PASS.
TA-DAAA!
AH! AN ALL-GIRL, BIKINI BATTLE! BEAUTIFUL!
YEAH, TALK ABOUT YOUR EYE-CANDY. BUT...
HOW COME THE OTHER TEAM IS WEARING NORMAL CLOTHES?
NO BIKINIS
HEH. WE HAVE THIS AS GOOD AS WON ALREADY. AFTER ALL, WE'RE THE ONES EQUIPPED WITH THE RARE "SWIMSUIT" COSTUMES, MAKING IT LOOK LIKE WE ARE THE LONG-TERM, MAX-LEVEL PLAYERS!
HUH? OOH!
YEAH, THAT DOES MAKE SENSE.
THE HUH AND THE WHAT NOW?!
Gamer Logic
THAT'S US!
HMPH! YEAH, NEW MAX-LEVEL PLAYERS WILL RUN AROUND IN THE RARE "SWIMSUIT" COSTUME FOR A WHILE, BUT EVENTUALLY IT JUST STARTS TO LOOK OUT OF PLACE AND THE REAL VETERANS SWITCH BACK TO THE DEFAULT COSTUMES.
OOH!
YEAH, I SEE WHAT SHE MEANS.
I DON'T HAVE THE FIRST CLUE WHAT YOU'RE TALKING ABOUT, BUT DON'T LET THEM TRICK YOU! NONE OF THEM WORE A BIKINI TODAY!!
More Gamer Logic

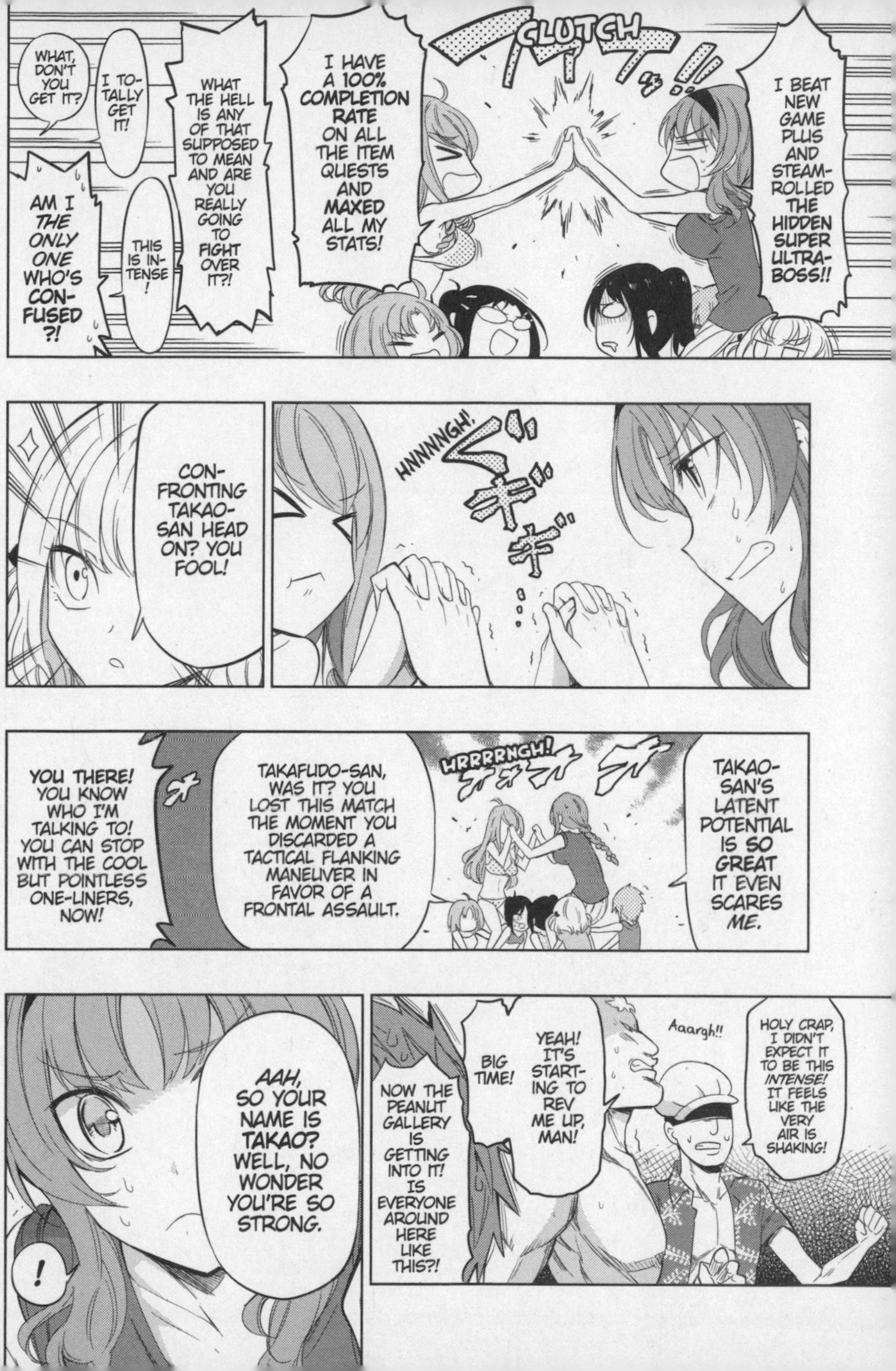
CLUTCH
I BEAT NEW GAME PLUS AND STEAM-ROLLED THE HIDDEN SUPER ULTRA-BOSS!!
I HAVE A 100% COMPLETION RATE ON ALL THE ITEM QUESTS AND MAXED ALL MY STATS!
WHAT THE HELL IS ANY OF THAT SUPPOSED TO MEAN AND ARE YOU REALLY GOING TO FIGHT OVER IT?!
I TO-TALLY GET IT!
THIS IS IN-TENSE!
WHAT, DON'T YOU GET IT?
AM I THE ONLY ONE WHO'S CON-FUSED?!
HNNNNGH!
CON-FRONTING TAKAO-SAN HEAD ON? YOU FOOL!
TAKAO-SAN'S LATENT POTENTIAL IS SO GREAT IT EVEN SCARES ME.
HRRRRNGH!
TAKAFUDO-SAN, WAS IT? YOU LOST THIS MATCH THE MOMENT YOU DISCARDED A TACTICAL FLANKING MANEUVER IN FAVOR OF A FRONTAL ASSAULT.
YOU THERE! YOU KNOW WHO I'M TALKING TO! YOU CAN STOP WITH THE COOL BUT POINTLESS ONE-LINERS, NOW!
HOLY CRAP, I DIDN'T EXPECT IT TO BE THIS INTENSE! IT FEELS LIKE THE VERY AIR IS SHAKING!
Aaargh!!
YEAH! IT'S START-ING TO REV ME UP, MAN!
BIG TIME!
NOW THE PEANUT GALLERY IS GETTING INTO IT! IS EVERYONE AROUND HERE LIKE THIS?!
AAH, SO YOUR NAME IS TAKAO? WELL, NO WONDER YOU'RE SO STRONG.
!

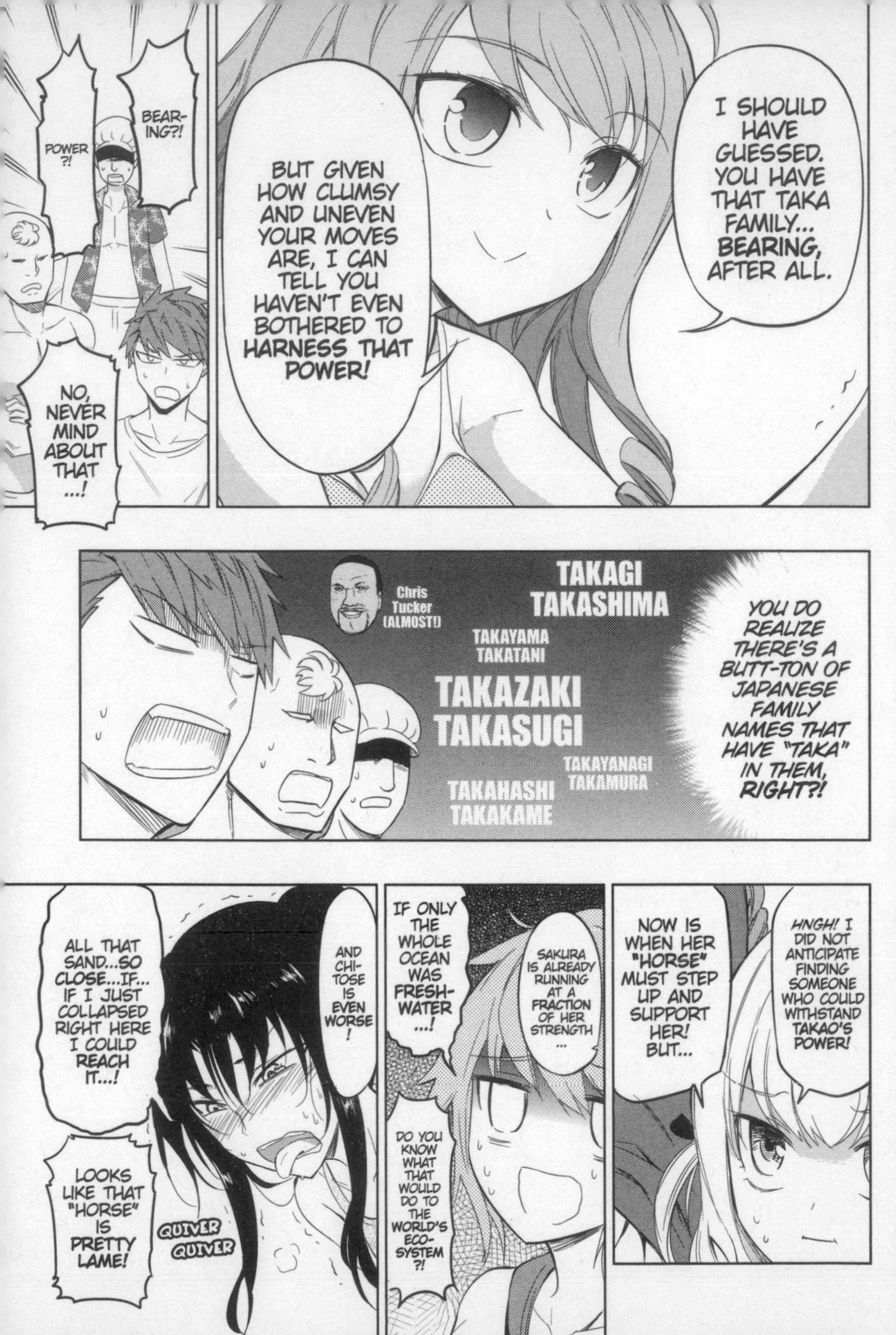
I SHOULD HAVE GUESSED. YOU HAVE THAT TAKA FAMILY... BEARING, AFTER ALL.
BUT GIVEN HOW CLUMSY AND UNEVEN YOUR MOVES ARE, I CAN TELL YOU HAVEN'T EVEN BOTHERED TO HARNESS THAT POWER!
BEAR-ING?!
POWER ?!
NO, NEVER MIND ABOUT THAT ....!
YOU DO REALIZE THERE'S A BUTT-TON OF JAPANESE FAMILY NAMES THAT HAVE "TAKA" IN THEM, RIGHT?!
TAKAGI
TAKASHIMA
Chris Tucker (ALMOST!)
TAKAYAMA
TAKATANI
TAKAZAKI
TAKASUGI
TAKAYANAGI
TAKAMURA
TAKAHASHI
TAKAKAME
HNGH! I DID NOT ANTICIPATE FINDING SOMEONE WHO COULD WITHSTAND TAKAO'S POWER!
NOW IS WHEN HER "HORSE" MUST STEP UP AND SUPPORT HER! BUT...
SAKURA IS ALREADY RUNNING AT A FRACTION OF HER STRENGTH ...
IF ONLY THE WHOLE OCEAN WAS FRESH-WATER ...!
DO YOU KNOW WHAT THAT WOULD DO TO THE WORLD'S ECO-SYSTEM ?!
AND CHI-TOSE IS EVEN WORSE !
ALL THAT SAND...SO CLOSE...IF... IF I JUST COLLAPSED RIGHT HERE I COULD REACH IT...!
LOOKS LIKE THAT "HORSE" IS PRETTY LAME!
QUIVER QUIVER

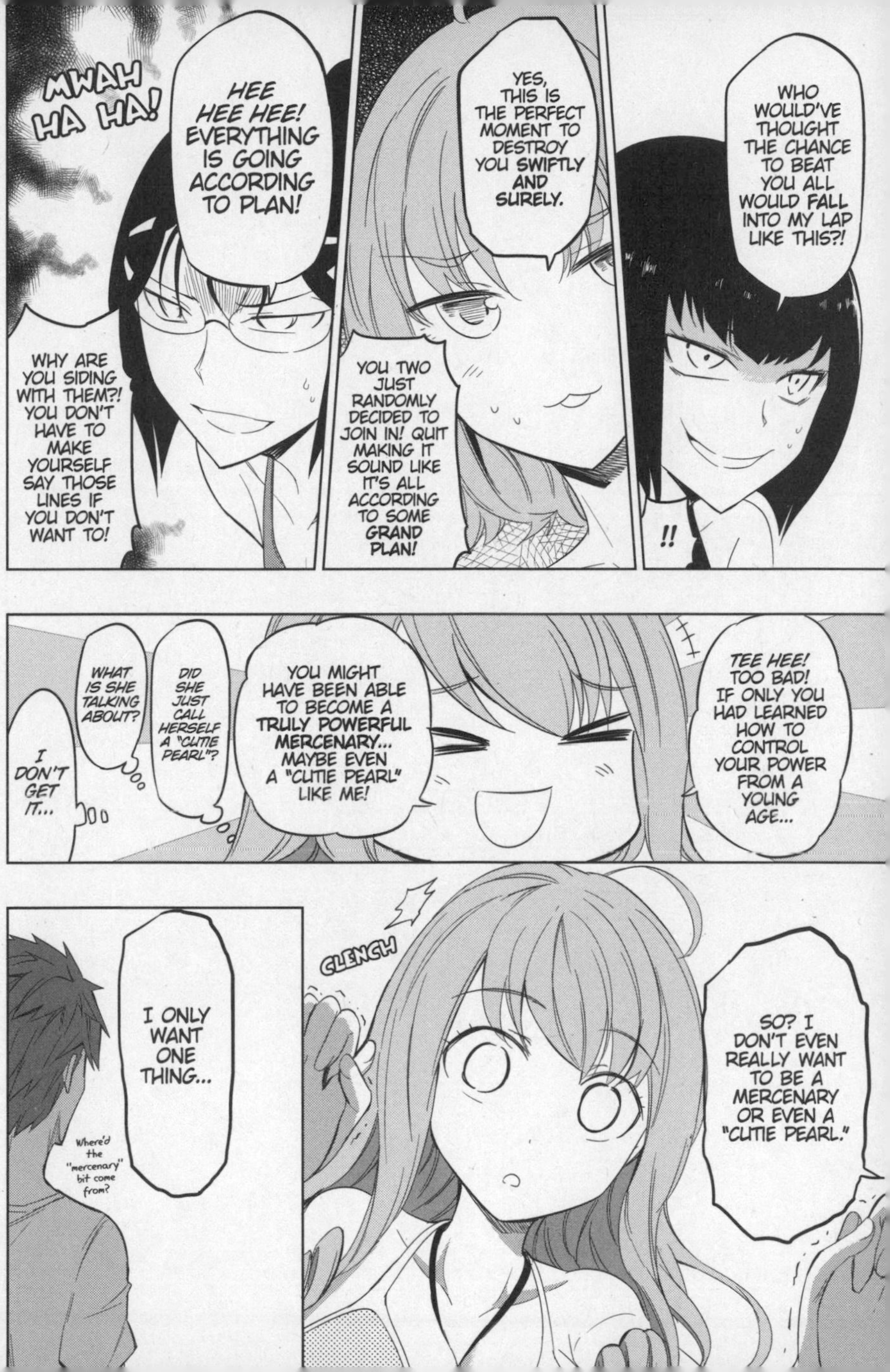

WHO WOULD'VE THOUGHT THE CHANCE TO BEAT YOU ALL WOULD FALL INTO MY LAP LIKE THIS?!
!!
YES, THIS IS THE PERFECT MOMENT TO DESTROY YOU SWIFTLY AND SURELY.
YOU TWO JUST RANDOMLY DECIDED TO JOIN IN! QUIT MAKING IT SOUND LIKE IT'S ALL ACCORDING TO SOME GRAND PLAN!
HEE HEE HEE! EVERYTHING IS GOING ACCORDING TO PLAN!
MWAH HA HA!
WHY ARE YOU SIDING WITH THEM?! YOU DON'T HAVE TO MAKE YOURSELF SAY THOSE LINES IF YOU DON'T WANT TO!
TEE HEE! TOO BAD! IF ONLY YOU HAD LEARNED HOW TO CONTROL YOUR POWER FROM A YOUNG AGE...
YOU MIGHT HAVE BEEN ABLE TO BECOME A TRULY POWERFUL MERCENARY... MAYBE EVEN A "CUTIE PEARL" LIKE ME!
DID SHE JUST CALL HERSELF A "CUTIE PEARL"?
WHAT IS SHE TALKING ABOUT?
I DON'T GET IT...
SO? I DON'T EVEN REALLY WANT TO BE A MERCENARY OR EVEN A "CUTIE PEARL."
CLENCH
I ONLY WANT ONE THING...
Where'd the "mercenary" bit come from?

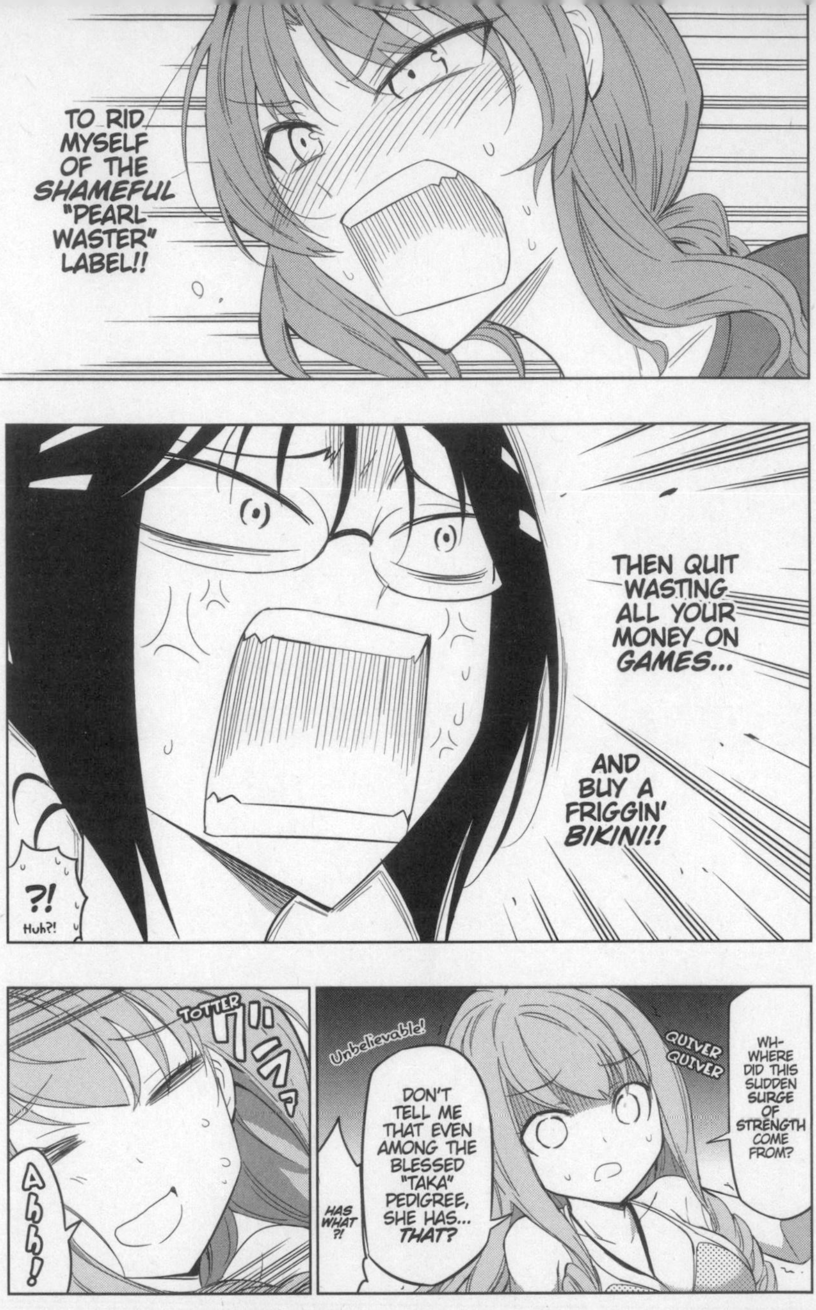
TO RID MYSELF OF THE SHAMEFUL "PEARL WASTER" LABEL!!
THEN QUIT WASTING ALL YOUR MONEY ON GAMES...
AND BUY A FRIGGIN' BIKINI!!
?!
Huh?!
QUIVER QUIVER
WH-WHERE DID THIS SUDDEN SURGE OF STRENGTH COME FROM?
Unbelievable!
DON'T TELL ME THAT EVEN AMONG THE BLESSED "TAKA" PEDIGREE, SHE HAS... THAT?
HAS WHAT?!
TOTTER
Ahh!

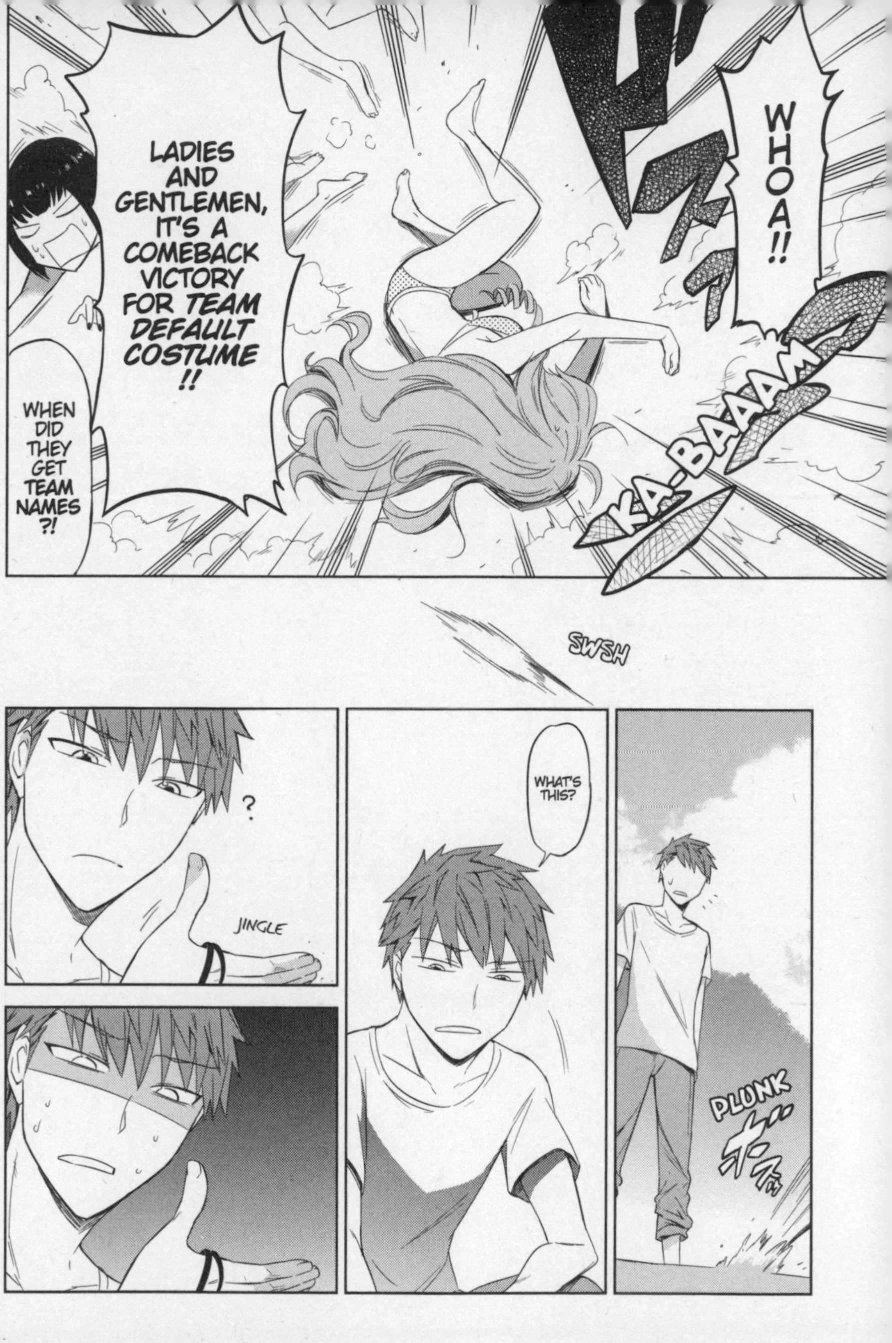
WHOA!!
KA-BAAAM!!
LADIES AND GENTLEMEN, IT'S A COMEBACK VICTORY FOR TEAM DEFAULT COSTUME!!
WHEN DID THEY GET TEAM NAMES?!
SWSH
PLUNK
WHAT'S THIS?
?
JINGLE

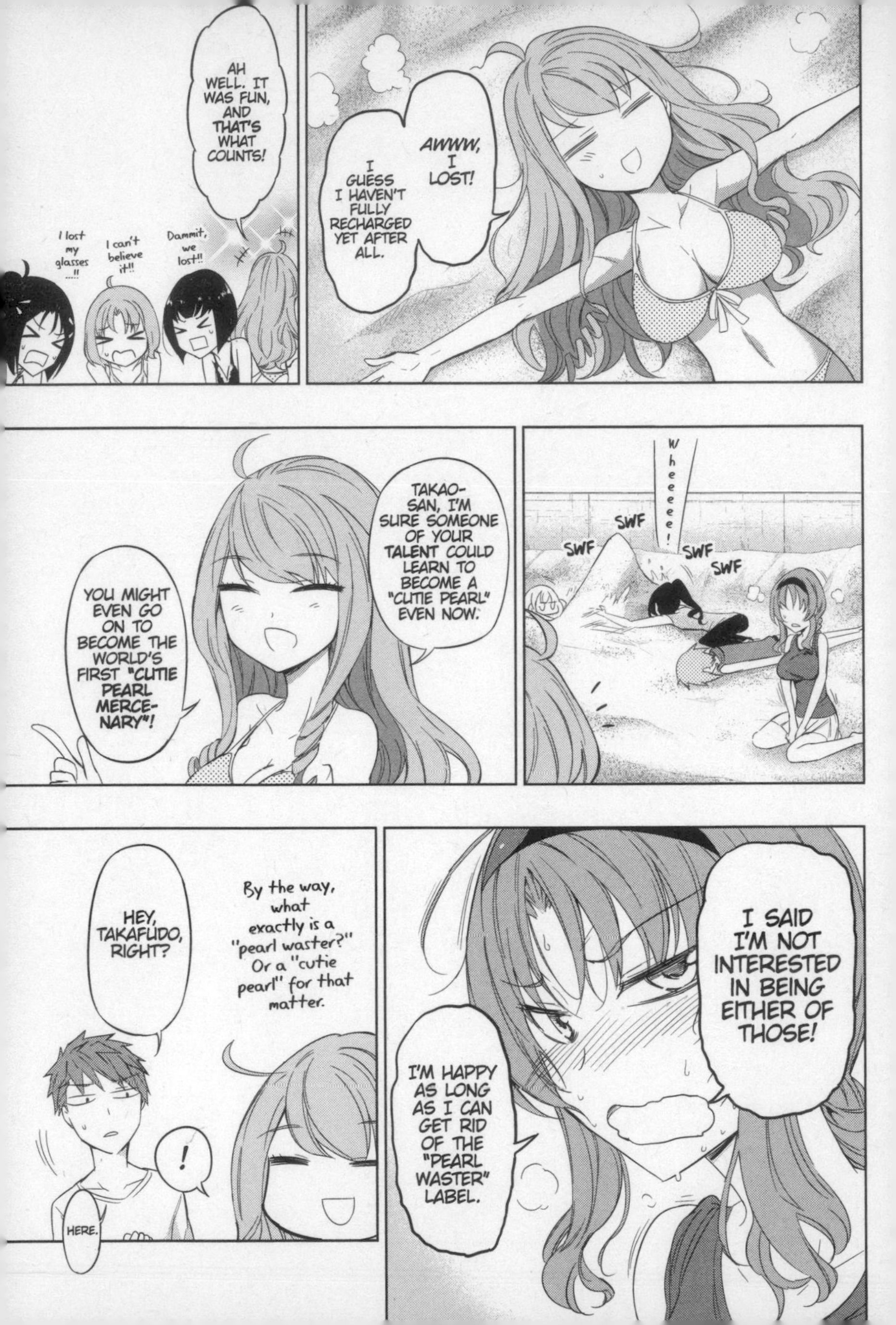
AWWW, I LOST!
I GUESS I HAVEN'T FULLY RECHARGED YET AFTER ALL.
AH WELL. IT WAS FUN, AND THAT'S WHAT COUNTS!
Dammit, we lost!!
I can't believe it!!
I lost my glasses .....!!
Wheeeee!
SWF
SWF
SWF
SWF
TAKAO-SAN, I'M SURE SOMEONE OF YOUR TALENT COULD LEARN TO BECOME A "CUTIE PEARL" EVEN NOW.
YOU MIGHT EVEN GO ON TO BECOME THE WORLD'S FIRST "CUTIE PEARL MERCENARY"!
I SAID I'M NOT INTERESTED IN BEING EITHER OF THOSE!
I'M HAPPY AS LONG AS I CAN GET RID OF THE "PEARL WASTER" LABEL.
By the way, what exactly is a "pearl waster?" Or a "cutie pearl" for that matter.
HEY, TAKAFUDO, RIGHT?
!
HERE.

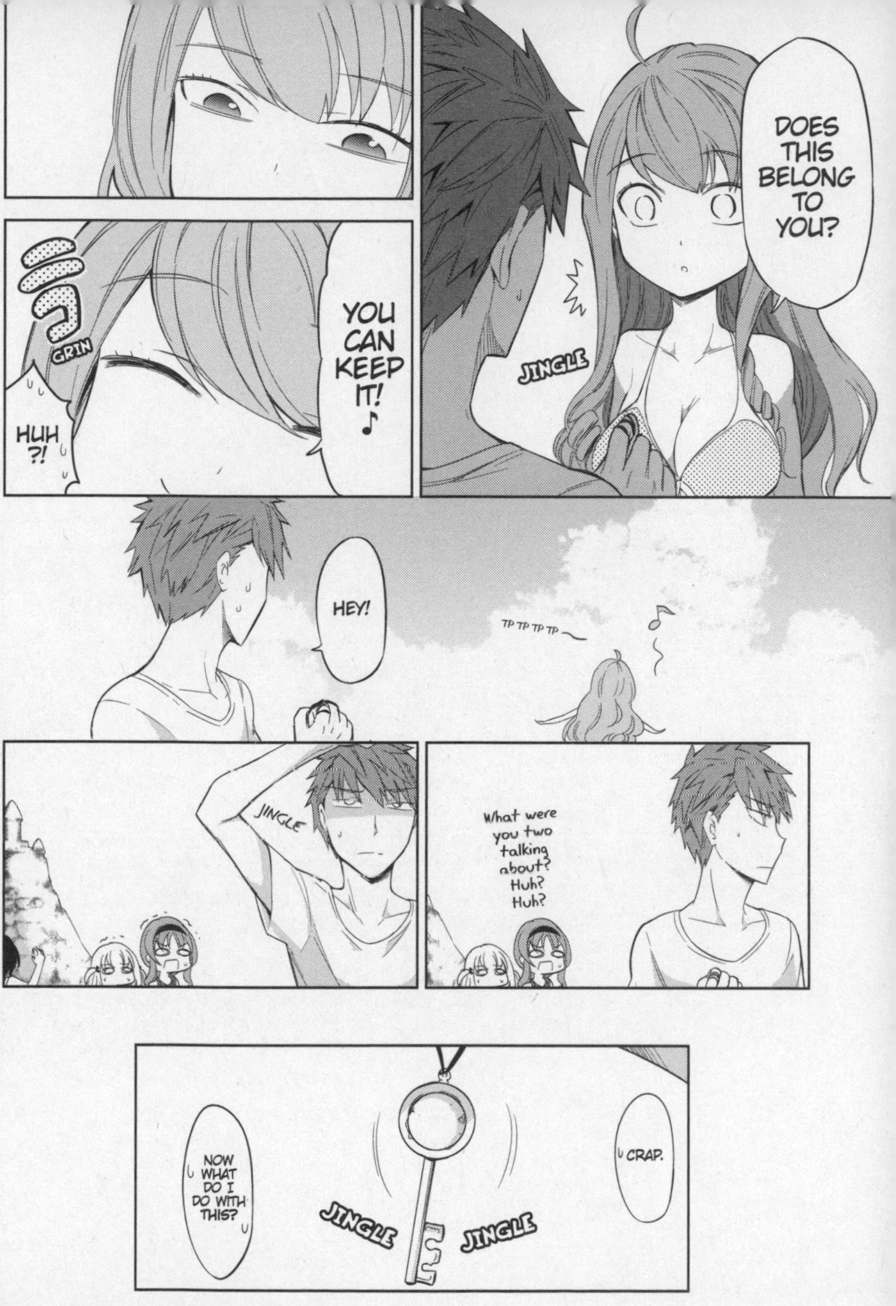
DOES THIS BELONG TO YOU?
JINGLE
YOU CAN KEEP IT! ♪
GRIN
HUH ?!
HEY!
TP TP TP TP
What were you two talking about? Huh? Huh?
JINGLE
CRAP.
NOW WHAT DO I DO WITH THIS?
JINGLE
JINGLE

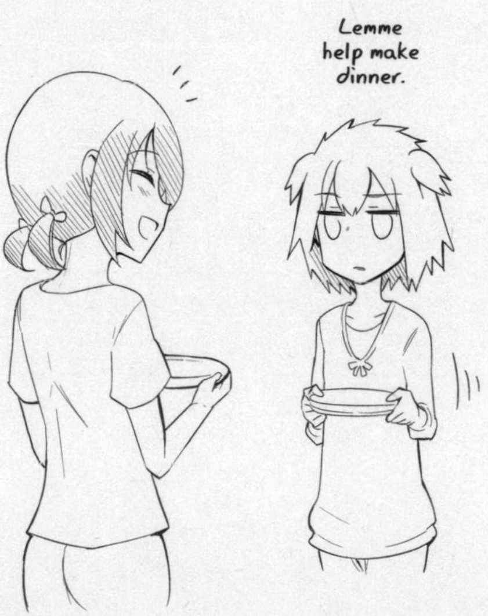
Lemme help make dinner.

D-FRAGMENTS

ディーふらぐ!

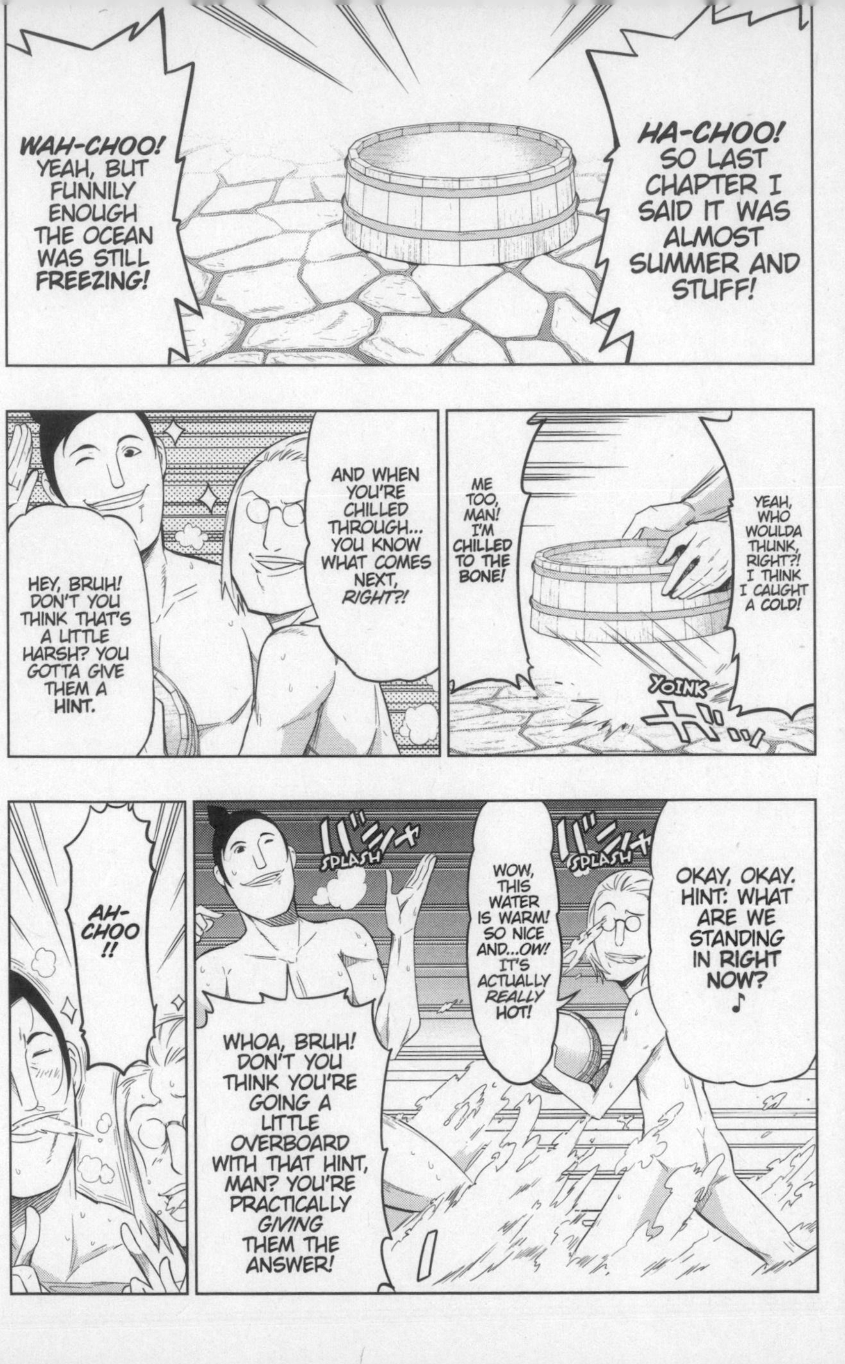
HA-CHOO! SO LAST CHAPTER I SAID IT WAS ALMOST SUMMER AND STUFF!
WAH-CHOO! YEAH, BUT FUNNILY ENOUGH THE OCEAN WAS STILL FREEZING!
YEAH, WHO WOULDA THUNK, RIGHT?! I THINK I CAUGHT A COLD!
ME TOO, MAN! I'M CHILLED TO THE BONE!
YOINK
AND WHEN YOU'RE CHILLED THROUGH... YOU KNOW WHAT COMES NEXT, *RIGHT?!*
HEY, BRUH! DON'T YOU THINK THAT'S A LITTLE HARSH? YOU GOTTA GIVE THEM A HINT.
OKAY, OKAY. HINT: WHAT ARE WE STANDING IN RIGHT NOW? ♪
SPLASH
WOW, THIS WATER IS WARM! SO NICE AND...OW! IT'S ACTUALLY *REALLY* HOT!
SPLASH
WHOA, BRUH! DON'T YOU THINK YOU'RE GOING A LITTLE OVERBOARD WITH THAT HINT, MAN? YOU'RE PRACTICALLY *GIVING* THEM THE ANSWER!
AH-CHOO!!

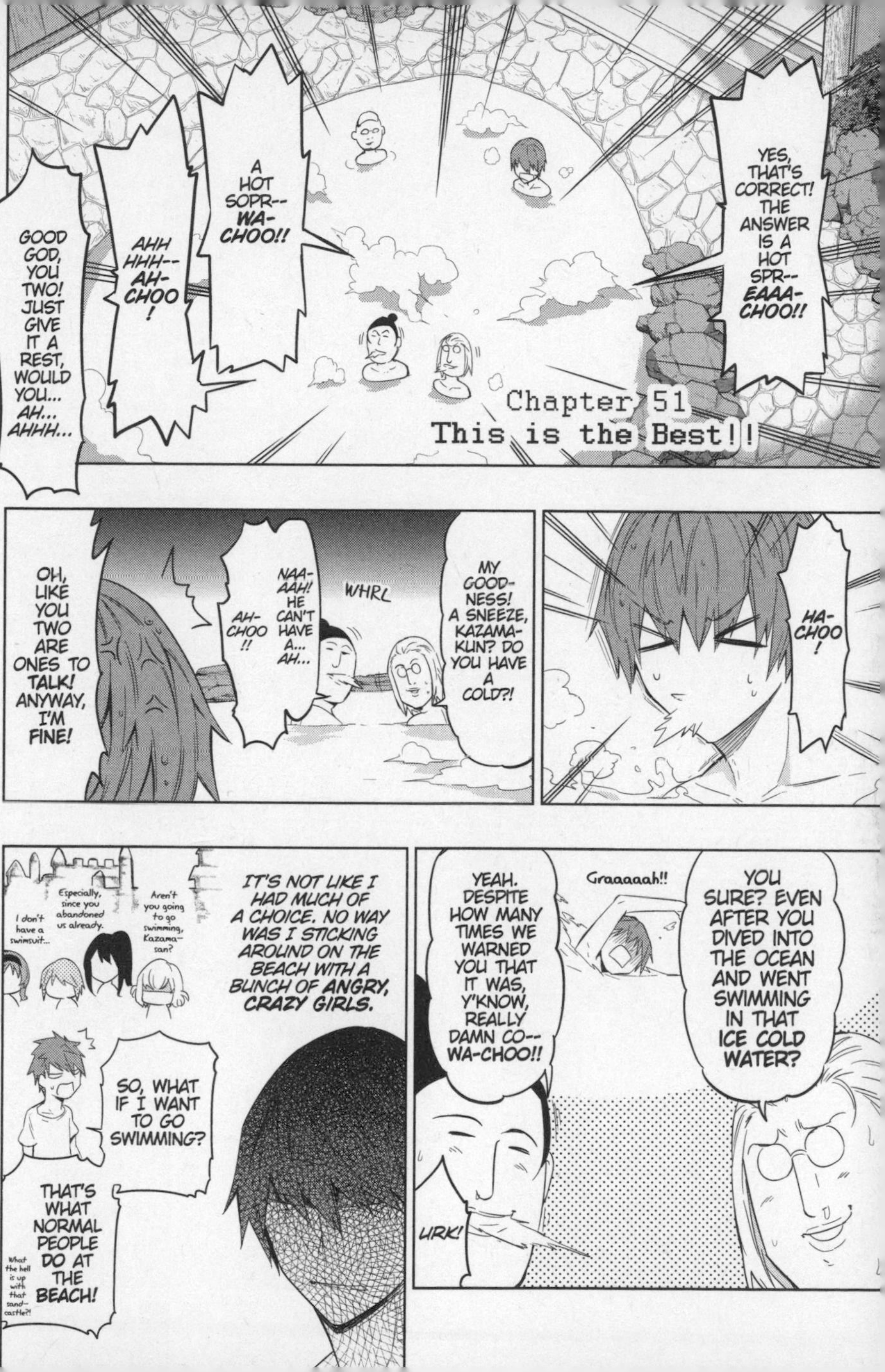
YES, THAT'S CORRECT! THE ANSWER IS A HOT SPR-- EAAA-CHOO!!
A HOT SOPR-- WA-CHOO!!
AHH HHH-- AH-CHOO!
GOOD GOD, YOU TWO! JUST GIVE IT A REST, WOULD YOU... AH... AHHH...
Chapter 51
This is the Best!!
HA-CHOO!
MY GOODNESS! A SNEEZE, KAZAMA-KUN? DO YOU HAVE A COLD?!
WHRL
NAA-AAH! HE CAN'T HAVE A... AH...
AH-CHOO!!
OH, LIKE YOU TWO ARE ONES TO TALK! ANYWAY, I'M FINE!
YOU SURE? EVEN AFTER YOU DIVED INTO THE OCEAN AND WENT SWIMMING IN THAT ICE COLD WATER?
Graaaaah!!
YEAH. DESPITE HOW MANY TIMES WE WARNED YOU THAT IT WAS, Y'KNOW, REALLY DAMN CO-- WA-CHOO!!
URK!
IT'S NOT LIKE I HAD MUCH OF A CHOICE. NO WAY WAS I STICKING AROUND ON THE BEACH WITH A BUNCH OF ANGRY, CRAZY GIRLS.
Aren't you going to go swimming, Kazama-san?
Especially, since you abandoned us already.
I don't have a swimsuit...
SO, WHAT IF I WANT TO GO SWIMMING?
THAT'S WHAT NORMAL PEOPLE DO AT THE BEACH!
What the hell is up with that sand-castle?!

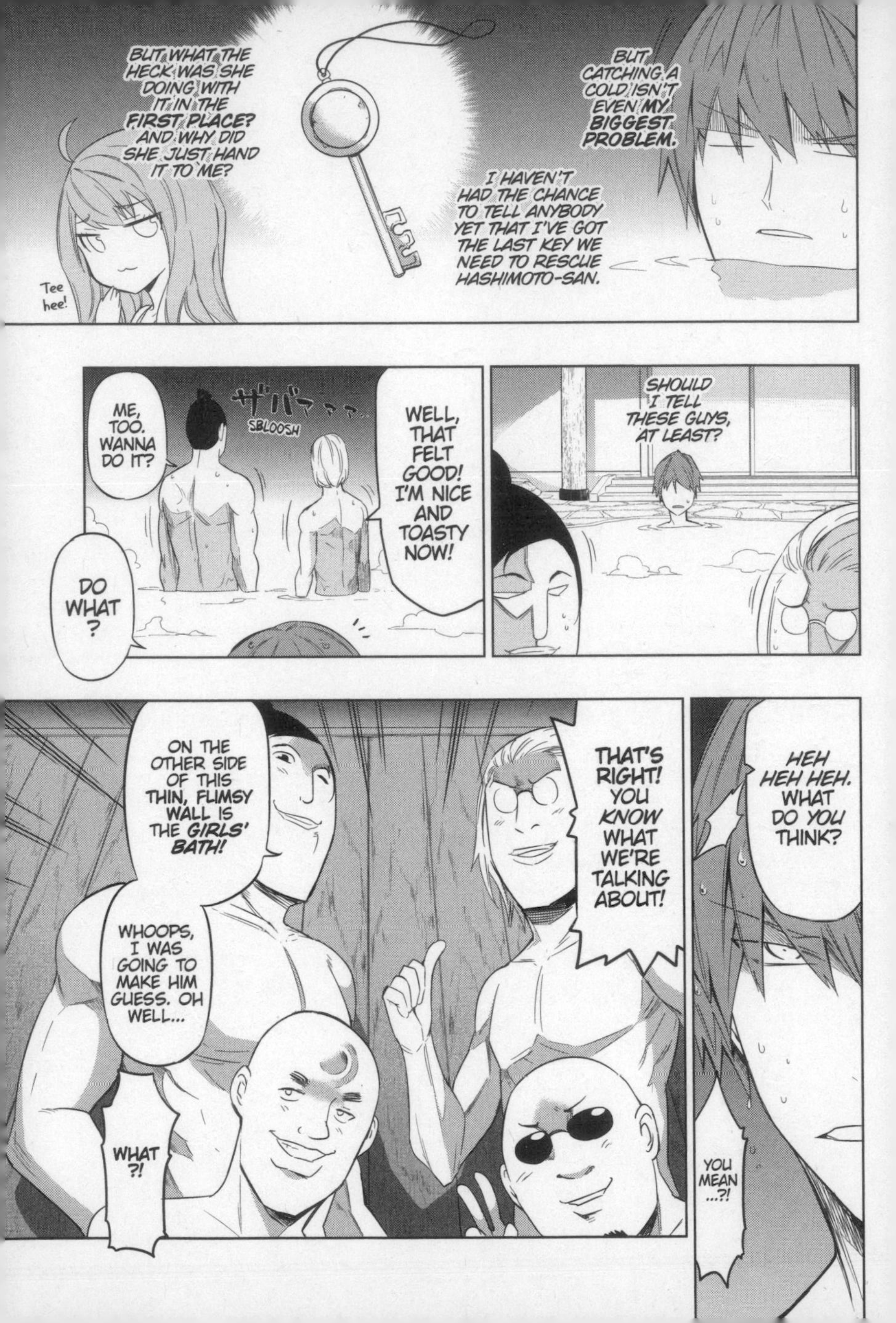
BUT CATCHING A COLD ISN'T EVEN MY BIGGEST PROBLEM.
I HAVEN'T HAD THE CHANCE TO TELL ANYBODY YET THAT I'VE GOT THE LAST KEY WE NEED TO RESCUE HASHIMOTO-SAN.
BUT WHAT THE HECK WAS SHE DOING WITH IT IN THE FIRST PLACE? AND WHY DID SHE JUST HAND IT TO ME?
Tee hee!
SHOULD I TELL THESE GUYS, AT LEAST?
WELL, THAT FELT GOOD! I'M NICE AND TOASTY NOW!
ザバァァァ
SBLOOSH
ME, TOO. WANNA DO IT?
DO WHAT?
HEH HEH HEH. WHAT DO YOU THINK?
YOU MEAN ...?!
THAT'S RIGHT! YOU KNOW WHAT WE'RE TALKING ABOUT!
ON THE OTHER SIDE OF THIS THIN, FLIMSY WALL IS THE GIRLS' BATH!
WHOOPS, I WAS GOING TO MAKE HIM GUESS. OH WELL...
WHAT?!

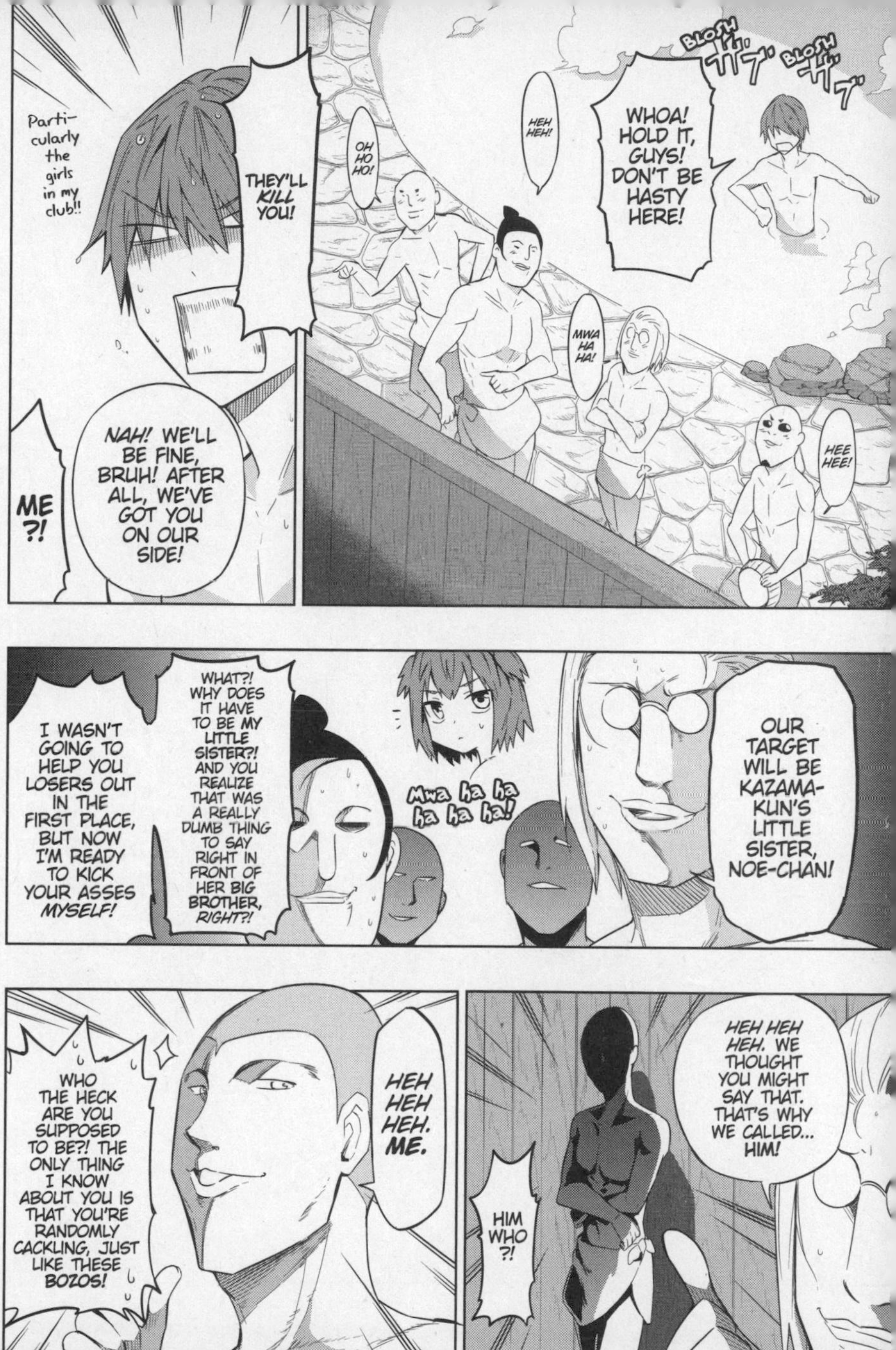
BLOSH
BLOSH
WHOA! HOLD IT, GUYS! DON'T BE HASTY HERE!
HEH HEH!
OH HO HO!
MWA HA HA!
HEE HEE!
THEY'LL *KILL* YOU!
Particularly the girls in my club!!
NAH! WE'LL BE FINE, BRUH! AFTER ALL, WE'VE GOT YOU ON OUR SIDE!
ME ?!
OUR TARGET WILL BE KAZAMA-KUN'S LITTLE SISTER, NOE-CHAN!
Mwa ha ha ha ha ha!
WHAT?! WHY DOES IT HAVE TO BE MY LITTLE SISTER?! AND YOU REALIZE THAT WAS A REALLY DUMB THING TO SAY RIGHT IN FRONT OF HER BIG BROTHER, *RIGHT?!*
I WASN'T GOING TO HELP YOU LOSERS OUT IN THE FIRST PLACE, BUT NOW I'M READY TO KICK YOUR ASSES *MYSELF!*
HEH HEH HEH. WE THOUGHT YOU MIGHT SAY THAT. THAT'S WHY WE CALLED... HIM!
HIM WHO ?!
HEH HEH HEH. ME.
WHO THE HECK ARE YOU SUPPOSED TO BE?! THE ONLY THING I KNOW ABOUT YOU IS THAT YOU'RE RANDOMLY CACKLING, JUST LIKE THESE BOZOS!

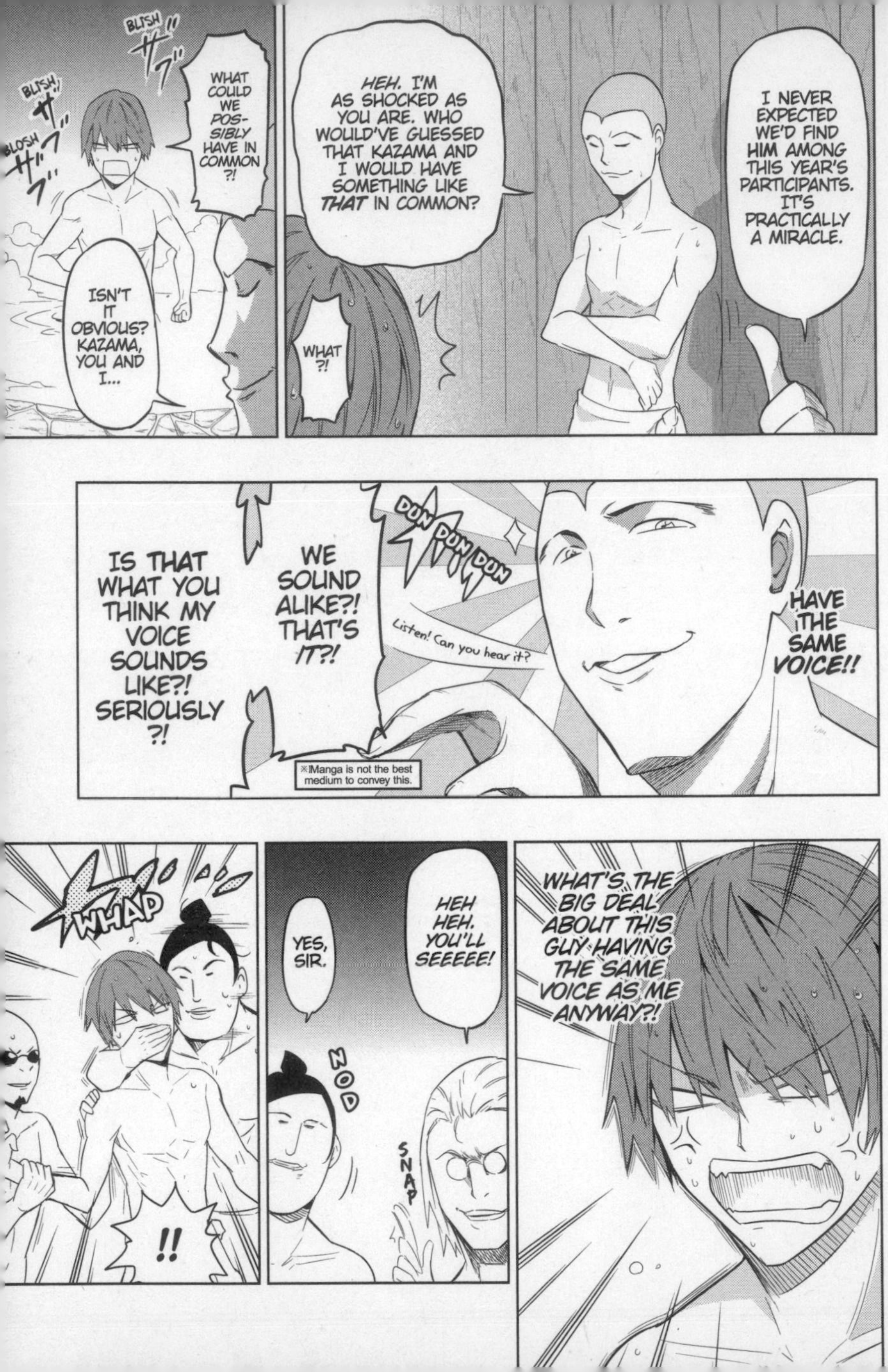
I NEVER EXPECTED WE'D FIND HIM AMONG THIS YEAR'S PARTICIPANTS. IT'S PRACTICALLY A MIRACLE.
HEH. I'M AS SHOCKED AS YOU ARE. WHO WOULD'VE GUESSED THAT KAZAMA AND I WOULD HAVE SOMETHING LIKE THAT IN COMMON?
WHAT ?!
BLISH
BLISH
BLOSH
WHAT COULD WE POS-SIBLY HAVE IN COMMON ?!
ISN'T IT OBVIOUS? KAZAMA, YOU AND I...
HAVE THE SAME VOICE!!
DUN DUN DUN
Listen! Can you hear it?
WE SOUND ALIKE?! THAT'S IT?!
IS THAT WHAT YOU THINK MY VOICE SOUNDS LIKE?! SERIOUSLY ?!
※Manga is not the best medium to convey this.
WHAT'S THE BIG DEAL ABOUT THIS GUY HAVING THE SAME VOICE AS ME ANYWAY?!
HEH HEH. YOU'LL SEEEEEE!
YES, SIR.
NOD
SNAP
WHAP
!!

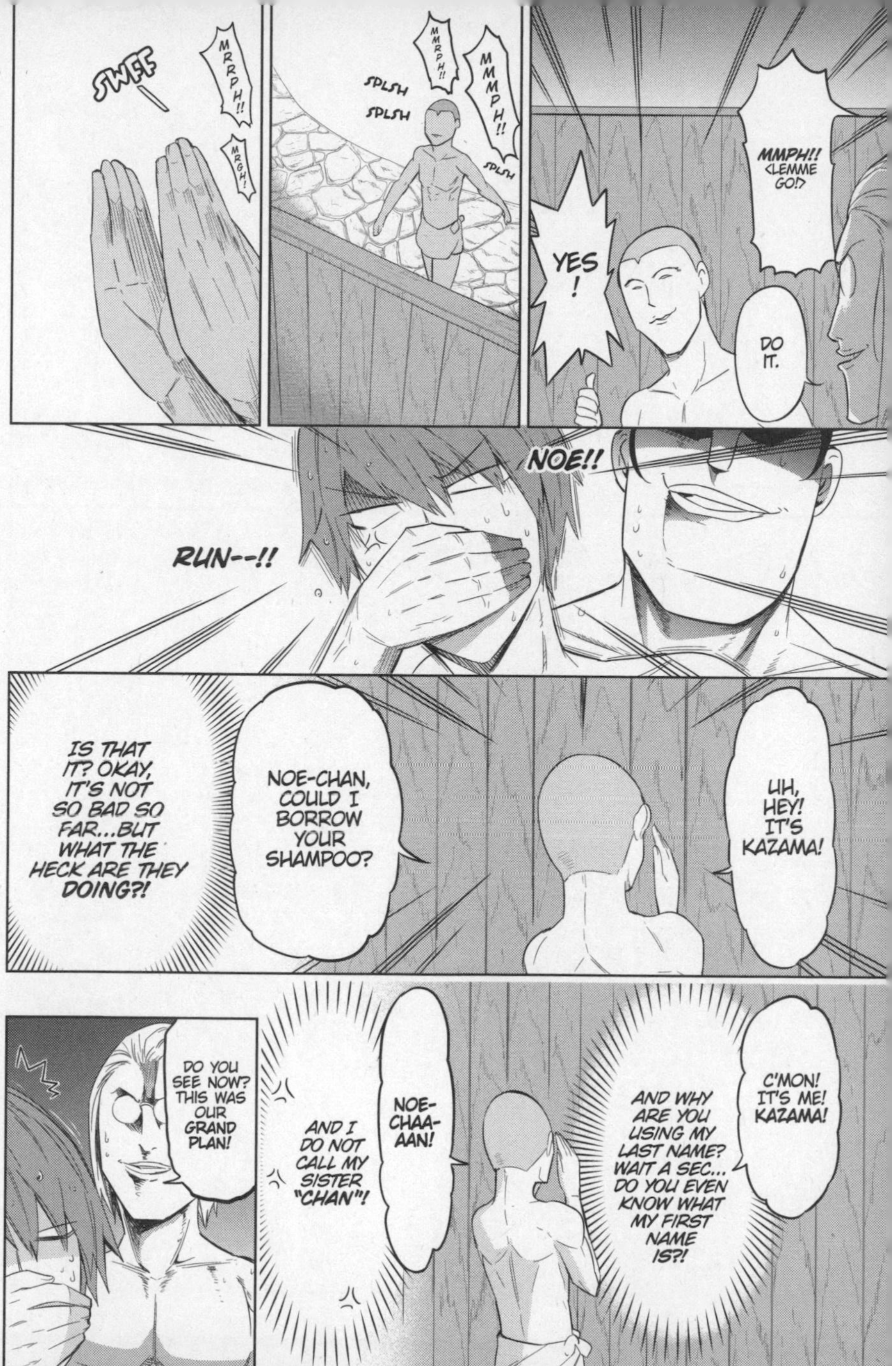
MMPH!! <LEMME GO!>
DO IT.
YES!
MMMPH!!
MMRPH!!
SPLSH
SPLSH
SPLSH
MRRPH!!
MRGH!
SWFF
NOE!!
RUN--!!
UH, HEY! IT'S KAZAMA!
NOE-CHAN, COULD I BORROW YOUR SHAMPOO?
IS THAT IT? OKAY, IT'S NOT SO BAD SO FAR...BUT WHAT THE HECK ARE THEY DOING?!
C'MON! IT'S ME! KAZAMA!
AND WHY ARE YOU USING MY LAST NAME? WAIT A SEC... DO YOU EVEN KNOW WHAT MY FIRST NAME IS?!
NOE-CHAAAAN!
AND I DO NOT CALL MY SISTER "CHAN"!
DO YOU SEE NOW? THIS WAS OUR GRAND PLAN!

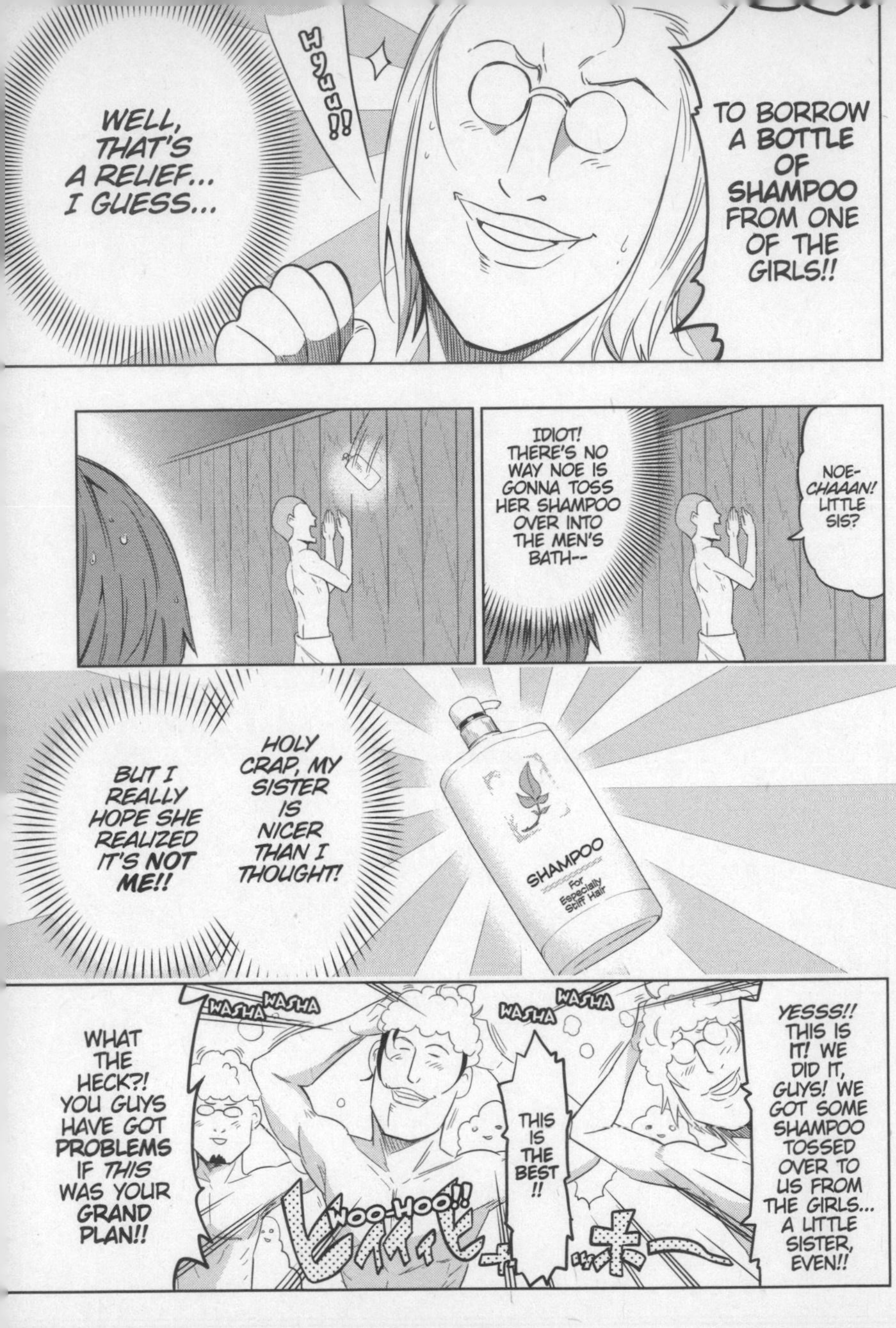
TO BORROW A BOTTLE OF SHAMPOO FROM ONE OF THE GIRLS!!
HYUUU!!
WELL, THAT'S A RELIEF... I GUESS...
NOE-CHAAAN! LITTLE SIS?
IDIOT! THERE'S NO WAY NOE IS GONNA TOSS HER SHAMPOO OVER INTO THE MEN'S BATH--
SHAMPOO
For Especially Stiff Hair
HOLY CRAP, MY SISTER IS NICER THAN I THOUGHT!
BUT I REALLY HOPE SHE REALIZED IT'S NOT ME!!
YESSS!! THIS IS IT! WE DID IT, GUYS! WE GOT SOME SHAMPOO TOSSED OVER TO US FROM THE GIRLS... A LITTLE SISTER, EVEN!!
WASHA WASHA
THIS IS THE BEST!!
WASHA WASHA
WOO-HOO!!
WHAT THE HECK?! YOU GUYS HAVE GOT PROBLEMS IF THIS WAS YOUR GRAND PLAN!!

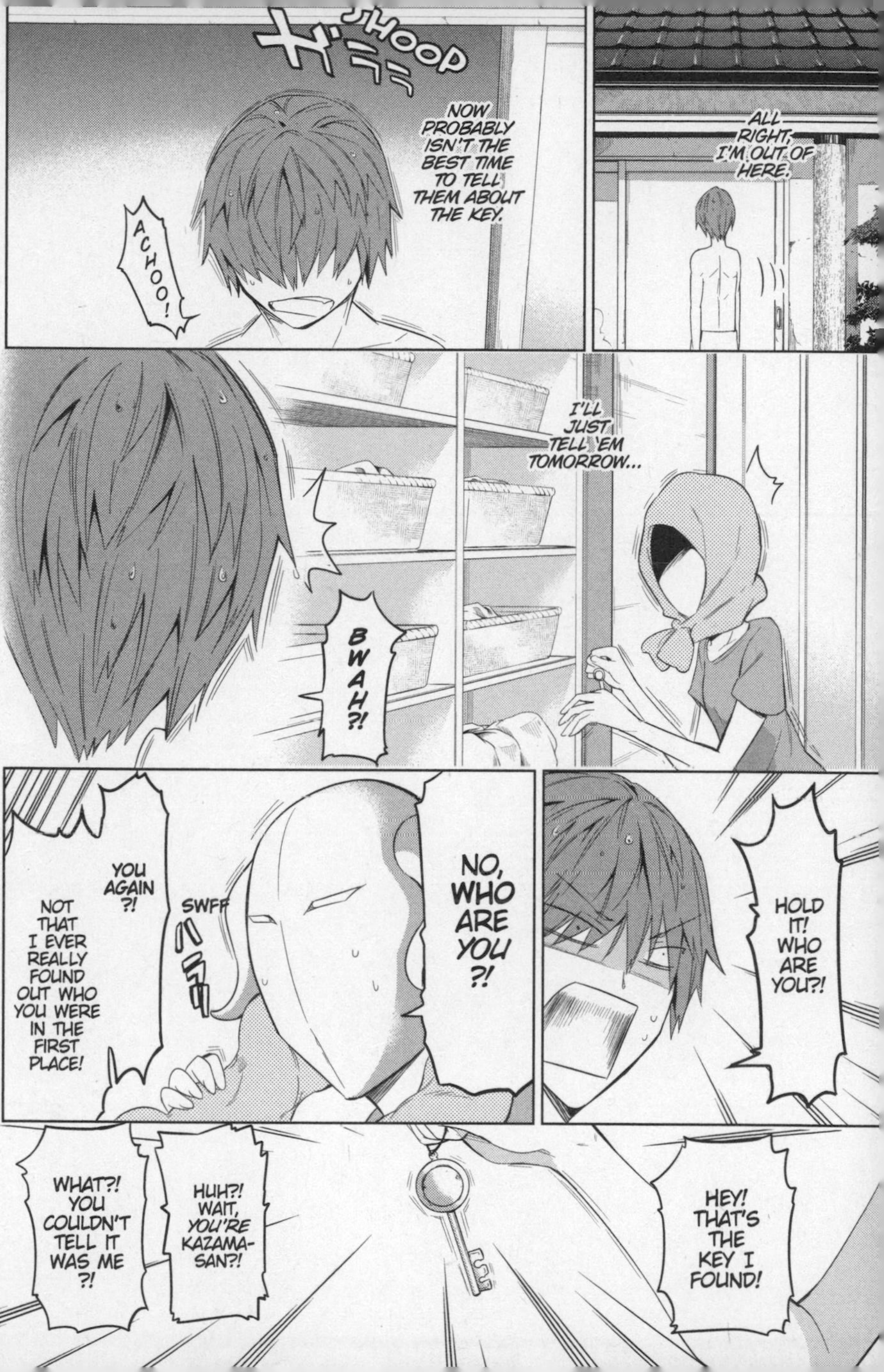
ALL RIGHT, I'M OUT OF HERE.
SHOOP
NOW PROBABLY ISN'T THE BEST TIME TO TELL THEM ABOUT THE KEY.
ACHOO!
I'LL JUST TELL 'EM TOMORROW...
BWAH?!
HOLD IT! WHO ARE YOU?!
NO, WHO ARE YOU?!
YOU AGAIN?!
SWFF
NOT THAT I EVER REALLY FOUND OUT WHO YOU WERE IN THE FIRST PLACE!
HEY! THAT'S THE KEY I FOUND!
HUH?! WAIT, YOU'RE KAZAMA-SAN?!
WHAT?! YOU COULDN'T TELL IT WAS ME?!

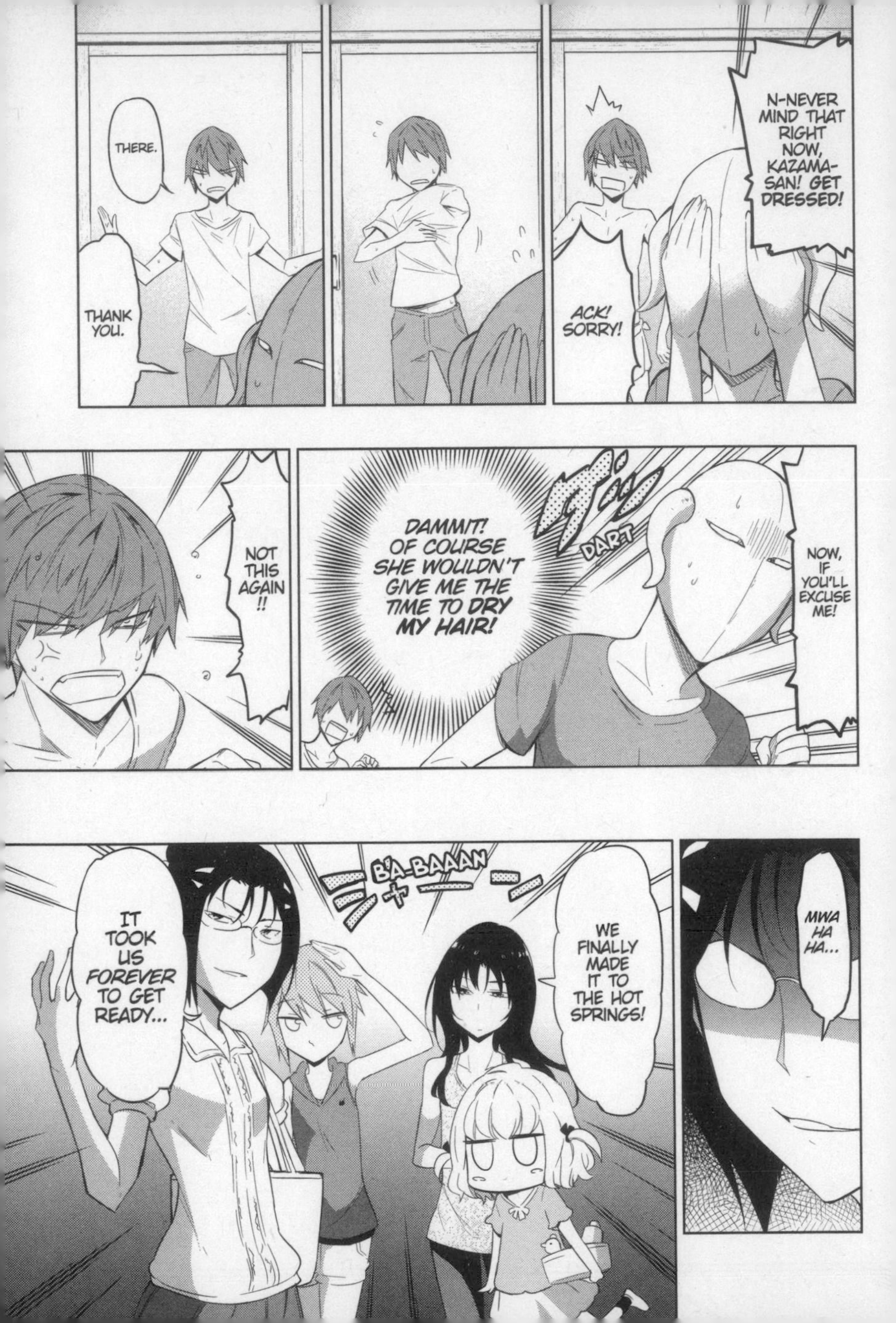
N-NEVER MIND THAT RIGHT NOW, KAZAMA-SAN! GET DRESSED!
ACK! SORRY!
THERE.
THANK YOU.
NOW, IF YOU'LL EXCUSE ME!
DART
DAMMIT! OF COURSE SHE WOULDN'T GIVE ME THE TIME TO DRY MY HAIR!
NOT THIS AGAIN!!
MWA HA HA...
WE FINALLY MADE IT TO THE HOT SPRINGS!
BA-BAAAN
IT TOOK US FOREVER TO GET READY...

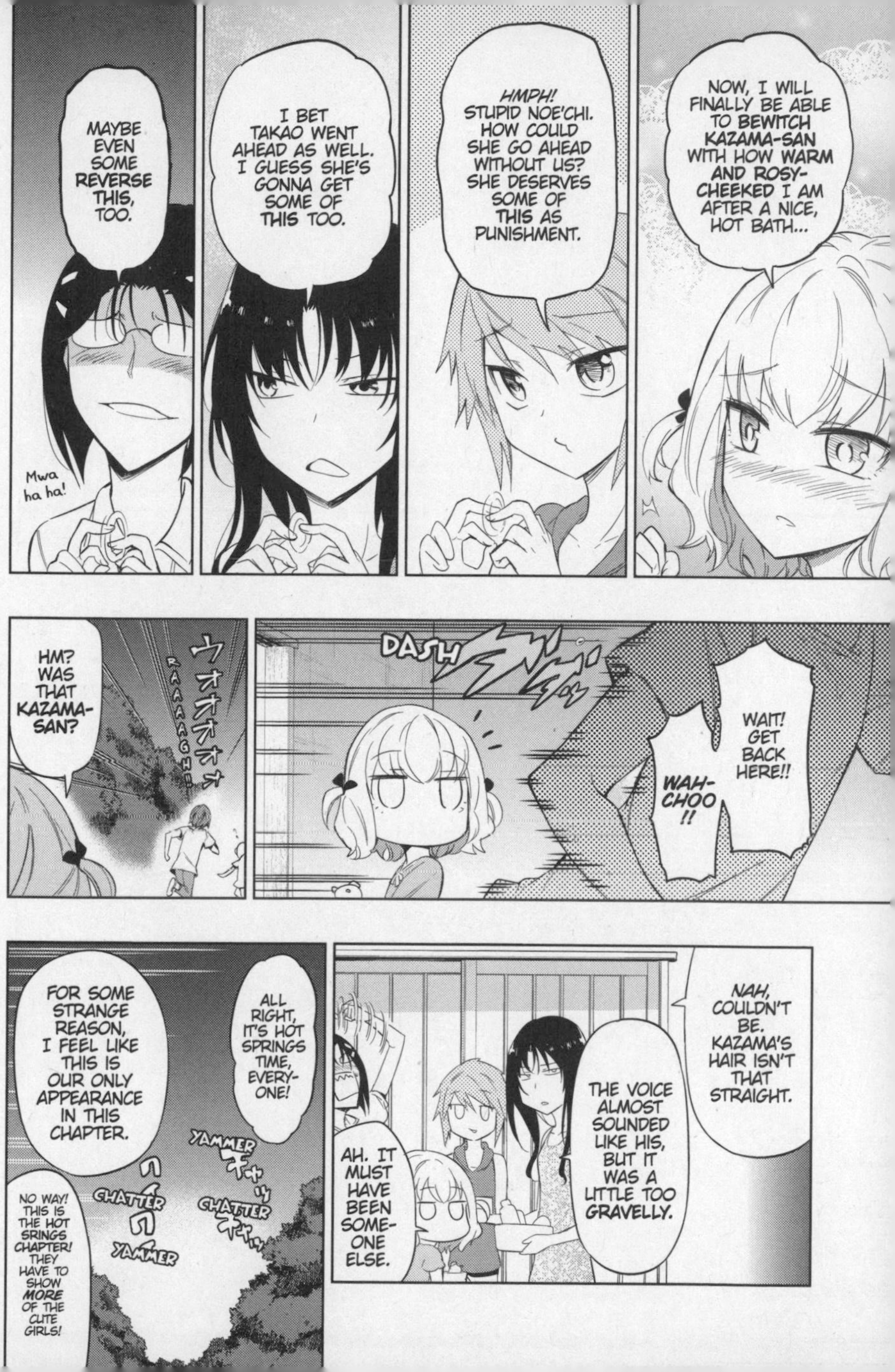
NOW, I WILL FINALLY BE ABLE TO BEWITCH KAZAMA-SAN WITH HOW WARM AND ROSY-CHEEKED I AM AFTER A NICE, HOT BATH...
HMPH! STUPID NOE'CHI. HOW COULD SHE GO AHEAD WITHOUT US? SHE DESERVES SOME OF THIS AS PUNISHMENT.
I BET TAKAO WENT AHEAD AS WELL. I GUESS SHE'S GONNA GET SOME OF THIS TOO.
MAYBE EVEN SOME REVERSE THIS, TOO.
Mwa ha ha!
DASH
WAIT! GET BACK HERE!!
WAH-CHOO!!
ウオオオオオ
RAAAAAGH!!
HM? WAS THAT KAZAMA-SAN?
NAH, COULDN'T BE. KAZAMA'S HAIR ISN'T THAT STRAIGHT.
THE VOICE ALMOST SOUNDED LIKE HIS, BUT IT WAS A LITTLE TOO GRAVELLY.
AH. IT MUST HAVE BEEN SOME-ONE ELSE.
ALL RIGHT, IT'S HOT SPRINGS TIME, EVERY-ONE!
FOR SOME STRANGE REASON, I FEEL LIKE THIS IS OUR ONLY APPEARANCE IN THIS CHAPTER.
YAMMER
CHATTER
CHATTER
YAMMER
NO WAY! THIS IS THE HOT SRINGS CHAPTER! THEY HAVE TO SHOW MORE OF THE CUTE GIRLS!

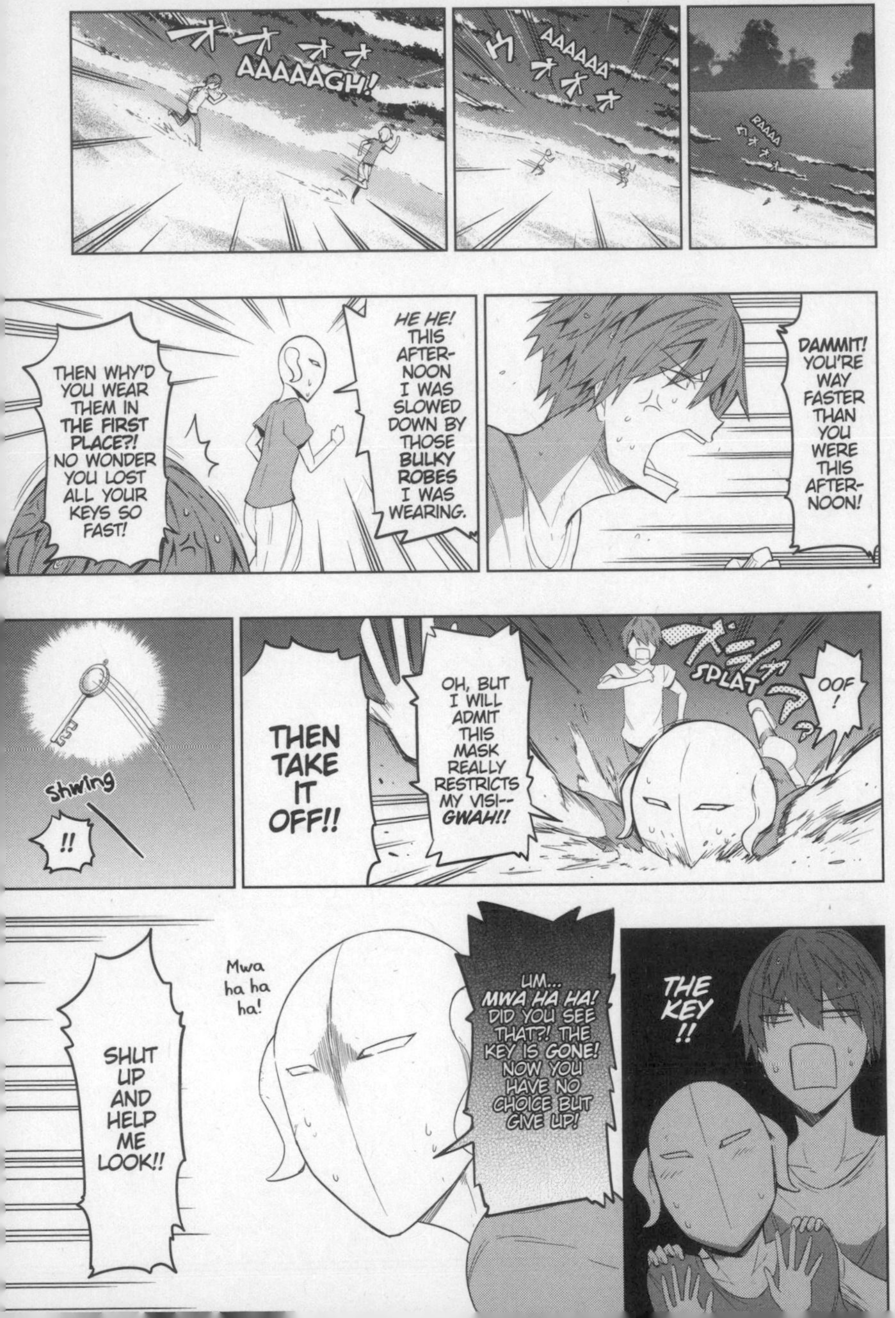
RAAAA
AAAAAA
AAAAAGH!
DAMMIT! YOU'RE WAY FASTER THAN YOU WERE THIS AFTERNOON!
HE HE! THIS AFTERNOON I WAS SLOWED DOWN BY THOSE BULKY ROBES I WAS WEARING.
THEN WHY'D YOU WEAR THEM IN THE FIRST PLACE?! NO WONDER YOU LOST ALL YOUR KEYS SO FAST!
OH, BUT I WILL ADMIT THIS MASK REALLY RESTRICTS MY VISI-- GWAH!!
SPLAT
OOF!
THEN TAKE IT OFF!!
Shwing
!!
THE KEY !!
UM... MWA HA HA! DID YOU SEE THAT?! THE KEY IS GONE! NOW YOU HAVE NO CHOICE BUT GIVE UP!
Mwa ha ha ha!
SHUT UP AND HELP ME LOOK!!

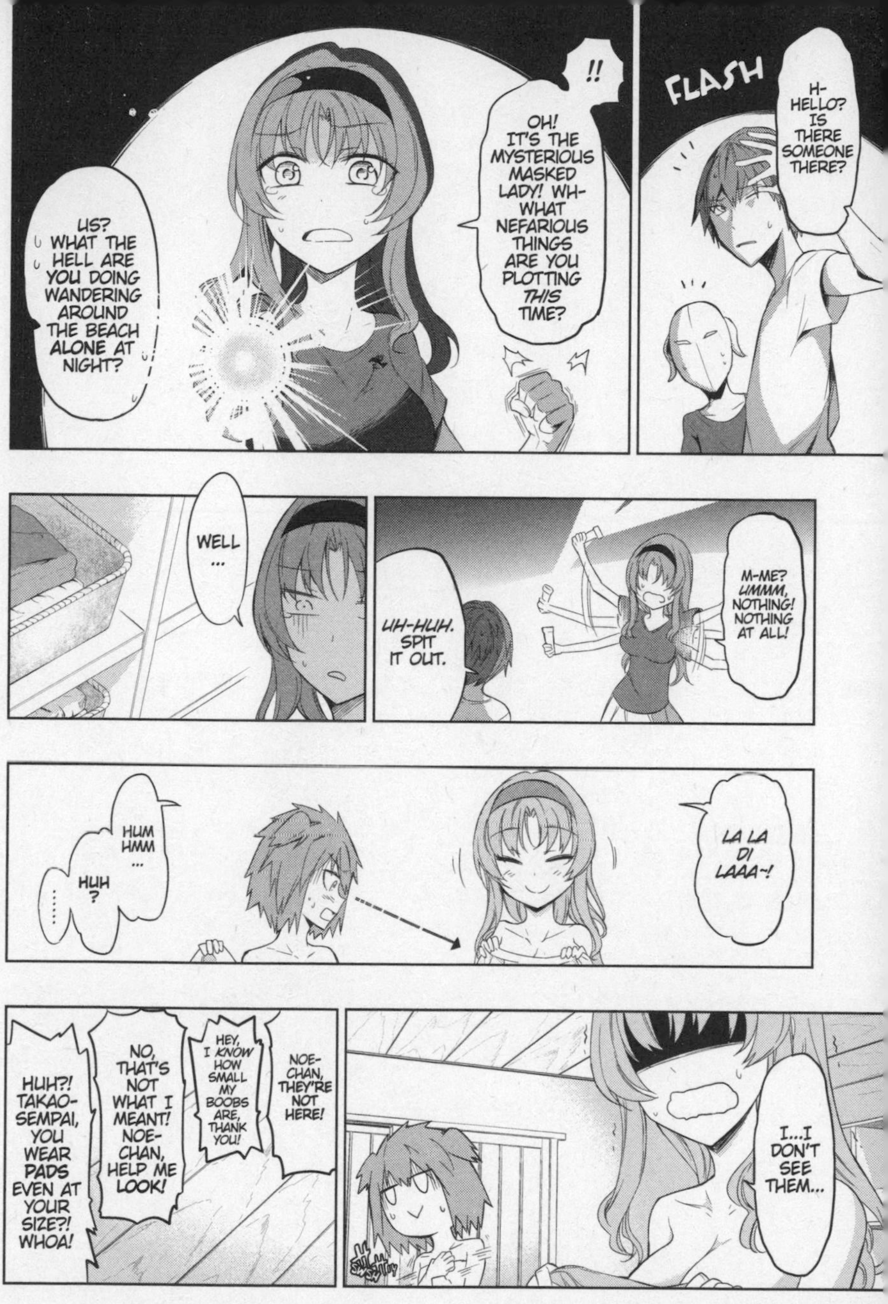
FLASH
H-HELLO? IS THERE SOMEONE THERE?
!!
OH! IT'S THE MYSTERIOUS MASKED LADY! WH-WHAT NEFARIOUS THINGS ARE YOU PLOTTING *THIS* TIME?
US? WHAT THE HELL ARE YOU DOING WANDERING AROUND THE BEACH ALONE AT NIGHT?
M-ME? *UMMM*, NOTHING! NOTHING AT ALL!
UH-HUH. SPIT IT OUT.
WELL ...
LA LA DI LAAA~!
HUM HMM ...
HUH ?
......
I...I DON'T SEE THEM...
NOE-CHAN, THEY'RE NOT HERE!
HEY, I *KNOW* HOW SMALL MY BOOBS ARE, THANK YOU!
NO, THAT'S NOT WHAT I MEANT! NOE-CHAN, HELP ME LOOK!
HUH?! TAKAO-SEMPAI, YOU WEAR PADS EVEN AT YOUR SIZE?! WHOA!

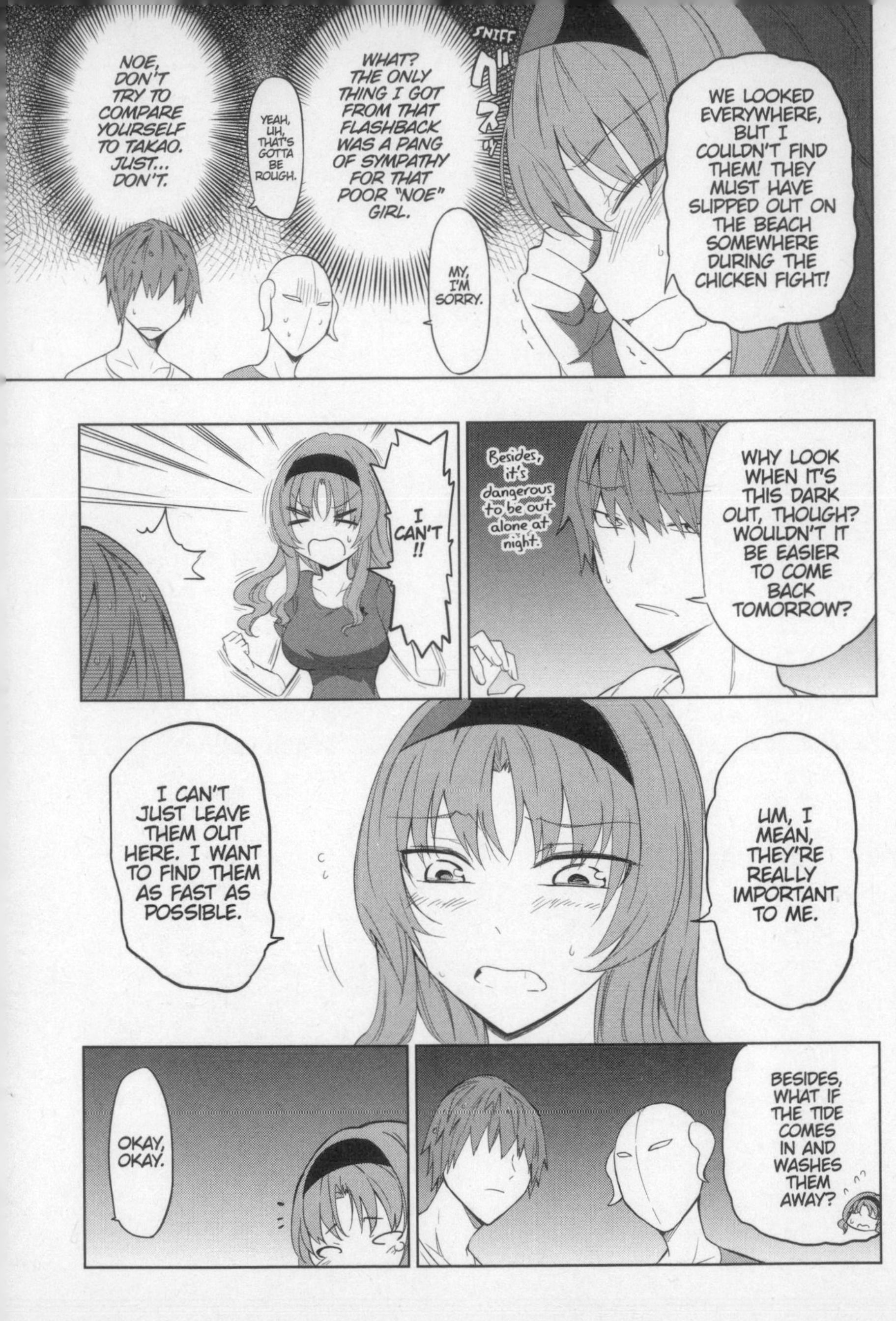
SNIFF
WE LOOKED EVERYWHERE, BUT I COULDN'T FIND THEM! THEY MUST HAVE SLIPPED OUT ON THE BEACH SOMEWHERE DURING THE CHICKEN FIGHT!
MY, I'M SORRY.
WHAT? THE ONLY THING I GOT FROM THAT FLASHBACK WAS A PANG OF SYMPATHY FOR THAT POOR "NOE" GIRL.
YEAH, UH, THAT'S GOTTA BE ROUGH.
NOE, DON'T TRY TO COMPARE YOURSELF TO TAKAO. JUST... DON'T.
WHY LOOK WHEN IT'S THIS DARK OUT, THOUGH? WOULDN'T IT BE EASIER TO COME BACK TOMORROW?
Besides, it's dangerous to be out alone at night.
I CAN'T!!
UM, I MEAN, THEY'RE REALLY IMPORTANT TO ME.
I CAN'T JUST LEAVE THEM OUT HERE. I WANT TO FIND THEM AS FAST AS POSSIBLE.
BESIDES, WHAT IF THE TIDE COMES IN AND WASHES THEM AWAY?
OKAY, OKAY.

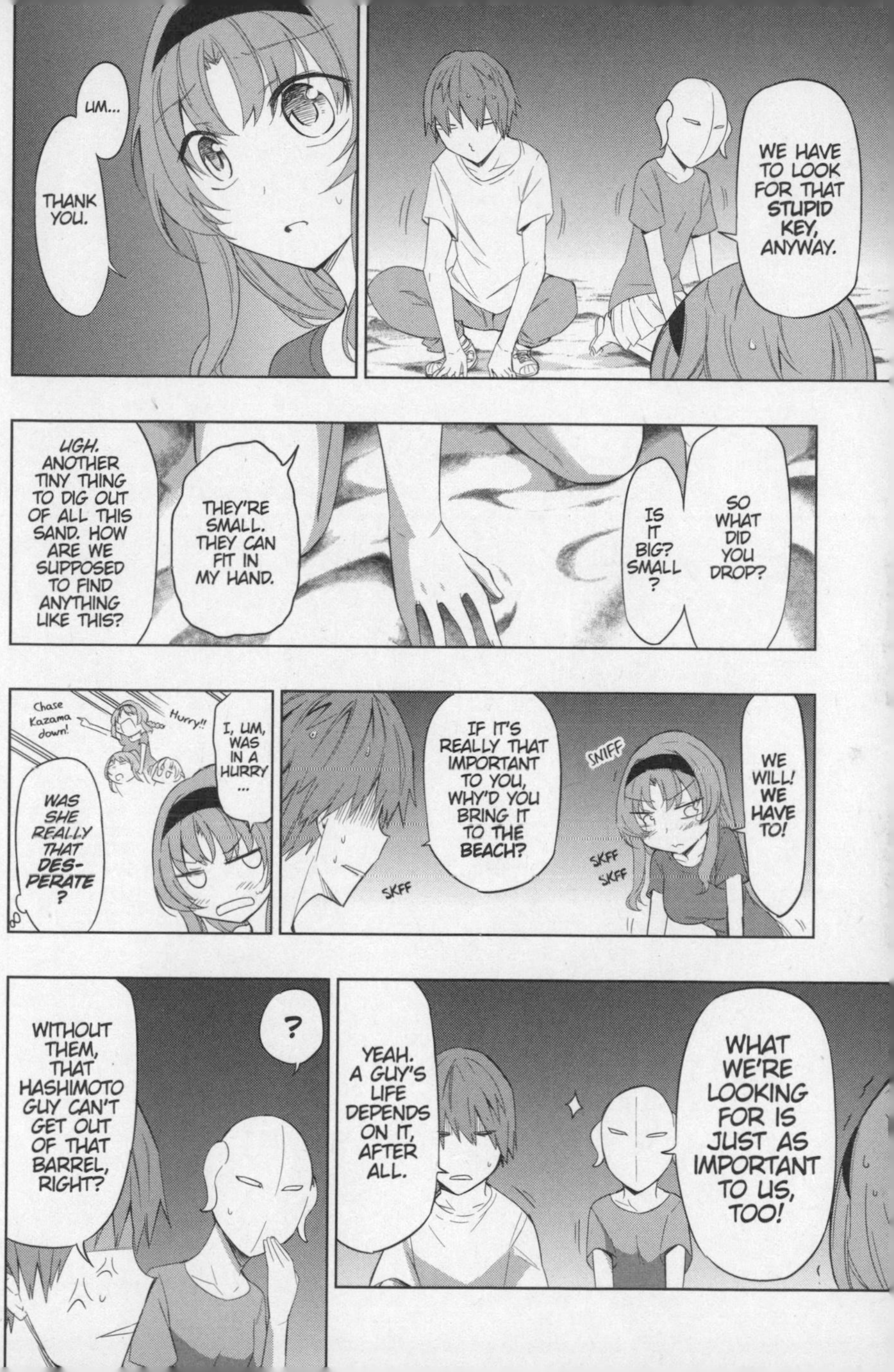
WE HAVE TO LOOK FOR THAT STUPID KEY, ANYWAY.
UM...
THANK YOU.
SO WHAT DID YOU DROP?
IS IT BIG? SMALL?
THEY'RE SMALL. THEY CAN FIT IN MY HAND.
UGH. ANOTHER TINY THING TO DIG OUT OF ALL THIS SAND. HOW ARE WE SUPPOSED TO FIND ANYTHING LIKE THIS?
WE WILL! WE HAVE TO!
SNIFF
IF IT'S REALLY THAT IMPORTANT TO YOU, WHY'D YOU BRING IT TO THE BEACH?
SKFF SKFF
SKFF
I, UM, WAS IN A HURRY...
Hurry!!
Chase Kazama down!
WAS SHE REALLY THAT DESPERATE?
WHAT WE'RE LOOKING FOR IS JUST AS IMPORTANT TO US, TOO!
YEAH. A GUY'S LIFE DEPENDS ON IT, AFTER ALL.
?
WITHOUT THEM, THAT HASHIMOTO GUY CAN'T GET OUT OF THAT BARREL, RIGHT?

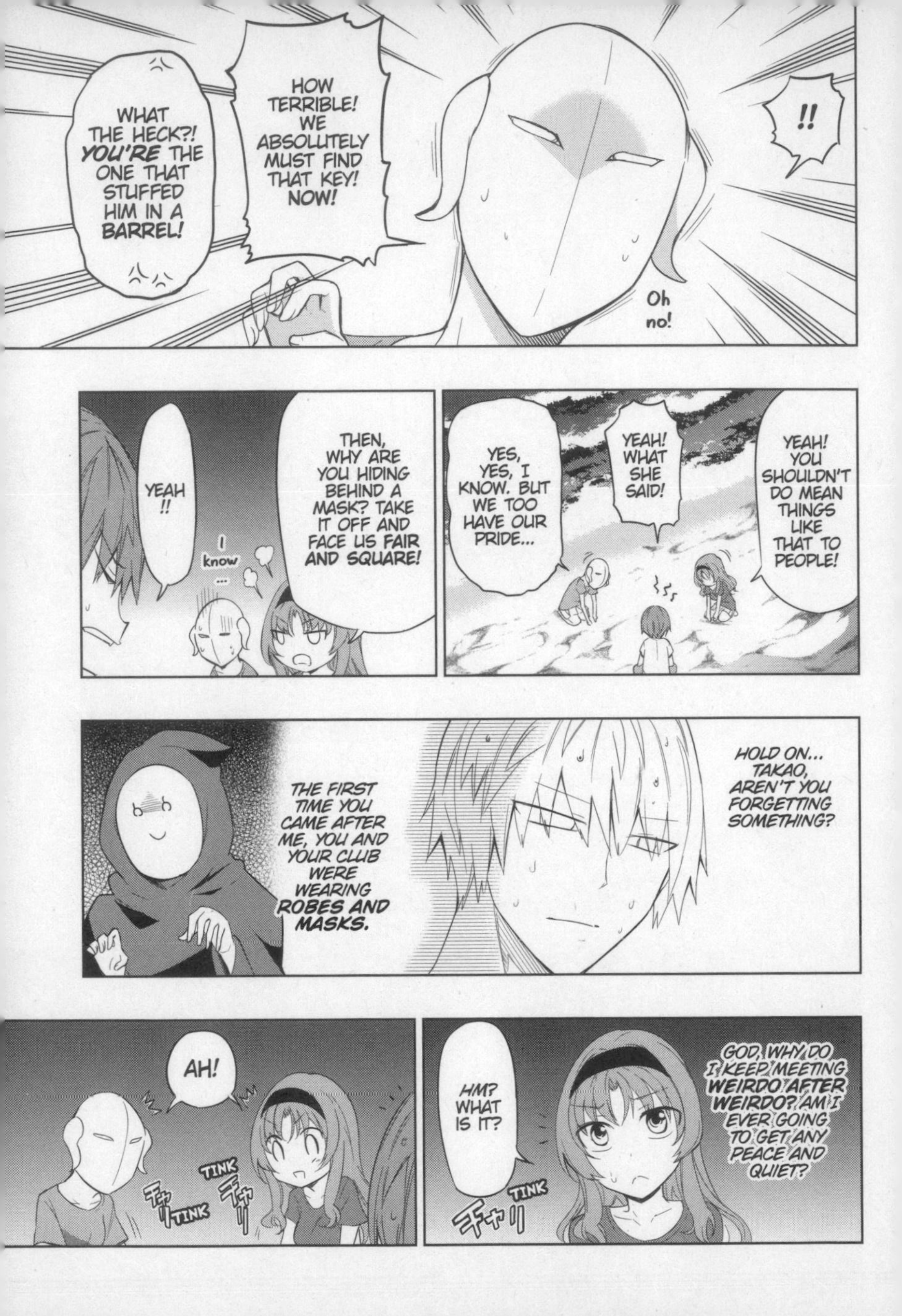
!!
HOW TERRIBLE! WE ABSOLUTELY MUST FIND THAT KEY! NOW!
WHAT THE HECK?! YOU'RE THE ONE THAT STUFFED HIM IN A BARREL!
Oh no!
YEAH! YOU SHOULDN'T DO MEAN THINGS LIKE THAT TO PEOPLE!
YEAH! WHAT SHE SAID!
YES, YES, I KNOW. BUT WE TOO HAVE OUR PRIDE...
THEN, WHY ARE YOU HIDING BEHIND A MASK? TAKE IT OFF AND FACE US FAIR AND SQUARE!
YEAH !!
I know ...
HOLD ON... TAKAO, AREN'T YOU FORGETTING SOMETHING?
THE FIRST TIME YOU CAME AFTER ME, YOU AND YOUR CLUB WERE WEARING ROBES AND MASKS.
GOD, WHY DO I KEEP MEETING WEIRDO AFTER WEIRDO? AM I EVER GOING TO GET ANY PEACE AND QUIET?
HM? WHAT IS IT?
TINK
チャリ
AH!
TINK
チャリ
TINK
チャリ

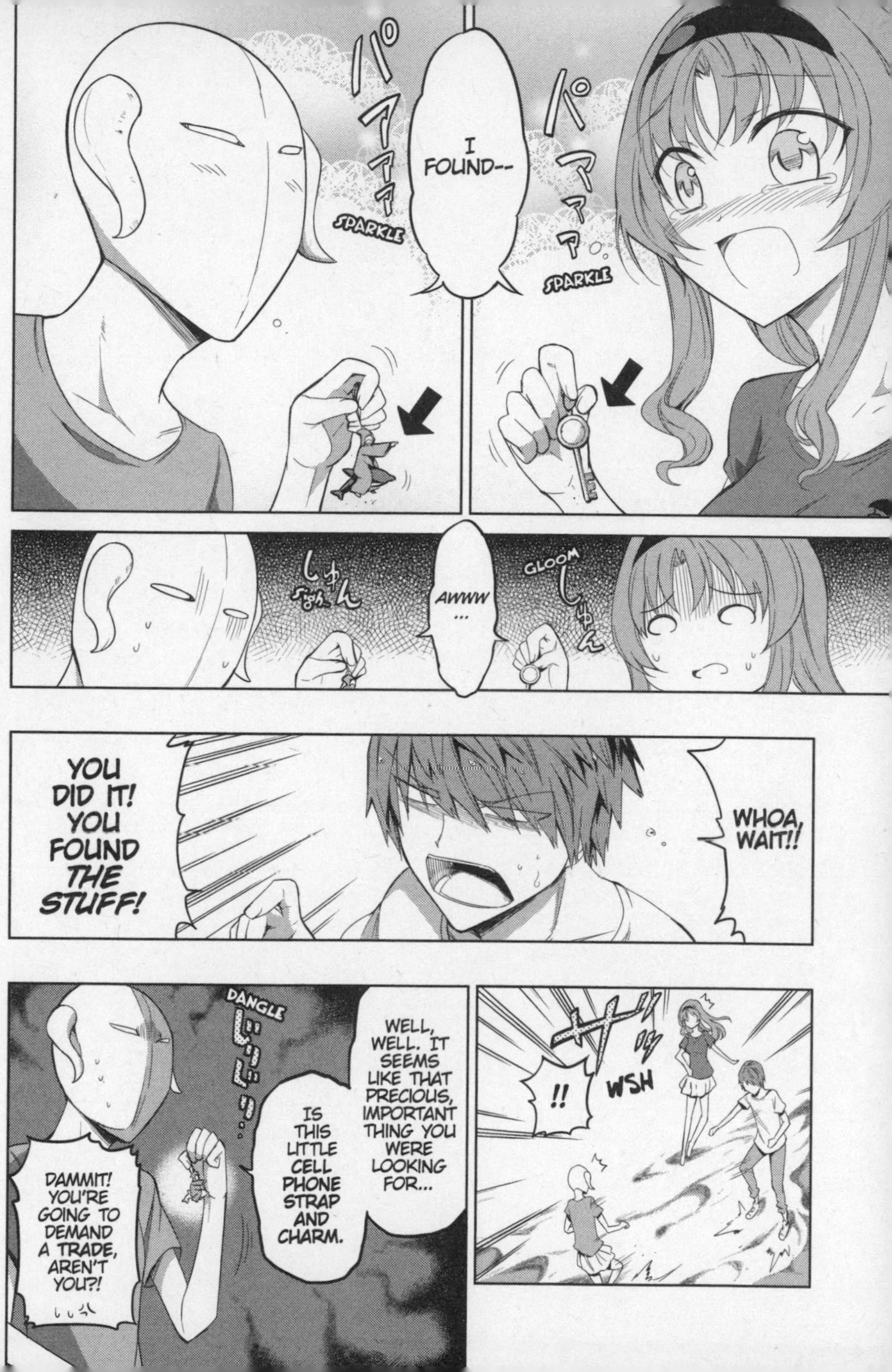
パァァァ
SPARKLE
I FOUND--
パァァァ
SPARKLE
GLOOM
しゅん
AWWW...
しゅん
sigh
WHOA, WAIT!!
YOU DID IT! YOU FOUND THE STUFF!
!!
WSH
WELL, WELL. IT SEEMS LIKE THAT PRECIOUS, IMPORTANT THING YOU WERE LOOKING FOR...
IS THIS LITTLE CELL PHONE STRAP AND CHARM.
DANGLE
DAMMIT! YOU'RE GOING TO DEMAND A TRADE, AREN'T YOU?!

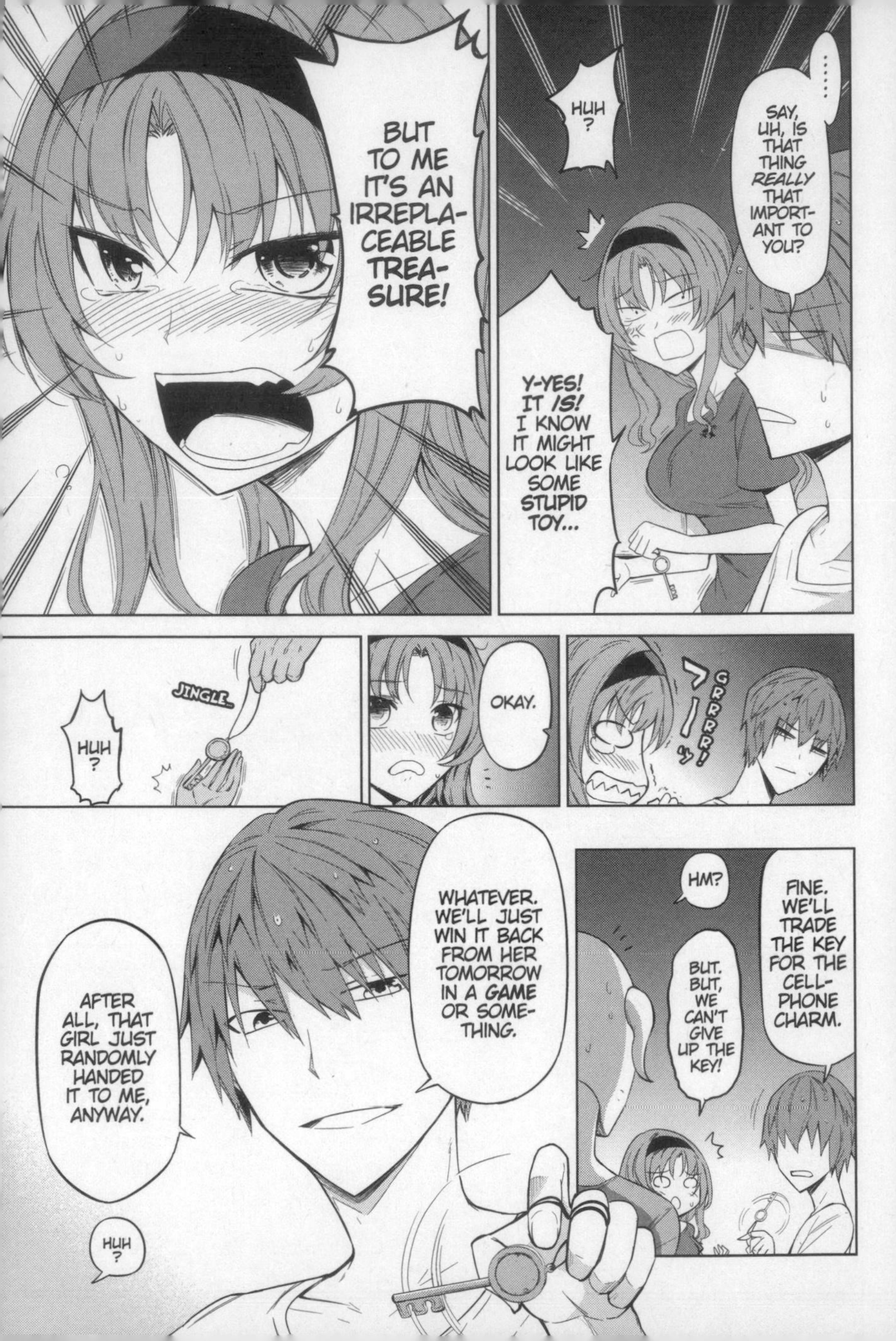
......
SAY, UH, IS THAT THING *REALLY* THAT IMPORTANT TO YOU?
HUH?
Y-YES! IT *IS*! I KNOW IT MIGHT LOOK LIKE SOME STUPID TOY...
BUT TO ME IT'S AN IRREPLACEABLE TREASURE!
GRRRR!
OKAY.
JINGLE..
HUH?
FINE. WE'LL TRADE THE KEY FOR THE CELLPHONE CHARM.
HM?
BUT. BUT, WE CAN'T GIVE UP THE KEY!
WHATEVER. WE'LL JUST WIN IT BACK FROM HER TOMORROW IN A GAME OR SOMETHING.
AFTER ALL, THAT GIRL JUST RANDOMLY HANDED IT TO ME, ANYWAY.
HUH?

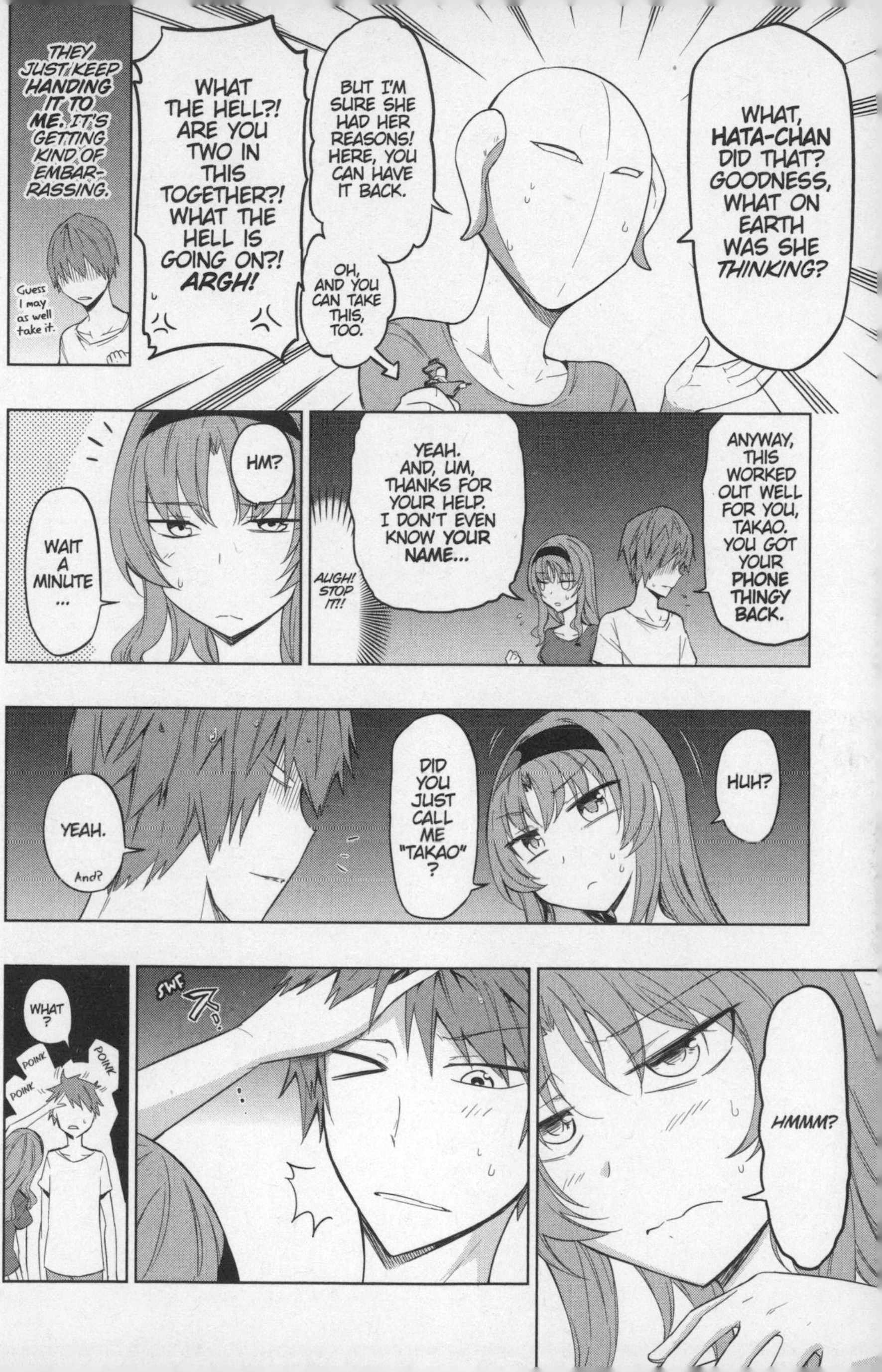
WHAT, HATA-CHAN DID THAT? GOODNESS, WHAT ON EARTH WAS SHE THINKING?
BUT I'M SURE SHE HAD HER REASONS! HERE, YOU CAN HAVE IT BACK.
OH, AND YOU CAN TAKE THIS, TOO.
WHAT THE HELL?! ARE YOU TWO IN THIS TOGETHER?! WHAT THE HELL IS GOING ON?! ARGH!
THEY JUST KEEP HANDING IT TO ME. IT'S GETTING KIND OF EMBARRASSING.
Guess I may as well take it.
ANYWAY, THIS WORKED OUT WELL FOR YOU, TAKAO. YOU GOT YOUR PHONE THINGY BACK.
YEAH. AND, UM, THANKS FOR YOUR HELP. I DON'T EVEN KNOW YOUR NAME...
AUGH! STOP IT!!
HM?
WAIT A MINUTE ...
HUH?
DID YOU JUST CALL ME "TAKAO"?
YEAH.
And?
HMMM?
SWF
WHAT?
POINK
POINK
POINK

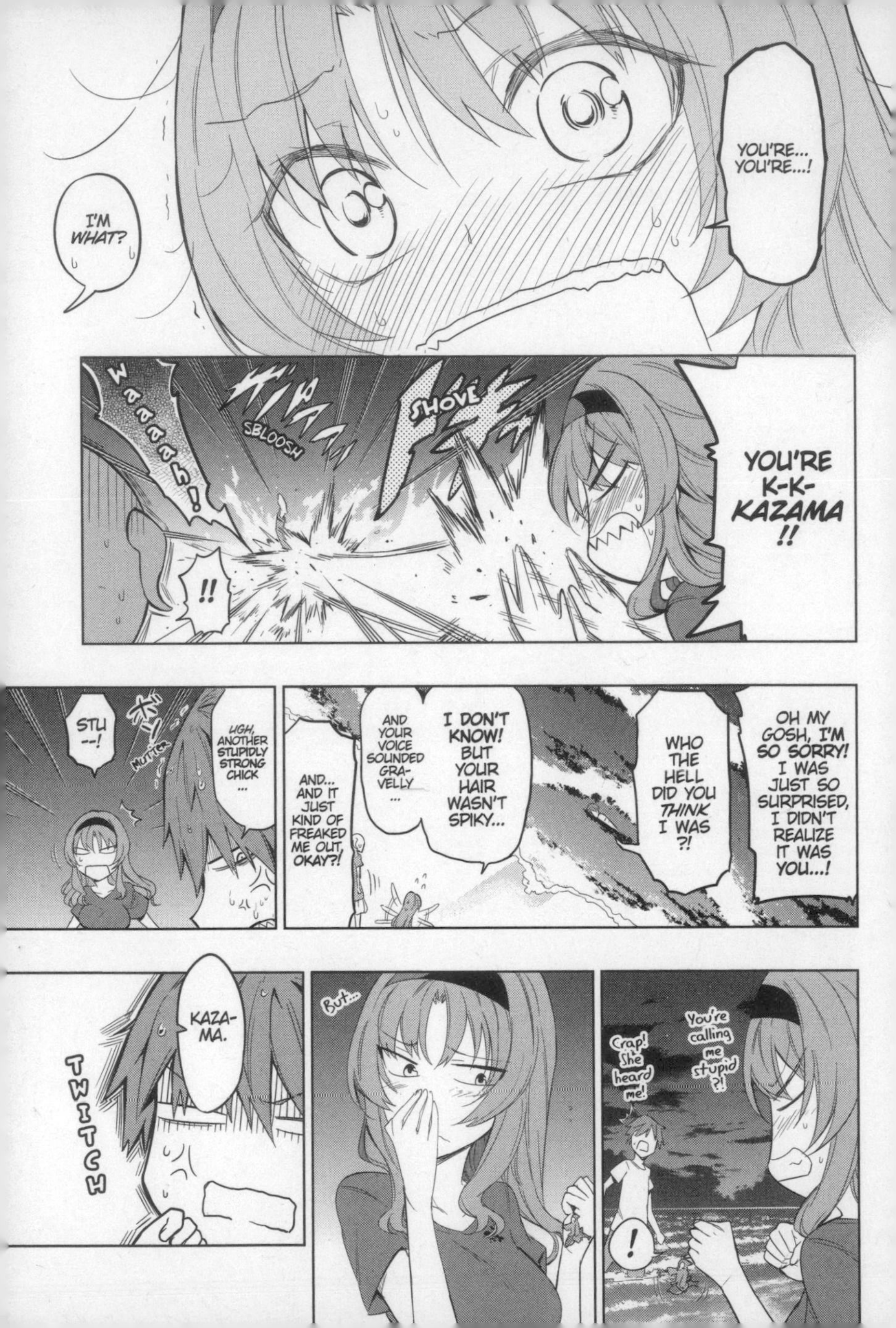
YOU'RE... YOU'RE...!
I'M WHAT?
YOU'RE K-K-KAZAMA!!
SHOVE
SBLOOSH
Waaaaah!
!!
OH MY GOSH, I'M SO SORRY! I WAS JUST SO SURPRISED, I DIDN'T REALIZE IT WAS YOU...!
WHO THE HELL DID YOU THINK I WAS?!
I DON'T KNOW! BUT YOUR HAIR WASN'T SPIKY...
AND YOUR VOICE SOUNDED GRA-VELLY...
AND... AND IT JUST KIND OF FREAKED ME OUT, OKAY?!
UGH, ANOTHER STUPIDLY STRONG CHICK...
MUTTER
STU--!
You're calling me stupid?!
Crap! She heard me!
!
But...
KAZA-MA.
TWITCH

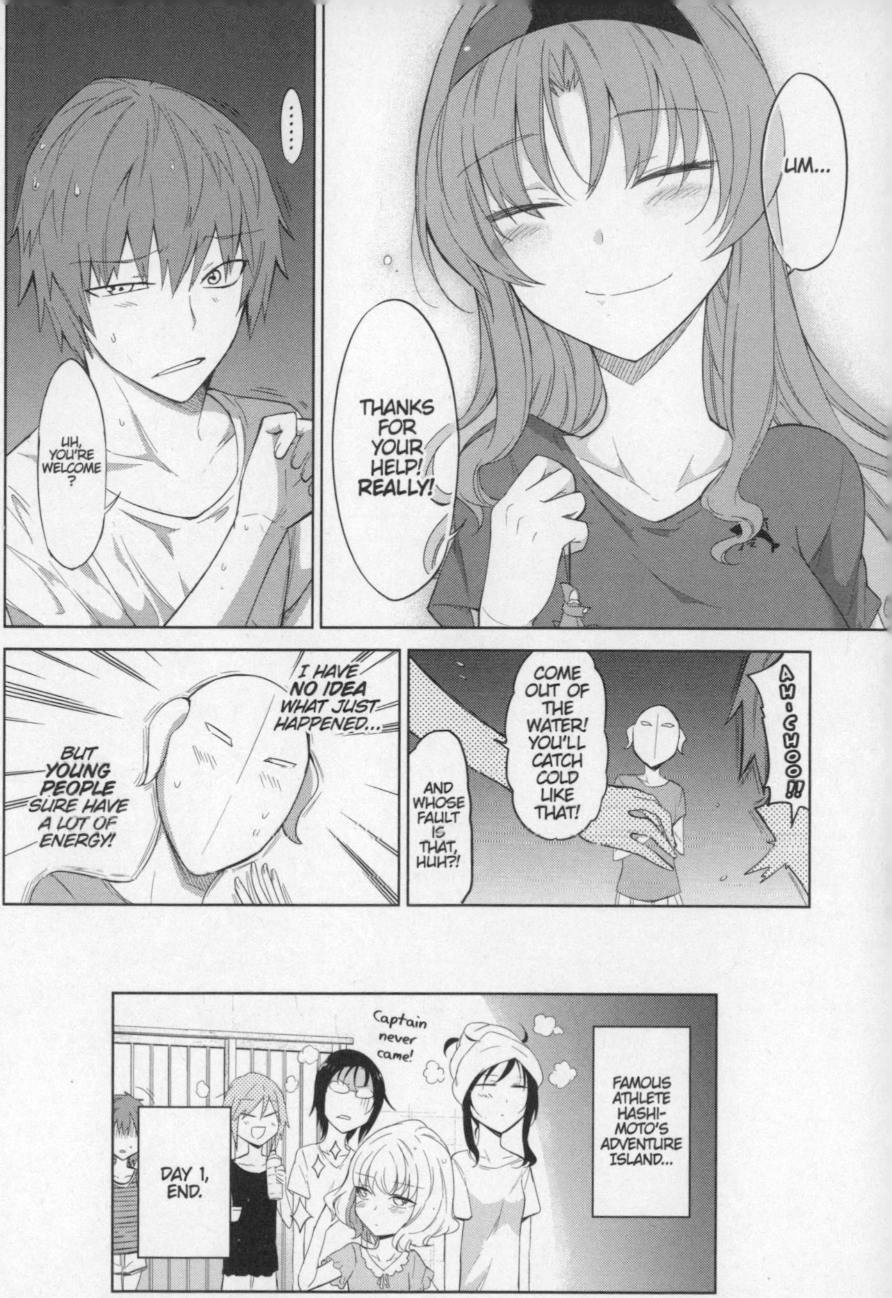
UM...
THANKS FOR YOUR HELP! REALLY!
......
UH, YOU'RE WELCOME?
AH-CHOO!!
COME OUT OF THE WATER! YOU'LL CATCH COLD LIKE THAT!
AND WHOSE FAULT IS THAT, HUH?!
I HAVE NO IDEA WHAT JUST HAPPENED...
BUT YOUNG PEOPLE SURE HAVE A LOT OF ENERGY!
FAMOUS ATHLETE HASHIMOTO'S ADVENTURE ISLAND...
Captain never came!
DAY 1, END.

NEXT: Vol.08...

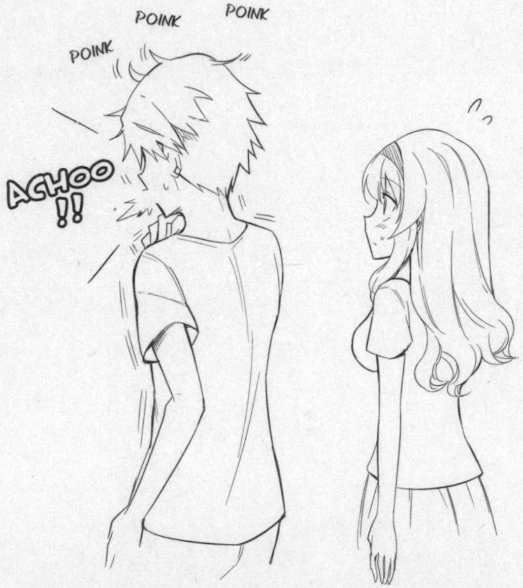

POINK
POINK
POINK
ACHOO !!

D-FRAGMENTS

ディーふらぐ!

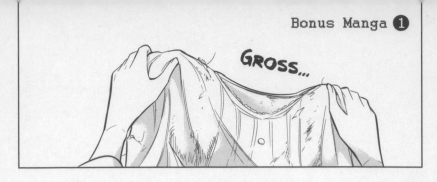

Bonus Manga ❶

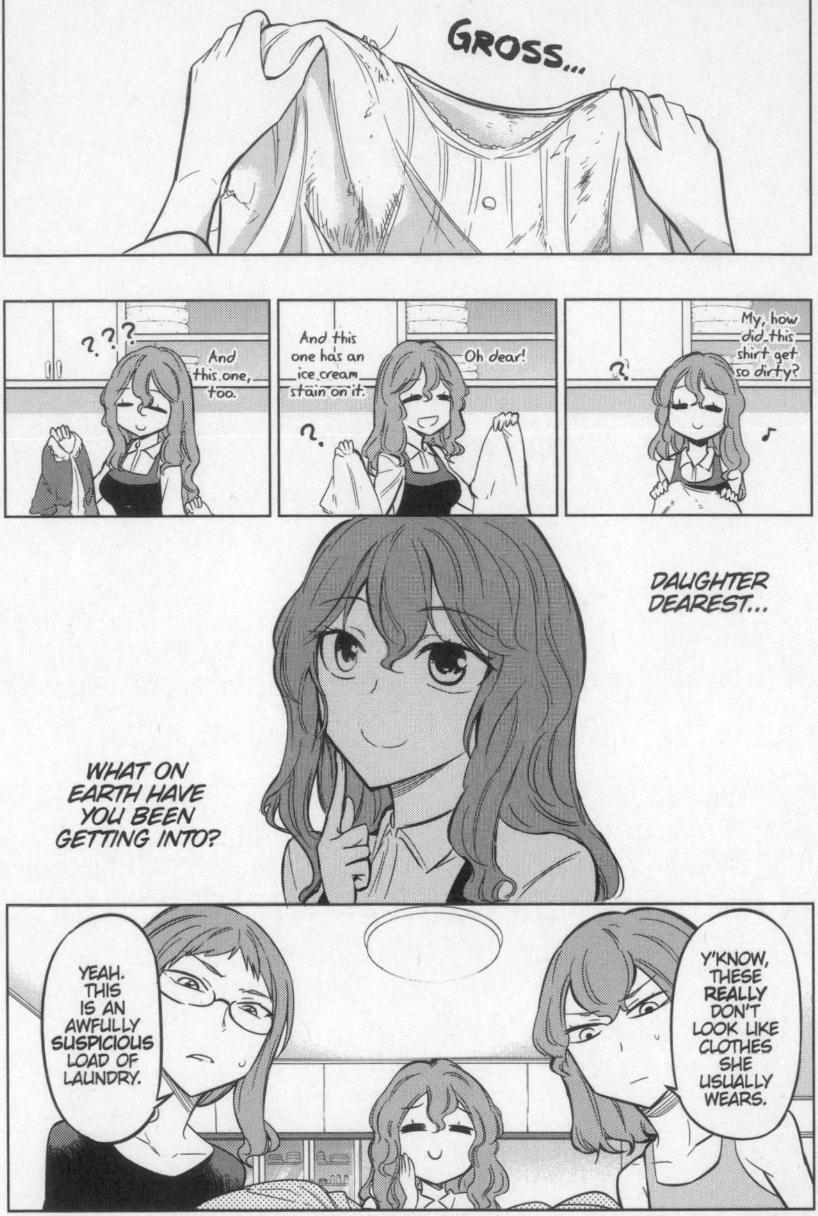
GROSS...
My, how did this shirt get so dirty?
Oh dear!
And this one has an ice cream stain on it.
And this one, too.
DAUGHTER DEAREST...
WHAT ON EARTH HAVE YOU BEEN GETTING INTO?
Y'KNOW, THESE REALLY DON'T LOOK LIKE CLOTHES SHE USUALLY WEARS.
YEAH. THIS IS AN AWFULLY SUSPICIOUS LOAD OF LAUNDRY.

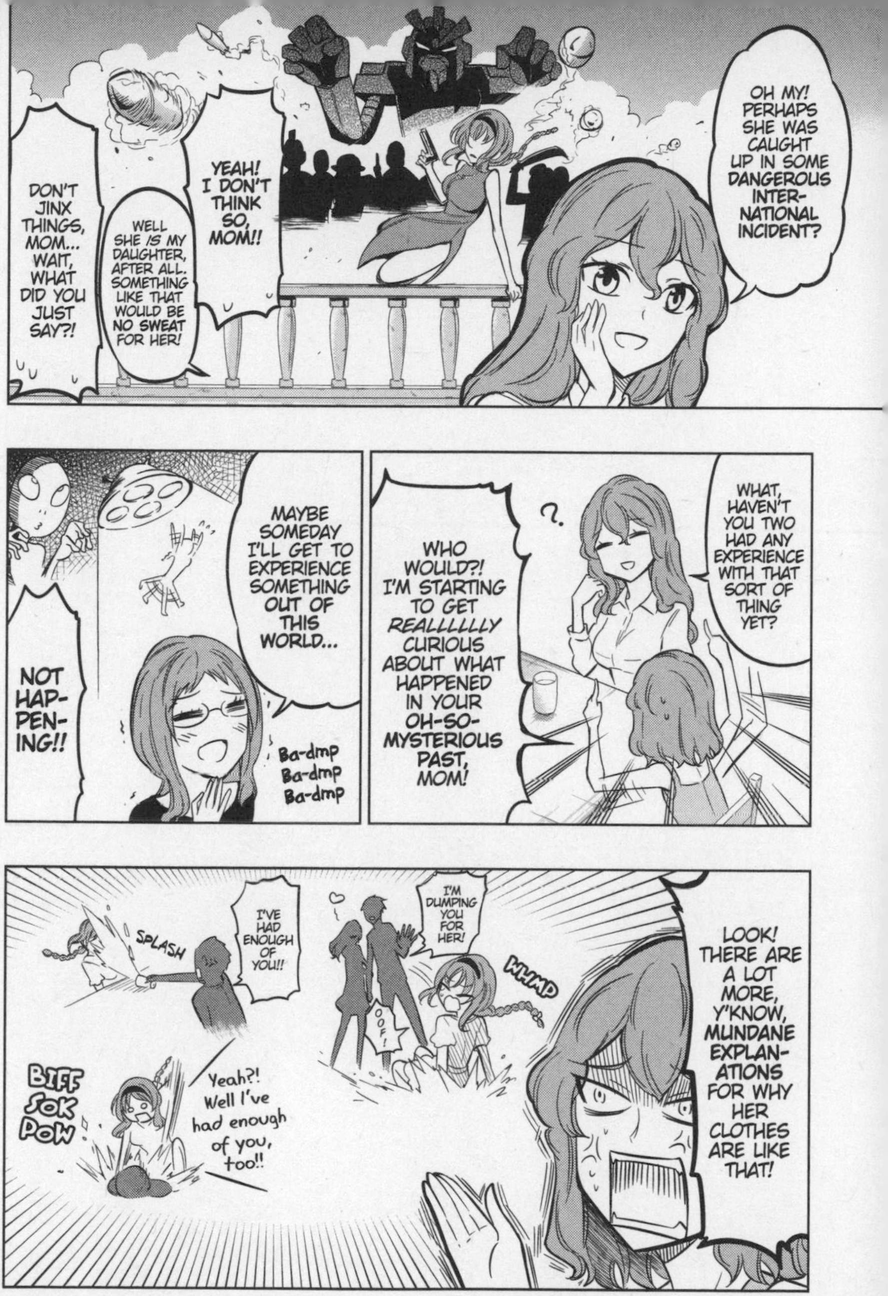
OH MY! PERHAPS SHE WAS CAUGHT UP IN SOME DANGEROUS INTER-NATIONAL INCIDENT?
YEAH! I DON'T THINK SO, MOM!!
WELL SHE *IS* MY DAUGHTER, AFTER ALL. SOMETHING LIKE THAT WOULD BE NO SWEAT FOR HER!
DON'T JINX THINGS, MOM... WAIT, WHAT DID YOU JUST SAY?!
WHAT, HAVEN'T YOU TWO HAD ANY EXPERIENCE WITH THAT SORT OF THING YET?
?
WHO WOULD?! I'M STARTING TO GET *REALLLLLLY* CURIOUS ABOUT WHAT HAPPENED IN YOUR OH-SO-MYSTERIOUS PAST, MOM!
MAYBE SOMEDAY I'LL GET TO EXPERIENCE SOMETHING OUT OF THIS WORLD...
Ba-dmp Ba-dmp Ba-dmp
NOT HAP-PEN-ING!!
LOOK! THERE ARE A LOT MORE, Y'KNOW, MUNDANE EXPLAN-ATIONS FOR WHY HER CLOTHES ARE LIKE THAT!
I'M DUMPING YOU FOR HER!
WHMP
OOF!
I'VE HAD ENOUGH OF YOU!!
SPLASH
Yeah?! Well I've had enough of you, too!!
BIFF SOK POW

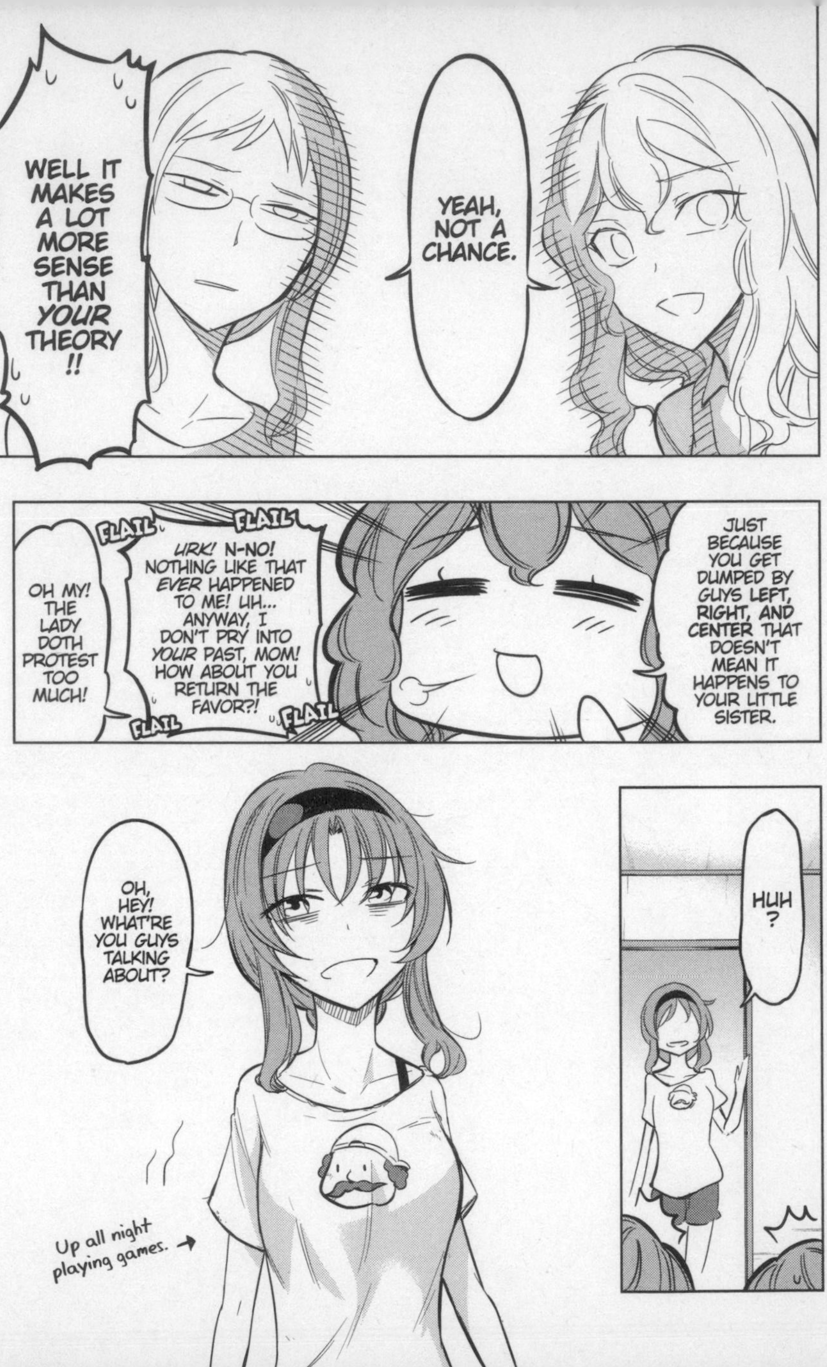
YEAH, NOT A CHANCE.
WELL IT MAKES A LOT MORE SENSE THAN *YOUR* THEORY!!
JUST BECAUSE YOU GET DUMPED BY GUYS LEFT, RIGHT, AND CENTER THAT DOESN'T MEAN IT HAPPENS TO YOUR LITTLE SISTER.
FLAIL
FLAIL
URK! N-NO! NOTHING LIKE THAT *EVER* HAPPENED TO ME! UH... ANYWAY, I DON'T PRY INTO *YOUR* PAST, MOM! HOW ABOUT YOU RETURN THE FAVOR?!
FLAIL
FLAIL
OH MY! THE LADY DOTH PROTEST TOO MUCH!
HUH?
OH, HEY! WHAT'RE YOU GUYS TALKING ABOUT?
Up all night playing games.

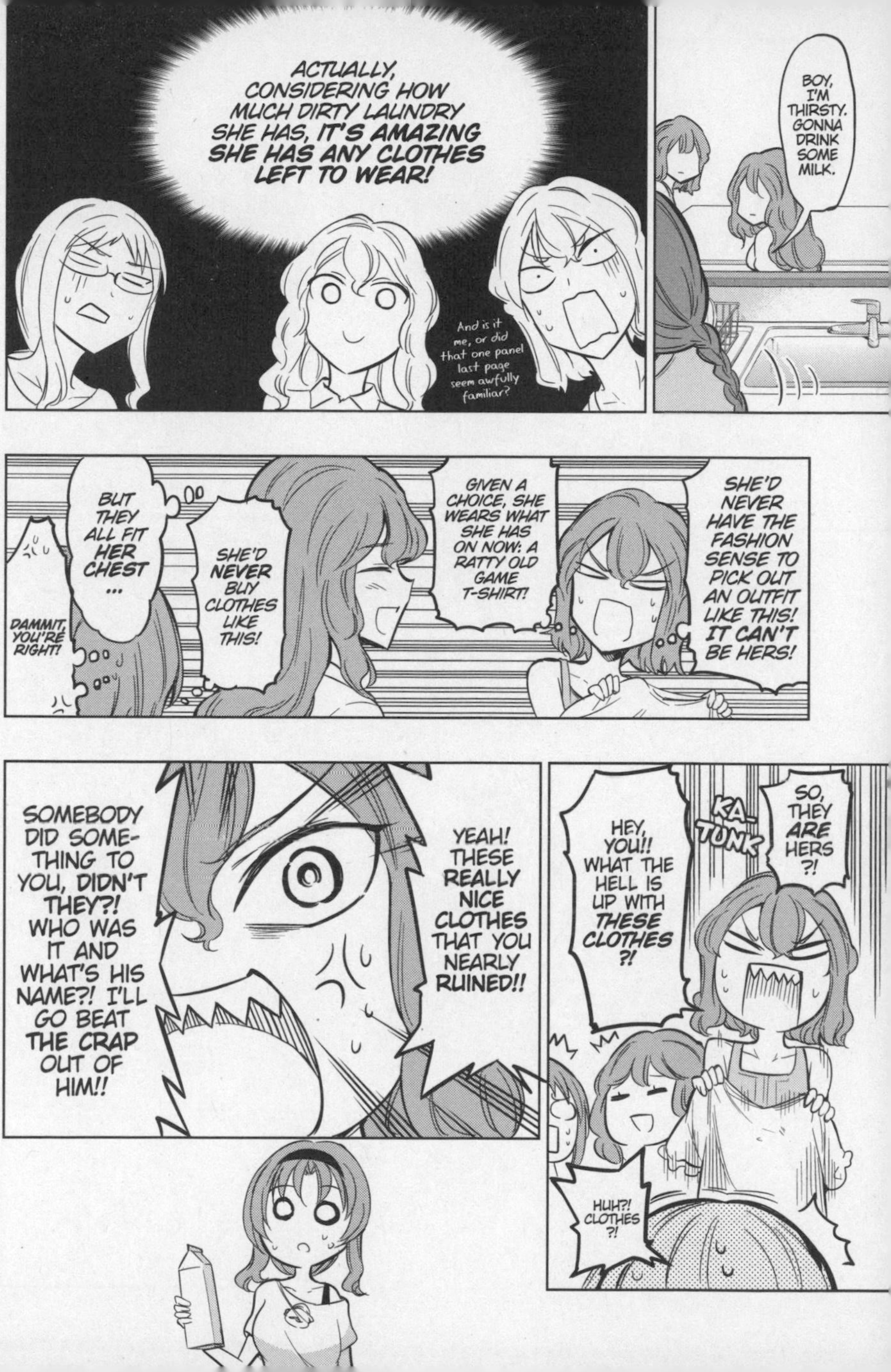
BOY, I'M THIRSTY. GONNA DRINK SOME MILK.
ACTUALLY, CONSIDERING HOW MUCH DIRTY LAUNDRY SHE HAS, IT'S AMAZING SHE HAS ANY CLOTHES LEFT TO WEAR!
And is it me, or did that one panel last page seem awfully familiar?
SHE'D NEVER HAVE THE FASHION SENSE TO PICK OUT AN OUTFIT LIKE THIS! IT CAN'T BE HERS!
GIVEN A CHOICE, SHE WEARS WHAT SHE HAS ON NOW: A RATTY OLD GAME T-SHIRT!
SHE'D NEVER BUY CLOTHES LIKE THIS!
BUT THEY ALL FIT HER CHEST...
DAMMIT, YOU'RE RIGHT!
SO, THEY ARE HERS?!
KA-TUNK
HEY, YOU!! WHAT THE HELL IS UP WITH THESE CLOTHES?!
HUH?! CLOTHES?!
YEAH! THESE REALLY NICE CLOTHES THAT YOU NEARLY RUINED!!
SOMEBODY DID SOME-THING TO YOU, DIDN'T THEY?! WHO WAS IT AND WHAT'S HIS NAME?! I'LL GO BEAT THE CRAP OUT OF HIM!!

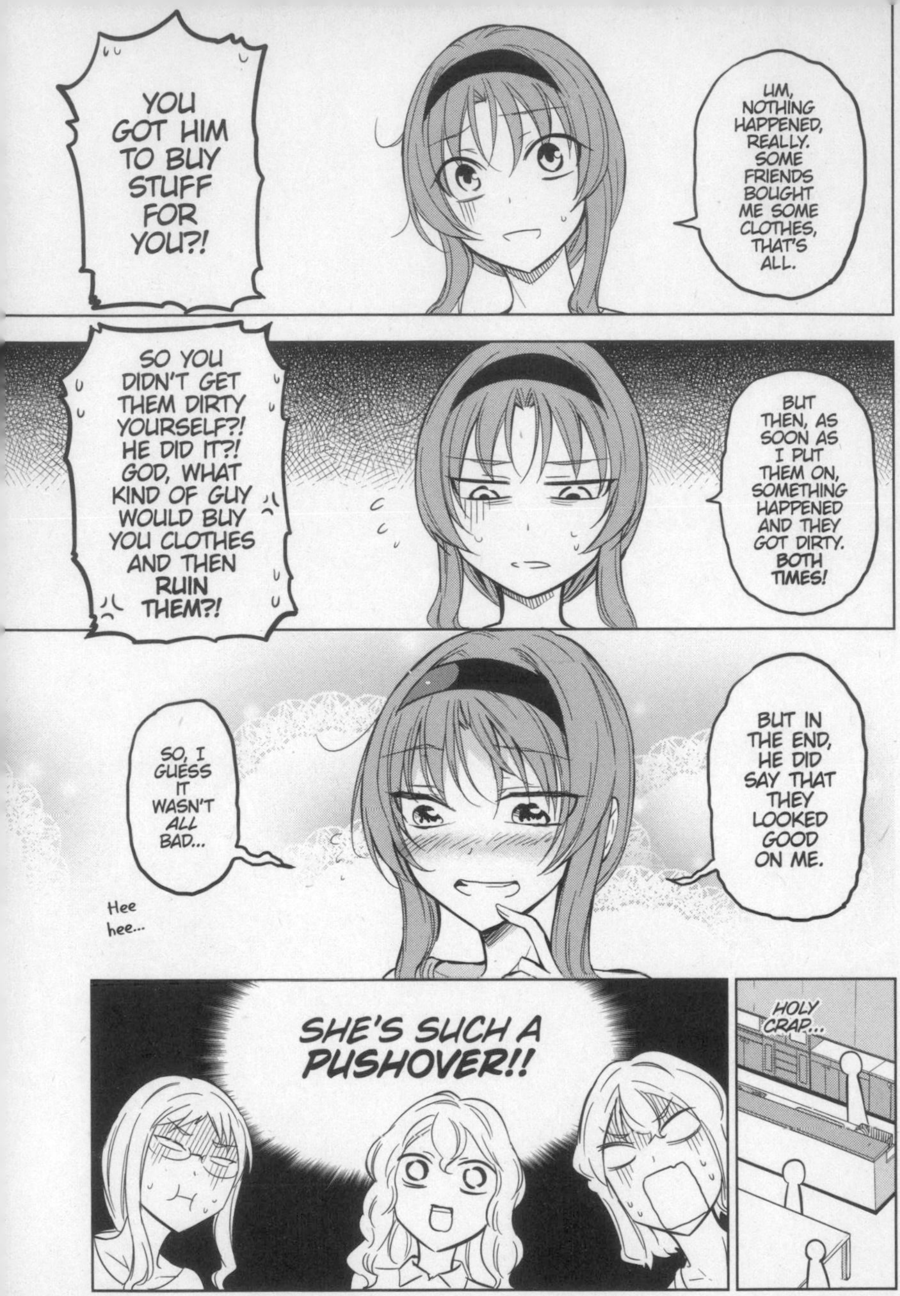
UM, NOTHING HAPPENED, REALLY. SOME FRIENDS BOUGHT ME SOME CLOTHES, THAT'S ALL.
YOU GOT HIM TO BUY STUFF FOR YOU?!
BUT THEN, AS SOON AS I PUT THEM ON, SOMETHING HAPPENED AND THEY GOT DIRTY. BOTH TIMES!
SO YOU DIDN'T GET THEM DIRTY YOURSELF?! HE DID IT?! GOD, WHAT KIND OF GUY WOULD BUY YOU CLOTHES AND THEN RUIN THEM?!
BUT IN THE END, HE DID SAY THAT THEY LOOKED GOOD ON ME.
SO, I GUESS IT WASN'T ALL BAD...
Hee hee...
HOLY CRAP...
SHE'S SUCH A PUSHOVER!!

END

Bonus Manga 2

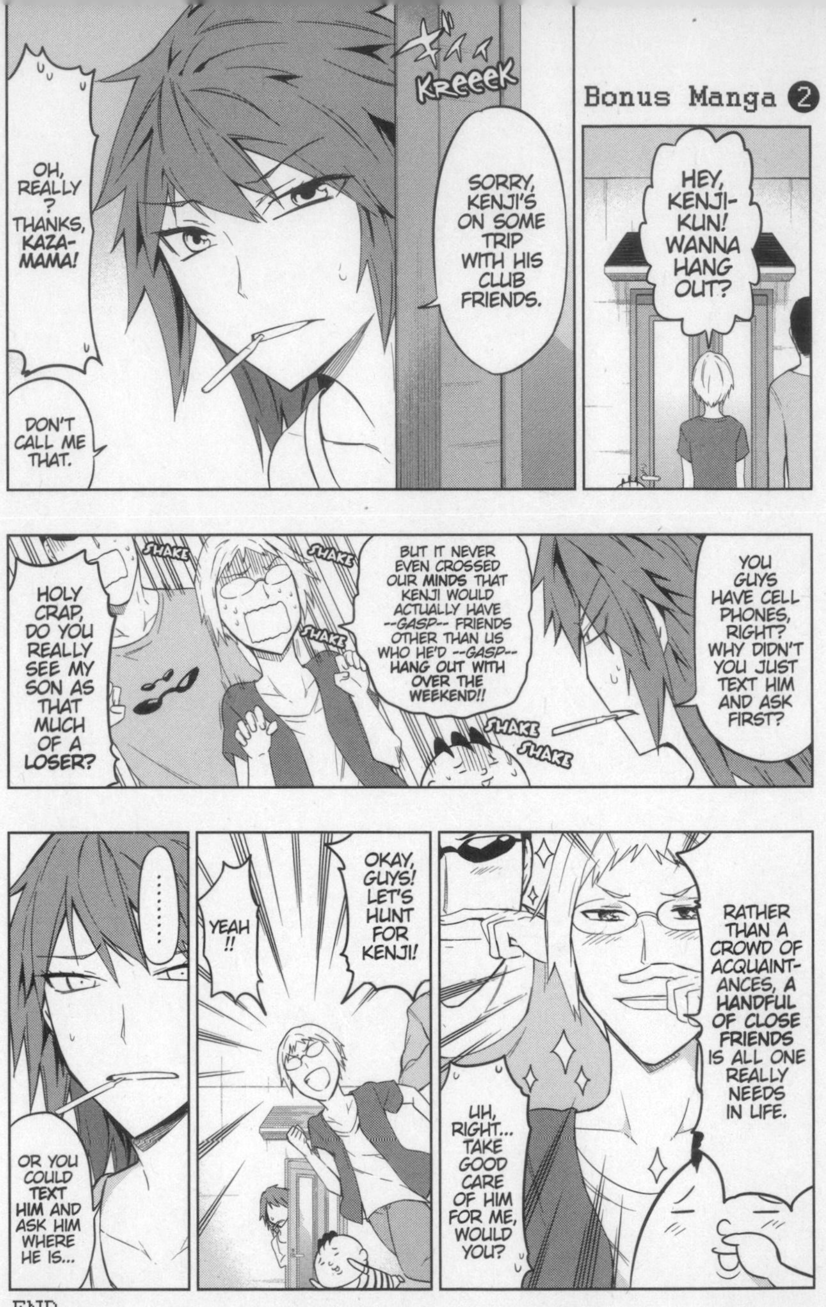
HEY, KENJI-KUN! WANNA HANG OUT?
Kreeek
SORRY, KENJI'S ON SOME TRIP WITH HIS CLUB FRIENDS.
OH, REALLY? THANKS, KAZA-MAMA!
DON'T CALL ME THAT.
YOU GUYS HAVE CELL PHONES, RIGHT? WHY DIDN'T YOU JUST TEXT HIM AND ASK FIRST?
BUT IT NEVER EVEN CROSSED OUR MINDS THAT KENJI WOULD ACTUALLY HAVE --GASP-- FRIENDS OTHER THAN US WHO HE'D --GASP-- HANG OUT WITH OVER THE WEEKEND!!
SHAKE SHAKE SHAKE SHAKE SHAKE
HOLY CRAP, DO YOU REALLY SEE MY SON AS THAT MUCH OF A LOSER?
RATHER THAN A CROWD OF ACQUAINT-ANCES, A HANDFUL OF CLOSE FRIENDS IS ALL ONE REALLY NEEDS IN LIFE.
UH, RIGHT... TAKE GOOD CARE OF HIM FOR ME, WOULD YOU?
OKAY, GUYS! LET'S HUNT FOR KENJI!
YEAH!!
......
OR YOU COULD TEXT HIM AND ASK HIM WHERE HE IS...

END

D-FRAGMENTS
ディーふらぐ!

Backstage Uran

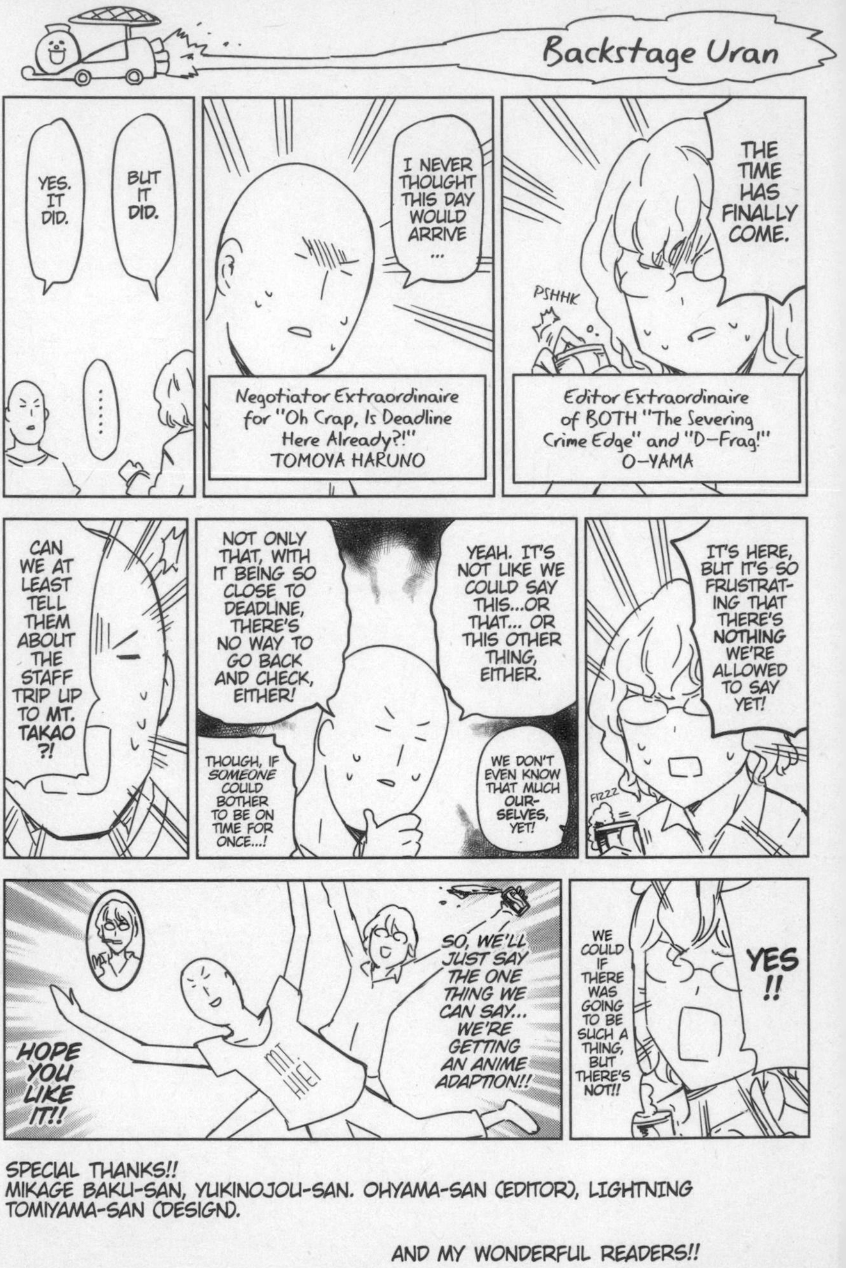
THE TIME HAS FINALLY COME.
PSHHK
Editor Extraordinaire of BOTH "The Severing Crime Edge" and "D-Frag!" O-YAMA
I NEVER THOUGHT THIS DAY WOULD ARRIVE ...
Negotiator Extraordinaire for "Oh Crap, Is Deadline Here Already?!" TOMOYA HARUNO
BUT IT DID.
YES. IT DID.
......
IT'S HERE, BUT IT'S SO FRUSTRATING THAT THERE'S NOTHING WE'RE ALLOWED TO SAY YET!
FIZZZ
YEAH. IT'S NOT LIKE WE COULD SAY THIS...OR THAT... OR THIS OTHER THING, EITHER.
NOT ONLY THAT, WITH IT BEING SO CLOSE TO DEADLINE, THERE'S NO WAY TO GO BACK AND CHECK, EITHER!
WE DON'T EVEN KNOW THAT MUCH OURSELVES, YET!
THOUGH, IF SOMEONE COULD BOTHER TO BE ON TIME FOR ONCE...!
CAN WE AT LEAST TELL THEM ABOUT THE STAFF TRIP UP TO MT. TAKAO ?!
YES !!
WE COULD IF THERE WAS GOING TO BE SUCH A THING, BUT THERE'S NOT!!
SO, WE'LL JUST SAY THE ONE THING WE CAN SAY... WE'RE GETTING AN ANIME ADAPTION!!
MT. HIEI
HOPE YOU LIKE IT!!

SPECIAL THANKS!!
MIKAGE BAKU-SAN, YUKINOJOU-SAN. OHYAMA-SAN (EDITOR), LIGHTNING TOMIYAMA-SAN (DESIGN).

AND MY WONDERFUL READERS!!

After the events of Chapter 51...

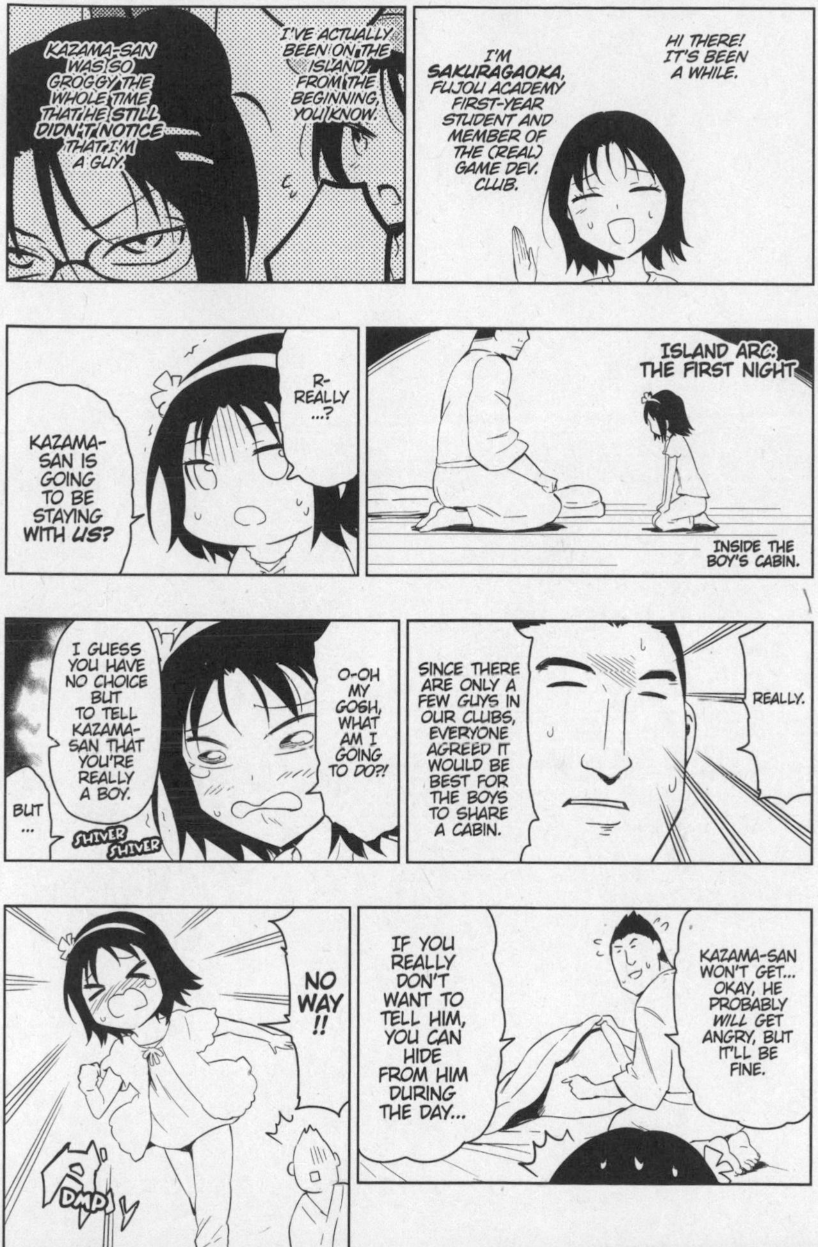
HI THERE! IT'S BEEN A WHILE.
I'M SAKURAGAOKA, FUJOU ACADEMY FIRST-YEAR STUDENT AND MEMBER OF THE (REAL) GAME DEV. CLUB.
I'VE ACTUALLY BEEN ON THE ISLAND FROM THE BEGINNING, YOU KNOW.
KAZAMA-SAN WAS SO GROGGY THE WHOLE TIME THAT HE STILL DIDN'T NOTICE THAT I'M A GUY.
ISLAND ARC: THE FIRST NIGHT
INSIDE THE BOY'S CABIN.
R-REALLY ...?
KAZAMA-SAN IS GOING TO BE STAYING WITH US?
REALLY.
SINCE THERE ARE ONLY A FEW GUYS IN OUR CLUBS, EVERYONE AGREED IT WOULD BE BEST FOR THE BOYS TO SHARE A CABIN.
O-OH MY GOSH, WHAT AM I GOING TO DO?!
I GUESS YOU HAVE NO CHOICE BUT TO TELL KAZAMA-SAN THAT YOU'RE REALLY A BOY.
BUT ...
SHIVER SHIVER
KAZAMA-SAN WON'T GET... OKAY, HE PROBABLY WILL GET ANGRY, BUT IT'LL BE FINE.
IF YOU REALLY DON'T WANT TO TELL HIM, YOU CAN HIDE FROM HIM DURING THE DAY...
NO WAY !!
DMP

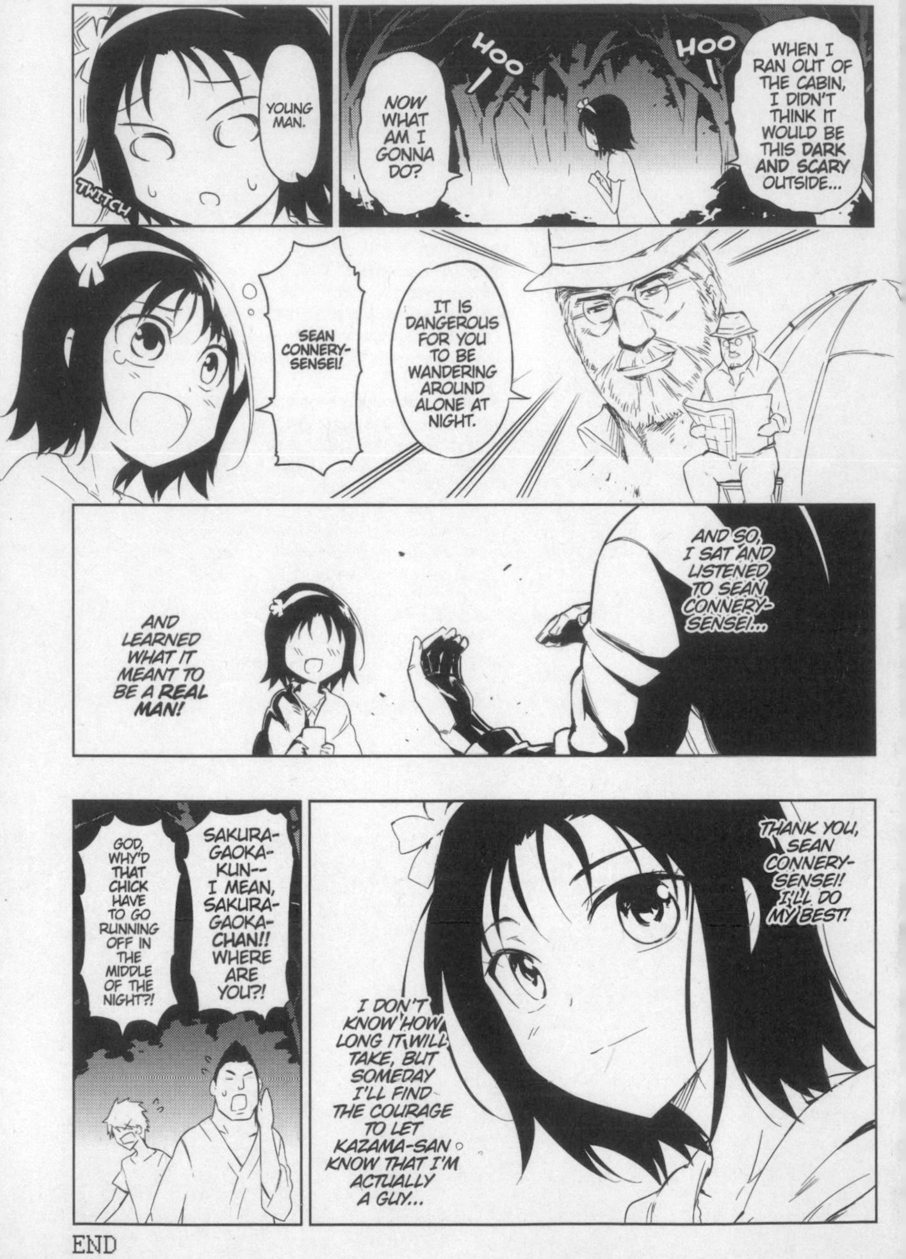
WHEN I RAN OUT OF THE CABIN, I DIDN'T THINK IT WOULD BE THIS DARK AND SCARY OUTSIDE...
HOO
HOO
NOW WHAT AM I GONNA DO?
YOUNG MAN.
TWITCH
IT IS DANGEROUS FOR YOU TO BE WANDERING AROUND ALONE AT NIGHT.
SEAN CONNERY-SENSEI!
AND SO, I SAT AND LISTENED TO SEAN CONNERY-SENSEI...
AND LEARNED WHAT IT MEANT TO BE A REAL MAN!
THANK YOU, SEAN CONNERY-SENSEI! I'LL DO MY BEST!
I DON'T KNOW HOW LONG IT WILL TAKE, BUT SOMEDAY I'LL FIND THE COURAGE TO LET KAZAMA-SAN KNOW THAT I'M ACTUALLY A GUY...
SAKURA-GAOKA-KUN-- I MEAN, SAKURA-GAOKA-CHAN!! WHERE ARE YOU?!
GOD, WHY'D THAT CHICK HAVE TO GO RUNNING OFF IN THE MIDDLE OF THE NIGHT?!

END

SEVEN SEAS ENTERTAINMENT PRESENTS

D-FRAG!

story and art by **TOMOYA HARUNO**

VOLUME 7

TRANSLATION
Adrienne Beck

ADAPTATION
Shannon Fay

LETTERING AND LAYOUT
Ma. Victoria Robado

LOGO DESIGN
Courtney Williams

COVER DESIGN
Nicky Lim

PROOFREADER
Lee Otter

ASSISTANT EDITOR
Lissa Pattillo

MANAGING EDITOR
Adam Arnold

PUBLISHER
Jason DeAngelis

Seven Seas books may be purchased in bulk for educational, business, or promotional use. For information on bulk purchases, please contact Macmillan Corporate & Premium Sales Department at 1-800-221-7945 (ext 5442) or write specialmarkets@macmillan.com.

Seven Seas and the Seven Seas logo are trademarks of Seven Seas Entertainment, LLC. All rights reserved.

ISBN: 978-1-626922-19-8

Printed in Canada

First Printing: December 2015

10 9 8 7 6 5 4 3 2 1

FOLLOW US ONLINE: *www.gomanga.com*

READING DIRECTIONS

This book reads from *right to left*, Japanese style. If this is your first time reading manga, you start reading from the top right panel on each page and take it from there. If you get lost, just follow the numbered diagram here. It may seem backwards at first, but you'll get the hang of it! Have fun!!

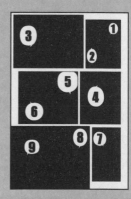